PENGUIN

FRIEDRICH HÖ
ESSAYS AND

FRIEDRICH HÖLDERLIN was born in Lauffen am Neckar in Swabia, south-west Germany, in 1770. From 1788 to 1793 he studied at the Stift (seminary) in Tübingen, years marked by an enthusiasm for the ideals of the French Revolution and for the philosophy of Kant. His fellow students and friends included Hegel and Schelling. On leaving Tübingen, to avoid continuing his intended career and becoming a parish priest, he took up the first of a series of jobs as a private tutor. In 1794–5 he was in Jena, then Germany's intellectual centre, and attended Fichte's lectures. In 1796 he moved to Frankfurt, and fell in love with his employer's wife, Susette Gontard, who went into his poetry as Diotima. Encouraged by Schiller, he published a novel, *Hyperion*, in two volumes in 1797 and 1799. After life in Frankfurt had become impossible, he tried in 1798–1800 to establish himself as a freelance writer in nearby Homburg, hoping to support himself by editing a literary journal. The attempt failed, but he produced a substantial unfinished tragedy, *The Death of Empedocles*, and a number of important philosophical and poetological essay-fragments. Other tutoring posts took him to Switzerland and Bordeaux, but on his return from France in 1802, when he learned that Susette Gontard had died of German measles caught from nursing her children, he began to show signs of mental break-down. The translations of Sophocles' *Oedipus the King* and *Antigone* that he published in 1804, now regarded as the very finest of their kind, met with general incomprehension, and his poems appeared only here and there in journals, not being properly collected and edited until the twentieth century. Declared clinically insane in 1805 and briefly institutionalized in 1806–7, he spent the second half of his life, until his death in 1843, in the care of a carpenter's family in Tübingen. He is now regarded as one of the greatest poets in German or in any language.

JEREMY ADLER is Emeritus Professor of German and Senior Research Fellow at King's College London. His edition of Hölderlin's *Selected Poems and Fragments* was published by Penguin (1998), as was his illustrated life of *Franz Kafka* (2001).

CHARLIE LOUTH was born in 1969 in Bristol. He is a Fellow of the Queen's College, Oxford, where he lectures in German. He is the author of *Hölderlin and the Dynamics of Translation* (1998).

FRIEDRICH HÖLDERLIN

Essays and Letters

Edited and Translated with an Introduction by
JEREMY ADLER *and* CHARLIE LOUTH

PENGUIN BOOKS

In memory of Michael Hamburger

PENGUIN CLASSICS

Published by the Penguin Group
Penguin Books Ltd, 80 Strand, London WC2R ORL, England
Penguin Group (USA) Inc., 375 Hudson Street, New York, New York 10014, USA
Penguin Group (Canada), 90 Eglinton Avenue East, Suite 700, Toronto, Ontario, Canada M4P 2Y3
(a division of Pearson Penguin Canada Inc.)
Penguin Ireland, 25 St Stephen's Green, Dublin 2, Ireland
(a division of Penguin Books Ltd)
Penguin Group (Australia), 250 Camberwell Road, Camberwell, Victoria 3124, Australia
(a division of Pearson Australia Group Pty Ltd)
Penguin Books India Pvt Ltd, 11 Community Centre, Panchsheel Park, New Delhi – 110 017, India
Penguin Group (NZ), 67 Apollo Drive, Rosedale, North Shore 0632, New Zealand
(a division of Pearson New Zealand Ltd)
Penguin Books (South Africa) (Pty) Ltd, 24 Sturdee Avenue, Rosebank, Johannesburg 2196, South Africa

Penguin Books Ltd, Registered Offices: 80 Strand, London WC2R ORL, England

www.penguin.com

This edition first published in Penguin Classics 2009
1

Selection, translation and editorial material copyright © Jeremy Adler and Charlie Louth, 2009
All rights reserved

The moral right of the translators and editors has been asserted

Set in 10.25/12.25pt PostScript Adobe Sabon
Typeset by Rowland Phototypesetting Ltd, Bury St Edmunds, Suffolk
Printed in England by Clays Ltd, St Ives plc

ISBN: 978-0-140-44708-8

www.greenpenguin.co.uk

Contents

Acknowledgements

This book was first conceived as a selection of Hölderlin's essays with Paul Keegan, formerly editor of Penguin Classics, about a decade ago. The plan was then altered to include a small number of letters on poetics and philosophy. The volume owes its present form to the generosity of Penguin Books, who accepted our joint proposal to include a larger selection of letters, making this the most extensive collection of Hölderlin's prose to appear in English to date.

The original versions of several of these translations were the first of any of Hölderlin's theoretical prose to appear in English. They were published, together with detailed introductions, by Dr E. S. Shaffer in *Comparative Criticism. A Yearbook*: 'Notes on the *Oedipus*', 'Notes on the *Antigone*' and 'The meaning of tragedies' (vol. 5, 1983); 'The declining fatherland . . .' and 'The Ground of the *Empedocles*' (vol. 6, 1984); and the *Pindar Fragments* (vol. 7, 1985). We are grateful to Dr Shaffer and to the Syndics of the Cambridge University Press for permission to reprint these translations in revised form.

Jeremy Adler wishes to record his gratitude to the late Dr Robin Harrison, who checked the first translations of the essays against the original texts; to the late John Lavery, for collating against the Greek Hölderlin's renderings of Sophocles and Pindar in the essays; and, especially, to Dr Stefanie Hölscher, who took substantial time from her own duties to check both the published versions and all the new translations of the essays with a scrupulous eye for detail. Charlie Louth would like to thank David Constantine for his watchful reading of the letters alongside the originals. To their careful work we owe numerous helpful suggestions. Needless to say, any remaining errors are our own.

The translations of the essays in *Comparative Criticism* were consulted by Thomas Pfau for his edition, *Friedrich Hölderlin: Essays and Letters on Theory* (New York, 1988), and in reciprocation the occasional helpful formulation has been borrowed from him.

We gratefully point out that the volume in its present form was made possible by Michael Hamburger, who put us in touch with one another; and, on a more personal note, Jeremy Adler wishes to record his debt to Charlie Louth for his patience during the long gestation of this edition. Finally, we wish to acknowledge our gratitude to Mariateresa Boffo of Penguin Classics and all the staff at Penguin Books who have helped this book see the light of day, and particularly to the copy-editor, Monica Schmoller.

JA and CL

Chronology

1770 *20 March* Johann Christian Friedrich Hölderlin born into the so-called 'respectability' class in Lauffen am Neckar. Hegel, Wordsworth and Beethoven born the same year.

1772 Death of father and birth of sister, Heinrike (Rike).

1774 Hölderlin's mother remarries and the family moves to Nürtingen.

1776 Half-brother, Karl Gok, born. Schooling begins in Nürtingen.

1779 Death of stepfather.

1781 Kant's *Critique of Pure Reason* published.

1783 First gets to know Schelling, five years his junior.

1784 Confirmed; enters Klosterschule (for pupils destined for the priesthood) in Denkendorf. First surviving poems from this year.

1785 First surviving letter.

1786 Moves up to Klosterschule in Maulbronn.

1787 Writing poems and reading Schiller, Klopstock, Ossian, Young.

1788 Kant's *Critique of Practical Reason* published. *June* Hölderlin first sees the Rhine. Gathers his poems together and translates first two books of Homer's *Iliad*. *October* Enters the Stift (seminary) in Tübingen at the same time as Hegel. Meets Neuffer there.

1789 French Revolution. Complaints about life in Stift, which gains a reputation for revolutionary sympathies among its students. Hölderlin breaks off engagement to Louise Nast.

1790 Along with other students, begins reading Kant; also

Leibniz and Herder. Works on his two examination disser-
tations: 'History of the Fine Arts among the Greeks' and
'Parallels between Solomon's Proverbs and Hesiod's *Works
and Days*'. Having passed examinations in philosophy in
September, gains the title of *Magister* and moves on to the
more narrowly theological part of his training. Writing
poems influenced by Schiller. Schelling joins the Stift, aged
fifteen. Kant's *Critique of Judgement* published.

1791 *April* Journey to Switzerland. First poems published.
Reading Rousseau.

1792 Begins work on his novel, *Hyperion*. France declares war
on the Austro-Prussian coalition, and French troops occupy
Mainz. *October* His sister marries and becomes Heinrike
Breunlin.

1793 21 *January* Louis XVI executed. 14 *July* Liberty Tree
raised in Tübingen by students including Hegel, Schelling
and Hölderlin. First contact with Sinclair. Reading Plato.
Meets Schiller, who recommends him for a post as house-
tutor in Waltershausen. After taking his final examinations,
arrives at Charlotte von Kalb's in Waltershausen at the end
of the year.

1794 Teaching Fritz von Kalb 9–11 a.m. and 3–5 p.m., otherwise reading Greek literature, Kant (*Critique of Judgement*
especially), Fichte, and working hard on *Hyperion*. Acquaintance with Wilhelmine Marianne Kirms. Execution of Danton
(*April*) and Robespierre (*July*). *November* Trip to Jena,
where he meets Schiller and Goethe and attends Fichte's
lectures. Moves to Weimar with the Kalbs. Writes 'There is
a natural state . . .' and 'On the Concept of Punishment'.

1795 *January* Leaves the Kalb household following troubles
with Fritz, and with Charlotte von Kalb's blessing returns to
Jena and lives next door to Fichte. Goes to his lectures, sees
much of Schiller, reads Goethe's novel *Wilhelm Meister's
Apprenticeship*. The publisher Cotta agrees to publish the
as-yet-unfinished *Hyperion*. Begins to get to know Sinclair
better and in *April* moves into his 'garden-house', where he
also meets Böhlendorff. Writes 'Being Judgement Possibility'
and 'Hermocrates to Cephalus'. *May* Matriculates at the

university, meets Novalis, and then suddenly quits Jena and goes home to Nürtingen via Heidelberg, where he meets Ebel. *July* Luise Agnese born (she died in September 1796), daughter of Wilhelmine Kirms and, very likely, Hölderlin. Several important conversations with Schelling in Tübingen and Nürtingen; becomes friends with Landauer in Stuttgart. *September* Accepts a new post and arrives in Frankfurt at end of the year. Publication of Schiller's *On Naive and Sentimental Poetry* and *On the Aesthetic Education of Man*.

1796 *January* Takes up job as house-tutor in the Gontard household in Frankfurt, teaching in the mornings. Soon falls in love with Susette Gontard. Contact with Sinclair and Schelling. *July* With the family, minus Jakob Gontard, flight from advancing French troops to Kassel, and to Driburg (*August*). *End of September* Returns to Frankfurt. Resists mother's urging that he return to Württemberg and become a priest. Perhaps writes 'Fragment of Philosophical Letters'. Between this summer and next spring (or possibly earlier: see note to Appendix), writes 'The Oldest Programme for a System of German Idealism', a collaboration between Hölderlin, Hegel and Schelling.

1797 *January* Hegel joins him in Frankfurt. *April* First volume of *Hyperion* appears. *22 August* Last meeting with Goethe. *17 October* Treaty of Campo Formio. Continuing work on *Hyperion*, begins his tragedy *The Death of Empedocles*, many poems.

1798 Life in Frankfurt becomes difficult and unhappy. *End of September* Leaves Frankfurt and moves to nearby Homburg. Sporadic secret meetings and exchangings of letters with Susette. *November* At the Rastatt Congress with Sinclair. Finishes *Hyperion*.

1799 In this year, in Homburg, most of the essays are written, some for the unrealized journal project (*Iduna*), conceived in *May* and abandoned in the autumn. Some also relating to *Empedocles*, which after going through several versions is also abandoned at the end of the year. *October* Second volume of *Hyperion* appears. *9 November* Napoleon becomes First Consul, and then declares the Revolution over.

'When the poet is once in command of the spirit . . .', the longest of the Homburg essays, probably written at the end of this year (and over into the next).

1800 Probably in this year translations of Pindar's Olympian and Pythian odes, closely connected with the deliberations of the essays. *Easter* Short visit home to Nürtingen. *8 May* Last meeting with Susette. *15 June* Treaty of Marengo, good prospects of peace. *June* Leaves Homburg for Nürtingen, then to Landauer's in Stuttgart (*20 June*). Gives private lessons; on the look-out for a new house-tutor post. Home to Nürtingen for Christmas. Writing poems, including the first elegies.

1801 *January* Travels to new job in Hauptwil, Switzerland, mostly on foot. *9 February* Peace of Lunéville. *April* Employment terminated. Back home to Nürtingen. *2 June* Last letter to Schiller. Writing elegies and hymns. *December* Sets off towards Bordeaux, where his last tutorship has been found. By foot to Strasburg.

1802 From Strasburg arrives in Lyons, then continues, still mostly on foot, to Bordeaux, arriving in the Meyer household end of *January*. Possibly begins translations of Sophocles here (*Oedipus* and *Antigone*). *10 May* Issued with a pass to Strasburg and leaves the Meyers without apparent ill-feeling on either side. Goes via Paris and sees some of the art treasures Napoleon fetched out of Italy. *June* Back in Stuttgart in a bad way. *22 June* Death of Susette Gontard. Summer in Nürtingen. *October* Attends congress at Regensburg with Sinclair. Completes Sophocles translations and their 'Notes' and looks for a publisher. Poems include 'Patmos' and 'Celebration of Peace'.

1803 *January* Sends 'Patmos' to the Landgrave in Homburg, via Sinclair. *June* Wilmans agrees to publish Sophocles translations. Meets Schelling. Late revisions to Sophocles versions; revises several poems, including the 'Night Songs'. Probably writes 'The meaning of tragedies . . .'.

1804 *April* Publication of *The Tragedies of Sophocles*. Sinclair involved in conspiracy against the Elector of Württemberg.

June Sinclair fetches him to Homburg via Stuttgart and Würzburg (last meeting with Schelling). Lodges with a French clockmaker, not far from Sinclair's, and receives sinecure as Court Librarian. Princess Auguste gives him a piano. *Pindar Fragments* perhaps written this year, following the publication of the 'Night Songs' in the autumn.

1805 *February* Sinclair arrested and accused of treason. During the trial inquiries are also made into Hölderlin's involvement, but he is spared trial by being declared clinically insane. *9 May* Death of Schiller. *July* Sinclair is released. Hölderlin moves to lodge with a saddler. Apparently working on Pindar.

1806 In August Sinclair writes to Hölderlin's mother saying that his madness has attained a 'high degree' and he can no longer look after him. Hölderlin forcibly removed to the University clinic in Tübingen.

1807 *3 May* Discharged from the clinic as incurable with 'at most three years' to live, and taken in by the carpenter Ernst Zimmer and his family. Their house is on the banks of the Neckar in Tübingen, Hölderlin's room forming a sort of tower overlooking the river.

1815 Death of Sinclair. Battle of Waterloo.

1820 First moves are made towards collecting Hölderlin's poems.

1822 *Hyperion* reprinted in one volume.

1826 Hölderlin's *Poems* appear (without many of the most important).

1828 Death of Hölderlin's mother, who seems never to have visited him during his time in Tübingen.

1831 Publication of an essay by Wilhelm Waiblinger, who had often visited Hölderlin when studying in Tübingen in the early 1820s (sometimes in the company of Eduard Mörike): *Friedrich Hölderlin's Life, Poetry and Madness*. Death of Hegel.

1832 Death of Goethe.

1838 With the death of Zimmer, responsibility for Hölderlin's care is taken over by his daughter Charlotte Zimmer.

1841 Begins signing poems 'Scardanelli', with fictitious dates.

1842 Second, expanded edition of Hölderlin's *Poems* (still far from complete).

1843 7 *June* Death of Hölderlin. Neither his sister nor his brother attends his funeral.

Introduction

Hölderlin is known best as a poet, and that is how it should be. There is no doubt where his main achievement lies: in the odes, elegies, hymns and fragments, most of which are gathered in the Penguin volume of his *Selected Poems and Fragments* (translated by Michael Hamburger), to which the present volume is intended as a companion. But for some time now he has been recognized as an almost equally important thinker in prose, whether in his letters, his mostly fragmentary essays or in his novel, *Hyperion* (not included here). His thinking occurs in a time and place – Germany at the turn of the nineteenth century – which, defined by the French Revolution on the one hand and by Kant's critical philosophy on the other, witnessed an explosion of philosophical insight and aspiration whose consequences continue to unfold and which is returned to again and again by thinkers and writers today. Hölderlin was in Jena in 1795, where he attended Fichte's lectures. Jena at this time was – to quote Nicholas Boyle – 'intellectually speaking the most exciting place in the world'.[1] And at the Protestant seminary (the Stift) he went to in Tübingen from the age of eighteen to twenty-three (1788–93), Hegel and Schelling, who became the two most influential post-Kantian philosophers, were among his fellow students and friends; all three kept in touch, and conversations with Hegel were continued above all in Hölderlin's Frankfurt and Homburg years (1796–1800; Hegel was in Frankfurt 1797–1800), those with Schelling in 1795 and later. The most tangible product of these conversations is the text known as 'The Oldest Programme for a System of German Idealism', a piece of collaboration between all three. Hölderlin is also part of a philosophical movement and moment, and in recent years it has become clearer than ever that he was a vital instigator and mover, as well as taking certain trains of thought further than anyone else.

But his friendship with Hegel and Schelling, as well as with Isaak von Sinclair, a political activist and writer, also served to focus Hölderlin on what was his particular domain and vocation: poetry. And just as his poetry encompasses philosophical and political concerns, so his theoretical prose is always poetic, both in the sense that it uses poetic means (particularly unconventional syntax and argument-by-rhythm), and in that it constantly explores and seeks to found the workings and function of poetry, especially its ability to encapsulate those aspects of experience and intimation which, precisely, escape conceptual discourse. The essay-fragments are thus frequently on the edge of themselves or of articulation *tout court*, defining the limits of their preoccupations as they extend them. And because poetry, for Hölderlin, has a religious and political import, his reflections touch again and again on fundamental questions such as personal development, the nature of history, our relation to the past and humankind's capacity for a better life, even as they examine the difference between literary genres.

In the notes to his translation of Sophocles' *Oedipus*, Hölderlin identifies a need to raise modern poetry to an equivalent of the '$\mu\eta\chi\alpha\nu\eta$ [mechane] of the ancients', $\mu\eta\chi\alpha\nu\eta$ meaning art, craft, technique, device, even machinery. And he himself, recognizing 'the sure, thoroughly purposeful and considered progression of ancient works of art' (to Neuffer, 4 December 1799), went about his work 'very deliberately'. The overriding concern of Hölderlin's thinking can be seen to be the question of manifestation: how things can be grasped, shown, realized and held on to; which means attending to the 'minute particulars' (Blake), the parts, the local, in which larger things become manifest. The poetic significance of this is obvious, and at the furthest reach of implication manifestation becomes epiphany: how and whether 'divine sense' ('The Archipelago'[2]) might appear in the world. But it also takes in the historical (how do new forms occur in time?), the political (what would they look like?) and the philosophical (how does the whole relate to, show itself in, its parts?). In thinking about how what he variously calls the spirit, being, unity, the whole, the original and many other designations manifests itself in the poem, Hölderlin is simultaneously, and often explicitly, investigating a general law of life.

Moments of transition are especially favourable to the workings of manifestation. Describing the shift from one historical epoch and political form to another in the fragment traditionally known as 'The Process of Becoming in Passing Away' ('The declining fatherland . . .'), Hölderlin writes that 'in the very moment and in that degree in which what exists dissolves, that which newly emerges, the youthful and possible, is also felt'. He understands himself to be living in such a time of radical change, of openness to possibility, which is both potentially propitious to poetry and badly in need of it to provide a 'hold' or 'purchase' amid the dissolution and uncertainty and so to cross the 'gap' (p. 272) as which the present is experienced. It does this, Hölderlin says, by giving pause and remembering and interpreting the course of change, allowing a distance from it, but more fundamentally by, as an instance of beauty, imparting a sense of unity. Poetry for Hölderlin is 'a live, intricately articulated, intense whole' and that is also what it can produce in its readers (to Karl Gok, New Year's Eve 1798/1 January 1799), that is the effect of beauty generally. In *Hyperion*, the hero calls poetry the 'beginning and end' of philosophy: because it makes beauty, understood after Heraclitus as unity-in-variety, manifest and so gives philosophy the premiss for its deductions and anatomies, and, because it offers it also an end point, a resolution of difference in aesthetic experience. The way in which poetry articulates beauty, in its parts, their interchange and altering, in the iridescence of its modulating structures, suggests that division and difference, so easily felt as sources of suffering and confusion, can also be, and are, the conditions of experiencing unity, are precisely that in which unity or wholeness manifests itself. Aesthetic experience thus provides a model for other kinds of experience and is indispensable for living in and understanding the world. All these passages of thought, these recurring preoccupations, grew out of Hölderlin's own life, which, as his letters show, was marked by division and conflict, and by wandering transitions and shifts in situation, among which his writing came to form the constant, the necessary 'hold'.

The Letters

Reading Hölderlin's letters allows us to trace the lines of his life, of his thinking and feeling, in their intersections with his friends and family and other correspondents. And also to trace his life as a writer, both in the reflections on his practice the letters contain and in the writing itself: there are passages which resemble the language of his novel, *Hyperion*, passages close to the reckonings of the essays, and gradually the letters or at least parts of them, beginning perhaps with those written just before the journey to Hauptwil in 1801, approach and arrive at the rhythms and clarities, the absolutely *necessary* tone, of his poems. Unlike some of the essays, which seem to have been written to himself, as a working out of ideas in the process of wording them, the letters are, by definition, always directed at another, they always occupy the particular space, what he once calls the 'psyche', between himself and his correspondent. Of course that is in a sense true of any letter, but Hölderlin's are particularly concerned, or even anxious, to create a rapport, to make the letter grow out of and reflect the precise contours of a relationship, and in so doing to actually establish and constitute that relationship within the letter (and his poems, too, very often address someone, invoke the presence and absence of a particular person as they speak): letters, poems and essays all seek to enact their theme as a real presence, not just as a reflection in words. For the letters this is complicated, but not invalidated, by Hölderlin's admitting at one point to his brother that he has written 'more for himself', or by the fact that many of the letters are drafts, and may not resemble what was actually sent. The form of the letter had a special significance for Hölderlin, and was a favourite form generally at the time. Like Rousseau's *Nouvelle Héloïse* and Goethe's *The Sufferings of*

Young Werther, Hölderlin's novel *Hyperion* is written in letters, and many of the bits and pieces he wrote for his failed magazine *Iduna* adopt the epistolary form. The fragmentary 'Philosophical Letters' likewise follow a seminal example, Schiller's *On the Aesthetic Education of Man: a Sequence of Letters*, and early in 1796, Hölderlin writes to Immanuel Niethammer that he and Schelling both think that 'new ideas' can best be presented in the form of letters, having the year before announced to Hegel the intention of making his 'image and . . . friendship' the 'conductor of [his] thoughts into the outer world of the senses' by writing him letters for him to 'judge and correct' (26 January 1795).

A letter always implies the idea of a correspondence. Unfortunately, with some important exceptions, most of the letters *to* Hölderlin have not survived. Of his own, enough are extant to form a good impression of him as a letter-writer, but still very many, possibly more than half, are thought to have been lost. Adolf Beck, in his unlikely-to-be-superseded edition, collected 313 items, of which 247 belong to the period before 1806. One more turned up in 1998. About a third of them are translated here. Really the letters should be translated complete, as they have long been into French, Italian and Japanese. But until we have them all in English too, a selection can helpfully single out the most important pieces – and perhaps avoid an element of repetition.

There is a large discrepancy between the numbers of letters from different periods of Hölderlin's life: from the time of the first period in Homburg (October 1798 to June 1800) forty-four letters survive, and we know that many more were written; but from the end of 1801, when Hölderlin left for Bordeaux, to June 1804, when he set off with Sinclair to Homburg for a further two-year stay, we have merely ten, and there may have been only a few more. Hölderlin's style in the letters both develops over time and varies from letter to letter, according to whom he is addressing and what he is writing about. The letters to Schiller, for example, span the years 1794 to 1801, an immense gap in terms of Hölderlin's development as a poet, yet they vary only slightly in tone and manner, seeming to remain locked within a repetitive pattern which psychoanalysis could certainly circumscribe. Something similar is true of the letters to his mother. In both these cases he is writing out of a position of embarrassment or even abjection, either begging or fending off, and this results in an awkwardness of expression and in an involved and sometimes self-defeating syntax which, at some risk to itself, the present translation has attempted to follow. Over the same period the language develops elsewhere into a tender, intense clarity which has no parallels and has left the occasional diffuseness and indirectness of earlier letters far behind.

The letters reveal the main stations of Hölderlin's writing life up to spring 1804 when his translations of Sophocles' *Antigone* and *King Oedipus* appeared. The letters written in Tübingen, after he had been declared clinically insane in 1805, are then a sad, immeasurably diminished coda, like a tragic waste. The present selection begins with the only extract from a very long letter giving an account of a journey on which Hölderlin saw, for the first time, the Rhine. The rivers of Germany, and rivers in general, the 'spirit of rivers' ('The Life-Giver'), were a constant source of Hölderlin's poetry (see 'The River Main', 'The Fettered River', 'Ganymede', 'The Rhine', 'The Ister', the *Pindar Fragment* 'The Life-Giver' and many other poems). Hölderlin had already written a lot and, though training to become a priest, was already firmly set on the course of becoming a poet. In Tübingen, where he went in 1788 to complete his theological training and formed important friendships with Neuffer, Hegel and Schelling, his main correspondents are his mother and his sister (over half of all the letters are written to his family, and well over half of those to his mother). The letters he writes them in the early years set the pattern for all his later letters to them: to his sister he describes his surroundings, talks about his everyday life in an intimate kind of way, and dwells on the difficulty of finding the right 'tone' or 'note' in which to address her, his mind taken up as it is by his studies and his writing (this antagonism is later expressed towards other correspondents as one between poetry and philosophy). And to his mother, as well as asking and thanking her for money, and justifying his position to her, he avows his commitment to writing and makes some religious reflections. His first letters to Neuffer also establish a pattern that varies little – their chief preoccupation or subject is poetry. Hölderlin clearly led something of a double life while at the Stift, pursuing philosophical (and political) concerns with one set of friends and poetic ones with another set, but joining both strands in much of his work. The letters to Neuffer contain the development of his poetical thinking until their friendship fades and his chosen intimate in poetry, at least on the evidence of the letters, becomes Böhlendorff. The first of the letters to Karl Gok, Hölderlin's half-brother, also belong at the end of the time in Tübingen – they become the main carriers of Hölderlin's hopes and beliefs and aspirations in a more general sense, not always attached to the particularities of poetry.

After leaving Tübingen in 1793 Hölderlin entered on an uncertain life whose only continuous thread is the 'most innocent of all occupations', his writing. But partly because his first job as a private tutor took him near, then to, Jena, then Germany's philosophical centre, he also set himself the task of coming to terms with modern philosophy, reading and re-reading Kant and Schiller, then Fichte, and working out the consequences in letters to his brother, to Neuffer and to Hegel, and in his first essay-fragments. He always seems to have read Plato alongside the modern thinkers. In Jena he made or consolidated many of his friendships, and he was fortunate in his friends. Whether he met them here or later, very many of them came to Jena at about this time, to study philosophy and to join the various radical groupings that were seeking to introduce the ideals of the French Revolution into German hearts and minds and soil. Nearly all his friends were radical democrats and shared his aspirations, which were so great and so uncompromising, of a kind hardly possible any more, that they rapidly had to assert themselves against a background of increasing disappointment. Some of the utopian energy of the prose of Hölderlin's letters, its ability to intensify into a sharp and rhythmical realization or anticipation, is close both to parts of the essays and to the poems, and derives perhaps from the contrast with the real prevailing political and social conditions (which the letters also register). Reaching out to the correspondents, the letters create an ideal community, construct the 'invisible church militant' (Letter 31, to Ebel, 9 November 1795) in the Here and Now of the writing, bridging the actuality of separation and insufficiency. In the end most of the letters have that idealistic purchase on reality, summoning up the world as it should and can be again and again. 'Every day I have to invoke the absent god again', Hölderlin begins a fragmentary draft to Susette Gontard (Letter 70, June 1799). The abstract quality many of the letters have derives from this too: he is calling into being a world that does not yet exist. His interest in philosophy perhaps has a similar cause. For though he later noted the 'tragic' state of affairs that even 'human thoughts and systems' are subject to local circumstances and the climate (Letter 61, to Sinclair, 24 December 1798), Kant's philosophy did not seem to grow out of the particular world of late eighteenth-century Germany but to apply generally, to all worlds, and thus to offer a way of fitting Germany to the forms of truth and beauty.

In Jena Hölderlin quickly became an independent mind, responding to the latest thinking as he heard it from Fichte's mouth (see especially Letter 24, to Hegel, 26 January 1795). He seems to have spoken to Fichte on several occasions, and these conversations may have had an influence on aspects of Fichte's philosophy. In Frankfurt, six months after leaving Jena, philosophy is still 'almost my only occupation' (Letter 34, to Niethammer, 24 February 1796) and the 'echoes of Jena' still resonate strongly. But though this letter goes on to detail the principles of his 'philosophical letters', he notes that they will not deal with philosophy alone, but move on to attend to poetry and religion, and he also makes a kind of confession which later magnifies into doubts about whether he should ever have given himself over to philosophy at all. 'Philosophy is a tyrant,' he writes, 'and I suffer its rule rather than submitting to it voluntarily.' In another frame of mind he can regard the 'metaphysical mood' as 'a certain virginity of the mind' (Letter 49, to Schiller, August 1797), as a natural stage, and it is probably true that his mature poetry capitalizes on his philosophical work rather than suffering from it as he feared. But the letters written in Frankfurt contain much less philosophical reasoning, and once in Homburg Hölderlin's theoretical concerns are primarily poetological rather than philosophical, though his thinking tends towards a unity of all things and is partly attempting to overcome such distinctions.

Three points should be made in this connection: much of Hölderlin's philosophical thought went into *Hyperion* (whose two volumes appeared in 1797 and 1799, the early fragment, with its important preface, as early as 1794); much of his thinking, and with it his influence on contemporary philosophy, took place in conversation, notably with Schelling and with Hegel, who joined Hölderlin as a private tutor in Frankfurt in 1797, but also with Sinclair and others; and the real turning-point of this period is meeting and falling in love with Susette Gontard who, by embodying for him the ideal, in a sense made philosophy superfluous. 'I write little and hardly do any philosophy any more', he writes to Neuffer (Letter 45, 16 February 1797), 'But what I do write has more life and form. My imagination is more open to the shapes of the world.' Philosophy he will now regard (or can regard) as a 'hospital' for sick poets (Letter 58, to Neuffer, 12 November 1798), though that did not prevent him from writing some of his most important essays after this date.

The entering of the concrete into his life and work also takes a political form, and Hölderlin now becomes more exposed than before to political events as the post-revolutionary fighting drives deeper into Germany and the Revolution becomes harder to idealize. From Paris he receives a letter from his friend Ebel, full of disappointment, and responds with an amazing summoning up of energy and hopefulness that also looks straight at 'reality, soiled as it is' (Letter 44, 10 January 1797). Though he continues to think of the times as 'destructive', as hostile to poetry ('We don't live in a climate for poets', to Karl Gok, Letter 52, 12 February 1798), he sets about overcoming what he calls 'being shy of experience' (see Letter 49, to Schiller, August 1797), which means above all letting experience, matter, into his poetry, finding ways of bringing his poetry into relation with the world.

The most important document of this process is the letter to Neuffer of 12 November 1798, written shortly after leaving the Gontard household in Frankfurt and moving to nearby Homburg. This letter contains a poetics in itself, and is perhaps the best introduction to the intense thinking about poetry and its place that Hölderlin embarked on in Homburg, a way into the intricacies, densities and vertiginous reach of the poetological essays. Its subject is 'life' or 'liveliness' in poetry (*das Lebendige in der Poesie*), something he longs to achieve but is conscious of lacking, and very characteristically he sees that lack as corresponding to one in his own life: 'I lack not so much strength as lightness, not so much ideas as nuances, not so much a main tone as a spectrum of diverse tones, not so much light as shadow, and all this for one reason: I shun the common and ordinary aspects of real life too much.' The rule that results from this self-diagnosis applies equally to life and poetry: 'Purity can only be represented in impurity and if you try to render fineness without coarseness it will appear entirely unnatural and incongruous.' This is the beginning of a long series of reflections on manifestation, at the heart of Hölderlin's poetics. Poetry cannot work, cannot make manifest, in isolation, but only in interaction with the world, by taking on the forms of immediate reality. This means both acquiring a degree of 'impurity', of 'coarseness', of ordinariness or 'body', *and* making the poem derive its shape, its breath, out of its relationship with the imperfect present. The epiphanies of the mature poems, their realizations of fulfilled life, are always undercut by a retraction or reservation, usually in the form of a reminder that that state is no longer, or not yet. They are part of a modulating structure, a particularly rich and harmonious chord, but set among dissonance and discordancy. As such they appear all the more forcefully, and by being exposed to the claims of reality in which the depicted states do not pertain end up more convincing because they do not 'appear entirely unnatural and incongruous', in shrill and unsubtle contradiction to the world, but have folded the contradiction, the discrepancy between poetry and life, into their workings.

In Homburg Hölderlin was able to devote himself to his writing uninterruptedly for the first time, and he rapidly achieved a new certainty: 'I am deeply conscious that the cause I live for is a noble one and, once it is brought to its proper expressiveness and formal perfection, one that is beneficial to mankind. And with this determination and purpose I live at peace in my occupations' (to his mother, Letter 80, 16 November 1799). The impossibility of his relationship with Susette Gontard, and the failure of his attempt to found a poetry magazine, also seem to have made him turn all the more uncompromisingly to his writing. Certainly the letters are as good an indication as any of the advances he was making. There is nothing in his prose before like the draft-fragment to Susette Gontard, probably of June 1799. The 'sure, thoroughly purposeful and considered progression' he saw in the works of the Greeks began to apply more and more to him. In June 1800, after a final parting with Susette Gontard on 8 May, he went back home to his mother's in Nürtingen, moving on almost immediately to live at his friend Landauer's in Stuttgart. He was fighting against depression, and slipping in and out of euphoria, but was in his richest phase of poetic production. There are few letters, and most of them short, confining themselves to the 'absolutely necessary' (Letter 88, to Heinrike Breunlin, Autumn 1800). He writes mostly to his sister, and a new tone occurs which is difficult to describe and harder to translate: by focusing on what is 'absolutely necessary' his language acquires a direct simplicity in which the distinction between statement and enactment disappears. Several letters speak of a reduced ability to communicate: 'often I really do feel like ice' (Letter 92, to Heinrike Breunlin, 11 December 1800), and it is as if the words he does find are forced to carry the weight of all that is unspoken. 'You too, dear Rike, are, I hear, firmer on God's ground again' (Letter 89, to Heinrike Breunlin, mid-October 1800). Or to his brother at the end of the year: 'You are preserved, saved up; the storm has passed

over you, be glad that you heard it from a distance in a place
of safety and have kept your soul pure and loving and fearless
for the better times that will come' (Letter 93, late December
1800). A growing restlessness and a need for peace and quiet
make him set off on his travels for a third time, to Switzerland,
crossing Lake Constance. The letters from Hauptwil are then
among his finest. At the news of the Peace of Lunéville in
February 1801 Hölderlin sought a correspondence for his joy
in the Alpine landscape: 'I can only stand there like a child and
wonder and rejoice in silence when I'm out on the nearest hill
and down from the ether come the heights stepping closer and
closer into the friendly valley whose slopes are thick with the
evergreen of fir woods and whose floor is seamed through with
lakes and streams, & that's where I live, in a garden, where
under my window willows and poplars stand by a clear water
I love to listen to at night when all is quiet and beneath the
serene starry sky I write and think' (Letter 98, to Heinrike
Breunlin, 23 February 1801).

The sense of wellbeing was short-lived. After leaving
Hauptwil in April Hölderlin returned home only to set off again
at the end of the year (1801) to his fourth and final job as a
private tutor, in Bordeaux. Before leaving he wrote the first of
two letters to Casimir Böhlendorff which have long had a
special status in Hölderlin's correspondence. It is a letter of
farewell, not so much to Böhlendorff as to Germany. But it is
also a difficult poetic reflection on the relationship between
antiquity and modernity which is extended in the letters to his
publisher Wilmans in 1803 and 1804 (Letters 111–115) and in
the 'Notes' to his translations of Oedipus and Antigone. The
confined tone, which seems to be holding back as much as it
expresses, but which is also a kind of innocence, returns: 'I shall
have to keep a hold of my wits in France, in Paris ... O my
friend, the world lies more brightly before me than usual, and
is more serious' (Letter 106, 4 December 1801). That tone
of simplicity and depth, it is tempting to call it mythic, now
dominates. To his mother, after a long and tough journey to
Bordeaux, most of it done on foot, he wrote: 'I am now hardened through and through, initiated as you could wish. I think

I shall remain so, in the main. . . . My accommodation is almost too grand. I would be happy with secure simplicity' (Letter 108, 28 January 1802). The time in Bordeaux was no longer than that in Hauptwil and by mid-June 1802 he was back in Stuttgart, having passed through Paris and seen the recently augmented collections of the Musée Napoléon. On his return he was greeted by news of Susette Gontard's death. Letters are now very sparse, but at the end of the year, still in Nürtingen where he remained until June 1804, he addresses the second letter to Böhlendorff, which uses the insights of the first to evoke his experience of France and, through it and the classical statues he saw in Paris, of Greece. This letter is like the poems Hölderlin was writing at this time, endlessly interpretable. It combines a sense of extreme exposure and great and precise purchase, and offers a direct view of Hölderlin's state of mind at this point. One passage repeats the movement of the quotation above from Hauptwil, but it is much more heavily freighted. It seems that Hölderlin has come home and into precariousness at once; it is a kind of culmination: 'the characteristicness of the woods and the coincidence in one region of different characters of nature, so that all the holy places of the earth are together in one place, and the philosophic light at my window, they are now my joy. May I keep in mind how I have come to where I am now!' (Letter 110, November 1802).

The remaining letters before what Michael Hamburger calls simply his 'change of personality' are all business letters of a sort; but they are far more than that. By now Hölderlin could not put pen to paper without an inevitability emerging from what he wrote. Every word seems right and unalterable. The letters to Wilmans are important because they talk directly about Hölderlin's writing and its premisses, not to an initiated friend like Böhlendorff but to a (discerning) publisher. Even so it is hard to imagine how Wilmans can have reacted to some statements, which have the whole weight of Hölderlin's poetic thinking behind them. And perhaps very few of the letters met with the exact correspondence they strove for, the taking up into a like mind. More and more they document a loneliness within the world. And from the last period before he was

definitively consigned to madness, the two years he spent in
Homburg under Sinclair's auspices with a sinecure as court
librarian, no letters survive.

Reading the letters, it is easy to discern the religious regard
Hölderlin had for the world, and his religious sense of poetry's
function and purpose in it, a function and purpose they come
close to fulfilling themselves. Religion for Hölderlin meant a
living relation with the world, and it is such a relation, one
of equilibrium, that he was always seeking to create in his
correspondence, against the odds, and sometimes against the
evidence. On 28 November 1798 he writes to his brother (Letter
59) that they have left their friendship 'without nourishment'
for too long: 'But the gods, though they do not need a sacrifice,
demand it nonetheless as a tribute. And so we too must again
begin to make sacrifice from time to time to the divinity between
us: the easy, pure sacrifice of speaking to one another about it,
of celebrating the god that unites us in the sweet letters that we
only exchange so rarely because they come from the heart and
not, as so often happens, from the pen.' Letters as tribute, as
sacrifice, to celebrate and thus to maintain and renew the 'god
that unites us'. A theology emerges here that had to wait for
Martin Buber to be realized fully, over a century later. The
conception recurs even more simply in the letter to his sister
from Hauptwil (Letter 98, 23 February 1801): 'all that is good
and sacred must be celebrated, and for that reason our correspondence should never remain interrupted for too long.' There
again the exchange of letters appears as a ritual, as a necessary
remembering of what is there. Hölderlin's poems, too, want to
celebrate, that is what propels them, but they are held back
from outright celebration, from fully espoused joy, by admitting
in their workings that the grounds for it are not yet present.
They actually inhabit a shifting ground, an intermediate region,
between an ideal past and a projected future idyll. They anticipate rather than celebrate, but their anticipations often seem to
begin to bring about, to do more than anticipate, what they
imagine. Behind the insistent conjurations of the letters we can
sometimes feel a similar movement, but it tends to work more
negatively: they attempt to refer to what is there, and cannot

protect themselves (as the poems can and do) from its absence. We can never know precisely what resonance most of his letters found, but it is hard to think many of them received what Keats (in a letter to Benjamin Bailey, 13 March 1818) calls 'a greeting of the Spirit', though they perilously solicit one. Like the poems, they largely lack the community they try to presuppose and to speak to. But to talk with another, to achieve a just relation across the gap of absence, *can* be to render the 'in-between' animate. 'Make sure you write to me soon', Hölderlin says in the second letter to Böhlendorff, 'I need your pure tones. Psyche among friends, the formation of thoughts in conversations and letters, is vital for artists.'

In the very last letters, written from Tübingen, where he spent the second half of his life, that living relation has gone, and more, it is hardly being looked for. The letters still have something ritualistic about them, but it has hardened into mere form, so that they read like parodies of the earlier letters, frighteningly hollow, and even seem to mock themselves. They are exercises in formula, fending off rather than connecting, and some consciousness of this can seem to peep through without disrupting the sense of naivety. In his dealings with most people (perhaps not his keepers) it was the same, and something analogous happened to his poetry. On occasion then the severe reduction the letters evince permits a striking phrase to emerge whose effect is like an echo, and their very emptiness is a sign.

The Essays

Hölderlin's philosophical essays form an essential part of his work and have increasingly come to be acknowledged as an achievement comparable in importance to his poetry. Yet the reader who approaches these essays with the standard assumptions of the genre will be in for a surprise. Instead of the conversational medium, the dialogue with the reader that we might expect, Hölderlin's musings are more often a dialogue with himself – solipsistic where the essay would be sociable; cryptic where it would illumine; and refractory, sibylline, obscure – operating at the very edges of the understanding –

where it would assist, simplify, explain. There are of course reasons for this, and with a few exceptions Hölderlin seems not himself to have thought of his theoretical writings as essays in anything approaching the normal sense. One aspect of the essay is however crucial to their gesture and mode, and that is the experimental, provisional aspect, the practice of taking a thought and seeing what can be made of it, how far the writing of it can conduct it out into uncharted territories of the mind. When we read Hölderlin's essays we seem to be catching the philosopher-poet in the very act of thinking. This phenomenon compels a tenacious commitment from the reader to follow Hölderlin's relentlessly advancing ideas through every conceivable permutation, until the ideal, the complete thought, is if not accomplished then at least shadowed forth in all its details.

By any standards, Hölderlin's essays, especially four or five of them, present the reader with substantial, intrinsic difficulties, but some of this difficulty can be explained and perhaps alleviated by making a few points about their context and composition. First, as mentioned Hölderlin often resorted to the essay to clarify ideas for himself, rather than to introduce a wider readership to his thought. Secondly, some of the most important essays are unfinished – it is just possible that in a few cases the final versions have not come down to us, but it is equally possible, and more likely, that he did not finish them and that their incompleteness is a consequence of their experimental nature. Thirdly, the essays were written in the throes of a German philosophical revolution, intended to be as significant as the political revolution in France, in which the key young thinkers – two poets, two philosophers: Novalis and Hölderlin, Schelling and Hegel – aimed to outdo Kant, the greatest and most difficult master of modern thought (and in vying with Kant, himself a writer of the utmost difficulty, they aimed to press forward their ideas to the limits of the thinkable). Fourthly, in aiming to go beyond Kant and Fichte, Hölderlin looked back to the gnomic utterance of the pre-Socratic philosophers, whose pithy apophthegms (sometimes framed in verse) provided him with a model quite unlike that of modern philosophical prose. And finally, even as a thinker, he remains a poet, using language not just in a reflective, abstract manner, but as the embodiment of his ideas, sometimes fusing philosophical and poetic streams of language, but sometimes causing them to conflict. In short, this blend of the philosophic and the poetic, of the tentative and the systematic, of the archaic with the modern, goes some way towards explaining the peculiar texture of the essays. The chief aim of these translations has been to remain as faithful to Hölderlin's remarkable rhythms, syntax and vocabulary as is consistent with English usage, retaining as many as possible of his often taxing linguistic idiosyncrasies, in the belief that his language forms an inseparable part of his meaning.

Hölderlin's philosophical thought unfolded over time in different media, and the reader wishing to follow his progress needs to pay equal attention to the expression of his ideas in each particular form, from the letters, as indicated, to the poetry, which is as permeated by philosophical ideas as it is grounded in experience, and from the early lyrical novel, *Hyperion*, to the fragmentary drama about an ancient Greek philosopher, *Empedocles*. In their turn, the essays interlock and engage with Hölderlin's writings in the other genres by exploring a series of connected themes in philosophy, poetics and history. Very often Hölderlin wrote reflective prose in the attempt to clarify and resolve a problem he had encountered in his more properly literary work, to try to understand where he had arrived, how he had got there and how he might proceed. His writings on tragedy in particular are deeply embedded in his work on his own unfinished tragedy and on his translations of Sophocles. But his essays are not all of a piece, and it is helpful to look at the different phases they pass through. They can usefully be divided into ten groups:

1. the earliest pieces from school and university, of which only five survive and which are not included in this collection;
2. the early essays, written between 1792 and 1799 but focusing on 1795–6 and influenced by Hölderlin's time in Jena, from 'I was slumbering, my Callias . . .' to 'The wise, however . . .';

3. the pieces probably linked with the abortive plan to found a 'poetic journal' in 1799, from the fragmentary 'Draft of the Journal Plan' to 'On the Different Modes of Poetic Composition';

4. 'The Ground of the *Empedocles*' and the fragment beginning 'The declining fatherland . . .' of the same year, closely associated with the last stages of Hölderlin's verse-drama;

5. the poetological essays, fragments and tables probably begun several weeks after the journal essays, from 'When the poet is once in command of the spirit . . .' to 'The tragic poet . . .';

6. a review of Siegfried Schmid's play *The Heroine* written in 1801;

7. the final essays on tragedy, i.e. the fragment 'The meaning of tragedies . . .', written after 1802, and the 'Notes' for Hölderlin's translations of *Oedipus* and *Antigone*, published in 1804;

8. the brief notes 'On the Fable of the Ancients', probably of 1804;

9. the *Pindar Fragments* of 1803–5;

10. the fragmentary manifesto jointly conceived with Hegel and Schelling and penned by Hegel in 1796/7, now known as 'The Oldest Programme for a System of German Idealism'.

The present edition is the most substantial collection of Hölderlin's essays in English, with only the earliest university pieces missing.

Hölderlin's essays begin with issues tackled by Kant, Schiller and Fichte – to consider the immediate external context – by continuing his own earlier preoccupations, first clearly voiced in *Hyperion*, concerning the self and being, beauty and art. To get to grips with his own position, we may go straight to the fourth and fifth essays in this collection, 'Being Judgement Possibility' and 'Hermocrates to Cephalus'. The former recapitulates and develops the position, also reached in *Hyperion*, regarding the relation between reflection and being. Indeed, this remarkable early essay defines what can broadly speaking be taken as a central idea in Hölderlin's literary and philosophical work, namely the unity of existence and the means by which it can be apprehended:

> Where subject and object are absolutely, not only partly, united, namely so united that no division can be executed without damaging the essence of that which is to be separated, there and nowhere else one can speak of a *being as such*, as is the case with intellectual intuition.

Hölderlin's understanding of the complex represented by the 'unity' of 'subject' and 'object' in the world and the faculty of 'intellectual intuition' as the means to grasp it represent his chief contribution to philosophy. The same ideas that drive his philosophy also feature in the poetological essays, for it is in literature that this unity can be represented, or, to put it more strongly, achieved: the aesthetic sphere intuits the unity that philosophy presupposes and examines theoretically. Rational thought, then, is inferior to poetry: as Hyperion recognizes in Hölderlin's novel, philosophy is ultimately 'blind', and only poetry represents the true 'beginning and end' of philosophy. Some of Hölderlin's most brilliant if tortuous formulations pursue this theme. Thus, the essay 'When the poet is once in command of the spirit . . .' introduces 'the concept of the *unity* of the *One*', where:

> among the harmoniously united, *one* as well as *the other* is *present in the point of opposition and union*, and . . . *IN THIS POINT THE SPIRIT IS FEELABLE IN ITS INFINITY*, which through the opposition manifested itself as finite.

The 'One', as Hölderlin understands it, is a complex entity entailing a unity of opposites. It is what Hyperion once calls *das Eine in sich selber unterschiedne* ('the One differentiated in itself'). It is a vision of wholeness that encompasses difference.

'Hermocrates to Cephalus' draws the consequences of such an object of thought, by rejecting closed systems and embracing an open-ended method. Although Hölderlin is here thinking of Fichte, his objection would apply also to Kant:

> So you seriously believe that the ideal of knowledge can be represented in a particular time in a particular system?
>
> . . .
>
> I have always believed that for its knowledge as for its actions mankind needed an infinite progress, an unbounded time, in order to approach the boundless ideal; . . . there will always be error, whether it contents itself with an individually determined boundary or simply denies a boundary that is in fact there, even though it ought not to be.

In recognizing the inevitable gulf between the perfectibility of the intellect and the imperfection of the world, Hölderlin commits himself to a boundless intellectual quest, a search for knowledge most clearly elaborated by Goethe's Faust and translated into a poetological principle by Friedrich Schlegel in his concept of *progressive Universalpoesie*. This is the endless journey of the Romantics, who by setting their sights on the Infinite courted failure and fragmentariness in their utterance. The incomplete state of Hölderlin's essays, then, can perhaps be understood not just as an accident of composition but as a consequence of his philosophy.

The position that Hölderlin first adumbrated in the penultimate version of *Hyperion* as early as spring 1795 and later developed in the essays is sometimes known as 'absolute idealism'. It has long been recognized, and was recently confirmed by Frederick Beiser, the historian of German idealism, that Hölderlin was the first to reach this position, and that it was he who transmitted the central idea of 'absolute idealism' to Schelling and Hegel. Besides the novel and the essay 'Being Judgement Possibility', this is evidenced by the letter to Hegel of 26 January 1795 (Letter 24), which, without elaborating Hölderlin's views, criticizes the inconsistencies in Fichte's thought.

The convergence between the thinking of Hölderlin, Schelling and Hegel can be deduced from the long-standing debate about the so-called 'Oldest Programme for a System of German Idealism', written some time in 1795-7, and given here as an appendix. The text has achieved iconic status in modern scholarship, not only as the earliest draft for a system of German Idealism, but because of the mysterious circumstances surrounding its composition and discovery. It is written in Hegel's hand, probably came from Hegel's papers, but did not enter the public sphere until 1913, when the Prussian State Library bought it at auction; however, its first editor, Franz Rosenzweig, argued that on internal grounds, and against the evidence of the handwriting, the essay should be attributed to Schelling. Since then it has also been claimed that the central role which the programme's author attributes to aesthetics indicates that Hölderlin had a key part in its composition. Although perhaps the strongest case has now been made for Hegel as author – and Hölderlin editions differ as to whether the fragment deserves even a supporting role in the canon (Schmidt includes it, Knaupp does not) – there is no immediate end in sight to the authorship dispute. We would not wish to make a case for Hölderlin's role beyond his inspiring a key idea in the text, but, following Beissner and others, print the 'Programme' as a significant fragment whose ideas belong in the ambit of Hölderlin's essays.

The crucial break with Fichte concerns the nature of the absolute, which Fichte locates in the 'I' or self. For Hölderlin, however, following Plato and Spinoza, the 'absolute' lies not in the subject, but in 'Being'. This was made clear in the passage from 'Being Judgement Possibility', which continues: 'But this being should not be confused with identity . . . identity is not a union of object and subject that takes place absolutely, therefore identity does not = absolute being.' The 'absolute' as Hölderlin understands it comprises a union of subject and object. In contrast to Kant's *Ding an sich* (the 'thing in itself'), Hölderlin's 'absolute' can be known and understood by means of 'intellectual intuition'. This is a faculty that made no sense to Kant, and whose very possibility he denied, but which plays a key part in the thinking of Fichte, Hölderlin and Schelling. For Hölderlin, the idea underpins both his philosophy and his

poetry, and accordingly his preoccupation with it continues
into the major poetological essays, 'When the poet is once in
command of the spirit . . .' and 'The lyric, in appearance idealic
poem . . .'. The latter contains one of the clearest statements
about his understanding of this difficult concept: 'The tragic
. . . *poem* . . . must be based on *one* intellectual intuition, which
can be no other than [the] unity with all that lives.' Unlike
Schelling, Hölderlin thought the intellectual intuition was not
a matter of self-consciousness, of the self divining itself, but
that it permitted an 'insight' into the unity of all things, the self
included. It was a union which threatened rather than secured
identity. But in his letter to Schiller of 4 September 1795 (Letter
30) he implied that the intellectual intuition is located in aesthetic experience and has no theoretical validity: 'the union of
subject and object . . . though possible aesthetically, in an act
of intellectual intuition, is theoretically possible only through
endless approximation'.

Allda bin ich / Alles miteinander, Hölderlin writes in one of
his fragments, 'And there I am / All things at once' (*Selected
Poems and Fragments*, pp. 312/313), and this emphasis on
unity helps to explain an apparent confusion as to whether
intellectual intuition is a mode of apprehension, a means to an
end, or the end itself, the totality that is to be experienced.
Insofar as the intuition makes the unity apprehensible, it creates
it, conveying the subject into the whole and overcoming the
division that made the apprehension possible and necessary.
The notion of unity as *totality* has important consequences,
because early on Hölderlin is clear about what totality implies.
The fourth of the notes known as 'Seven Maxims', or 'Reflection', begins: 'Only that is the truest truth, in which even error,
because it is placed within the whole of a system, in its time and
in its place, becomes truth.' Unity is made up of 'harmoniously
opposed' antitheses; it is not a stable condition, but on the
contrary a precarious organization of conflicting elements. If
the question for poetry is how this various unity can be made
manifest, part of the answer seems to be that it is through
poetry's itself adopting the structures of 'truest truth', and the
aphorism carries on: 'This is also the highest poetry, in which

even the unpoetic, because it is said at the right time and in the
right place in the whole of the work of art, becomes poetic.'
Poetry must integrate what might at first seem to lie outside it
– the unpoetic – in order to be itself, to be its 'highest' form.
To be whole, it must be inclusive and open to the other. It is its
ability to do this, to be 'receptive' (p. 284), that makes it
peculiarly apt to body forth the wholeness divinable in and
through the intellectual intuition, which is similarly constituted.

Hölderlin's poetics, as already noted, revolve round the problem of how things may be made manifest in poetry. Poetry, and
art more generally, is understood as having a vital role in human
affairs because it allows being, the feeling of totality, to be
revealed. Perhaps, as Hölderlin's writing sometimes seems to
suggest, it actually produces, as opposed to *re*producing, the
feeling of totality, the absolute, in the world, and so makes our
divided and damaged experience (momentarily) complete. A
poem, Hölderlin says, is a 'metaphor', it literally 'carries' something 'across' (according to the Greek sense of *meta-pherein*)
into sensible form, it is the translation of something. This something doesn't have to be as grand as an intellectual intuition. A
lyric poem, he writes several times, is the metaphor of '*one*
feeling' ('The lyric, in appearance idealic poem . . .'). The fundamental premiss of his poetics is that nothing can be expressed
directly, it can only be expressed in some form of division,
opposition or complex modulation, as and through something
other; and several times he suggests that a thing finds best
expression in its opposite, in what is most unlike itself.
Although there must be an underlying analogy to make the
metaphor viable in the first place, the poet's 'total feeling' can
be preserved 'more certainly' in the chosen subject 'the more
alien this subject is in its analogy' ('The Ground of the *Empedocles*'). The intent of most of Hölderlin's poetological investigations is towards devising a law, a precise pattern, according
to which different kinds of material can be articulated in the
workings of a poem.

Hölderlin is unusual among poets in having tried so
thoroughly to theorize his practice and to work his way towards
it by writing technical prose. Like Coleridge, he believed that

poetry has 'a logic of its own, as severe as that of science' (*Biographia Literaria*, 1817), but he attempted to formulate it in detail, and at a level of abstraction and ambition unlike anything in Coleridge or elsewhere. Partly this is a phenomenon of his time and of his place in the German tradition: German Romanticism generally, to which Hölderlin does and does not belong, began, in theory, with the composition of its famous fragments (by Novalis and Friedrich Schlegel), and these anticipations of a dreamt-of ideal reality often summoned up far more than they could convert into certain good. Like Coleridge, who of course depended heavily on what he had gathered on his trip to Germany in 1798–9 and supplemented thereafter, Hölderlin's poetological concerns are always braided together with more purely philosophical ones, but in all his very intricate, exacting and quasi-mathematical deliberations, his attempts to arrive at a 'calculable law' of poetry, he insisted on 'the living sense which cannot be computed' ('Notes on the *Oedipus*') and he knew that what he was trying to focus on in the philosophical idiom of the time would in the end escape him. One way of trying to understand the import of Hölderlin's poetics, then, is to think of them as a response to the complexity of the world and to a sense that it would somehow always elude philosophy. As he puts it in the 'Notes on the *Antigone*', philosophy 'always treats only one faculty of the soul', and proceeds by logic, whereas poetry 'treats the various faculties of a human being', and proceeds by 'rhythm . . . in a higher sense'.

Hölderlin's poetic theory aims to discover and define this 'rhythm in a higher sense'. Part at least of what he means by this rhythm is a sequence of modulations in the texture of a poem, a lively and enlivening variety and fluency. To theorize this movement he worked out a series of 'tones' or 'notes', which are derived from the three genres of classical poetics: epic, lyric and drama (drama for Hölderlin meant almost exclusively the tragic, but he wrote a review (pp. 312–15) in which we can see him attending to the comic too). In the discursive writings we can see that the idea of tone as a fundamental aspect of a poem evolved out of considering characters in Homer. In what is probably the last of the essays written or begun for the failed journal *Iduna* in 1799 (which for that reason is written in a more patient and lucid idiom than some of those Hölderlin seems to have written primarily for his own use), 'On the Different Modes of Poetic Composition', he writes of the 'natural tone' proper to epic, and quotes part of Phoenix's speech to Achilles in Book 9 of the *Iliad* by way of illustration, characterizing it as 'expansive, constant, really true'. As the word 'tone' itself suggests, but as commentators looking for the application of Hölderlin's tone-poetics in his own poems have tended to ignore, it is thus more a matter of *how* something is said than of *what* is said. This 'natural' tone, at home in the epic, he later called the naive tone, and from the other genres he subsequently derived an 'heroic' tone (proper to tragedy) and an 'ideal' tone (proper to the lyric).

'On the Different Modes of Poetic Composition' observes that Achilles, the express subject and hero of the *Iliad*, would hardly be distinguishable from his surroundings had not Homer removed him 'so tenderly carefully from the fray', and that it is in his tent that he appears 'properly before our eyes'. There is no more than an implication, then, that Achilles' *heroic* quality appears best in the contrasting *naive* mode, and that the 'naive tone' that characterizes the epic is therefore not its only tone, but simply the dominant, apparent, expressive one. According to a later formulation, the 'basic tone' (*Grundton*) of the epic is indeed heroic, and the naive tone is the 'artistic character' (*Kunstkarakter*) or 'language' or 'style' of the poem and not its unique tone (the proliferation of different terms for the same phenomenon is a constant of Hölderlin's essays). This 'metaphoric' shift becomes the vital element of Hölderlin's poetics, and it is already present in embryo in an earlier and fuller reflection on the dynamics of tone, the important letter to Neuffer of 12 November 1798 quoted earlier. Here Hölderlin says that as a writer he lacks not a 'main tone' but a 'spectrum of diverse tones', that if he is to articulate his 'innermost', his most intimate, self, he must make use of the inimical aspects of life he finds assailing him, he must take them into himself in order to 'reproduce them as subordinate tones among which the tone of my soul will spring forth with all the more life'

(p. 109). That is, nothing can appear in isolation, in a pure state, in monotone, but is truly expressed as part of a complex, in polytone. Hölderlin was quite an accomplished musician, playing the flute and the piano and with a good singing voice, and as his novel, *Hyperion*, and other writings show he was fond of thinking of the chord as an image of diverse but harmonious life: the tonic or key-note of a chord resonates more fully, more richly, when part of that chord than when played on its own; in a way its true (composite) character emerges. The chord is not a precise analogy, but still perhaps a helpful one, for suggesting what Hölderlin means when he talks about basic tone and its manifestation in and through other tones.

This though is only the beginning of Hölderlin's tone-theory. As the letter to Neuffer intimates, it is not merely a matter of expressing one basic tone through another tone (so, in the case of epic, expressing the heroic through the naive), but of devising a *sequence* of tones, what at one point he refers to as an 'alternation of tones' ('Note on Homer'), in which each genre (epic, lyric, tragedy) finds its ideal embodiment. In a series of tables Hölderlin attempted to set out the operation necessary for each kind of poem, the premiss being that every genre requires its own modulating sequence and has to pass through a number of different modes. To continue the musical analogy, the chords are arranged so as to form a discrete melody. One consequence of this is that since the tones are drawn one from each genre (naive=epic, heroic=tragic, ideal=lyric or, if we follow the basic tones, naive=lyric, heroic=epic, ideal=tragic – see 'The Poetological Tables') but are all present in each sequence, every genre is a modulation of the others, all are different permutations of a basic set of tones which derive from different faculties of human nature, i.e. feeling (naive), passion (heroic) and imagination (ideal), or from different aspects of existence, i.e. reality (naive), necessity (heroic) and possibility (ideal). This insight into the fundamental mixedness of the genres puts Hölderlin into the company of German Romantics such as Friedrich Schlegel again, who at much the same time (1798) was speaking of 'unifying the separate genres of poetry'.

According to the tables in their most developed form, each

genre works through a sequence of seven tone pairs (or chords), with the 'artistic character' tone in the first pair (which in the lyric sequence is ideal) returning in the same position in the final pair, obeying a basic rule of musical composition. The other striking feature of the sequences is that the fourth pair (at the middle of the poem) is an inversion of the third. In the manuscripts Hölderlin has grouped these two pairs (third and fourth) together with bracket-like lines, drawing attention to the moment of inversion. The reversal interrupts the normal sequence of basic tones (which as the tables show goes from ideal to naive to heroic in a repeating series), such that for each genre the key basic tone associated with it (so for the lyric the naive tone) is absent from the sequence for two consecutive steps, causing a kind of crisis and perhaps a negative presence. Hölderlin seems to call this phenomenon 'catastrophe' ('Does the idealic catastrophe . . .'), where again, as in his use of the word 'metaphor', he is remembering the etymological, literal sense of 'down-turn', 'overturning'. This notion of a decisive and revelatory moment of reversal is a constant of Hölderlin's poetics, and can be found in the idea of the caesura in the Sophocles 'Notes'. What he says about this might also be said of the tone-tables, and shows the continuity of Hölderlin's poetological thinking: 'the rhythmic succession of ideas, wherein the *transport* manifests itself, demands a counter-rhythmic interruption, a pure word, *that which in metrics is called a caesura*, in order to confront the speeding alternation of ideas at its climax, so that not the alternation of the idea, but the idea itself appears' ('Notes on the *Oedipus*').

This figure can also be found in Hölderlin's longest and most difficult disquisition into the workings of poetry, the essay 'When the poet is once in command of the spirit . . .', also known by the title drawn from an expression in the text itself, 'On the Procedure of the Poetic Spirit'. Though the chronology is uncertain, Hölderlin probably wrote this just before completing the tables. It appears to have been written at speed, and unlike some of the other comparable Homburg writings such as 'The declining fatherland . . .' is all but complete. 'When the poet is once in command of the spirit . . .' enquires into the precise nature of the interaction between spirit and matter that constitutes a poem; it tries to describe, but at points perhaps also to enact, the process whereby spirit might enter into or manifest itself in poetry. Fundamental to this is a 'necessary conflict', necessary because only through it, in its dialectical warring, can the spirit be felt, as it merges with the sensuousness of matter and breaks out of its pure, unfeelable form. This conflict involves both 'opposition and union', and 'in this point the spirit is feelable in its infinity', the spirit becomes part of the poem, it bends the language to its progress and submits to the channelling of form. The poetic is a matter of opposing and relating, and through it *must* be possible, Hölderlin says, what might at first look impossible: the grasping of spirit (which he also calls the 'pure', or 'original poetic individuality', or the 'poetic I', or a number of other formulations), the grasping of spirit in such a way that nothing that it is is impeded or traduced by the grasping. The spirit must be able to grasp itself because, and here Hölderlin at first resorts to Kantian reasoning, it is defined by freedom and so must also have the freedom to do this. But the essay as a whole goes beyond this philosophical move to suggest that the spirit experiences a kind of completion or extension in the encounter with matter – the spirit becomes feelable not just to others but to itself and so takes on a new quality: 'the pure, which in itself conflicted with the organ, is *present* to *itself* in this very organ and only by that means *is a living thing*'. The essay is a continuation of Hölderlin's reflections in his letter of 12 November 1798, where he says that 'Life in poetry is what now occupies my thoughts and senses more than anything else.' *Lebendiges* (liveliness) is, according to 'When the poet is once in command of the spirit . . .', what has consciousness of itself, and the poem permits a 'reflection' in which the spirit is grasped but not held. It is not life itself or the spirit itself, but what the essay-fragment 'The Standpoint from which we should consider Antiquity' calls 'real reciprocal relation' (*reelle Wechselvereinigung*) between the two.

Large parts of 'When the poet is once in command of the spirit . . .' concern the workings of the poem, but it begins by talking about the poet, and in fact Hölderlin sees an analogy between the 'course and the destiny' of poetry and the 'course and the destiny of mankind as such' (p. 296). According to his triadic pattern of thinking, which is also present in the tone-theory, and in various different forms was a staple of contemporary thought, from Mozart's symphonies to Novalis's concept of history and Hegel's dialectic, a 'naive' state of life (childhood) passes into an 'heroic' one (a state of conflict) which is followed by an 'ideal' state, the 'pure echo of the first life' (p. 296), in which life is fully apprehended and lived for the first time, as the givenness of childhood is replaced by the freely constituted and conscious life of maturity. The successful arrival at a poem, the finding of language, is a version of the same process, and 'creative reflection' – which is another way of talking about the process of opposing and unifying we have already encountered – 'gives the heart everything back that it took from it' (p. 296). What is ideally true of the individual human life is also true of the poet's transposition of his experience into language and of the spirit's interaction with substance in the poem. The law that governs all these operations is: 'Put yourself *through free choice* in harmonious opposition with an outer sphere, just as you in yourself are in *harmonious* opposition, by nature, but unrecognizably, as long as you remain in yourself' (p. 290). The step outside of oneself is thus an entering into oneself, self-exposure is self-recognition, we need the other to know ourselves. What we then discover is that the initial state, that which we leave to learn, is in itself already 'harmoniously opposed', a delicate structure of tensions and resolutions rather than the stable condition of unity it seemed to be, and similarly the poetic spirit is something not of a totally and inaccessibly different order, but already intrinsically partakes of the structures of life and can for that reason coincide with them. The poem creates not some equivalent of spirit, an analogous, allusive process, but, according to the highest pitch of Hölderlin's theory, actually bodies it forth.

It is obvious that Hölderlin's thinking, at least in his Homburg period (1798–1800), is marked by a thorough interconnectedness: every aspect is related to every other, history, poetry, the self, all have analogical structures, everything is imbricated in everything else. In keeping with this mode of thinking, the three genres are versions of each other, shifts of emphasis rather than radically different forms. But gradually Hölderlin was more and more drawn to the tragic as the supreme genre, the one in which 'the immediate God' becomes 'wholly One with man' ('Notes on the *Antigone*'), as he puts it in the more mythical language he now prefers over the philosophical idiom in which he had previously spoken of tragedy as the metaphor of an intellectual intuition.

Tragedy, 'the strictest of all poetic forms' as he calls it in another letter to Neuffer (Letter 71, 3 July 1799), forms the focus of Hölderlin's deliberations primarily in connection with his work on his unfinished tragedy, *The Death of Empedocles*, and then with his translations of Sophocles' *Oedipus the King* and *Antigone*, which were in part a renewed attempt to write modern tragic drama having abandoned *Empedocles*, which seems to have happened late in 1799.

The two fragmentary essays, 'The Ground of the *Empedocles*' and 'The declining fatherland . . .', can be read as exploring the horizontal, synchronic axis, and the vertical, diachronic axis of tragedy respectively. The 'Ground' analyses the tragic hero as an expression of his era and as a resolution of its conflicts, whilst 'The declining fatherland . . .' focuses on the epoch itself as a time of transition. Both essays are intimately connected with the evolution of Hölderlin's play on Empedocles. The manuscript evidence shows that Hölderlin wrote the 'Ground' as a way out of the impasse at which the first two versions of his play had arrived, and that it enabled him to begin a third version which breaks off at about the point that 'The declining fatherland . . .' sets in. This then enables a plan for the continuation of the third version which seems never to have been realized. For a long time the connection of the latter essay to the drama complex went unrecognized, and it is true that its implications are very much wider than the horizon of the play, but though no mention is made of Empedocles and the level of abstraction is very great, it is now clear that it belongs in this context even though it also shows how

Hölderlin's demands on and understanding of the form of tragedy were exceeding any specific realization.

Hölderlin's thinking about tragedy belongs at the start of a German tradition that reaches forward to Nietzsche and beyond. Peter Szondi defined the tradition in his now classic study *Essay on the Tragic* (1961; English translation 2002), where he points out that a new view of tragedy begins when the empirical poetics in the train of Aristotle was supplemented by a philosophy of the tragic, a metaphysics of tragedy. The first three thinkers in this line were Schelling, Hölderlin and Hegel. As Hegel's treatment of it in *The Phenomenology of Spirit* indicates, tragic art occupied a key place in post-Kantian idealism. Indeed, Szondi maintained that the birth of Hegel's dialectic coincided with his thinking on tragedy. But it was Schelling who first developed the concept of the tragic in his *Philosophical Letters on Dogmatism and Criticism* of 1795; Hölderlin followed in his writings of 1798–1803; while Hegel's earliest thoughts were published in 1802–3. The connecting threads that link these three are various. They include: the concern with classical tragedy, and Sophocles in particular; the dialectic structure which emerges in their definitions of the tragic; the central place the tragic assumes in their thinking; and the great, indeed religious, significance located in the tragic action. It is now clear that both in philosophical reach and poetic conviction Hölderlin's thoughts go beyond anything in the work of his peers, and it is generally accepted that his thinking had a considerable influence on the others', though of course their discussions will have been a three-way process.

Because the earlier of Hölderlin's reflections on the tragic are associated with *The Death of Empedocles*, it will be helpful to say a few words about Hölderlin's fragmentary play. It is not insignificant that a philosophy of the tragic arose from work on a play about a philosopher. Indeed, the very structure of the tragic which Hölderlin envisages arises out of Empedocles' philosophy. *Empedocles* incorporates many features of the historical figure, as one would expect. Clearly enough, the play was to conclude with his mythical death in the volcano of Mount Etna. More significant, however, is the way in which

Hölderlin integrates the facts of Empedocles' life into a pattern derived from his philosophy. A central element of this is his doctrine of the cosmic cycle of Love and Strife, which forms the basis for Hölderlin's view of tragedy in the 'Ground', and introduces that pre-Socratic force to his theory still evident in the Sophocles 'Notes'. In a fragment preserved in Simplicius, Empedocles himself puts the doctrine as follows:

> There is a double coming into being of mortal things and a double passing away. One is brought about, and again destroyed, by the coming together of all things, the other grows up and is scattered as things are again divided. And these things never cease from continual shifting, at one time all coming together, through Love, into one, at another each borne apart from the others through Strife.[3]

Here lies the origin of both 'The Ground of the *Empedocles*' and 'The declining fatherland . . .'.

In the 'Ground', Empedocles' first principle, Love, becomes *Innigkeit*, 'intimacy', while Empedocles' second principle remains the same: *Zwist* (strife). Like Empedocles, Hölderlin conceives of 'intimacy' and 'strife' as engaged in a three-part cycle, which – we may gather from the drafts and the 'Ground' – was to have determined the course of Empedocles' life in *Empedocles*. All three versions of the play focus on the second stage of the cycle as manifested in Empedocles' own life. The first, 'intimacy', is recalled retrospectively from the vantage-point of the second, the desolation of 'strife'; whilst the third, a renewed, truer and freer 'intimacy', is foreshadowed by Empedocles himself. Here again we find a variation on the triad naive-heroic-ideal. The conclusion is inevitable: final union with nature and the gods through death in the volcano. Empedocles, the worshipper of the sun, will return to the element of fire. Having been a darling of the gods and then found himself abandoned by them, he anticipates a regained intimacy with them and the elements.

This, then, is the basic constellation developed with almost unbearable intricacy in the 'Ground', and it is a model that implicitly has a wider application to tragedy in general. The essay's first section presents the basic pattern in broad outline. The second, the 'General Ground' is preserved only in part, but seems to repeat the structure of the first on a larger scale. The third and longest section appears to break with the previous argument – but only to introduce two new terms: the two categories whose combination it is that produces 'intimacy'. These are 'nature', or as Hölderlin terms it, 'the aorgic';[4] and 'art', or 'the organic'. Their union produces the 'divine' which typifies the height of 'intimacy'. The dialectical relationship between 'art' and 'nature' occupies the rest of the essay. Thus Hölderlin grafts his own concepts onto the ancient pre-Socratic framework.

In 'The declining fatherland . . .' the triadic pattern assumes a different but related form as it is applied to history. The three phases are past, present and future, where the present (the 'real') is characterized as a period of conflict and confusion ('strife'), and past and future (the 'ideal') are viewed as analogous to one another in that they escape the bewildering complexity of the actual and clarify into discrete shapes. The focus of the essay is transition, and transition has a similar function (and literal meaning) in the realm of history as we saw that metaphor did in the context of the poem. In the opening paragraph time or history and language are both regarded as sites or processes in which the absolute ('the world of all worlds, the all in all') can appear, and the analysis of the present as a constant going-over from one thing to another, which the old dissolves into and the new arises out of, makes us acutely conscious of the infinite potential of each passing moment, but also of the fragility of the particular constellation reality seems to have taken on. This present is always in motion, under way, is always a process of passing away and becoming at the same time. Hölderlin is interested in the end of an epoch (this being the connection to *Empedocles*, which tries to locate itself at the shift from a monarchical order to a republican one), in 'decline', but wants to make us see that the course of decline and the emergence of the new are one and the same process, this being the nature of the present.

The problem is how, in the moment, this double nature of the present can be understood, given that the immediate feeling of living in it is one of confusion and disorientation ('fear'), of the time being 'out of joint'. This is where tragedy comes in (Hölderlin treats tragedy, as also later in the 'Notes' to Sophocles, as being particularly concerned with transitions between epochs, but most of what he says about it might also apply to poetry in general and to how he understood his own poetry's role in the present). The 'gap' between epochs, the fearful, negative moment in which only dissolution can be felt and not the new crystallization it also is, is filled and traversed by tragedy's anticipating the future and looking back (from an imagined future perspective) on the process of dissolution, and comprehending it, clarifying it, into a meaningful progression by portraying it as 'the secure unimpedable bold act, which it actually is' ('The declining fatherland . . .'). Thus, 'real dissolution' becomes 'ideal dissolution', it is grasped as 'necessary', and tragedy enables the crossing into the new epoch, gives us a model of how uncertainty can be traversed, and in so doing actually effects the transition. The words Hölderlin uses to describe this faculty of 'the free imitation of art' are 'memory' or a 'reproductive act', terms which recur in 'When the poet is once in command of the spirit . . .'. Through 'remembering' the dissolution, tragedy orders it and reality takes on the composed and clarifying structure of a work of art. This is how art may have political effect. Hölderlin's theory is worked out with great intricacy and philosophical consequence, and in abstract terminology, but its kernel is adequately expressed in Seamus Heaney's words: 'If our given experience is a labyrinth, then its impassability is countered by the poet's imagining some equivalent of the labyrinth and bringing himself and us through it.'[5] It is the imagining itself, the memory, which brings us through the labyrinth.

It is not certain when Hölderlin began his translations of *Oedipus* and *Antigone*, but his interest in Sophocles was long established, and *Empedocles* was intended as a Sophoclean drama. He appears to have had a complete draft (at least) of his versions ready by autumn 1802, when he began looking for a publisher, and this makes it possible that work on them began not long after *Empedocles* was abandoned at the end of 1799. First though, he seems to have translated the greater part of Pindar's Olympian and Pythian hymns (in the first half of 1800). There are then several mentions of the tragic in the letters (such as in that to Mehmel, probably written in late autumn 1800) which show that it was a continuing preoccupation, and there are certainly continuities between the 'Notes' accompanying his translations and his earlier thinking on tragedy. The form of that thought, on the other hand, has changed considerably: the philosophical language, though not ambition, has largely yielded to a more poetic and radically individual style which seems to owe something to the language of the translations themselves. Just as the earlier pieces grew out of the work on *Empedocles*, the 'Notes' are not merely comments on the translations but continuous with them, the product of the experience of translating tragedy and discovering some common ground joining his method and its object. Tragedy, for Hölderlin at this stage, was a matter of violent coupling and splitting, and his practice as translator also forced the German language into a kind of interlinear intimacy with the Greek that opened up as much difference as consonance. This curious interrelatedness of tragedy and translation is an unspoken theme of the 'Notes'.

Hölderlin's thinking and language in these late reflections is of great intensity and intellectual beauty. Though they present us with a rigorous itinerary of thought which has now received extensive exegesis, they are like Hölderlin's poems in their resistance to it. Their fascination partly derives from the independent life they appear to lead as unimpeachable imaginary structures. We can come at them first by looking at the short text 'The meaning of tragedies . . .', which may be a vestige of the 'introduction' to Sophocles' tragedies Hölderlin promised in letters to his publisher Wilmans in late 1803 but seems not to have written. This fragment, if such it is, syncretizes pre-Socratic thought with German idealism and modern scientific thinking to present, in miniature, an entire system. Hölderlin develops a metaphysics which relates man to (the totality of) the world. Nature ('the primal') uses man ('the sign') in order to manifest itself. Where nature most completely appears ('straight out', 'in its strongest gift'), man becomes least significant ('= o'). Thus Hölderlin establishes tragedy as a natural phenomenon, expressible as a mathematical law: the meaning of the sign is inversely proportional to the appearance of the primal – tragedy discloses nature's infinite power in the death of the tragic hero. This is certainly Hölderlin's most radical, autarchic definition: for it sets up 'the tragic' as a pure idea, free from traditional poetic categories.

This idea also underpins the 'Notes', and of course the tension between nature and the individual was previously explored in *Empedocles* and its accompanying prose deliberations. As the 'Notes on the *Oedipus*' have it, in tragedy the 'natural power ... removes man from his orbit of life, the very mid-point of his inner life, to another world, and tears him off into the eccentric orbit of the dead'. The antithesis takes many forms in the 'Notes', such as consciousness and time, form and spirit, the organic and what Hölderlin called the aorgic, but the overriding one is that between man and God. The point of tragedy is to bring God back into human affairs, epiphany.

The form of the 'Notes' can itself be understood as part of this drama of opposition in that it tries to compel the bursting multiplicity of ideas (that constitute, in condensed form, an entire philosophy) into an apprehensible whole. The two sets of 'Notes' are written to the same pattern, and can be read like an essay in six parts. The arrangement into sections is largely based on a dialectic of observations about form and content which mirrors the dialectic of tragedy the 'Notes' describe. In each set, the first part deals with the plays' form and in particular their 'calculable law' or 'rhythm'. The second part focuses on the main character and proceeds by exegesis of central passages: in each case, Hölderlin picks on the moment when the hero(ine) comes into contact with the inimical forces that threaten his or her individuality, where Oedipus interprets the oracle 'too infinitely' and Antigone espouses the gods in her conflict with Creon. The third part, which consciously begins by sharing the same wording, then attends to a more general idea of the tragic, and moves on to show the consequences of this for dramatic structure and the function of the chorus, that is, for 'tragic representation'; before turning to the historical dimension of tragedy, its role in the 'course of the world' ('Notes on the *Oedipus*') or in the 'spirit of the age' ('Notes on the *Antigone*'). So the two essays unfold in parallel, and their reading is facilitated and enriched if we bear the correspondences in mind.

By basing tragedy in nature or founding it theologically, Hölderlin removes the tragic from the aesthetic sphere, and sets it squarely in life. Tragedy has its time and place at particular moments of historical change. This aspect of the 'Notes' follows on closely from 'The declining fatherland . . .'. Tragedy expresses, finds a language for, historical experience, and in so doing ensures that there is no 'gap' (p. 272) in time, that passage from one epoch to the next is possible. In his remarks on *Antigone*, Hölderlin locates a historical transition from the Greek phase of world history to the 'Hesperian' (modern, Christian), what he calls 'a national reversal, where the whole shape of things changes, and nature and necessity, which always remain, tend to a new shape' ('Notes on the *Antigone*') within the drama of *Antigone* itself. The moment of transition becomes language and so occurs, the historical moment is 'dramatized'. His translation cannot simply be a repetition of that, it must, by bringing Sophocles wholly into the Hesperian era (into the German language), act on Hölderlin's own post-revolutionary times; and accordingly he reads 'the form of reason which here [in his translation of *Antigone*] shapes itself tragically' as 'political, and specifically republican'.

The distinction between 'Greek' and 'Hesperian' (on which see the two letters to Böhlendorff, Letters 106 and 110: 4 December 1801, November 1802) forms an important theme in the 'Notes'. It is his very insight into their differences which justifies Hölderlin's changes in the text. He explains this in his letter to Wilmans of 28 September 1803 (Letter 111) as correcting an 'artistic bias' the Greeks had to make; to which the 'Notes' add the deeper, more radical hermeneutic insight that 'the Greek ideas alter' ('Notes on the *Antigone*'). The first and last sentences of the 'Notes', taken as an essay in six parts, flank the entire argument with references to the demands which an era imposes on its poets, with respect to what can be learnt from the Greeks. It is this which rounds off the 'Notes' and brings them home: the search for a reliable law, to express the spirit of Hesperia. From the start, behind this objectivity, stands the plea for a secure living; and indeed, the objectivity also subdues a ferocious analogy between the poet and his hero in Greece, and in Hesperia between the tragic drama and its translator. The 'calculable law' would be a calculus for holding on to the incalculable and dangerous totality of life, which manifests itself at its purest in tragedy.

Hölderlin's nine *Pindar Fragments*, which survive only in manuscript, seem to derive from the practice established in the middle sections of the Sophocles 'Notes' of quoting a brief extract of verse and following it with an esoteric and yet closely involved prose commentary. The difference is that whereas Hölderlin selected the passages from Sophocles, these fragments of Pindar have only made their way down to us by being quoted in other authors; they are vestiges of poems since lost, the remains of a past age which Hölderlin now carefully preserves and puts into dialogue with his own age and concerns. Translation already does this, and the commentary is therefore like an extension of the work of translation, distancing and recovering at the same time. The *Pindar Fragments* can be thought of as a kind of poetic archaeology or archaeological philosophy. It is likely that they were written some time after the work on Sophocles, possibly even as late as summer 1805, when there is evidence of Hölderlin's continuing interest in Pindar. They are as fine as anything Hölderlin wrote. Once regarded as proof of his weakening powers and incipient madness, it has since become clear that they represent a new kind of literary text, *sui generis*, a blending and confrontation of translation, poetry and philosophy. In treating Sophocles, Hölderlin changed the text and added a commentary. Here, he keeps close to Pindar's wording, and confronts it with his own Hesperian viewpoint. The work itself tells us this: while the opening fragment ends

'think otherwise in another age', the third specifies this 'other'
by distinguishing the 'Greek sons of Nature' from the Hesperian
'men of learning', i.e. the active, natural ancients from the
reflective moderns. The work as a whole connects the two
perspectives, represented by poems and commentary, through
quasi-Pindaric allusiveness, and binds all nine pieces into a new
whole by a structure which recalls Pindar's (and Hölderlin's)
triadic mode of composition. One can also note the way in
which these triads employ the 'alternation of tones' explored
in Hölderlin's poetics. The hybrid character is perfectly sym-
bolized by the centaur: the central figure in the opening and
closing pieces. Like the centaur the *Fragments* join the apparently irreconcilable in a totally convincing form.

The *Pindar Fragments* can be thought of as post-tragic.
Against his earlier focus on tragedy as a realm in which the
immediate can manifest itself, Hölderlin now affirms (in the
fifth and central text, 'The Highest') that 'the immediate, strictly
speaking, is impossible for mortals, as it is for immortals'. He
is no longer in pursuit of the poetic law, the calculus which will
fetch the divine directly into the human sphere, but attends to
the law of institutions, 'of church and state . . . the inherited
statutes' which 'more strictly than art . . . hold fast the living
affairs in which, in time, a people has encountered itself and
continues to.' Since the worlds of God and man are separate,
they can only meet in a third, and this for Hölderlin is the
function of law. 'Law' in German (*Gesetz*) has in its etymology
to do with fixing, setting, placing; laws are the firm traces of
tradition which make orientation possible, marks of what is
reliable. The stray lines from Pindar which Hölderlin selects
are traces of this sort: the translation posits them and the
commentary then derives out of them, paces out their contours,
shows their validity. They offer a hold, and the 'Fragments'
keep coming back to the idea of holding on, of finding a purchase, and also to the idea of how things 'hang together',
connect, keep their identity. The rhythms of the language are
easy, reflective, subdued, but it is clear that this quietness is
partly protective, a means of self-preservation, an attempt to
found life away from extremes and locate a dependable core, a

mode in which each thing is centred in itself. 'At this time', 'Of the Dolphin' says, 'every creature gives its own note, its loyalty, the way it hangs together in itself', and the time he means is that of song, where each note (or tone) rings true and fits together into a melody.

The emphasis on self-fidelity and on following tradition, which might seem to pull in different directions, recurs in the final fragment, 'The Life-Giver', about centaurs and rivers. The river makes 'a course and a boundary ... on the originally pathless and upwards growing earth', that is, it forms one of the traces of which the other fragments speak, the marks or signs that create and guide civilization. 'The Life-Giver' reminds us of the violent origin of these traces and of the fact that they are dynamic, not static, the product of contest and opposing forces. Here, the stream turns into a river as the banks grow firmer and establish trees, bushes and vines; the river and its banks shape one another mutually; the channelling of energy is form itself. Similarly, to observe the laws is to shape them, to maintain a living tradition – just as Hölderlin enlivens Pindar by conducting his fragments into the 'poetic prose' (p. 298) of the apparent commentaries and forging a continuity between old and new.

The *Pindar Fragments* are very likely the last work Hölderlin wrote before succumbing to madness. They concentrate all his concerns, poetic and philosophical, reflective and translative, archaic and modern, into a unique form which seeks to hold on and hang together. Their seeming repose and frequent gentleness is the product of a great effort of attention: 'the world always shouts / Away from this earth, so that it strips / It bare; where humankindness does not hold it'.[6]

CL and JA

NOTES

1. Nicholas Boyle, *Goethe: The Poet and the Age*, vol. 2 (Oxford, 2000), p. 468.

2. This and the other poems mentioned in the Introduction are to be found in the companion volume, *Selected Poems and Fragments*, trans. Michael Hamburger (Penguin, 1998/2007).

3. Quoted after G. S. Kirk and J. E. Raven, *The Presocratic Philosophers* (Cambridge, 1957; reprinted, 1981), Fragment 423, pp. 326f.

4. See 'The Ground of the *Empedocles*', note 46.

5. Seamus Heaney, *The Redress of Poetry* (Oxford, 1990), pp. 2–3. The wording in the revised text of Heaney's inaugural Oxford lecture (in *The Redress of Poetry* (London, 1995)) is slightly different and not so close to Hölderlin's meaning.

6. From the poem 'The Only One', third version. This version of the poem is not included in *Selected Poems and Fragments*.

Further Reading

Hölderlin Editions

Sämtliche Werke, Friedrich Beissner and Adolf Beck (eds.), 8 vols. (Stuttgart, 1943–85)

Werke und Briefe, Friedrich Beissner and Jochen Schmidt (eds.), 2 vols. (Frankfurt, 1969)

Sämtliche Werke, D. E. Sattler and others (eds.), 20 vols. (Frankfurt, 1975–2008)

Sämtliche Werke und Briefe, Michael Knaupp (ed.), 3 vols. (Munich, 1992–3)

Sämtliche Werke und Briefe, Jochen Schmidt (ed.), 3 vols. (Frankfurt, 1992–4)

Theoretische Schriften, Johann Kreuzer (ed.) (Hamburg, 1998)

English Translations

Poems and Fragments, Michael Hamburger (trans.) (4th edn; London, 2004), includes German

Selected Poems and Fragments, Michael Hamburger (trans.), Jeremy Adler (ed.) (2nd edn; London, 2007), includes German

Hymns and Fragments, Richard Sieburth (trans.) (Princeton, 1984), includes German

Selected Poems, David Constantine (trans.) (2nd edn; Newcastle upon Tyne, 1996)

Ode and Elegies, Nick Hoff (trans.) (Middletown, Conn., 2008)

Hyperion, Willard Trask (trans.) (New York, 1965)

Hyperion, Ross Benjamin (trans.) (New York, 2008)

The Death of Empedocles, David Farrell Krell (trans.) (New
  York, 2008)
Hölderlin's Sophocles: Oedipus and Antigone, David Constan-
  tine (trans.) (Newcastle upon Tyne, 2001)
Essays and Letters on Theory, Thomas Pfau (trans.) (New
  York, 1988)
*The Poet's Vocation: Selections from Letters by Hölderlin,
  Rimbaud and Hart Crane*, William Burford and Christopher
  Middleton (trans.) (Austin, 1968)

Books in English which Deal with Hölderlin's Essays and Letters

M. B. Benn, *Hölderlin and Pindar* (The Hague, 1962)
Josef Chytry, *The Aesthetic State: A Quest in Modern German
  Thought* (Berkeley, 1989)
David Constantine, *Hölderlin* (Oxford, 1988)
Ian Cooper, *The Near and Distant God: Poetry, Idealism and
  Religious Thought from Hölderlin to Eliot* (Oxford, 2008)
Aris Fioretos (ed.), *The Solid Letter: Readings of Friedrich
  Hölderlin* (Stanford, 1999), with very full bibliography of
  writing on Hölderlin in English
Véronique M. Foti, *Epochal Discordance: Hölderlin's Philos-
  ophy of Tragedy* (New York, 2007)
Howard Gaskill, *Hölderlin's Hyperion* (Durham, 1984)
Emery E. George, *Friedrich Hölderlin: An Early Modern* (Ann
  Arbor, 1972)
R. B. Harrison, *Hölderlin and Greek Literature* (Oxford, 1975)
Jean Laplanche, *Hölderlin and the Question of the Father*, Luke
  Carson (trans.) (Victoria, 2007)
Charlie Louth, *Hölderlin and the Dynamics of Translation*
  (Oxford, 1998)
Eric L. Santner, *Friedrich Hölderlin: Narrative Vigilance and
  the Poetic Imagination* (New Brunswick, 1986)
Martin Simon, *Friedrich Hölderlin: The Theory and Practice
  of Religious Poetry* (Stuttgart, 1988)
George Steiner, *Antigones* (Oxford, 1984)
Richard Unger, *Friedrich Hölderlin* (Boston, 1984)

Andrzej Warminski, *Readings in Interpretation: Hölderlin, Hegel, Heidegger* (Minneapolis, 1987)

Context

Karl Ameriks (ed.), *The Cambridge Companion to German Idealism* (Cambridge, 2000)

Ernst Behler, *German Romantic Literary Theory* (Cambridge, 1993)

Frederick Beiser, *German Idealism: The Struggle against Subjectivism, 1781–1801* (Cambridge and London, 2002)

Andrew Bowie, *Aesthetics and Subjectivity from Kant to Nietzsche* (Manchester, 1990)

David Farrell Krell, *The Tragic Absolute: German Idealism and the Languishing of God* (Indiana, 2005)

Peter Szondi, *An Essay on the Tragic*, Paul Fleming (trans.) (Stanford, 2002)

PART 1

LETTERS

Translated by Charlie Louth

1. *To Johanna Christiana Gok* (extract)

Maulbronn, June [1788]

During the morning I had had a pretty good look round Speyer. And so in the afternoon I wanted to go out into the open and rest my eyes on the surrounding countryside. I spent the whole afternoon walking about and covered virtually the whole area around Speyer without finding anything that especially attracted my attention. It was almost evening when I came to the place they call the Gran (where merchandise is unloaded from the boats). The sight that stretched before me brought me back to life, like being reborn. My feelings expanded, my heart-beat quickened, my mind sped into the distance – my eyes were amazed – I did not know what I was looking at, and stood there like a statue.

Imagine the majestic, peaceful Rhine, coming from so far away that the boats were barely visible – and so far across that almost it could be taken for a wall of blue, & on the opposite bank thick, wild woods – & beyond the woods the darkening hills of Heidelberg – & down one side an immense plain – & all so full of the Lord's blessings – & so much going on around me – here boats being unloaded – there others putting out for the sea, with the evening wind filling their sails – I went home moved, and thanked God that I could feel where thousands rush by indifferently, either because they are accustomed to the sight or because they have hearts like lard.

2. *To Immanuel Nast*

[Maulbronn, 6 September 1788]

Dear Nast,

In a fortnight I'll be with you! Not a day earlier – or later! I'll ride with Elsner and get to Höfingen by midday, and from there on to Leonberg. But the very next day I *must* be off again.

You'll come with me (I won't hear of anything else) all the way to Nürtingen, even if it's only for a day or two, and then I'll go back to Stuttgart with you where Bilfinger will be waiting for us, and he'll accompany you back to Leonberg. How would that suit, dear friend? *I* shall keep my word, even if the emperor himself tried to hold me back.

So then, at about 2 o'clock in the afternoon in a fortnight I'll be at yours! Ah, brother, just for the bliss of our first embrace I'd travel days and days! You cannot possibly love me as much as I love you – no! impossible! It would be an unforgivable vanity on my part – if I were to believe it. Let me tell you – my mother & brother & sister, & heaven knows I love them dearly – I've taken leave of them a few times now – but it was never so hard as leaving you. We'll go and see Landbek and Hiemer together – when we're in Stuttgart. Oh brother, brother, why do I feel so good at the moment? – Because the day before yesterday I finished something which for the past few weeks has been making my head glow –

I can see it's no bad thing – that everything I encounter in the world goes awry for me – I keep myself for myself that way – and feel more real joys and have no need to be annoyed by so many inanities.

I long to see you & Landbek friends. I'd like to bet you'll be inseparable! Imagine a handsome – gentle – tender painter of 20, your height, & that's what he's like. And Hiemer – well, he's a jolly poet, quite the *bon homme*! And as for me I'm nothing other in God's wide world than your very own

Hölderlin

3. *To Christian Ludwig Neuffer*

[Nürtingen, December 1789]

Dear Neuffer,

A long time since I was in touch with you – here I am at last. I'd have written often from Tübingen if it hadn't been for all

the unpleasantnesses, the pettinesses and injustices I've had
to put up with, which made me feel indifferent even about
friendship. And, dear Neuffer, my fate is beginning to seem
pretty bizarre, if only because the day before your arrival, of
all days, I went and hurt my foot and, since the very next day
I was granted leave to travel, I had to go away for four weeks
without seeing you. If only you had been in Tübingen none of
this would have happened. I'd have had no cause to plead so
hard to be allowed to go on leave, wouldn't be a burden to
my mother, nor be making life so difficult for myself in my
frustration. O dear brother, what a way to find out what you
mean to me! – And things are pretty unpoetic in my head at the
moment. What I did force onto paper were brief outpourings
of my moods, which a few days later I could no longer bear to
look at. Immediately after the holidays I wrote a little song to
go with that lovely tune. Things looked better then. In a few
lucky hours I worked on a hymn to Columbus that will soon be
finished, though it's a lot shorter than my others. Shakespeare's
going to get a hymn too – what do you think? The other day I
came across a marvellous book – a collection of old German
legends. Said to be by Bürger. Neuffer, it gave me so much
pleasure. There I found Gustavus portrayed with such warmth,
such veneration – and such valuable details about his death,
that I made a solemn vow to go back to my notes again as soon
as I return to Tübingen and in particular to concentrate what
little powers I have in the hymn on his death. The judgement
of our beloved predecessor on the hymns to Gustavus struck
me suddenly as juster than anything I'd ever heard. Städlin is
really a marvellous man. Once my mother has taken advice
from a clear-sighted person or two and, if it turns out according
to my desires, I'll soon be following his example of how to earn
one's living. I'm telling this to no one but you and should like
to have your advice too. And in general, dear Neuffer, I beg
you for our friendship's sake, let me hear from you as often
and as much as possible. You have total control over my moods
and fits of low spirits and whatever you want to call the devils
that plague me. Give my greetings to M. Hoffman, and say that

soon I'll be sending the guardroom a shipment of potatoes, as promised. Goodbye, beloved friend.

Yours,
Hölderlin

4. To Maria Eleonora Heinrike Hölderlin

[Tübingen, mid-November 1790]

Good morning, dear Rike,

I won't be able to match up to you this time. My head is so heavy this morning from working into the night that I'll have trouble getting anything down on paper at all, not to speak of writing a letter as full of bright good humour as yours was. It upsets me that you should think the trouble I have writing letters, with my head taken up with study (and here I am in the same old trouble again), has anything to do with you. Dear Sister, nothing could be further from the truth.

Today it's the fair. Rather than getting pushed around in the hustle and bustle I'm going for a walk with Hegel, who is in the same room as me. We're going to the chapel at Wurmlingen with the famous view.

How am I getting on in my room? Marvellously, dear Rike. My repetitor is the best man in the world. The room is one of the best, looks east, is very spacious and only on the second floor. There are seven people from my year. I don't have to tell you that's a lot more agreeable than 6 strangers. And the few others are also good people, among them Breyer and Schelling.

My congratulations to dear Karl on mounting the rostrum. That's how Demosthenes and Cicero appeared before their people, only the scene will have been rather more ample. Just let him become a proper man, our dear Karl. He must think and work every minute his constitution allows him to. Rike, it is an amazing thing: *the desire to learn can consume all other desires*. Believe me.

Goodbye. Thanks very much for what you sent. Look after yourself, dear Rike.

Your affectionate brother,
Friz

If you find any more of my papers please send them. There are still a few missing.

5. *To Johanna Christiana Gok*

[Tübingen, ~ 14 February 1791]

Dearest Mamma,

You have quite put me to shame with your kindness. I am still so far behind you in goodness and you give me so many opportunities to follow your example. Forgive me, dear Mamma, if in my last letter I said anything that may have lacked the respect I owe you as a son. – I am quite serious about not coming to Nürtingen after all. In the short time I have I could rarely spend time with you as I should like, and I won't get permission to come for longer. But if possible I'll come later this month. – Here is the sermon I gave yesterday (on Sunday). This time I was a little more expansive than in my first. I took pleasure in developing a subject it every day becomes more important for me to improve and refine my knowledge of. The part where I say that if we look at the matter closely *there can be no religion at all, no certainty of God and immortality, without belief in Christ*, that's the thought that for some time now has been preoccupying me more than usual. There are many good Christians, I think, who are not fully convinced of this idea. It is not that they don't believe it if it is explained to them, but they never find themselves in situations where they realize the necessity of the *Christian* religion from this point of view. Allow me to tell you, dear Mamma, the steps that have led me to this conclusion. I had been studying the area of philosophy that deals with the *rational proofs* for the existence of God and with those of his qualities we are supposed to recognize in nature, and I had an interest in it I am not ashamed of though for a while it did lead me into thoughts you would perhaps have found unsettling had you known what they were. For I soon came to see that these *rational proofs* for the existence of God, and also for immortality, were so imperfect that a fierce opponent could knock them down completely or at least in their main lines. At this point I came across writings by and about *Spinoza*, a great and noble man from the last century, and yet strictly speaking an *atheist*. I found that if one looks at the matter closely, with *reason*, *cold* reason untouched by the heart, one is *forced* to accept his ideas in order to explain everything. But I was still left with the faith of my heart, which is so incontestably full of the longing for eternity, for God. But don't we most doubt precisely what we *desire*? (I say this in my sermon.) Who can help us out of these labyrinths? – Christ. He shows us by his miracles that he is what he says he is, God. He teaches us the existence of divinity and love and wisdom and the omnipotence of God so clearly. And he must know there is a God and what God is, for he is bound up with divinity in the most intimate way. Is God himself.

That is the course my insights into the nature of God have taken over the past year.

All my love to dear Rike and to Karl – tell him to send me something again soon. – I should be very pleased if my dear uncle were to become vicar in Löchgau. Perhaps that's the little place where I might spend a few peaceful years as a curate one day. – A thousand thanks for what you have sent me . . .

I am
your most obedient son
Friz

6. To Johanna Christiana Gok

[Tübingen, ~ June 1791]

Dearest Mamma,

I imagine I can now greet besides you – but only in writing, alas – my dear cousins & Rike, who is now the damsel errant just as at Easter I was the knight errant. I should have loved to come to Nürtingen for a few days if I'd had any hopes of obtaining leave of absence.

The piece of news you gave me *reassures* me a good deal – for reasons you will have no difficulty in guessing. Love doesn't tarnish with time! The good child still thought of me, as I learnt on many occasions – & had I not been guided by the wisdom of my 21 years I might not have resisted many a relapse. I admit the news also set my poor heart pounding for a few moments! But we don't need to go into that. A propos, I must tell you that for a long time now it has been my firm intention never to marry. I mean this quite seriously. My odd character, my moods, my tendency to be full of projects, & (if I am quite honest about it) my ambition – all traits which can never quite be eradicated with impunity – do not put me in hopes of finding happiness in the calm of married life, in some peaceful parish. But that will perhaps change in years to come.

Forgive me for chatting away like this. The wisdom of my 21 years very often deserts me.

I still have 3 guilders left of the money you sent and I'm being very careful with them. Next post-day, when that little amount will probably be all gone, I'll present you with my accounts.

I always take my wine money. So far I've sometimes spent it on an innocent amusement, sometimes on a good book. But this summer it will be kept for necessary expenses only.

I will do all I can to get the grant.

Here's my washing. I'm sorry I had to be reminded a second time about the white scarf.

7. To Christian Ludwig Neuffer

Tübingen, 28 November 1791

My dear Neuffer,

Since getting your last letter I must have said to myself a thousand times how you are just the same as you always were, understanding and good-natured despite my neglect and flightiness. Given the extravagant disorder of our money affairs you could excuse me easily enough for being so slow to pay my debts, but that I have not written a line to tell you which way my little boat was pointing is once again asking a great deal of your patience, since you must have known I had need of your sympathy and that things must be bleak with me and within me, it must have annoyed you that I was too lazy to brighten up my life for an hour and open my heart to you. Neuffer, since I've been back here I feel as if my best energies had been left with those I hold dear, I am indescribably stupid and indolent. Rarely are there any *lucida intervalla*. And when I think of how you and Magenau are coming alive, growing in the strength that happiness and love give, of how charged with pride and courage I felt in the heavenly hours I spent with you in Stuttgart, and that I could be a different person altogether if I weren't in a situation which for me could not be worse – then I want to get out.

But that's the way things are. Despite everything I won't give up completely. My girl still has a sweet hold on me even though she keeps me at a distance. But after a fortnight and more languishing, the recompense is right royal. Yesterday was such a day. As each day passes I am more certain of it: love and friendship are the wings with which we shall reach every goal.

I will soon have finished my 'Hymn to Humanity'. But then it is a work of the lucid intervals, and they are far short of being a clear sky. Otherwise I haven't done much: learnt a few things about the rights of man from the great Jean-Jacques, and on clear nights fed my eyes on Orion and Sirius and the twin gods Castor and Pollux, that's all. Seriously, dear Neuffer, I am annoyed with myself for not having woken up to astronomy sooner. This winter I intend to devote myself to it in earnest.

I've done my best with what you asked me to see to. I nearly lost my temper with the landlord of the Adler. He said he had already delivered instructions to Uhland but would still send you the money if he had been paid after the vacation. I summoned up all my powers of persuasion, and eventually, after much toing and froing, we agreed that if possible he would send you the proportion* of the grant you had promised him this year and wait for a more convenient time. I haven't quite sorted out the business with the coffee yet. I told Frau Sch. that I was to give her in your name 4 florins 42 but she brought me the enclosed bills and claims you owe 14 florins 24. Just tell me what I should do, I won't let the rogues cheat you. But make sure you do it soon, dear friend, while you still remember the details. – *Saltus dithyrambicus!* The Swabian *Almanac* hasn't been reviewed yet. I got a wonderful letter from Magenau yesterday. It made me happy as a child. – If you like, dear Neuffer, we can respond to each other's verses in writing like in our golden days together. If you think it's a good idea you could have a word about it with Magenau when he comes to see you. I'll write to him soon anyway. – The reason I'm still in the seminary is that my mother wishes it. I suppose I can waste a year or two for her sake.

Send me some of your poems soon. There is more in them for our souls than in letters. Isn't that true?

Yours,
Hölderlin

Here are the books for your brother.
All my love and remembrances in Stuttgart.

*or perhaps the 20 florins are the whole grant? To avoid any misunderstanding.

8. *To Heinrike Hölderlin*

[Tübingen, early March 1792]

Dear Rike,

A thousand thanks for your lovely letter. There was really no
need to apologize for writing it in a hurry.

I'm looking forward even more to my Easter holidays now
that it has been brought home to me so keenly that the best
place to be is with my nearest and dearest. We had quite a hard
frost along the way. But the journey did me not the slightest bit
of harm. On the contrary I think it has been very good for my
health. Christlieb sends his thanks again. If I'm not mistaken,
Karl asked me to do something for him. What it was though,
I've quite forgotten. I never found that table-knife either.

Kamerer could have made the detour. Give me a week and
I'll try to write something definite about these statutes of ours.
It would be a shame if they were devised so that no reasonable
person could subscribe to them without forfeiting his honour,
and if we turn out not to be able to oppose them; if that's the
case – I'm firmly resolved to find myself somewhere else to go,
even if I have to earn my bread in the sweat of my brow. God
knows how dear my family is to me and how much I desire to
live as they would wish, but I cannot possibly let absurd and
pointless laws be imposed on me and stay in a place where my
best energies would go to ruin. Providence, I hope, will make
sure that in future things will turn out well for me somewhere
else, as long as I do what I can to become a man, especially as
by the time I can expect to serve as a priest the government will
probably have changed. For if Prince Wilhelm (as a Protestant)
comes to the throne, the giving out of clerical positions is a
matter of his whims, just as much as secular ones. – I am far
from the only one to have come to this decision. The greater
part and the best of our repetitors and scholarship-holders will
leave if this happens. And even if I were the only one – all the
same I want to do all I can to save my honour and my energies.
I'd give a lot for all this to be empty anxiety – but I fear . . .
The latest news doesn't sound good at all. Georgii was the

only one to protest against the Duke's interventions but was
outvoted, and so the matter is supposed to be going forward
very soon. There's no doubt of its importance. We must show
our country and the world that we are not made of stuff that
will suffer becoming the playthings of arbitrary power. And a
good cause can always hope for God's protection.

Farewell, dear Rike. Don't let our dear mother be too anxious! I can't let myself think of that if I want to avoid losing all
courage. The battle between a child's love and honour is a hard
one, that's certain. Farewell!

Your affectionate brother
Friz

9. *To Heinrike Hölderlin*

[Tübingen, June 1792]

Dear Rike,
I don't know what will become of our correspondence in the
end. There are always thousands of things going through my
head that much to my regret I can't talk to you about. That is
the blessing and the curse of solitariness, I think – our minds
tend to be wholly taken up with what we are reading or writing.
But it really is bad if there's something else we should be
attending to and the untimely guests, the thoughts about our
reading or writing, take up the place of the thoughts that should
be there. –

Everything will soon come to a head now between France
and the Austrians. It's true they report in Professor Elben's
paper that the French have suffered total defeat – but don't
forget the news comes from Koblenz, and we should never
quite trust that source whenever the news is favourable for the
Austrians. And what makes the news more than likely a lie is
that yesterday in the Strasburg paper news came in dated the
15th of June saying that Luckner and Lafayette, 2 French gen-
erals, have enclosed the Austrian army completely and hope to
force the Austrians to surrender unconditionally.

So things will soon come to a head. Believe me, dear Sister, we'll be in for bad times if the Austrians win. The abuse of princely power will be terrible. Take my word for it and pray for the French, the champions of the rights of man.

Forgive me for going on so. But then I have Fräulein Stäudlin as an example. I confess that her letter gave me great pleasure.

The moment for taking my month's break will be determined by when Prof. Flatt stops his lectures for a month. In a week's time I'll know that for sure & give you a definite idea then.

My humble thanks for what you have sent. *Adieu*, dear Rike.

Your affectionate brother,
Friz

10. *To Christian Ludwig Neuffer*

[Tübingen, July 1793]

You are right, my friend, your genius was with me these last days. Indeed I rarely felt the permanence of your love for me with such certainty and quiet joy. For a while now your genius has transmitted to me your very nature, I think. I have written to Stäudlin telling him of the many blissful moments I enjoy now. It was because your soul was alive within me. Your calm, the lovely contentment with which you look on the present and the future, on nature and man, I came to feel it all. And the bold hopes with which you look on our splendid goal, they were in me too. It is true I wrote to Stäudlin: Neuffer's quiet flame will be burning more and more brightly when my straw-fire will perhaps long have died out; but this thought doesn't always put me off, least of all in the heavenly hours when I return from the quickening embraces of nature or from the grove of plane trees by the Ilissos where, lying among Plato's disciples, I have watched the great man's flights through the obscure distances of the beginning of the world or followed him into the vertiginous depths, into the remotest reaches of the country of the spirit, where the soul of the world sends out its life into the myriad pulses of nature to which the issuing forces, at the end of their immense cycle, return; or when, intoxicated by the Socratic cup, and by Socratic friendship, I have sat at the banquet listening to the sweet and fiery talk of the enthused youths paying tribute to sacred love, with Aristophanes the joker throwing in his flashes of wit until at last the master, divine Socrates himself, with his heavenly wisdom, teaches them all what love is – then, my beloved friend, I admit I am not so despairing and sometimes I think I must be able to instil into my little work some spark of the sweet flame that warms & illuminates me at such moments, into my *Hyperion*, which at present is the life & soul of what I am, and also manage from time to time to produce something else for the delight of men and women.

I soon found that my hymns win me few hearts among the sex that in the end is more capable of beautiful feelings, & this strengthened my resolve to write a Greek novel. I'll leave it to your noble female friends to judge from the fragment I'm sending to Stäudlin today whether my Hyperion might not one day take his place among the heroes who provide rather better entertainment than all the knights with their adventures and fine phrases. I'm particularly keen to hear the judgement of the person you do not name. I hope what is to come will reconcile her and others to a harsh passage on her sex that Hyperion had to unburden his soul of. Let me know your own judgement too, dear friend. The point of view I should like this fragment of a fragment to be considered from I have set out in the letter to Stäudlin in a rather long-winded fashion. I'd like to be able to tell you the main points now too, but I don't think I'll have time. Let me just say that if this fragment gives more the impression of a mixture of accidental moods than of the considered develop- ment of a definite character that is because as yet I have left the motives behind the ideas and sentiments unclear, & this for the reason that I wanted to appeal to the faculty of taste, by de- picting ideas and sentiments (for aesthetic pleasure), rather than to the understanding, by presenting a regular psychological development. But of course in the end everything has to be precisely traceable back to the character & the circumstances that influence him. Whether this is the case in my novel the rest will show.

The fragment I have chosen is perhaps the least interesting. The necessary foundations, without which what is to follow can no more be appreciated than the second book without the first (which still awaits completion), these necessary foundations had to find a place somewhere. – What you say so well about the *terra incognita* in the realm of poetry is particularly true of the novel. Plenty of predecessors, but very few who have come upon new, fertile land, & still a measureless expanse to discover and develop! I give you my solemn word, if the complete *Hyperion* isn't three times better than this fragment I'll throw it on the fire without mercy. Altogether, if posterity is not to be my judge, if soon I can't make that claim with prophetic certainty, like you I'll strip every string from my lyre and bury it in the rubble of the times. Your song did me a great deal of good, especially the last strophe. Dear Neuffer, that last strophe is one of those that give us a glimpse behind the veil covering the divinities of philosophy. What I envy you most for, as I think I have often said, is your luminous powers of depiction. I am struggling after the same with all my strength. But this dear guest, your song, would have met an even friendlier countenance if it had come in the company of your hymn. I am tempted to believe that with this hymn you're behaving as many a rogue may have done in wrestling matches. He kept himself back until his opponent entered the ring quite sure of himself, and humiliated the poor lad then all the more with his unexpected victory. Come on then! I'm ready for anything. I've sent my hymn to Stäudlin. The magical light I saw it in when I had finished it, & even more when I read it to you on that unforgettable afternoon, has now dissipated so entirely that only the hope of soon writing a better poem can offer me some consolation for its imperfections. – How do things stand with the journal? – Have you written to Matthisson yet? – I haven't. Here's my Hesiod.

Oh how right you are when you say what a fine, productive

time it would be if we could live together again like before.
I will do all I can to be with you soon. And now goodbye.

Yours,

Hölderlin

The packet for Stäudlin was already made up when your kind
letter arrived this morning. Would you mind giving it to him?

11. *To Karl Gok*

[Tübingen, September 1793]

It was good of you to write to me again, dear Karl. I guessed
you would share my joy in the new acquaintance I have made.
I too shall never forget how close we were as boys and as we
grew up together. And that's what I thought, dear Karl, when
you complained about not having a friend. I know it well, this
awakening of a youthful heart, I too have lived through the
golden days when warm and fraternal feelings bind us to everything and such sympathy with *everything* is not enough, and
we need one person, a single friend, to mirror and gladden our
souls. To be honest, this lovely period is almost over for me. I
no longer attach myself so fondly to *individuals. My* love is for
humankind, though not of course in the corrupt, slavish, torpid
form which, however restricted our experience, we only too
often find it in. But I love the great and beautiful potential even
corrupt people have. I love the generations of the centuries to
come. For this is my keenest hope, the belief that keeps me
strong and active: our grandchildren will be better than we are,
freedom will come one day, and virtue will thrive better in the
holy warming light of freedom than in the icy zone of despotism.
We live in a period when everything is working towards better
times. These seeds of enlightenment, these quiet aspirations and
efforts of individuals trying to shape the human race, will spread
and gain strength and bear splendid fruit. That's it, Karl, that's
what my heart yearns for. This is the sacred goal of my aspirations and of all I do – that I might in our age germinate the

seeds which will come to ripeness in a future one. And so it is,
I think, that I attach myself with slightly less warmth to individual people. I should like my work to have a general effect.
The general doesn't exactly permit us to ignore the particular,
but once we have made it the object of our aspirations and
efforts the particular does cease to claim all our soul's attention.
But still, that doesn't mean I can't be a good friend, perhaps
not as *tender* a friend as before, but a true and active friend.
Oh and if I find a soul who like me strives for that goal, there
is nothing more sacred or dearer to me in the world. And that
goal, Brother of mine, *the shaping, the improvement of the
human race*, the goal that in our life here we will perhaps only
attain imperfectly but which the better generations to come will
attain the more easily the more we have helped prepare for it
in our particular sphere of activity – dear Karl, that goal lives,
I know, in your soul too, perhaps just not with the same clarity.
If you want me as a friend this goal shall be the bond that
from now on will join our hearts together more firmly, more
inseparably and more intimately. Oh, there are brothers everywhere, but few are friends of that kind. Goodbye. Give my love
to our dear mother.

Yours,
Friz

Matthisson's poems I've lent to someone. Here's something
else. *The discussion between Marquis Posa and the King* is my
favourite bit. (p. 259).

12. *To Johanna Christiana Gok*

Waltershausen, 3 January 1794

Dearest Mamma,
Comfort and happiness from above for the new year! And a
thousand thanks for all your love in the last year, and in all the
past years!

   Tomorrow I shall have been here for a week. And I can truly

say that not a day of it has not gone well. Major von Kalb, the most cultivated and obliging man in the world, received me like a friend, and his attitude has not changed. Frau von Kalb is still in Jena. My charge is such a good, bright and handsome boy that one cannot fail to like him. This is what my life is like: in the mornings my coffee is brought up to me in my room between 7 and 8 o'clock and I am left to my own devices until 9 o'clock. From 9 to 11 o'clock I give my lessons. After twelve we have lunch. (N.B. since you pitied me so much because of Saxon cooking I mustn't forget to say that the cook is Viennese and the table full of good things.) After lunch, as also in the evening, I can stay with the Major, go out with the little one, do some work, or do anything else, just as I like. From 3 to 5 o'clock I give lessons again. The rest of the time is my own. They dine in the evenings here too and the excellent beer which is drunk at table makes it easy for me to forget our Neckar wine. And I feel very well on it. My journey here will be paid for, as I came to hear. It is a very beautiful area. The house lies on a hill overlooking the village, and I have one of the most pleasant rooms. And the people here, as far as I have been able to get acquainted with them, are of a very good sort. With the rector especially I'm already on the best of terms. In conditions like these I have no need to be in a town. I can use the major's horses whenever I like. He likes his peace and quiet, is rarely away, and never sees many people. 'I have spent long enough gadding about the world, by land and sea,' he says, 'now I'm all the fonder of my wife and child, my garden and my house.' Only three years ago he was serving in the French army, and he took part in the American War of Independence under Lafayette. His features have much in common with those of the Court Councillor in Nürtingen (to whom and all his household please send my compliments).

The most enjoyable part of my journey was the time I spent in Nuremberg. Stäudlin had given me a letter of introduction to Schubart, secretary of the Prussian legation. With its gothic palaces and busy inhabitants Nuremberg is a place with a certain dignity and looks very inviting on the open plain where it lies surrounded by forests of fir on all sides. In the reading society and in a house in the country I met some very cultivated people. I spent Christmas day very enjoyably in Erlangen with a compatriot and cousin, the son of the physician Jäger in Stuttgart. And also heard there a beautifully lucid sermon by Prof. Ammon. I'll write to Blaubeuren and Löchgau next week. All my love and remembrances. And a good morning to my dear Karl!

Yours,

Friz

Remember me to all in Nürtingen!
My letter from Coburg you have I hope got by now.
My address is: Hölderlin, tutor in the household of Major von Kalb in Waltershausen, near Meiningen.
(paid for as far as Nuremberg)

13. *To Johanna Christiana Gok*

Waltershausen, 23 January 1794

I've settled in now, dearest Mother. My health seems to be growing stronger with my way of life here rather than ailing at all. If my job means I have had to put a bit of a stop to my mind's usual nourishment, the body is all the better for it. – Your concerns about the war still seem to me, as before, a little exaggerated. Even if we don't have peace by Easter, as it is very likely we shall, it really doesn't look as if the French are going to advance much beyond their own territory. The major has already announced to me that as soon as they were completely over the Rhine I should have to move together with Fritz to Jena, because if it came to that he too would be a bit anxious. – At the moment I am in charge here in the house. The major is off travelling, and her ladyship is still in Jena. The letters she writes me evince an intelligence equal to the goodness of her heart. I live quite without the kind of constrictions which etiquette and pride usually place on someone in my position. I've not yet had the chance, given the weather and all I've had to do, to explore the area much. But next Sunday I'm going on a little excursion to Königshofen, a town near Würzburg 2 hours from here, to meet with a couple of friends from home who were at university with me, Troll, a secretary, and Kleinmann, who is tutoring, both of them employed 6 hours away from here at Herr von Wöllwarth's in Birkenfeld. Swabians soon track one another down wherever they are. – My travelling expenses will probably be paid when Frau von Kalb arrives. I don't like to request anything before then.

I got your lovely letter yesterday, on the 22nd. So it didn't take much more than a week to get here. I'd like to write to Löchgau too, if I still had time enough to. I'd better say now, dear Mamma, that you mustn't take offence if you often have to wait rather a long time for my letters, and if they're often also very hurriedly written. I often only find out that a messenger is going to Meiningen an hour beforehand. No one goes regularly. A thousand greetings to Karl, and to Löchgau and Blaubeuren.

Ever yours,
Friz

14. *To Friedrich Schiller*

[Waltershausen, ~ 20 March 1794]

In a moment when the presence of a great man gave me unusual seriousness of purpose I promised to do honour to humanity in my present activity, which in its consequences may have such far-reaching effects. I promised this to *you*. I give account of myself here.

To form my pupil into a *human being*, such was and is my aim. Convinced that all humanity that does not also bear the name of reason, or is not in exact relation to it, cannot be so called, it was my belief that I could not develop the most noble faculty in my pupil too soon. It was no longer possible for him to remain in the innocent state of nature, and indeed he was already past this stage. The child could not be watched over, to cut off all influence of society on his wakening powers. So if at this point it was possible to create in him a consciousness of his moral freedom, to make of him a being capable of assuming responsibility for his actions, this was what must happen. Now it is true that for the time being he hardly has anything, it seems to me, in the way of proper cognizance of moral relations in the wider sense, but he does in the narrower sense, and of these friendship seemed to me the only applicable one in this case.

I did not seek to win his favour. I also sought to discourage him from trying to win mine, and here nature did not require any great resistance. For my part I simply followed the promptings of my heart which in good hours led me to feel a properly fraternal bond with the boy's cheerful, lively and apt nature. He understood me, and we became friends. To the authority of this friendship, the most innocent I know of, I sought to connect everything that should and should not be done. But because any authority we might connect human thought and action to sooner or later begins to make for great disadvantages, I gradually ventured to add that everything he did or did not do was not merely to be done or not for his and my sakes, and I am certain that if he has understood me on this point he has understood the summit of all he needs to know.

This is what I base the means to my end on, to a greater or lesser extent. I do not want to burden you with the details. The deep respect for you, with which I grew up, with which I so often fortified or humbled myself, which even now prevents me from any slackness in my education and in that of my pupil, this respect does not permit me to become too talkative.

This respect is endlessly strengthened by your kindness towards me, to which I owe my present situation, favourable in so many ways.

The uncommon energy of mind I admire Frau von Kalb for will, I hope, be a succour to my own mind, all the more so as everything is conspiring to provide the conditions for untroubled hard work. If only I can realize the motherly hopes this noble lady has for me!

She has been here for a week. She asked me to send you her compliments, with the assurance that she will write soon.

She told me that I might have had the good fortune of living near you for a few months. I feel deeply what a chance I have missed. I have never foregone so much by my own doing before. Let me entertain this belief, great and noble man! Being near you would have worked wonders for me. Why is it I must be so poor and take so much interest in the richness of a single mind? I shall never be happy. Still, I must be willing, and I am. It is my will to become a man. Be so good as to turn your attention towards me from time to time. A person's good will is never quite in vain.

I take the liberty of enclosing some verses whose worthlessness in my eyes is not so incontrovertible that I should think it an obvious act of insolence on my part to importune you with them, but of which my estimation is not sufficient either to put me out of the rather apprehensive frame of mind in which I write this down.

Should you deem the verses worthy of appearing in your *Thalia*, that would be to do this relic of my youth a greater honour than I dared hope for.

I am, with the sincerest esteem,

your most devoted admirer,

M. Hölderlin

15. *To Karl Gok*

Waltershausen, near Meiningen, 21 May 1794

Dear Brother,

It was good of you to give me a sign of your existence and of your brotherly thoughts again. I have often thought of you since the moment we parted on the heath and found it so hard to take leave of one another.

The distance between us now always seems so vast, and I often say to myself I should make a quick dash over to see you all. But before that happens we'll probably be a good bit older.

I doubt whether I'll be leaving my present situation in a hurry. I have leisure for my personal education, as well as promptings from the world around me, and on good days my other occupations allow me to rest and recuperate. As yet it is uncertain whether I shall spend next winter in Jena as well as Weimar. Both possibilities, as you can imagine, are very agreeable indeed. Here I live very quietly. I remember only few periods of my life spent in such constant and equal composure and calm.

You know, dear Brother, how much value there is in not being distracted by anything. You are lucky enough to enjoy this too. Make the most of it. If one has only a single hour over from the rest of the day to devote to the free use of the mind, when one can attend to one's most pressing and noblest needs, that is a great deal and, at the least, enough to gain strength and spirit for the rest of the time.

Brother, hold up your better self and don't let it be pushed down by anything, by anything at all! It is of great importance to me to know the direction your mind is taking. Make sure, dear Karl, you keep me informed as often as you can. Very soon I will give you an account of my own occupations. I am in the middle of working on something now that I don't want to talk about until I've got it clear in my mind.

If you can get hold of the most recent issues of Schiller's *Thalia* or Ewald's *Urania*, or of the Swabian journal *Flora*, look out for my name and think of me. For the most part it's only small things you'll find there. Virtually the only thing I'm reading at the moment is Kant. His magnificent mind reveals itself to me more and more.

I am very glad to hear that dear granny is there with you all. Give her all my heartfelt respects. She's quite better again now, isn't she? That my little niece is thriving so well was also a piece of news I was very pleased to hear.

I'm going to write to Blaubeuren. Frau von Kalb asks dear mother to wait with the cherry spirit until the cherries here are ripe, and then to send it in jars in a small crate. Fritz is quite well again and is always a source of great joy. It wouldn't be easy to find a child as good as him.

God preserve you, my dears!

Yours,
Friz

What's our friend Hiemer up to?

16. *To Christian Ludwig Neuffer*

[Waltershausen, early July 1794]

My dear Neuffer,

With every letter from you the mutual communication of our natures and their fluctuating states becomes more indispensable to me. I truly share your pain at the blow that has struck your beloved girl and with her you yourself. You will have felt for the first time all that you are to each other. It is my heart's innermost desire that this fine union should endure in all its rare intimacy. When I imagine to myself that one day I too could be with such a woman, with hearth and home not far from you and your Rosie, I sometimes manage to set a proper limit on my endless longing from one part of the world to another, from one activity to another, or rather, I understand it better, especially as from my present situation I can see so clearly that a confined, quiet scope and sphere of influence, so long as one has become completely familiar with it, keeps our faculties in unremitting activity and, precisely because we are not wearied and distracted by the multifariousness of the world, preserves our strength and purity. And it also conceals many hidden joys that we can never be aware of if we flit by in a hurry. But as the sacred fates determine! We cannot make mountains into valleys, and valleys into mountains. But up on the mountains we can enjoy their high grandeur, the broad sky and the open air, and down in the valleys the peace and the silence and make ourselves all the more familiar there with the lovely and wondrous things we would not have seen from above. Or even better: if something needs doing up in the mountains we'll climb up there, and if we can plant and build in the valley we'll stay down below.

Forgive me, dear Neuffer. But it is not so easy to let go a chance thought if it corresponds in some small way with our own nature, and one ends up chattering. – In response to the passage in your letter where you talk about the unproductiveness of your mind let me copy you out a passage from Herder's *Tithonus and Aurora*: 'What we call the self's survival is, in finer souls, only the sleep before a new awakening, a slackening of the bow before it is put to use again. Thus the field lies fallow so that it may yield the more abundantly; the tree dies in winter so that it can send out new sap and shoots in the spring. The fates do not abandon a good man as long as he does not abandon himself and give in to self-doubt. The spirit that seemed to have left him returns at the proper time and brings new activity, happiness and joy. *Often a friend is such a spirit!*' Dear Neuffer, if you write to me soon saying I have been something like that to you it will make me very happy.

Your translation of the *Catiline* is of particular interest to me because it is still familiar from last year, when I read it. It is just the thing to be doing at the moment. You are right, translation is like gymnastics, and does the language a lot of good. It becomes nice and supple when it has to adapt to foreign beauty and grandeur, and often to foreign whims too. But though I have a great deal of admiration for your ability to prepare the means to your ends so doggedly, I warn you I'll have a few words to say if you start a new translation once you have finished the two you are on now. Our language is the organ of *our* minds, *our* hearts, the sign of *our* imaginings, *our* ideas; it must obey *us*. If it has lived too long in foreign service there is, I think, the danger that it will never again become quite the free and pure expression of our minds, shaped entirely from within, thus and not otherwise, that it should be. I would gladly go into this in more detail, my dear Neuffer, if I wasn't pressed by the post which is about to go. – This afternoon I was interrupted while writing by Frau von Kalb. She saw that I was writing to you and asked me to thank you warmly for your greetings, to tell you that from all that she knew about us she had more faith in the lastingness of our friendship than in any other, for once two individuals join hands with the idea of strengthening and helping one another through partaking of all that concerns the spirit and the heart, all that raises, expands and magnifies our being, they are bound together for ever because their love is unending, like the process of their perfection. That is almost word-for-word what she said. And she went on: – to talk of you is also to include Rosie in the conversation and there should be no division of what is inseparable – she'd like to meet the person who would not be gladdened by a love so rare in our day and age and so on. I think that from these words which I have faithfully relayed to you you can divine a part of her nature. – My pupil is of a good disposition, honest, cheerful, tractable, with harmonious and in no way eccentric mental faculties, and pretty as a picture from head to toe. I would gladly tell you a bit more about myself, about my novel, my study of Kant's aesthetics, a journey I recently made over the Rhön hills into the Fulda region and many other things if I didn't have to stop. Do you happen to know if Stäudlin has sent my poem to boldness into the *Urania*? I'd like to know as I might do something else with it.

Yours,
Hölderlin

Be so kind and send the enclosed letter to Hegel's house and remember me when you do to Fräulein Hegel. Tell her Hesler sends his regards too, and that if I hadn't been in such a rush I'd have taken the liberty of writing to her myself. Ask her if I might do so when I write to her brother in future.

17. To G. W. F. Hegel

Waltershausen, near Meiningen, 10 July 1794

My dear friend,

I am certain you will have thought of me from time to time since we parted with the watchword 'Kingdom of God!' By that watchword we would, I believe, recognize each other after every possible metamorphosis.

I am certain that whatever may happen to you the passage of time will never wear away that trait in you. And I think that will also be the case with me. It is this trait, after all, that each of us especially loves in the other. And so we are assured of the eternity of our friendship. But still I have often wanted to be near you. You were so often my genial spirit. I have a great deal to thank you for. Only since we parted do I feel it fully. I should like to learn a thing or two more from you, and also let you have something of my own thoughts from time to time.

Letter-writing can only ever be a makeshift; but something nevertheless. For that reason we shouldn't abandon it altogether. From time to time we must remind ourselves that we have great claims on each other.

I think you will find that in many respects your surroundings suit you not at all badly. But I have no cause to envy you. My own situation does me just as well. Things are clearer in your mind than they are in mine. You welcome having a bit of distraction nearby. I need peace and quiet. There is pleasure here for me too. You find it wherever you go.

From time to time it would be nice to be among your lakes and Alps. The grandeur of nature has an ennobling and strengthening effect on us that we cannot remain immune to. On the other hand I live in the ambit of a rare spirit, of a compass and depth and refinement and elegance that are extraordinary. I doubt very much you'll find a Frau von Kalb in Bern. It would do you a power of good to sun yourself in her light. Were it not for our friendship you'd be a little annoyed that your good fortune has on this occasion gone over to me. And she too must almost think that she has lost out to my blind good luck, after all I've told her about you. She has many times urged me to write to you. On this occasion too.

Frau von Berlepsch was in Bern, may still be. And Baggesen. Tell me all you can of them in a letter. – So far Stäudlin has only written to me once, Hesler too. I think we're going to have to work very hard if we're to prevent the latter from making us blush with shame. I live in hope of meeting up with him somewhere before long.

Is Mögling in Bern? – Send him my love. You'll be spending many happy hours together.

Write me as much as you can of what you're doing and thinking at the moment, dear friend! –

My preoccupations are pretty focused at the moment. Kant and the Greeks are virtually all I read. I am trying to become particularly familiar with the aesthetic part of the critical philosophy. Recently I made a short excursion over the Rhön hills into the Fulda region. It is like being in the Swiss mountains, with the colossal heights and pretty, fertile valleys where, overshadowed by firs, among streams and herds of cattle, the little houses lie dotted about at the foot of the hills. Fulda itself is also in a very lovely setting. The hill-people are, as always, rather curt, and naive. For all that they may well have many good sides that our civilization has erased.

Write to me soon, dear Hegel. I cannot possibly do without communication from you entirely.

Yours,
Hölderlin

14th

In haste I must add that I got the enclosed sheet, in all honesty, only a few days ago. I am very angered by the impertinence of a lawyer from Hildburghausen whom Hesler entrusted the letters to at Easter time and who probably only sent them on to Meiningen a few weeks ago, which is where I got them from, by what occasion I don't know. For that they come from Hildburghausen I conclude from a letter received yesterday from Hesler in which he appears to express a sense of embarrassment, as he ought to have enquired about the matter earlier.

As I said, the affair upsets me a great deal, especially as my carelessness in such matters is something you are all too familiar with from the past. But this would exceed even my carelessness, and I have given my word of honour. To put your mind at rest I should add that I know Hesler's seal, and it was intact on the letter I got from him. Write soon. I'll be writing to you about Hesler's letters as soon as I can.

18. *To Karl Gok*

Waltershausen, 21 August 1794

I have owed you a letter for a long time now, my dear Brother. But in the contract between our hearts it is not written that we should exchange many words and write great long letters, but that we should become men and only on this condition acknowledge each other as brothers. We mature to manhood by restless activity, by striving to act out of duty even if it doesn't afford much joy – even if it seems a very slight duty, so long as it *is* duty, we mature into manhood. By renouncing desires, by denying and overcoming the selfish part of our being which always wants to have things nice and comfortable, by patiently biding our time until a wider sphere of influence opens up, and with the conviction that it is also great to limit our energies to a restricted sphere of influence if something comes of it and no wider sphere of influence does open up, amid a calm undisturbed by any human weakness or vanity, which no illusions of grandeur and no supposed humiliation unsettle or confuse, whose only interruption comes from the sorrow and joy provoked by the wellbeing or sufferings of mankind or from the feeling of our own imperfections, we enter into manhood. And through unremitting efforts to improve and expand our ideas, following the unshakeable maxim that when judging all possible claims and actions, their legitimacy and raison d'être, absolutely no authority is to be acknowledged other than our own, following the sacred, unshakeable maxim not to let our conscience be seduced by pseudo-philosophies of any sort, including our own, nor by enlightenment that is clear as mud or the kind of worldly-wise nonsense which defiles so many sacred duties by calling them prejudices, but equally through not letting ourselves be led astray by fools or rascals who by talking of free thinking and the zeal for freedom seek to condemn or ridicule a thinking spirit, a being who feels his worth and rights in the person of humanity, – through all this and much more besides we enter into manhood. We must make great demands of ourselves, Brother of mine! Do we want to be like the poor in spirit who are so at ease in the consciousness of their little worth? Believe me, I get a strange feeling when I think of the hopes attaching to the coming century and set them beside the stunted, small-minded, coarse, presumptuous, ignorant, lethargic young people there are so many of and who one day are supposed to play their part. The few who are exceptions to this must encourage and support one another. And another thing! At this point in time it is necessary to say: be shrewd, say nothing, however true it is, if you are sure it will achieve nothing. Never sacrifice your conscience to shrewdness. But be shrewd. 'Do not cast your pearls before swine' is the golden rule. And whatever you do, never do it in the heat of the moment. Reflect coldly! And then act with fire! – I am certain you are of one mind with me here: brothers must speak to one another in this way. The enclosed letter is from Frau von Kalb to our dear mother. It shows how rarely tutors take proper responsibility for their charges when someone who acts according to his own general convictions and conscience is regarded as something unusual despite the hundreds of mistakes he makes.

Last Sunday I was on the Gleichberg, which dominates the open plain an hour from Römhild. To the east I had the Fichtel hills (on the border between Franconia and Bohemia), to the west the hills of the Rhön which form the border between Franconia and Hesse, to the north the Thuringian forest that forms that between Franconia and Thuringia, and over towards my beloved Swabia, to the south-west, the Steigerwald on the distant horizon. That would be the best way of studying the geography of the two hemispheres, if only it were possible! Let me know all you're doing as well, and tell me about the joys and anxieties of our dear mother, the circumstances our beloved relatives find themselves in, about my acquaintances, about H., B., G. etc., and about anyone you know who might be of the slightest interest to me. Give them all my warmest regards when you see them. –

That Robespierre had to pay with his head seems just to me, and will perhaps bring some good with it. Only let the twin angels of humanity and peace come and the cause of humankind will be sure to thrive! Amen.

Yours,
Friz

19. To Christian Ludwig Neuffer

Waltershausen, near Meiningen, 10 October 1794
I was a good few days nearer you than usual, on an estate belonging to the Kalbs in the Steigerwald, in the Bamberg area, and awaited there your last letter which despite all protestations would have determined me to make haste to you and show you that you still have something loyal in the world had this letter not contained such happy, marvellous news. I got it very quickly; before leaving here I had made every arrangement for it to be sent on to me without delay. So it would have been no great sacrifice, dear friend, as I was already almost half-way and nature has equipped me with a sturdy pair of legs. But then your letter arrived and only I can know how glad I was that you didn't need me. It was one of those moments when our joy gives us strength for months. I have a deep and permanent wish in my heart that this fine love may endure, with all the blessings and virtues it brings, with all its blossoms and fruits. When I compare it to the times we live in it always seems to me like a nightingale in autumn. – Believe me, my dear, good friend, the dissimilarity between our situations in this regard, which has more to do with fate than with my own nature, doesn't prevent me from recognizing with joy and respect all the beauty and all the worth of this relationship. I do not say 'with respect' idly,

for without that which demands respect, without the nobility and steadfastness of a moral being, such a relationship could certainly not exist. And I have something too: the bond with you – it will endure, with its blossoms and fruits, like the ties of your love. I mean this very seriously, dear Neuffer! My conviction, which is confirmed every day, that a friendship such as ours is not to be found on every street corner, ensures that I shall hold on to it for ever. It is almost my only comfort, when I need comfort, that my heart stands in a lasting relationship with *one* being, that I have *one* friend whom I can trust and depend on. That I need this comfort you will not find hard to believe because like me you know how most people are perfectly well disposed towards themselves, but if they could would deal with others pretty much as they do with their pots and pans, or their chairs – they take care not to break them for as long as they're still of use or haven't gone out of fashion. And of course I don't allow myself to be broken, and I only let people use me up to the point where I can make better use of myself. But that's not a great deal.

It is now often the case that I find my official job burdensome. I dare admit that to you. I had been keeping it even from you because to you in particular I have given all too much reason to suppose me discontented with everything that does not have a gold or silver lining, an endless bewailing that the world is not an Arcadia. I'm pretty much beyond such childish weak-heartedness. But I am a human being. After all, I'm bound to hope that conscientious and often very strenuous efforts should have some success. And so it's bound to hurt if they have virtually no success because of the very average talents of my pupil and because of an extremely badly managed upbringing earlier on in his childhood and other things I'll spare you. That it pains me would be of little importance in itself, but that it inevitably disturbs me in my other occupations seems to me less unimportant. I think you would also find it very disagreeable to have half your day go by on lessons from which you gain nothing more than a bit of patience and more often than not have the other half spoilt by the realization that your pupil has gained nothing from it at all. – Still, I try to hold up, as far as

possible, and as long as the sun shines in through my windows
I mostly get up in a cheerful mood and make what use I can of
the early morning, the only hours I actually have any peace and
quiet. These were mostly spent this summer on my novel, which
you will find the first five letters of in the *Thalia* this coming
winter. I have now virtually finished the first part. Hardly a line
is left from my old drafts. The great transition from youth into
the substance of a man, from affect to reason, from the realm
of imagination to the realm of truth and freedom always seems
to me to merit such a slow treatment. But still, I look forward
to the day when I'll have the whole thing in fair because then
I'll be able to move straight on to another project which is
almost closer yet to my heart, a play on the death of Socrates,
done according to the ideals of Greek drama. I've written very
little poetry since the spring. The poem to Fate, which I began
before I left home, reworked almost completely last winter and
sent off in a letter to Schiller sometime around Easter, seems to
have found his approval, judging by what he says in his reply
to my last letter, when I sent him the *Hyperion* fragment. He
intends to put it in an almanac he is shortly to become the
editor of, and I am going to send in a few more things, as he
has requested. Whether I'll be able to send you anything for
Reinhard's *Almanac* and the *Academy* and Conz's *Museum*
will depend on how productive I am. I should not want to
disgrace you and it would be very shoddy of me to reward your
comradely offer in such a way – so I want to avoid bothering
you with things written in haste. Perhaps I'll be able to send
you an essay on *aesthetic ideas*; as it can be considered a commentary on Plato's *Phaedrus*, taking a passage from it as its
express starting-point, it might interest Conz. In essence it is to
contain an analysis of the beautiful and the sublime in which
the Kantian analysis will be simplified and also, from another
perspective, varied and extended, as Schiller has already done
in part in his treatise on 'Grace and Dignity', though he has
ventured a step less beyond the Kantian borderline than he
should have done in my opinion. Don't smile! I may be wrong;
but I've checked, and checked again and again at the cost of
much effort. – At the moment I'm working on a new version of

my poem to the genius of youth. – At the beginning of November I'm probably going off to Jena. People have noticed that my physical self, together with my other faculties, is suffering in my present situation, and in order to preserve me it has been decided to send me there for six months with my charge, who also needs to go for several reasons. I'll see how it goes. I expect little enjoyment from it, and that is not what I'm after; but if I'm not mistaken it will contribute something to my education. Many thanks for the kind greetings from your noble girl. I return them with all my heart. Your poem was a delight to read, especially the strophe before last, as poetry and as an outpouring of your heart. Frau von Kalb sends you her regards. Yours to her gave her great pleasure, she says. I'm running out of time and must stop sooner than I want to.

Yours,
Hölderlin

Tell me something about Gotthold too. Has Hiller gone to America? Do you think Fräulein Hegel has sent my letter on to her brother? And the other good friends, what are they all doing? You have no idea how welcome bits of news from your parts and circles are to me at the moment.

20. To Christian Ludwig Neuffer

Jena, November 1794

I'm now here, as you can see, dear friend, and I have good reason to be glad of it, not so much because I am here, as because being here confirms me in the belief that we manage to accomplish something from the moment we are not simply carried to our destination but set out to go there on our own two feet, without worrying if we feel the odd sharp stone underfoot. I know very well there are greater destinations, and greater effort, more work and more gain; but of great things in this world we rarely have more than small instances.

My head and heart are now full of what I want to carry out

in my thinking and writing, and, as is also my duty, in my actions, though this last naturally not on my own. The proximity of truly great minds, and also the proximity of truly great, independent, courageous hearts, casts me down one minute and raises me up the next. I shall need to work my way out of half-light and slumber, use both gentleness and violence to wake and form my half-developed, half-withered faculties, if I am not to end up taking refuge in a dispirited resignation with only the other dispossessed and helpless people to console myself with, letting the world take its usual course and looking on from my peaceful corner at the rise and fall of truth and justice, the flourishing and fading of art, the life and death of everything that concerns mankind as humans and, at the most, confronting the demands of mankind with my negative virtue. I'd rather die than live like that! And yet I often have virtually no other prospect. Dear old bosom friend, in such moments I often miss having you close by, with your comfort and the visible example of your steadfastness. I know your courage sometimes deserts you too, I know it is the general fate of those souls who have more than animal needs. Only not to the same degree. A passage I came across today in the preface to Wieland's collected works still burns at my heart. There it says: Wieland's muse arrived at the beginnings of German poetry, and is leaving him in its *decline*. Marvellous! Call me a child, but that kind of thing can ruin a whole week for me. But even if . . . ! If it comes to it we'll break our miserable instruments and *do* what the artists have *dreamt of*. That's how I console myself. – Now some news from here. Fichte is now the life and soul of Jena. And thank God he is. I've never met a man of such depth and energy of mind. To seek out and determine in the remotest regions of human knowledge the principles of this knowledge, and with them the principles of justice, and with equal force of mind to think out the remotest and boldest conclusions deriving from these principles, and despite the powers of darkness to write them down and present them with a fire and a lucidity which without this example would have seemed to me in my insufficiency impossible to combine, – this, dear Neuffer, is certainly to say a great deal, but no more than is fit for a man like him. I go to his lectures every day. Speak to him sometimes. I've already been at Schiller's too, once or twice, the first time not altogether successfully. I went in, was greeted warmly, and barely noticed at the back of the room a stranger whose appearance, and what little he said at first, did nothing to suggest anything special about him. Schiller told him my name, and told me his too but I didn't catch it. Coldly, almost without looking at him, I greeted him and was totally taken up, inwardly and outwardly, with Schiller. For a long time the stranger didn't speak a word. Schiller brought in the *Thalia*, which contains a fragment of my *Hyperion* and my poem to Fate, and handed it to me. As Schiller then left us for a moment the stranger took the journal from the table, flicked through the fragment as I stood beside him, and didn't say a word. I felt myself getting gradually redder and redder. Had I known what I know now, I'd have gone white as a sheet. He then turned to me, enquired after Frau von Kalb, the area and the neighbours round our village, and I answered all this in monosyllables, in a way I think I rarely do. But luck was simply against me. Schiller came back, we talked about the Weimar theatre, the stranger let fall a few words weighty enough to make me suspect something. But I suspected nothing. The artist Meyer from Weimar also joined us. The stranger conversed with him on various subjects. But I suspected nothing. I left, and learnt the same evening in the Professors' Club (have you guessed?) that *Goethe* had been at Schiller's that day. Heaven help me to make good my misfortune and my stupid behaviour when I get to Weimar. Later on I had supper at Schiller's – he comforted me as much as he could, and with his wit and his conversation, which revealed the full force of his extraordinary mind, made me forget the disaster that had befallen me on the first occasion. I am also at Niethammer's occasionally. I'll tell you more of Jena next time. Make sure you write soon too, dear Neuffer.

Yours,
Hölderlin

My address is: – in Voigt's garden.

21. *To Johanna Christiana Gok*

Jena, 17 November 1794

So here I am, dearest Mother, going to classes, visiting Schiller and occasionally a public circle, and otherwise I'm at home buried in work of various kinds. The half of the day I have to sacrifice to my pupil it is true I give up much less readily here, now that much incites me to work of my own, something that could never happen in Waltershausen. The journey here from Franconia I had to make by mail-coach, to my annoyance, and so it was impossible to visit Friemar, which lies towards Gotha. But I was told by a vicar from around there who was travelling with us that he knew of people called Heyn in a nearby village, though not in Friemar itself. I'll definitely do the journey back on foot and whatever happens will make sure my route takes me through Friemar. I don't have much to tell you about the journey, except that Schmalkalden, a town in Hesse, is anything but modern in aspect, though there is a great deal of industry there; and that the view you have from the heights of the Thuringian forest is very grand, with a large part of Franconia behind you, with its hills and woods, the great plains of Saxony before your eyes, and the Harz mountains darkly in the distance. One might well envy the happiness of the inhabitants of the valleys in the Thuringian forest, who have the prosperity and uprightness and good health we know from the Black Forest at home, were it not for the thought that amid the tribulations of civilized life we are perhaps of more use and can do more to help. We have to go through the night, and happy he who can lend a hand and has work to do. Gotha is a pretty place, but the people lead a luxurious life there. I don't want to do anyone an injustice though, and freely admit that my judgement is only a hasty one, with very little to go on. Erfurt is enormous, but deserted. Coadjutor Dalberg is the life and soul of this town; otherwise it doesn't seem to have much in the way of a soul; remarkable, though, the number of beautiful faces you see in the street. I won't say anything about Weimar until I've gone over for a visit and with any luck seen more, heard and gained more than on the fleeting journey through. Here I live in a garden, on the outskirts, with a couple of nice rooms, good food (or what passes for good food in Jena), and with the advantage that my landlord is a bookseller and has a large reading club where I can always get the most recent things first-hand for a day or two. But my work usually only lets me make use of this opportunity at table and in the evenings. Fichte's new philosophy now absorbs me entirely. I go to his lectures and nobody else's. Schiller behaves very amiably towards me. And Paulus has also given me a courteous welcome. I've not been to his house yet. With the professors one is not well acquainted with it is better to seek them out when they have decided to give their time to society, that is in the public circles, of which there are plenty here, and where there is quite a good atmosphere, especially as far as men are concerned, for so far as I've got to know the ladies with my own eyes and from what I've heard there's something rather obliging about them that is hardly grace, and something off-putting that is hardly dignity. In any case I attend these circles only very seldom, if I have to and want to. I meet up with Hesler sometimes. The area around Jena is splendid . . .

My address is: to — in Voigt's garden.

22. To Johanna Christiana Gok

Jena, 16 January 1795

Don't be surprised, dearest Mother, at my writing to you from here, when from my last letter you perhaps thought I would be in Nuremberg by now.

I think you will not be too displeased at this unexpected news once I have explained myself properly.

I am living here at my own expense and have no need for the moment to be at all dependent on you. – For good reasons I have never been completely open to you about my situation up to now. I thought I would be able to overcome the difficulties and intense suffering I have to an unusual degree encountered in my chosen work by dint of dogged and well-directed efforts, and did not suspect that it would in the end come to the point where I cannot very well avoid telling you several things I had kept from you up until now, being obliged as I am to justify to you the change in my circumstances. That my pupil, besides having no more than indifferent gifts, was at the point when I took over his education at an advanced stage of ignorance, was certainly not welcome but not in itself grounds for not embarking on his education with all seriousness, and this I did, as God is my witness and as his parents also acknowledge, with all conscientiousness and according to my best lights.

But that he was quite insusceptible to all rational instruction with which I attempted to work upon his uncivilized character, that firm words were as unsuccessful in inspiring respect as kind ones were in eliciting a devotion to goodness, was, I admit, a bitter discovery for me. I sought the cause of this almost unrelieved stubbornness in the beatings which to all appearances had been practised on him to excess prior to my arrival. Often it seemed that I had woken him from his sleep; he was open, sensible, and not a trace of his brutishness seemed to remain. And on such days he made inconceivably rapid progress in his studies. I was idolized, as if I had performed miracles with the child, the good old parish priest in Waltershausen shook me warmly by the hand and confessed to me that after all the attempts he had made himself with the child he had given up hope and had been put to shame by me, and even the less educated members of the household and the people in the village could feel the happy transformation the child had undergone. That cheered me and gave me courage. But just as quickly and without warning he fell back again into extreme apathy and lethargy. His father, though with too much consideration for my feelings, had drawn my attention to a vice the child had occasionally shown traces of. His disposition and state of mind gradually made me even more attentive and unfortunately I discovered, partly due to his own admission, more than I had feared. I cannot possibly express myself to you more clearly. I hardly left him for a moment, watched over him anxiously day and night. Body and soul seemed to recover, and

I regained hope. But in the end he found ways of escaping my vigilance, and his obduracy, the consequence of this vice, grew, especially towards the end of the summer, to such a degree that it virtually robbed me of my own good health and of all good spirits, and so also prevented my mental powers from functioning properly. I made every effort to help, but in vain. On several occasions I frankly declared the chagrin that all these failed initiatives were causing me, asked for advice, for support. They consoled me and asked me to persist for as long as I could. As some compensation for so many bitterly wasted hours, and also to give the lad some diversion and more exercise by sending him to dancing lessons and the like, we were dispatched to Jena. By dint of indescribable efforts, almost constant surveillance during the nights, the most forceful pleas and admonishments, together with a proper severity, I managed for a time to reduce the evil, and once again there were corresponding improvements in his moral education as well as in his studies. But it didn't last long, the total impossibility of having a real influence on the child, and of helping him, began to make inroads into my state of health and my wellbeing. The anxious staying up at night muddled my head and rendered me virtually incapable of doing my work by day. Meanwhile Frau von Kalb arrived. The noble woman was greatly distraught with the child, and also with my situation. She and Schiller asked me to give it one last try. The major also sought to console me, and himself, and wrote asking me to keep at it for as long as I could. We left for Weimar and as there the vice increased with every day despite the endeavours of the doctors and my own continuing exertions, whereas my health, my courage, my spirits decreased commensurately, as was unavoidable, Frau von Kalb declared that she could no longer bear to see me suffer, she didn't want me to be worn down for no purpose, and advised me to go to Jena and maintain myself here for as long as I could, promising me to use all her influence to assist my future happiness and providing me with three months' money. Given the reduced circumstances in which I live I think I'll get by quite well with 7 carolins until Easter. Schiller is being very kind and looking after me. If by Easter I finish a piece of work I began several years ago I won't need to be dependent on you then either. I am now in a period that is probably of great importance for the whole of my future life. Herder too, whom I visited once in Weimar, shows great interest in me, so Frau von Kalb says in a letter I've just received, and he has asked her to tell me I should visit him whenever I'm in Weimar. And this will happen fairly often; I had to promise Frau von Kalb that when I took my leave. She intends to remain in Weimar and has only taken on a day-tutor for her son. Precisely because she was staying in Weimar, she no longer had much need of a resident tutor. She means to write to you any day. I also spoke to the great Goethe when I was there. To meet and talk with such men sets all one's faculties into activity. – My plan now is to carry on attending lectures here until the coming autumn and then to either give classes here or look round for a new job as a tutor in Switzerland or somewhere, or perhaps to become the travelling companion to some young man. Of course all these things do not depend entirely on me. But insofar as they do, I am trying to ensure my success by working hard and keeping my strength up, and for the rest I hope the fates, and people generally, will be well disposed towards me. Help me preserve my spirits by following the course of events with kindness and sympathy. Dearest Mother, don't let any unfounded anxiety disrupt the hopes you will certainly have for me, for what mother can leave off expecting something of her son? Grant me the uninterrupted use of my energies, something I have now almost for the first time since my boyhood. Believe me, the motives that have led me to prefer the frugal meal I take once a day to a well-laden table and even, for the moment, to my hearth and home, are not childish ones. And so I feel now as I write a new surge of energy and courage within me. Only one thing, dear God, just one thing I'd like to arrive at, and that is that my mother should be able to say from the bottom of her heart: all the efforts and worries expended on him were not in vain! – I hope all is well with you. Give my love to all the family. From now on I'll write more often again. In my recent unsettled situation it was almost impossible. Write to me as soon as you can. I long for a letter from you. And the heartfelt joy I'll get from it you will grant me, I'm sure. All my good wishes.

Yours,

Friz

I was provided with new clothes before I came here. I'm paying 5 thalers for my lodgings until Easter. 14 groschen a week for food. A jug of beer costs me 3 cr. a day and breakfast about 6 cr. I'm living – *next to Fichte's house*, that's the address you can give for my lodgings, they don't have a name.

23. *To Christian Ludwig Neuffer*

Jena, 19 January 1795

I have lots to write to you, dear Neuffer! – First of all I must tell you that I have left my former situation and am now living here independently. You will well understand that I fairly had to pluck up my courage before taking this step. I know that you'll give it your blessing. I would scarcely have done it had the just desire to make a serious go of my life not been compounded by the particular circumstances of my former arrangements. Before my departure from Waltershausen I wrote to you saying how much my tutoring work was disrupting me in my personal development. I suffered more, dear Neuffer, than I liked to say. I saw how the child got worse day by day, and could do nothing to help, very likely even a more accomplished tutor could have done nothing. We came here, I virtually gave up all thought of benefiting from being in this place, with the sole purpose of making one final attempt to save my pupil. I risked my health through continually staying up at night, for his vice made that necessary and I also wanted to make up in part for the wasted day. Often I seemed to be succeeding, but there only followed even sorrier relapses, and I also began to suffer from headaches to an alarming extent from being up all night and probably also from the frustration of it. Your letter was a nice surprise in those unhappy days and did me a power of good despite the contrast between your congratulations and my feelings at the time. Seeing Schiller also helped me keep my spirits up. At the end of December Frau von Kalb arrived to fetch us because she had suddenly decided to move to a town and so no longer found it necessary to keep us here in Jena. We left for Weimar, and I should have made more of many precious hours if my health and state of mind had not been so damaged.

I was at Herder's, and the warmth and generosity he showed me made an unforgettable impression on me. His style and manner are present in his conversation too. But I sensed a simplicity about him also and an easy nature which one would hardly guess in the author of the *History of Mankind*, it seems to me. I expect I shall visit him again quite often. I also made Goethe's acquaintance. My heart was pounding as I went in through his door; you can imagine what it was like. I didn't actually meet him at his house, but later at Frau von Kalb's. Calm, with majesty in his eyes, and love too, extremely simple in his conversation, though now and then it's spiced with a sharp jab at the idiocy around him and an equally sharp look on his face, and then again with a flash of his genius which is far from diminished – that's how I found him. People said he was proud; but if you understand by that a condescending and off-putting attitude towards people like us, it was a lie. Sometimes it is like having a father in front of you, full of affection. Just yesterday I spoke to him here at one of the gatherings. I also had some good conversations in Weimar and here with the painter Meyer, his constant companion, a simple honest Swiss and rigorous in his art. – Have you read Goethe's new novel, *Wilhelm Meister*? – Only Goethe could have written it. What you'll like best is the serenade beneath Marianne's window and the conversation about poets. – But I'm forgetting my own story. On leaving Jena I had already made it clear to Frau von Kalb, and she had told Schiller, that I would like to stay. Frau von Kalb and Schiller pressed me to give it one final go, there now being doctors on the case, in such terms that I really had no choice. But when things got no better in Weimar, and since the need for a tutor isn't so great anyway as the boy

can have tuition there out of house, and in any case the help
and attention I can give is not nearly adequate given present
circumstances, Frau von Kalb offered of her own accord to put
an end to my misery and I took her at her word, but she didn't
want me to leave so suddenly. I put it to her that for my health
I had to get peace and quiet as soon as possible and that I also
wanted to go back to Fichte's lectures, and in the end she gave
in, provided me with money for another quarter, promises to
do everything to make an extended stay here possible, asked
me to make sure to come and visit several times a month and
showed as we parted all her magnanimity and, I do believe, her
sincere affection towards me. – I wanted to account for my
decision to you, hence all the detail. I now work all day long
for myself. Just go to Fichte's lecture in the evenings and, as
often as I can, to Schiller's. He is very attentive and loyal
towards me. What will come of it I don't know myself. The
only thing missing here is you, dear Neuffer! When shall we see
each other again? Believe me, I often feel that nothing means
as unalterably much to me as you. What you are to me I'll never
find anywhere else. And if ever in my life I've spoken from the
bottom of my heart, it's now. I'd often like to be with you too
to cheer you up as best I could. That this noble love should
have such clouded days! Send love to your Röschen, tell her I
mean to have a proper celebration the day I hear of her complete
recovery. Whatever happens, don't let your old spirit slip, dear
Neuffer! I worry about that often. But you were always the one
who set such a good example. You will find part of your *Aeneid*
in the latest *Thalia*. Schiller's new journal, the *Horae*, will be
the foremost journal of its kind in Germany. Whatever you do,
don't give up what you wrote to me about serious satire. Schiller
too says that now is the time to put the public into thorough
indignation if there is to be any effect. He spoke sympathetically of your tireless work on your *Aeneid*. And showed me the
Nisus and Euryalus episode in Conz's journal. Don't let Voss
put you off. Come out into the open, and let people marvel at
the man who dared compete with Voss. All the better for you!
Will you send me some poems for Schiller's future almanac? I
can't understand what he's done with the ones I gave him in

Swabia on your behalf, but think he must be saving them for the almanac. He told me to send you his regards.

Yesterday I also met Woltmann, who is the recently appointed professor of history here and, as you will remember, has had a few poems in Bürger's almanac. He is a slight, dainty figure – quite in the Göttingen style. – Niethammer too, who is very friendly towards me, sends his regards.

You ask how things stand with my Tübingen affairs. Much the same. I said to you before I left, if I remember rightly, that I had passed many happy hours with her, and, it's true, bitter ones too; but that having got to know her better would never have desired a closer union. I wrote to her again not long ago, but only the sort of letter you might write to anybody. God, what blessed days they were when without knowing the girl I transposed my ideal into her and lamented my unworthiness. If only we could remain forever young. Tell me why you asked in the first place. The girls and women here leave me cold as ice. In Waltershausen I had a friend in the house I was sorry to lose, a young widow from Dresden who is now a governess in Meiningen. She is an extremely intelligent, dependable and good woman, made very unhappy by a bad mother. It will interest you to hear more about her and her story some other time.

A visit this afternoon got in the way of writing to you and now I must hurry. Write when you can, and this time as soon as you receive my letter. Even more than usual, I long for a few lines from you. Keep a part of your heart for me! I'll never be able to do without it, not in my whole life.

Ever yours,
Hölderlin

One more thing. Do you think you could visit my mother and, if you should find that she is not quite content with the change in my situation, reassure her? I intend to do everything not to be a burden to her and accordingly am living very thriftily, have only *one* pretty middling meal a day and over a mug of beer think of our Neckar wine and the lovely hours that blessed it. Farewell, dear friend.

24. *To G. W. F. Hegel*

Jena, 26 January 1795

Your letter was a happy welcoming for me on my second arrival in Jena. At the end of December I had departed for Weimar together with Frau von Kalb and my pupil after spending 2 months with him here on my own, and did not imagine myself I might be back again so soon. The many and various miseries I was exposed to in the business of tutoring – which were due to the particular circumstances surrounding my pupil – my weakened health and the need, which was only increased by my stay here, to concentrate on myself for at least a certain period, induced me even before departing from Jena to set before Frau von Kalb my desire to leave her employment. I was persuaded by her and Schiller to have one more try but couldn't keep it up for more than a fortnight, in part because it cost me almost all my rest at night, and so I went back to Jena with perfect peace of mind to an independence which, really, I am enjoying for the first time in my life and which I hope will bear some fruit. My work is now almost entirely directed at reshaping the raw materials of my novel. The fragment in the *Thalia* is one of these rough-hewn blocks. I expect to have it finished by Easter, prefer to keep quiet about it till then. I've sent a reworked version of 'The Genius of Boldness', which you will perhaps remember, in to the *Thalia*, together with a few other poems. Schiller does a lot for me and has encouraged me to write for his new journal, the *Horae*, as well as his planned *Muses' Almanac*.

I have spoken to Goethe, dear friend! It is the finest pleasure in life to find so much humanity with so much greatness. He talked with me so gently and amiably that I can really say my heart laughed, and laughs still when I think of it. Herder was also very warm towards me, took me by the hand, but was a bit more the man of the world; he often spoke every bit as allegorically as you would expect him to. I shall probably see them again from time to time. Major and Frau von Kalb are likely to stay in Weimar (which is also why the boy no longer needed me, enabling my earlier departure) and the friendship between us, especially with Frau von Kalb, will mean I can visit them fairly often.

Fichte's speculative pages – *Basis of a Total Theory of Knowledge* – and also his published *Lectures on the Vocation of the Scholar* will interest you greatly. At first I heavily suspected him of dogmatism. He really does seem, that would be my conjecture, to have stood, still stands, at a parting of the ways – he seeks to get beyond the fact of consciousness *theoretically*, a great many of his remarks show that, and this is just as certainly transcendental, and even more strikingly so, as when the metaphysicians we've had up till now have wanted to get beyond the existence of the world – his absolute *I* (= Spinoza's substance) contains all reality; it is everything, & outside it there is nothing; therefore for this absolute *I* there is no object, for otherwise all reality would not be in it; but a consciousness without an object is not conceivable, and if I myself am this object then as such I am necessarily limited, even if only in time, and therefore not absolute; therefore no consciousness is conceivable in the absolute *I*, as an absolute *I* I have no consciousness, and insofar as I have no consciousness I am (for myself) nothing, therefore the absolute *I* is (for me) nothing.

These are the thoughts I wrote down while still in Waltershausen, when I read the first parts, immediately after reading Spinoza; Fichte confirms my [*missing text*] His examination of the reciprocal determination of the *I* and the *Not-I* (in his language) is certainly curious; also the idea of striving etc. I must break off, and must ask you to regard all that as as good as not written. That you're getting to grips with the concepts of religion is certainly good and important in many respects. The concept of providence I imagine you're dealing with in exact parallel to Kant's teleology; the way in which he connects the mechanism of nature (and so also of destiny) with its purposiveness really seems to me to contain the whole spirit of his system. Of course it is the way he solves all antinomies. In regard of the antinomies Fichte has a very curious thought, but I'd prefer to write to you about it on another occasion. For a long time now I've been thinking about the ideal education of the people, and because you are in the middle of dealing with a part of that, religion, perhaps I'll choose your image and your friendship as the conductor of my thoughts into the outer world of the senses and write *in good time* what I would perhaps have written later in letters to you which you can judge and correct.

25. *To Karl Gok*

Jena, 13 April 1795

I have owed you a letter for a long time now, dear Brother. But the joy you gave me with the full and varied utterances of your pure kindred heart can never be repaid in words. Altogether I do not know what I have done to deserve the love I receive from you all.

The kindness of our dear mother puts me so endlessly to shame. Even if she was not my mother, and if it was not I that experienced this kindness, I would still be infinitely glad that a soul like hers exists on earth. Oh Karl, how much easier our responsibility is made us. We would have to lack feeling hearts for the sympathy of such a mother not to give us infinite sustenance in our intellectual development. – I think you are on the right path, dear Brother. Your heart is full of the unselfish sense of duty, your mind unfolds this sense with the help of other noble minds whose writings are your companions, the feeling of your heart is becoming an unerring principle, clarified by your thinking, which does not kill it – thought secures it and makes it firm. On this concept of duty, i.e. on the principle: a human being should always act in such a way that the conviction that forms the basis of his action could be a valid law for everyone, and he should act in this way solely because he ought to, because it is the sacred unalterable law of his being (as everyone can ascertain by checking with unbiased eye his conscience, the feeling of the law that manifests itself with each individual action) – on this sacred moral law then you ground the judgement of your rights. To approach ever closer to this sacred law is your final purpose, the aim of all your striving, and you have this aim in common with all that can be called human. Now whatever is necessary as a means to this supreme end, whatever is indispensable for your never completed process of moral perfection, all that you have a right to. And here of course the most indispensable thing of all is free will. (How could we do a good thing without wanting to? Whatever occurs by compulsion is not the action of a good will and thus not good in the proper sense, useful perhaps, but not good, legal perhaps, but not moral.) And so not one of your energies may be restricted in a way that would make it at all unfit for your purpose, and the same goes for the products of your energies, and each time you resist such a restriction of your energies or their products you assert a right, whether in words or in deeds. Naturally therefore, every human being has *in this sense* equal rights; we cannot dispute the entitlement of anyone, as long as he is a human being, to use his energies or their products if it would prevent him from coming nearer to his aim of the greatest possible moral perfection. –

But since this aim is impossible in this world, since it cannot be attained within time and we can only approach it in infinite progression, we have need of a belief in an *infinite* extent of time because the *infinite* progress in good is an uncontestable requirement of our law; but this infinite extent of time is inconceivable without faith in a Lord of nature whose will is the same as the command of the moral law within us, and who must therefore want us to endure infinitely because he wants us to make infinite progress in good and, as the Lord of nature, also has the power to realize that which he wants. Of course this is to speak of him in human terms, for the will and the act of the infinite being are one. And so the sacred law within us is the basis for the rational belief in God and immortality, and also, insofar as they are not dependent on us, in the wise governing of our destinies. Just as certainly as the supreme aim is the greatest possible moral perfection, just as we must needs take this purpose for the supreme one, equally we need to have faith that when our capacity of will is exceeded, whatever course things take they still work towards that supreme purpose, i.e. that they are bound into this purpose by a wise and holy being whose power goes beyond ours. I see that there is a lot more I could say, but I'll break off here because I should also like to convey to you, as far as can be done in a few words, a chief characteristic of Fichte's philosophy. 'There is in human beings a striving towards the infinite, an activity which refuses to let any limit become permanent and makes stasis a sheer impossibility, always endeavouring to go beyond itself, to become more free and independent – this activity, which according to its instinct is infinite, is limited. This activity, according to its instinct infinite and without limits, is necessary to the nature of a conscious being (of an *I*, as Fichte puts it), but the limitation of this activity is also necessary to a conscious being, for if this activity had no limits, nothing in which it fell short, it would be everything, and outside it there would be nothing; if therefore our activity did not come up against any resistance from without there would be nothing outside ourselves, we would have no knowledge of anything, we would have no consciousness. If nothing was *against* us, there would be no *objects* for us. But however necessary limitation, resistance and the suffering brought about by resistance are for consciousness, the striving towards the infinite, an activity which according to its instinct is boundless, is equally necessary in the conscious being, for if we did not strive to be infinite, free of all limits, we would not feel that something is set against this striving and so in turn we would not feel anything different from ourselves, we would have no knowledge of anything, we would have no consciousness.' – I have expressed myself as clearly as I could in the brief space available. At the beginning of the winter, before I had worked my way into it, the whole thing sometimes gave me a bit of a headache, especially as my study of Kant's philosophy had given me the habit of testing everything before accepting it. – Niethammer has also asked me to contribute to his *Philosophical Journal* and so I've got a good bit of work ahead of me this summer. Schiller has got Cotta in Tübingen to take on the little work of mine I have mentioned before. How much he will pay me is, according to Schiller's wishes, to be decided when Cotta comes over here, which is due to happen in about a fortnight. I hope not to have to be such a trouble to our dear mother in future. I thank her for what she has sent with my whole heart. I shall never forget that in my present situation I was given so much kind support.

Schiller is likely to stay here. I'll probably present myself for examination here in the autumn if I stay. Only if I fulfil that requirement will I be permitted to hold lectures. I am not concerned about the title of professor, and very few professors here receive any salary worth the name. Many have none at all. – I have a bit more to relate about a little journey I made – I badly needed to stretch my legs after the constant sitting during the winter and happened to have a few French thalers spare. But I'll save it for a letter to dear Rike. – I'll be very happy to have the fine waistcoat promised me. Perhaps though dear mother will not be offended if I confess I still have some unused cloth for a waistcoat in my trunk (a present I brought with me from Waltershausen). On the other hand I'm in great need of a pair of trousers. That was rather indiscreet of me, Karl, wasn't it? I shall have to write to dear Rike next Wednesday, there's not time enough today.

Goodbye, all my love to everyone.

26. To Christian Ludwig Neuffer

Jena, 28 April 1795

Dear Neuffer,

I'd been hoping to find a good moment in which to impart myself to you once again entirely, together with all the little occurrences that keep me in motion. But really I think I'll have to reserve that pleasure for the day we see one another again. And I'd have written earlier if I hadn't broken the happy monotony of my life by going on a pleasant journey. In the latter part of the winter I was slightly unwell due to lack of exercise, perhaps also because I was not yet quite strong enough for the diet of nectar and ambrosia to be found in Jena; I remedied this by doing a walk via Halle to Dessau, and from there back via Leipzig. I'm not the one to bother you with travel descriptions, I never really had any patience for that genre, probably because I have no gift for it, I'm mostly content with the total impression and even when something does strike me I prefer not to risk a verdict on it in passing. People of my sort especially, who every day God sends see through a different pair of glasses (come from who knows where), are not to be trusted. I had a good time with Heydenreich and Göschen. Heydenreich seems to be a refined and clever man, with all the experience in the world. Göschen, who has a rare cultivation of understanding and taste for someone in his position, has managed to preserve an even rarer warmth and naturalness.

Now I'm enjoying the spring. I'm living in a house in a garden, on a hill above the town from where I can survey the whole of the splendid Saale valley. It resembles our Neckar valley in Tübingen except that the Jena hills are grander and stranger. I hardly ever come out and see people. I still go to Schiller's, where more often than not I meet Goethe now, who has been staying here for quite some time. Schiller sends his regards and asks for some poems for his almanac. He says you can just send them to me. I'm absolutely delighted you're more yourself again, your last letter put the one before quite to shame; the pleasure you got from what Heyne said I feel as if it were my own – we'll stubbornly persevere, won't we, dear Neuffer, we'll not let ourselves be driven off the path our natures singled out for us by any adversity in the world. I understand now why you like translating so much. Schiller has got me to translate Ovid's Phaethon into stanzas for his almanac, and I've never got up from any other piece of work in such good spirits. There is less passion involved than in a production of one's own, and yet the music of the versification occupies the whole person, not to speak of the other attractions such work has. – Cotta in Tübingen has paid me 100 fl. for the first volume of my novel. I didn't like to ask more, so as not to appear to be acting the Jew. Schiller found the publisher for me. Don't be scandalized by my little book. I'm writing it to the end because I've begun it and it's better than nothing at all, and comfort myself with the hope that I'll soon rescue my reputation with something else.

This summer at least I'll be living in total peace and independence. But the way people are, they always lack something, and what I miss – is you, and perhaps someone like your Röschen. It's curious – probably I'll never fall in love except in my dreams. Hasn't that been my case so far? And since I've had eyes to see with I don't fall in love at all any more. It's not that I want to renounce my past acquaintances – and by the way, you were going to write to me one day about Miss Lebret: why don't you? – But compare that to your love with its joys and pains and pity me! Is your sweet good girl quite well again now? You must spend heavenly days together. In the end it's the only thing there is in the way of happiness on earth, the happiness of loving in mutual respect, having put one another to the test. I think you will find me purer and more understanding when once again we're together and you talk to me into the night again about your Röschen.

God preserve the two of you as you are! – How are you otherwise, dear Neuffer? We don't go into enough detail in what we tell each other about ourselves. But I think that's the way it always is with letter-writing. Next autumn I'm coming for sure, even if it's only for a few days. I need to warm myself again with you and my dear family. – Dear Neuffer, I had all kinds of things to write to you, but I've got into a tone I'm going to find it hard to get out of for today. All I'd do is repeat myself, and perhaps get a bit too sentimental. More soon!

Yours,
Hölderlin

27. To Christian Ludwig Neuffer

Jena, 8 May 1795

I will try and see, poor dear brother, whether I can pull myself together in my pain sufficiently to spare you in yours. I confess, it overwhelms me too, and I do not know what to say to you when I see in my mind's eye the noble irreplaceable being who lived for you and have to say to myself: this is death! O my friend, I cannot comprehend this nameless thing that delights us for a while and then rends our heart; my thoughts fail at the way things pass, where our heart, the best thing we have, the only one still worth listening to, begs for survival in the midst of all its pain – may the God I prayed to as a child forgive me for it: I cannot conceive of death in his world! – Neuffer, you should be sacrosanct in your grief, the sorry confusion I find myself in about everything, which the pain of what has happened to you has brought home to me for the first time or – I myself don't know which it is – perhaps brought about, I ought not to mention this confusion to you. I am a miserable consoler. I grope around in the world like a blind man and should be showing my brother a light in his suffering, to gladden him in his darkness. Your beloved had a better lesson to give you, didn't she, dear friend? You will find her again, will you not? Oh, what if we were only here to dream a while and then to become the dream of another – don't hate me for these wretched words, you have always remained true to nature, your pure, untroubled mind will give you comfort, the sacred girl will not be lost to you, and that you no longer hear the dear words in which her noble spirit revealed itself to you, and that she no longer stands before you in her unchanging loveliness – brother, can your heart bear the words of comfort with which I would so gladly soothe my own – her spirit will greet you in every virtue, every truth, you will recognize her in every instance of grandeur and beauty with which despite all the world delights us from time to time. How weak I must seem to you. I look at your letter again, which will for ever be sacred to me, and I find you telling me that she will accompany you your whole life long, that her constant presence will keep you in the elevation and purity in which you always have lived with her – how glad I am the dear blessed girl will have this eternal springtime at her grave, the springtime of your heart! For it is my hope for you and the blessings which her memory will recompense you with: the best part of your heart will never age; every day you will be able to look forward to having become more worthy of her and more like her.

The love between you was unique, a wonder in the present

heartless and diminished world. Is it not a love for eternity? Believe me, my beloved friend, in the future you will sometimes say, when I feel keenly all you are to me and tell you that only you can make me forget the neediness of life, you will say to me then: I have her to thank for it, she helped me up out of the indifference life bestows, in her more appeared to me than most people even believe possible, more than thousands of people can be, she gave me belief in myself, she went before me in life and in death, and I struggle my way after her through the night. – Dear brother, I am by your side, I follow the same path, I share your pain and want also to share its fruits; you are right, our life must be a melody over her grave, a better melody than anything our poor lyres can give her. – The wonder of it! My pain was truly inexpressible, I had nothing but tears and had to do a violence to myself even to write you these few poor words, and the best consolation came from your letter again – if only mine could be of some help to you! Oh if only we could be more to one another in general! Being far from you now increases the pain threefold. I wrote to you recently that I wanted to come in the autumn. If possible I'll come sooner. If you were here there would be no reason not to stay. But as it is I'll never manage it. The two of us now wander about the world so depleted, neither of us has anything but what we are to one another, except for the possibility of a better world in and above us, dear Neuffer, and we are supposed to live in this way, only half for one another? I'll come soon, and you can lead me to her grave. Dear God, I didn't think to see you again in such conditions. – Couldn't you come and fetch me, dear brother, or visit me even earlier? It would definitely do you good. You would find friends everywhere here. Do it, if it's at all possible. I'll write to you when the post next goes. If you can bring yourself to, do the same yourself soon. Many here suffer with you and with me. We must suffer as she would have done in our place. Preserve yourself for the world and for me. Farewell, good and noble friend.

Yours,

H.

28. *To Friedrich Schiller*

Nürtingen, near Stuttgart, 23 July 1795
I well knew I would not be able to remove myself from your proximity without doing my innermost self sensible harm. Now I feel it more keenly every day.

It is odd that one can thrive under the influence of a great mind even without its working on one through conversation, merely through its proximity, and that with every intervening mile one feels more deprived. Despite all the motives I had I would hardly have persuaded myself to go were it not precisely this proximity that in other respects had so often unsettled me. I was always tempted to see you, and the only effect of seeing you was to feel that I could be nothing to you. I can see that the pain I so often carried within me was the necessary atonement for my proud demands. Because I wanted to be so much to you I was forced to tell myself that I was nothing to you. But being only too well aware of what I wanted, I do not reproach myself for this in the slightest. If it had been vanity seeking its gratification in this way, begging a friendly glance from a great man recognized as such in order to use this unde-served gift as consolation for its own shortcomings, not caring much who the man was so long as he did the job of flattering its petty desires, if my heart had debased itself to such an insulting courtiership, then indeed I should hold myself in the deepest contempt. But I am glad to be able to say with absolute certainty that there were many happy hours when, in as far as I am able to measure it, I had a pure sense of the worth of the mind I admire so much, and that my striving to mean much to it was at bottom nothing but the just desire to approach in one's whole person the good, the beautiful and the true, whether it is unattainable or attainable; and if one is reluctant to rely entirely on oneself to judge in this matter, that is certainly human and natural.

It is odd that I have given you this apologia. But precisely because this attachment really is sacred to me I try to separate it in my consciousness from all that could degrade it by any apparent kinship, and why should I not write to you about it as it appears to me since after all it belongs to you? I'd just like to visit you once a month, and enrich myself for years. And what of you I brought with me I try to use thriftily and profitably. I am living very solitarily and think it does me good. I enclose some poems by my friend Neuffer. He will take the liberty of offering you another one he still wants to rework.

If you permit, I will also send a few more poems soon.

As for the enclosed it often depressed me that the first piece of work I have undertaken at your direct behest did not turn out better. With everlasting respect I remain

Your admirer,
M. Hölderlin

29. To Johann Gottfried Ebel

Nürtingen, 2 September 1795

My esteemed friend,
You gave me great pleasure by writing to me so kindly. The good fortune of living among people who share with me my needs and convictions becomes a rarer thing with each day; all the more reason to thank the person who makes me believe he finds in me a part of his own being.

You are so kind as to enquire after the rest of my journey. For the most part it was very entertaining, for it was for the most part an echo of what you had communicated to me during the good hours we spent together.

I can tell you I have small hope of finding elsewhere days like those I look forward to spending in your company, and from no other possible situation do I expect the benefit for my inmost being that I would have to thank the uncommon people for that your friendship and my own willingness will perhaps bring me into contact with. So you can see that I had every reason to keep myself free all this time. – The cruel failure of my efforts would perhaps have determined me not to get involved with education again in a hurry, did I not believe that it is impermissible and inappropriate to trace everything back to oneself, & that in the world as it is private tutoring is more or less the only refuge where one can escape with one's hopes and efforts for the education of mankind. Such was the extent to which people and nature were against me in my previous situation!

You need not fear therefore, my dear friend, that I shall expect wonders of myself or of the child! I know too well how many special disadvantages attend every particular method of education, and how very often with me the execution lags behind the project, to expect wonders of myself. And I know too well that nature only evolves by stages and that it has distributed the degree and the content of its forces among all individuals, to expect wonders of the child. – I believe that the impatience with which one rushes to one's goal is the rock which often precisely the best people founder on. The same goes for education. It would be so nice to complete one's work of creation in six days; the child is often required to satisfy needs it doesn't yet have, and to listen to and grasp rational things before it has reason, and then, since they fail to reach their object by the proper course, this makes the teachers tyrannical and unjust, and makes teacher and pupil equally miserable.

I am certain that here as in everything justice is the first law to be followed and I am much inclined to think that here as in everything a thoroughgoing justness, consistent in the last detail, is also the most astute way to proceed.

On these grounds I would not demand rational behaviour of my charge (rational in the strict sense) before he had reason, before he had arrived at a consciousness or a feeling of his higher and highest needs. But not to demand reason of him before he has it is not to demand *anything at all* from him until he has given me the right to consider him a rational being. For what I would *demand* of him I would only demand for the sake of *reason*, or however else one wants to call or represent the highest principle out of which a person should act. (For no doubt you will agree with me that it is only sensible, in demanding something of a child, to appeal to the principle of action not as it is represented in some philosophical system but as it can be represented to the child according to his years and his individual character.)

Rousseau is right: *la première et plus importante éducation est de rendre un enfant propre à être élevé.*

I must lead the child out of his state of innocent but limited instinct, out of the state of nature, onto the path where he moves towards civilization, I must waken his humanity, his higher needs, and only then place in his hands the means whereby he must seek to satisfy these higher needs, and once these higher needs are wakened in him I can and must *demand* of him that he keep these needs forever alive and that he forever strive to satisfy them. But Rousseau is wrong in patiently waiting for humanity to awaken in the child and in so doing contenting himself for the most part with a negative education, only fending off the bad impressions and not attending to good ones. Rousseau felt the injustice of those who wanted to expel the child from his paradise, from his happy animal state, if not with the flaming sword then with the cane, and ended up, if, that is, I understand him rightly, at the opposite extreme. If the child were surrounded by another world than the one we have at present, then Rousseau's method might be more adequate. This other better world is what I must surround the child with, not impose it on him; without all pretension, in the way nature meets him, I must conduct towards him those objects that are great and beautiful enough to awaken in him his higher needs, the striving for better, or if you like his reason. I believe that the history of better times can form this world for the child if it is dealt with *selectively* and *vividly*, as it is appropriate for the child in general and for the particular individual I have before me; an example might be Roman history in the lively detail of Livy and Plutarch. But I would never ask the child whether he had remembered what had been said, for the point is not history itself but its influence on the heart, and as soon as the child began to consider history as a memory exercise or as an intelligence test the intended effect would be lost.

As I say, I should not like to *demand* anything from my pupil at this stage, and yet it does seem necessary to give him some instruction which he might be less receptive to later on, and because of this I would have to solicit the urges which are already present and sufficient for this purpose, such as the urge to imitate and the urge to be curious etc. I can't think there are many children who don't wonder what may lie behind the next hill. So long as geography is not, as it usually is, reduced to something dead and papery; so long as the maps are enlivened with suitably adapted travel accounts, this subject can be communicated to the child, I believe, without demanding too much or imposing too many constraints. If the child can come to notice day by day that arithmetic is part and parcel of many useful activities he will very likely take pleasure in doing it, and I confess that I set great store by this element of teaching because as with mathematics in general it gives better than anything else an idea of strict order. To teach a child a language systematically will be very difficult if it is to occur before the child is even capable of working towards a freely chosen goal, given that constraints and unjustified demands cannot well be avoided in this case. Yet it is possible to become fairly familiar with a language through conversation. This would probably work best with French. – Constraint I would only use when the law of reason must always lay claim to it: if someone wanted to do illicit violence to himself or others.

I should not have troubled you with these remarks if I did not hold it necessary to acquaint you and your worthy friends above all else with my conception of this occupation. And yet for this purpose I have said far too little. Words so rarely give evidence of our intentions. But still let me say that I expect my interest in the children to be as pure and loyal as that shown by their own noble parents. I should also not be lacking in vigour and energy if only I might be granted a few hours each day to devote to the peaceful cultivation of my own personal needs. In this way, and in the company of the educated and accomplished people who would receive me in their home, I would maintain my strength and fortify my spirits for my pupils. –

Should you be looking for a tutor for the other family I would suggest a young scholar who is presently living in Switzerland

and whom I can imagine so well in such a post that to my mind
he would virtually be ideal. I suspect that he would be available.
– Be so kind as to give my regards to your esteemed friends.
With true respect,

Yours,

M. Fr. Hölderlin

30. *To Friedrich Schiller*

Nürtingen, near Stuttgart, 4 September 1795
You will forgive me, estimable Court Counsellor, for the late-
ness and inadequacy of the contributions you have allowed me
to make. Illness and discontentment have prevented me from
carrying out what I intended. Perhaps you will not be vexed if
I send you this a little later. After all I belong to you – at least
as a *res nullius*; and likewise the unripe fruits I offer.

Dissatisfaction with myself and my circumstances has driven
me into the realm of the abstract. I am attempting to work out
for myself the idea of an infinite progress in philosophy by
showing that the unremitting demand that must be made of
any system, the union of subject and object in an absolute . . .
I or whatever one wants to call it, though possible aesthetically,
in an act of intellectual intuition, is theoretically possible only
through endless approximation, like the approximation of a
square to a circle; and that in order to arrive at a system of
thought immortality is just as necessary as it is for a system of
action. In this way I believe I will be able to prove how far the
sceptics are right, and how far they are not.

I often feel like an exile when I think back to the hours when
you imparted yourself to me without ever becoming frustrated
by the tarnished, uneven mirror that you often found it impossible to recognize your expression in.

I believe that it is the property of exceptional people to be
able to give without receiving, to be able to 'warm themselves
on ice'.

All too often I sense that there is nothing exceptional about me. I am rigid with cold in the winter that surrounds me. The sky above me is like iron, and I am like stone.

In October I will probably take up a post as private tutor in Frankfurt.

I could excuse my chit-chat, perhaps, by saying that I consider it virtually a duty to give you some account of myself, but that would be to go against my heart. Almost the only pride, the only consolation I have is to be able to write to you and to tell you something of myself.

Ever your admirer,
Hölderlin

31. To Johann Gottfried Ebel

[Nürtingen,] 9 November 1795

My esteemed friend,

I have put off writing to you from one week to the next. If I wanted to write the truth, I was obliged to tell you about the difficult situation I find myself in, and that could not very well happen without a touch of indiscretion. As I am now driven by necessity I console myself with your kind request that I should let you know if I were forced to change my circumstances. You are probably unaware how much we Württemberg theologians are at the beck and call of our consistory; among other things these gentlemen are also free to determine our place of residence. Because I am not at the moment employed in a public occupation, and particularly with the Christmas holidays getting closer, I can expect to be sent to work with a parish priest any day if before then or at the latest immediately afterwards I do not enter into some other legitimate engagement. Now it is true I have recently been offered another job as tutor in Stuttgart; but you yourself can judge how much self-denial it would cost me to relinquish the hopes you have entitled me to.

I admit that it is not without a certain resignation that I make this avowal to you. However great the temptation of soon being with you and your noble friends, or at least of being able to assure myself it will happen, it goes right against my way of thinking to show signs of impatience towards a friend who is quite rightly hesitating in his choice, and even more to seem to wish that he should renounce other more substantial considerations in my favour.

I heartily beseech you, dear friend, to believe what I say to you until you have the opportunity to convince yourself of it properly. If you can offer some comfort to me please do so as soon as you can!

I would also deeply regret not seeing my friend Sinclair. You will share my conviction that the precocious maturity of mind and even more the incorruptible purity of soul that inhabit this man are a rare find in this world.

It would be so good for me to find sustenance for my inner life again. It's not that the soil here at home is poor, but it is unploughed, and the piles of stones that weigh down on it prevent the sky from acting upon it, and so I mostly walk among thistles and daisies.

My best wishes to you! Give my regards to the noble household that will perhaps take me in.

If I don't see you soon, be so kind as to tell me more about your literary work and other things that engage you in heart and mind. Even if I can give you nothing in return but the proof that I have understood you, surely it won't have been in vain. You know that spirits must communicate with each other everywhere there is the slightest stirring of living breath, combine with everything that does not have to be expelled, so that out of this union, out of this invisible church militant the great child of time, the day of days may proceed which the man closest to my soul (an apostle whom his present imitators understand as little as they do themselves) calls *the coming of the Lord*. I'd better stop, otherwise I'll never stop at all.

                                      Your sincere friend,
                                      Hölderlin

Give my love to Sinclair if you happen to speak to him before the letter I have only half finished today reaches him in Homburg.

32. To G. W. F. Hegel

Stuttgart, 25 November 1795

You do me an injustice, dear friend, if you put my silence down to neglectfulness on my part. I am being held up by the people in Frankfurt, because of the war, they say. I have waited from one week to the next to give you definite news and even now have none, either as regards your affairs or my own.

In any case it looks as if I shall have to do without you in Frankfurt because the child is only 4 years old and you don't seem much inclined to take on a burden like that. – You ask my advice about the repetitorship? You intend to let yourself be determined by my decision? Hegel, now you're doing yourself an injustice. First of all I have no pretensions of that kind and am simply unfit for such a post, as for any position where one has to deal with a variety of characters, a variety of situations, and then alas I have quite particular reasons due to my former foolishness in Tübingen. But for you it would be something like a duty in that you could perform in Tübingen the role of a waker of the dead. It is true that the Tübingen gravediggers would do their utmost against you. When I think that your work might be in vain then it really seems to me you would be betraying yourself by taking on that wretched lot. But whether you would have a better sphere of action where you are in Switzerland or at home in Swabia is certainly a difficult question. Perhaps you could get a travel grant once you were here, which would be no bad thing. If I don't find a suitable private tutorship soon I'll become an egoist again, look for no official occupation for the moment and take up going hungry.

Renz will probably become a repetitor from what I hear. The two of you could have a fine time together. Just don't neglect your literary occupations. I was thinking that a paraphrase of the Pauline epistles according to your conceptions would be well worth undertaking.

More next time. I'd like our correspondence to come to an

end, for a while at least. If we cannot talk there's very little advantage in it for you, at least in what I write.

Goodbye.

Yours,
Hölderlin

Fichte is in Jena again and this winter is lecturing on natural law. Sinclair is now in Homburg at his parents'. He sends his best wishes and holds you in high regard, as ever. Remember me to Mögling.

33. *To Johann Gottfried Ebel*

Nürtingen, 7 December 1795

My esteemed friend,

I gratefully accept your kind invitation. I hope to be able further to convince you and your worthy friends how much I appreciate that what I desired has been made possible.

I hope to be able to set off next week. I have been a little unwell recently, but still the signs are that it won't last more than another week at most.

It is very good of you to go to the trouble of looking for lodgings for me. Should it be possible to live somewhere near you, that would be a great pleasure, or perhaps I could win your company at table. Should you trouble yourself with this matter too, and perhaps make arrangements, I would ask that you attend only to the midday meal. If it is purely a matter of my own choice, I do not eat in the evenings.

Assure your friends in advance that they will notice enough dross, natural and unnatural, original and incidental, in me, flaws caused by many a bad situation, but that I have courage and strength of will enough to be improved, among other things by their example or displeasure. It was my firm intention, before I had any hope of being tried and tested in this way, to spell out everything that I am fighting against in me and that I would particularly fight against as a tutor, but it occurred to me on the other hand that to risk such a frank confession would look like trying to make one's vices into virtues and turning one's weakness into an advantage.

It is with reluctance that I break off so soon. But at the moment I am too distracted and pressed upon by other occupations to be able to talk to you peacefully any longer, and I will of course make up for it. Believe me, I know how lucky I am soon to be able to enrich myself in your company and that of your friends.

Goodbye for the time being. Assure your worthy friends of all that you can read in my soul.

Your true friend,
Hölderlin

Would you be so kind and send this letter to Sinclair?

34. *To Friedrich Immanuel Niethammer*

Frankfurt am Main, 24 February 1796

My esteemed friend,
I have put off writing to you from one day to the next. And I would probably have waited yet longer before writing the letter I owe you if you had not reminded me of my promise. You do this so gently that it puts me quite to shame. You enquire how I feel in my new situation and whether I will soon have the essays ready which I promised to write for you when still in Jena.

The new conditions in which I now live are the best possible. I have plenty of free time for my own work, and philosophy is once again almost my only occupation. I am busy with Kant and Reinhold and in this element hope to collect and strengthen my mind again which became distracted and weakened by fruitless efforts that you were witness to.

But the echoes of Jena still ring too powerfully within me, and memory still has too great a hold, for the present to be able to have a healing effect on me. Various different lines are intertwined in my head and I am unable to untangle them. I am not yet collected enough for the kind of continuous, concentrated work required for the philosophical task I have set myself.

I miss having you to talk to. Even now you are still my philosophical mentor, and your advice to beware of abstractions is as precious to me today as it was before, when I let myself get caught up in them whenever I was at odds with myself. Philosophy is a tyrant, and I suffer its rule rather than submitting to it voluntarily.

In the philosophical letters I want to find the principle that will explain to my satisfaction the divisions in which we think and exist, but which is also capable of making the conflict disappear, the conflict between the subject and the object, between our selves and the world, and between reason and revelation, – theoretically, through intellectual intuition, without our practical reason having to intervene. To do this we need an aesthetic sense, and I shall call my philosophical letters *New Letters on the Aesthetic Education of Man*. And in them I will go on from philosophy to poetry and religion.

I saw Schelling before I left and he is glad to be collaborating on your journal and to have you introduce him to the academic world. We did not always agree in what we said to each other but we were at one in the opinion that new ideas can be presented most clearly in the form of letters. With his new convictions he has, as you will know, taken a better path, before having gone to the end of the less good one. Let me know what you think of his most recent things.

Remember me to all who still have fond memories of me and maintain the friendship which has been so precious to me. It would be a fine reward for me soon to offer you fruits which I will be able to say your care and attention have helped to bring to maturity.

Yours,
Hölderlin

35. *To Karl Gok*

Things are still going well with me; I'm in good health and have
no anxieties and that is all one needs, at least to carry out the
day's work untroubled.

You say you want to occupy yourself with aesthetics. Don't
you think that the *definition* of concepts must precede their
union, and that for this reason the subordinate *parts* of knowledge, e.g. the theory of right (in the pure sense), moral philosophy etc., must be studied before approaching the *cacumina
rerum*? Don't you think that in order to get to know the neediness of knowledge, and so to sense something higher above it,
one must first have perceived this neediness? It's true it is also
possible to start from the top – to the extent that the pure ideal
of all thought and action, unrepresentable and unattainable
beauty, must be present to us everywhere, one has to – but it
can only be recognized in all its completeness and clarity when
one has found one's way through the labyrinth of knowledge
and only then, having keenly missed one's homeland, arrived
in the quiet land of beauty.
[*But Hölderlin just wants to give him something to reflect on.
Not wishing to be thought an authority on this subject, he
frankly confesses to not having thought it over fully as yet.*

*Had a visit from a member of the Breunlin family who was
on his way to Wetzlar.*]

36. *To Karl Gok*

Dear Brother,
Your last letter gave me endless joy. Goethe says somewhere:
'Love and pleasure are the wings of great doings'. – And so it
is with truth: whoever loves it will find it. Whoever's heart rises
above the anxious, selfish field of vision which is what most

people grow up in and which, alas, we encounter again almost
everywhere on the patch of earth which is vouchsafed us for
our rest and peregrinations, whoever's feelings are not narrowly fenced in, his mind certainly won't be either in any real
sense.

Your strivings and tusslings make your mind ever stronger
and more nimble, dear Karl! You seem to me to be going more
profoundly into things and taking more than just one direction.

For this is what true thoroughness is: complete cognizance
of the parts, which we must ground and comprehend together
as One, and, penetrating to the utmost point of knowledge, deep
cognizance of what does the grounding and comprehending.
Reason, we can say, *lays the ground*, and understanding *comprehends*. Reason lays the ground with its principles, the *laws*
of *acting* and *thinking*, insofar as they are related purely to the
general conflict in the human being, that is, to the *conflict
between the striving for the absolute and the striving for limitation*. But reason's principles in turn are themselves grounded
by reason, in that it relates them to the ideal, the highest ground
of all; and the *Ought*, which is contained in the principles of
reason, is in this way dependent on (ideal) being. Now if the
principles of reason, which *firmly* command that the conflict of
that general, self-opposed striving be *unified* (according to the
ideal of beauty), if these principles in general are exercised on
this conflict, then every unifying of the conflict must produce a
result, and these results of the general unifying of the conflict
are then the general concepts of the understanding, e.g. the
concepts of substance and accident, of action and reaction, duty
and right etc. These concepts are then to the understanding
precisely what the ideal is to reason: just as reason forms its
laws according to the ideal, so the understanding its maxims
according to these concepts. These maxims contain the criteria
and conditions under which any action or object is subject to
those general concepts. E.g. I have the *right* to appropriate a
thing which does not dispose of a free will. General concept:
right. Condition: the thing does not dispose of a free will. The
action subject to the general concept: the appropriation of a
thing.

I'm writing all this for you the way one puts a quick drawing or something into a letter, to entertain you for a quarter of an hour or so.

That your fate often lies heavily on you I can well believe, dear Brother. Be a man and overcome it. The slavery that presses against our hearts and minds on all sides in early youth and in adulthood, the abuse and suffocation of our noblest powers, also gives us a marvellous feeling of self-achievement if in spite of it all we carry out our better aims. I will do what I can to help too. Another employment I cannot and do not want to find you. What you need now is simply time of your own; you must be able to live for yourself before you can live for others. It is this consideration that leads me to suggest, contrary to things I've said in the past and having thought about it more fully, that you go to a university. If my precarious fate maintains me in my present situation I can quite easily do without 200 fl. towards the end of next winter. I'll send you that and you'll go to Jena and can, I think, reckon on the same sum from me every year, probably even a bit more, and the little bit extra you're bound to need our dear mother will not refuse you. Whatever you do don't thank me, I am following my convictions, and the fulfilment of such a behest admits of no other reward than that of attaining our goal. And what doubt could there be about that, dear Brother!

Unfortunately I've got little or nothing to write to you about important acquaintances in the sense you mean.

Let the world go its way; if it can't be stopped we'll go ours.

I hope to get more done this summer than I have so far. The urge to produce something out of ourselves that will remain when we quit this life is the only thing in the end that attaches us to it.

I admit that we often long to pass out of this middle state of life and death over into the infinite being of the world in all its beauty, into the arms of eternally youthful Nature, which is where we began. But everything takes its steady course, and why should we pitch ourselves too soon where our desires take us?

Don't let's be put to shame by the sun, after all. It rises over good and bad – and we can also dwell a while among mankind and its doings, within our own limits and weaknesses. – I'll try to do something for your friend H. if I can. Sinclair, whom I've just visited again, sends his best wishes. He sorrows, as we do.

Fichte has published a *Natural Right*. I've just got it this minute from the bookseller and so cannot yet make a judgement on it. But all the same I think I can advise you with good grounds to purchase it.

All my love to our dear mother and the rest of the family and friends.

Farewell, dear Karl.

Yours,
Hölderlin

Cotta is keeping me waiting which is annoying. With any luck he'll have sent the money, or will do soon, even though they're only starting now with the printing of my book.

37. To Christian Ludwig Neuffer

Frankfurt [, June/July 1796]

If only I had you with me, dear friend, so that we could delight our hearts again together. The written word is to friendship what opaque vessels are to a golden wine. Just enough shimmers through to distinguish it from water but it is much preferable to see it in a crystal glass.

I should like to know how things are with you at the moment. I would like them to be as they are for me. I am in a new world. Before I may have thought I knew what was good and beautiful, but since I have it before me I have nothing but laughter for all my knowledge. Dear friend, there is a being in the world on which my mind can dwell for thousands of years, and will do, without ever forgetting how inept all our thinking and understanding is when faced with nature. Loveliness and majesty, and peacefulness and life, & spirit and soul and form is a blessed unity in this being. You can take my word for it that anything comparable has seldom been intimated in this world, and will hardly be found there again. You well know how I used to be, how the commonplace left me cold, you know how I lived without faith, how chary my heart had become, and how miserable I was for that reason. Could I have become what I am now, happy as an eagle, if this, this one thing, had not appeared before me and rejuvenated, strengthened, heightened, magnified my life, which no longer meant anything to me, with its spring light? I have moments when I find all my old worries as completely foolish and incomprehensible as children would.

And it is really often impossible to think of anything mortal in her presence and that is why so little can be said about her.

Perhaps now and then I will succeed in catching a part of her nature in a happy turn of phrase and if I do it will not remain unknown to you. But it will need to be a solemn, completely undisturbed hour if I am to write about her. –

That I now spend more time writing than ever you can imagine. You'll be seeing something by me again soon.

What you sent me has reaped you a splendid reward. She read it, liked it, wept over your laments.

Oh, be happy, dear Neuffer! Without joy eternal beauty cannot flourish within us as it should. Great pain and great pleasure are the best shapers of a man. But to live like a cobbler, who sits on his stool day after day doing what he could do in his sleep, that fetches the spirit to the grave before its time.

I cannot write now. I'll have to wait until I feel less happy and youthful. All the best to you, true, proven and always beloved friend. If only I could press you to my heart. That would be the true language for us two now.

Yours,
Hölderlin

10th June

I'm leaving for Hamburg later today because of the war ... Goodbye, my dear Neuffer! Time presses. I'll write again soon if I can.

38. *To Friedrich Schiller*

Kassel, 24 July 1796

I take the liberty, esteemed Counsellor, of sending you a short contribution for the coming anthology. I should rather have brought it and enjoyed being near you again. Your health is better, as I hear, and that is an extra spur for me to make a pilgrimage to you and see you. But before then I must be patient for at least a few months more. I am now in flight with the family with whom I have been living very happily since last winter in Frankfurt. The people I am with are truly of a rare sort, and I value them all the more because I found them at just the right time, several bitter experiences really having made me mistrustful of relationships of all kinds.

I wanted once again to appear to you in all my neediness, wanted to ask your opinion on many matters that are preoccupying me at the moment, and wanted by some roundabout route to capture a few friendly words from you, but I am forced to break off.

Would you be so kind as to give my regards to your wife?

Yours ever,

M. Hölderlin

39. *To Karl Gok*

Kassel, 6 August 1796

I hope, dear Karl, that the post will now make it possible to give you some news once again and also to receive word from you. For you can easily imagine that in all sorts of ways I have a great need to know exactly what the particular circumstances of the great events that have taken place at home are, and especially all that concerns my dear family.

I should probably torment myself with disquieting probabilities more than I do, were my imagination not becoming more acquainted with the war here in the Rhine country too.

I pity our good mother with all my heart, and am concerned for her as I know how much she suffers under such circumstances, being sensitive and modest as she is.

You, Karl, will be strengthened in your inmost soul by the proximity of such an extraordinary spectacle as the one granted by the giant strides of the republicans.

It is altogether easier to be told about the Greek thunderbolts that thousands of years ago sent the Persians hurtling out of Attica across the Hellespont and down into barbarian Susa than it is to see such a pitiless storm passing over your own house.

It is true you don't witness this new drama without paying for it. But so far, I reckon, you've come off not too badly. Just today I read in the paper that General Saint-Cyr is pursuing the Austrians through Tübingen, Reutlingen and Blaubeuren, and this made me worried about our dear sister and her household. I am also anxious because of Condé's monstrous lot, who contaminate the land and wreak so much havoc amongst you. Make sure you write by return when you receive this letter, dear Karl. In my own situation nothing is wanting apart from peace of mind about my family. For three weeks and three days now I've been living very happily here in Kassel. We travelled via Hanau and Fulda – quite close by the thundering of the French cannon but still safely enough. I wrote to you on the day of my departure saying we were going to Hamburg, but this place is of such interest to Mme Gontard, in so many regards, that once we'd arrived here she decided to stay for some time. (She sends her greetings to our dear mother and you and advises you to look on your situation as cheerfully as possible.) We also have Herr Heinse, the famous author of *Ardinghello*, living with us here. He is really a thoroughly excellent man. There's nothing finer than the kind of bright serenity this man has in his old age.

These past few days we've had spectacles of our own here too, only more peaceful ones than yours. The King of Prussia was visiting the local Landgrave and was received with great pomp and ceremony.

The natural surroundings here are grand and attractive. And

the art is a pleasure too: the Augarten here and the Weisser Stein have parks that are among the foremost in Germany. We have also got to know some good artists.

The picture gallery and several statues in the museum have given me days of real happiness.

In the next weeks we're setting off into Westphalia, to Driburg (a spa not far from Paderborn). I enclose the address where you can safely send me a letter. If peace comes we'll be in Frankfurt at the beginning of winter.

Goodbye, dear Karl. Don't give up on any of your hopes, which you are quite right to have. Write to me soon and at length and in detail and always from the heart.

Send my love to our good mother and all the dear family over and over again and assure them I am with them in my heart.

Yours,

Friz

40. To Karl Gok

Frankfurt, 13 October 1796

I am now a good bit closer to you again than I have been for a while, and feel it. My last letter you received from Kassel. From there we travelled into the German Boeotia, to Westphalia, through wild and lovely regions, over the Weser, over bare hills and through muddy, indescribably poor villages on even muddier and poorer bumpy roads. This is my brief and faithful account of the journey.

In our spa town we lived very peacefully, made no further acquaintances and did not need to since we lived among glorious hills and woods and were our own best company. Heinse travelled with us the whole time. I used the baths a little and drank the delicious, fortifying and purifying mineral water and felt uncommonly well from it, still do. It will give you particular pleasure to hear that we were only staying about half an hour from the valley where Arminius defeated the legions of Varus.

Standing on the spot I thought of the beautiful May afternoon
when we sat on a rock in the woods near Hardt and read
Hermanns Schlacht together over a jug of cider. What lovely
walks we had together, dear Karl! We shall, I hope, have even
lovelier walks when we see each other again. I should like to
hear our dear mother's considered opinion on the proposal
I made this summer to improve your situation.

We mustn't rush her. I'm sure she will tell us the precise
economic reasons for her decision if she is not of our opinion.

You *must* study philosophy, even if you only have enough
money to buy a lamp and oil and the only time you can find is
from midnight to cock-crow. Let me at least repeat that – and
I know you think the same.

If it comes to it you can do without professors and universi-
ties, but, dear Brother, I should like you to have the chance of
satisfying your most noble needs without having too hard a
time of it.

It would give me so much pleasure to see combined in you
one day, as is proper, the thinker and the administrator.

If Jena doesn't come off, you must at least come to Frankfurt.
I want you to have a thoroughly good time with me here.
Before the Christmas holidays (for at that time the roads will
be completely calm), so before the Christmas holidays I'll send
you the money for the journey and you can buy yourself a
warm coat, get on the mail-coach, stay here a few days, go and
visit dear Sinclair in Homburg and then back to the office full
of energy, without its costing you anything.

This only for if you don't go to Jena.

I'm very well. You will find I'm in less of a revolutionary
frame of mind when you see me again. I am in good health too.
I'm sending you a piece of cassimere for a waistcoat. The fair
here is very empty this year. I hope that Württemberg and my
dear family are safe now from new troubles. I don't like to say
much about the political misery. For a while I have been very
quiet about everything going on in our country.

Remember me to everybody – our dear mother and sister and
grandmother, and all the others in Löchgau and Blaubeuren.

If mother doesn't mind I should like her to write a few words

as well the next time. I long to see something from her too.
I trust she's well and holds nothing against me?

Yours,

Friz

41. To G. W. F. Hegel

Frankfurt, 24 October 1796

Dearest Hegel,

Things are finally on the move again.

You remember that at the beginning of the summer I mentioned an extremely advantageous position and said my greatest
wish, for you and for me, was that you should come here to
live with these good people in question.

The disruptions of the war were probably the main reason
why I received no answer for so long. Also I was in Kassel and
Westphalia throughout the summer and thus quite unable to
give you any news about the matter.

The day before yesterday Herr Gogel came round quite
unexpectedly and told me that if you were still free and interested in the post he would be glad to have you. Your main task
would be to see to the education of two good boys of 9 or
10; you would be able to live in his household without any
constraints, have, which is important, your own room, with
the boys in the neighbouring one, and would be perfectly content with the financial conditions. He said it would be better
not to write too many good things about him and his family
because raised expectations are always disappointed, but if you
wanted to come his door stood open to you any day.

Now the footnotes! You are very unlikely to get less than
400 carolins. Your travelling expenses will be paid, as mine
were, you can probably count on 10 carolins. Every fair you'll
receive a very substantial present. And everything will be paid
for, apart from little things like the hairdresser's, the barber's
and so on. You will have very good Rhine wine or French wine
to drink at table. You will be living in one of the finest houses

in Frankfurt, on one of the most beautiful squares in Frankfurt.

You will find Herr and Frau Gogel to be unpretentious, easy, sensible people who, though you might expect them to be gregarious and sociable given their wealth and conviviality, in fact live largely amongst themselves because, especially Frau Gogel, they prefer not to get involved with and sullied by the Frankfurt society people who with their stiffness and poverty of heart and spirit would spoil their domestic happiness.

Believe me, that says it all. But last of all, dear friend, let me put this to you. – A man who despite a variety of changes of situation and character has remained true to you in heart and mind and spirit and will be your friend more fully and warmly than ever and gladly and willingly share in every concern of your being and every aspect of your life, who in his happy situation lacks nothing but you, this man will be living just round the corner from you if you come.

Really, my friend, I need you and think you will also be able to make use of me.

If one day we are on the point of splitting wood for a living or dealing in boot-polish and pomade, then let us wonder whether it might not be better to become a repetitor in Tübingen. For me, through the whole of Württemberg and the Palatinate, the seminary smells like a bier that's already been attacked by the worm. Seriously, dear friend, you have no right to be so wilful and put your spirit through such an unpleasant ordeal.

As proof that you can rely on what I've said to you about the financial arrangements you should know that all the businessmen here have almost exactly the same observance in this regard. You can be quite certain of the main sum. That I have from a good source. I have told Herr Gogel that I'll ask you to write to me expressing as far as you see fit your thoughts on this situation and your particular desires in a letter I will give him to read. So you can clarify anything further this way or, if you prefer, just come. Only let's try to make sure things move on now as quickly as possible. Though Herr Gogel did say that if need be he could wait a few months more. There are lots of other things I'd like to say but your coming here will have to be the preface to a long long, interesting and *unlearned* book by the two of us.

Yours,
Hölderlin

42. To G. W. F. Hegel

Frankfurt, 20 November 1796

Dearest Hegel,

The whole thing is settled. You will receive, as I thought, 400 carolins, with free laundry and service at home, and Herr Gogel will reimburse your travelling expenses when you get here or if necessary send you a bill of exchange in Bern. These are his own words which I've had from him this instant.

If you did want a bill of exchange in Bern, to avoid any possible difficulties, write to me by return and I'll make sure to take care of it promptly without putting you out at all.

That you're not coming till the middle of January Herr Gogel is bearing with more patience than I am; I wish it was New Year's Eve today. Herr Gogel has read your letter and as I expected was very content with it. If you haven't changed you will find in his character and way of expressing himself a great deal in common with your own habits.

The substance and form of the tuition will as is natural be left to you. Your expertise in French Herr G. takes as a rare and important bonus.

His boys, there are two of them, are good, he says, one of his 2 girls, who you will only teach the odd thing to from time to time, is a bit stubborn. But that shouldn't put you off too much. She'll probably be able to remember that Germany is in Europe for you. You won't have anything against a quarter of an hour's talk with a nice little thing like her.

Even though teaching children is often a bit of a burden you'll be better off occupying yourself with the boys than with church and state as they are at the moment. And for things we cannot be expected to teach like handwriting, arithmetic, drawing, dancing or fencing, masters are usually engaged who can be completely entrusted with the children, so that you will be able to have plenty of rest.

We will share all our troubles and joys like brothers, old friend of my heart! It is a good thing the evil spirits I brought with me from Franconia and the ethereal spirits with metaphysical wings that accompanied me out of Jena have left me since I arrived in Frankfurt. It will mean I'll be some use to you still. I can see that your situation has made you lose a little of your accustomed cheerfulness too. You wait. By next spring you'll be your old self again. What you say about leading and guiding, my dear, cherished friend, pained me. You have so often been my mentor when my disposition turned me into a simpleton, and you will have to be again many a time.

You will find friends here of a sort you don't meet every day.

Last week I visited Sinclair in Homburg. He is also delighted you're coming. I tell you, my dear friend, you need nothing more than your house and mine for your time here to be full of happiness. The day we see one another again will give us a new lease of life. I will come to meet you in Darmstadt if only I can arrange it. Then I'll take you round to my house first and have my fill of seeing you again and then I'll bring you to the good Gogel's house.

The day before yesterday I dreamt of you, you were still making all kinds of circuitous journeys round Switzerland which was driving me mad. Afterwards the dream gave me great pleasure.

Goodbye, dear Hegel. Write to me again soon. If only you had already left the district of Bern!

Yours,
Hölderlin

43. *To Friedrich Schiller*

Frankfurt, 20 November 1796

Esteemed Sir,

It often saddens me that I can no longer speak to you from my heart as before I could, but your total silence towards me quite takes my courage away and I always have to have at least some small pretext if I am to bring myself to mention my name to you again.

The pretext on this occasion is the request that you be so kind as to let me have back the unhappy verses which there was no space for in your *Almanac* this year, so that I can go through them again; for the manuscript I sent you from Kassel was the only one I had.

I hope you will also consider it worth your while to enclose your judgement on them, for in this regard too anything is easier to bear than your muteness.

I still remember very clearly every slightest sign of your interest in me. You also wrote me once, when I was still living in Franconia, a few words that I always repeat to myself when I feel misunderstood.

Have you changed your opinion of me? Have you given me up?

Forgive me these questions. An attachment to you which I often fought against in vain when it grew into a passion, an attachment which still continues, forces me to ask such questions.

I should reproach myself for it, were you not the only man to whom I have lost my freedom in this way.

I know I shall not rest until by some achievement and success I once again catch a sign of your pleasure in me.

Do not, because I say nothing of my occupations, believe that I have been idle. But it is hard to hold out against the dejection which comes from losing the kind of favour I used to enjoy or dreamt I did.

I am embarrassed and scrupulous over every word I say to you, and yet otherwise, when I find myself in other people's presence, I have more or less got over youthful anxiety.

Just say a friendly word, and you will see that it transforms me.

Your unfeigned admirer,
Hölderlin

44. *To Johann Gottfried Ebel*

Frankfurt, 10 January 1797

My dear friend,

The only reason I have hesitated so long before answering your
first letter is that I felt how full an answer it needed, and because
no moment when I had the time to write to you was rich enough
to say to you all that I wished.

Dear Ebel, it is splendid to be as hurt and disappointed as
you are. Not everybody has such a concern for truth and justice
that he even sees them when they are not there, and if the
observing mind is swayed by the heart like this then probably
the heart is too noble for the century it belongs to. It is almost
not possible to look with the naked eye at reality, soiled as it
is, without falling ill; the eyes do well, for as long as they can,
to shut themselves against the motes and the smoke and dust
blowing up, and it can also be a fine instinct in a human being
to look cheerfully on things that do not directly concern him.
But you hold out despite it all and I admire you just as much
for still wanting to see now as for not seeing in quite the same
way before.

I know, it is infinitely painful to take our leave of a place
where we have seen all the fruits and flowers of humanity rise
up in our hopes again. But we have ourselves and a few others,
and it is also good to find a world in ourselves and a few others.

As for the general situation, I have one consolation, which is
that all fermentation and dissolution must necessarily lead
either to annihilation or to new organization. But there is no
such thing as annihilation, and so the youth of the world must
come back again, out of our decomposition. One can say with
some certainty that the world never looked so motley as now. It

is an immense multifariousness of contradictions and contrasts.
Old and new. Civilization and barbarity. Malice and passion.
Selfishness in sheep's clothing, selfishness in wolf's clothing.
Superstition and unbelief. Servitude and despotism. Unreasoned
wisdom – unwise reason. Feeling without thinking – thinking
without feeling. History, experience, tradition, without philosophy – philosophy without experience. Energy without principles – principles without energy. Discipline without humanity
– humanity without discipline. Feigned obligingness – shameless impertinence. Precocious young boys – silly old men. – This
litany could be continued from sunrise to midnight without
having named more than a thousandth part of the chaos that
is humanity. But that's how it should be! This characteristic of
the better-known part of the human race must certainly be seen
as a harbinger of extraordinary things. I believe in a future
revolution of attitudes and ways of seeing things that will make
all we have had till now go red with shame. And Germany can
perhaps contribute a great deal to this. The more quietly a state
grows, the more splendid it will be when it reaches its maturity.
Germany is quiet, modest, there is a lot of thinking going on, a
lot of work, and great movements are afoot in the hearts of its
young people which do not spill into fine phrases as elsewhere.
A lot of development, and what is infinitely more: workable
material! – Goodnaturedness and industry, hearts of children
and minds of men are the elements which an excellent people
is formed from. Where are these things to be found in greater
measure than among the Germans? It's true that vile mimicry
has done a lot of damage, but the more philosophical they
become, the more self-sufficient. You say yourself, my dear
friend, that from now on we should live for the mother country.
Will you do so soon? Come! Come here! I won't understand
you if you don't come. You are a poor man in Paris. Here
your heart is very, very rich, richer than perhaps you realized
yourself, and I think your spirit will not want either. You have
friends here, you have even more than that. I did not know that
you were so difficult and hard to satisfy. Now I do. I do not
measure people with a small stick and am certain I know your
innermost self, my dear Ebel, and am bound to say I do not

understand how you could be discontented with people, or at least with one good soul in particular, – she herself said to me recently she knew no one more perfect than Ebel, and she had tears in her eyes; but I shouldn't really be revealing this. – In other respects too you will feel quite at home again in our circle. Since I started this letter Hegel has arrived. You will definitely grow fond of him.

Herr and Frau Gontard send you their regards. And Henry too! Good wishes. Come soon.

Hölderlin

Hegel had entered into employment here with Gogel before your last letter arrived. But I'll look for someone else who might suit you.

45. To Christian Ludwig Neuffer

Frankfurt, 16 February 1797

My dear friend,
I have sailed round a world of joys since we last wrote. I should have liked to have written to you during that time if I had ever stood still and looked back. I was carried along on a wave – my whole being was always too much involved in life to reflect on itself.

And it's still like that. I am still as happy as at that first moment. It is an unending, joyous, sacred friendship with a being who has strayed into this poor unspirited and orderless century. My sense of beauty is now proof against all disruption. It orients itself for ever by this madonna. My intelligence schools itself on her, and my contradictory soul is soothed and brightened every day by her self-sufficient peacefulness. I tell you, my dear Neuffer, I am on the way to becoming quite a good boy. And in other aspects too I am also a bit more content with myself. I write little and hardly do any philosophy any more. But what I do write has more life and form. My imagination is more open to the shapes of the world, my heart is full of

desires. And if holy fate allows me to maintain this happy life I
hope to do more in the future than I have so far.

I can well imagine, dear friend, that you will be eager to hear
me speak of my happiness in more detail. But I can't! I have
often wept and raged at a world in which the best thing of all
cannot even be named on a piece of paper to send to a friend.
I enclose a poem to her that I wrote at the end of last winter.

Over the summer I lived in Kassel and in a spa town in
Westphalia, in the area where ancient Arminius fought his
battle, mostly in the company of Heinse whom you will know
as the author of *Ardinghello*. He is a splendid old man. I have
never encountered such a vastly cultivated mind together with
such child-like simplicity.

The first volume of my *Hyperion* will appear by next Easter.
Circumstances have delayed its publication so long.

Being forced to quit Frankfurt and the distractions of the
journey prevented me from being able to send in anything in
time for Schiller's *Almanac*. Next year I hope to appear along
with you once again, dear friend. The song I found in there by
you obviously had a lot of work put into it. Write and tell me
all about what you're working on, your tastes and moods. Let's
correspond more often again. To have Hegel here with me is
doing me a power of good. I like calm, rational people because
you can orient yourself so well by them whenever you can't
make out where you stand with yourself and the world.

My dear Neuffer, I wanted to write you so much but the
poor moments I have to do it are so little in which to convey to
you what lives and moves within me. And it is always the death
of our quiet happiness to want to put it into language. I prefer
to wander in joyful, lovely peace like a child, without counting
up what I have and am, for what I have cannot be grasped
entire by any thought. If I could just show you her picture
words would no longer be necessary. She is beautiful as an
angel. A face full of tenderness, spirit and serene loveliness! Oh,
the manifesting of this modest quiet soul is so inexhaustibly rich
that I could spend a thousand years in blissful contemplation of
her, oblivious of myself and everything. Majesty and delicacy,
cheerfulness and gravity, and sweet play and sovereign sorrow

and life and spirit, everything in and about her is united into one divine whole. Good night, dear friend. 'Whom the gods love receives great joy and great sorrow.' To navigate a stream needs no skill. But when our hearts and fates cast us down to the bottom of the sea and fling us up into the sky, that forms the helmsman.

Yours,
Hölderlin

46. To Friedrich Schiller

Frankfurt, 20 June 1797

My letter and what it contains would not have been so late if I had been more certain of the reception you would deign to give me. I have sufficient courage and independence of mind to free myself from the influence of other masters and critics, and so to go my own way with the necessary calm, but my dependence on you cannot be overcome. And because I feel how much difference a word from you makes to me, I often try to forget you so as not to become anxious as I work. For I am certain that precisely this anxiousness and inhibition is the death of art, and for that reason can well understand why it is harder to bring nature to its proper expression at a period where there are already masterpieces on every side than at a period where the artist is virtually alone with the living world. He is too familiar with this world, not different enough from it, to have to resist its authority or give in to it. But this bad dilemma is almost unavoidable as soon as the mature genius of a master, with more force and clarity than nature, but also, precisely because of this, more subjugatingly and positively, begins to bear on the younger artist. Child no longer plays with child, we no longer have the primal equilibrium that existed between the first artist and the world, now the boy has men to deal with, and he will scarcely become familiar enough with them to forget their superiority. And if he feels this he is forced to become wilful or submissive. Or is he not? At any rate I should not want to react like those weak-minded gentlemen who in such cases, as you know, tend to take the path of the mathematicians and by infinite reduction make infinity and finitude one and the same. Even if one could forgive this disgraceful practice which is committed against the best of things, it's such a poor consolation: $o = o$!

I take the liberty of enclosing the first volume of my *Hyperion*. You took an interest in the book when, affected by an unfavourable state of mind and almost completely unmerited slights, it was quite disfigured, and so brittle and needy I cannot bear to think of it. I have begun it again with a clearer, more open mind and happier in myself, and I ask you to be so kind as to have a read of it when you can and to let me know by one means or another what you think. I feel that it was unwise to issue the first volume without the second because it is part of a whole and does not stand well on its own.

I hope the enclosed poems might be judged worthy of a place in your *Muses' Almanac*. – I must admit that I have too much of a stake in them to be able to wait patiently until the publication of the *Muses' Almanac* to know my fate and so I beg you to do one more thing: to address me a few lines saying what you have seen fit to include. If you permit me to, I'll send on reworked versions of one or two of the poems that came too late last year.

I must appear rather needy to you, speaking this way, but I am not ashamed of needing encouragement from a noble mind. I can assure you that I am not one to console myself with vain gratifications and that otherwise I am very quiet about my doings and aspirations. I remain with deep respect

Your humble servant,

M. Hölderlin

47. *To Christian Ludwig Neuffer*

Frankfurt, 10 July 1797

My dear Neuffer,

It is a long time since I last wrote. And it is often impossible. I am about to tell you how things are and they have already changed. Fate drives us forward and round in a circle and we have no more time to stop a while with a friend than someone whose horses have bolted. But the pleasure is then the greater when we do pause again and try to tell an intimate friend what we are about, and in so doing learn it again for ourselves. – I often miss you, dear Neuffer. Philosophy, politics, and so on – we can talk about them with all sorts. But the people we can reveal our weakest side to, and our strongest, are few and far between. I have almost completely forgotten what it is to open myself to a friend in total confidence. I would like to sit with you and warm myself first on your loyalty a while – then I could speak to you out of my heart. – Oh, dear friend, I say less and less, and gradually a burden heaps up on me that will all but crush me in the end, or at least give my mind a definitively sombre cast. And that precisely is what makes me unhappy: my eyes have lost the clarity they once had. To tell the truth I think I was more balanced than I am now, with a better judgement of myself and others, when I was 22 and still lived with you, my dear Neuffer. Oh, give me back my youth! I am torn apart by love and hate.

But vague utterances of this kind are only going to frustrate you. And for that reason I would do better to keep quiet.

You too have been happier than you are. But you have peace and quiet. And without that life is no better than death. That's what I want too, dear friend, peace and quiet.

You say that for some time now you have left your harp hanging on the wall as you put it. That's all right too, if you can do it without pangs of conscience. And your sense of yourself reposes on other appropriate activities, so you are not reduced to nothing if you are not a poet. For me, every other possibility, anything else I could do, is ruined, and nothing delights me except when from time to time I allow myself, in the heat of the moment, to be pleased by a few lines written down in the excitement of invention. But you yourself know how fleeting that pleasure is. My official duties, it's in their nature, have too intangible an effect for me to be able to feel my strength in them.

Won't you write and tell me what sort of reception the first volume of my *Hyperion* is enjoying among you and your friends, and what your own particular judgement is?

The poem 'To Diotima' I sent you last time is already intended for Schiller, so I can't very well let it appear in Lang's almanac. And since the version you have is the final one and I don't have a copy myself, I trust you won't mind if I ask you to copy it out and send it to me as soon as ever possible, otherwise it might be too late to get in. I'd be very pleased if you put something of your own in with it.

Goodbye, my dear Neuffer!

Yours ever,
Hölderlin

48. *To Karl Gok*

Frankfurt [, August 1797]

Dear Karl,

Your concerns were quite unfounded. I haven't got your letter to hand, and there's not time enough to look for it, otherwise I would painstakingly dispel every one of your doubts.

You ask me about my state of mind, about my occupations. The first is a weave of light and shadow, as in everything, except that with me the masses they form are often weightier and in greater contrast. My occupations on the contrary are much as they were. I write, teach my charges and from time to time read a book. And I don't like to stray from my timetable. Anyone who has never been deprived of it, as I have, has no idea of the value of a day spent steadily working, at peace with oneself. For most people life is too drowsy. For me it is often too lively,

small as the circle is in which I move. Only a few years ago
I could not understand how any situation that hems in our
powers could be called favourable in any respect. Now sometimes I feel what happiness lies in it when I compare it with
other situations which often take us too far away from ourselves
and are to us what rapeseed is to fields, sucking too much strength
out of us and rendering us useless for what comes after.

Let your life go on being as insignificant as it is! It will gain
importance enough in due course. I wanted to spin you all sorts
of arguments. But the night is too beautiful. The sky and the
air embrace me like a cradle-song, and it's best to be still.

My *Hyperion* has already earned me great praise. I'm looking
forward to having got right to the end of it. I have made a very
detailed plan for a tragedy, and the subject of it engrosses me.

A poem of mine with the title 'The Traveller' is in the latest
issue of the *Horae*, where you can read it. You'll also find a few
things by me in Schiller's next almanac.

The day's business has made me a bit tired, dear Karl. You
won't mind then letting me off saying more this time. I'll write
again soon, with more life, and more warmth! As ever,

yours,
Friz

49. *To Friedrich Schiller*

[Frankfurt, August 1797]

I shall never be able to forget the nobility of your letter. It has
given me a new lease of life. I have a deep sense of how accurately you have judged my truest needs, and I am all the more
willing to follow your advice because I had already begun to
go in the direction you point me in.

I now consider the metaphysical mood as a certain virginity
of the mind and believe that being shy of experience, however
unnatural it is in itself, is as a phase in life perfectly natural and
for a time just as beneficial as any other avoidance of particular
circumstances because it contains our strength and preserves it,

restrains the prodigality of our youthful life until it grows to an abundance that propels it into the diversity of different objects. I also think a more general activity of the mind, and of the life, precedes the more particular actions and conceptions not just in the nature and substance of things but actually in *time* too, in the historical development of human nature – the idea comes before the concept, and the tendency before the (particular, regular) act. I regard reason as the beginning of understanding, and when the will delays and resists becoming a useful intention I find that just as characteristic of human nature in general as it is characteristic of Hamlet that he finds it so hard to do *something* with the *sole* purpose of revenging his father.

I have always had the habit of letting my unnecessary trains of thought run away with me when I write to you, but somehow I need a preamble of that kind before addressing you more properly and directly, and you understand the reason for it and pardon it.

You will wonder how the new translation of *Kabale und Liebe* the English translator is sending you comes to pass through my hands.

A friend of mine, Mögling, secretary of legation in Stuttgart, visited me on his way back from London where he had spent some time accompanying the Prince of Württemberg, and knowing I have the honour of being acquainted with you he gave me the duty, or, really, he wanted to let me have the pleasure, of sending it on to you. The publisher of the book, who was the one who passed it on to my friend, sends you his compliments as well and expresses the wish to receive your most recent works as soon as they appear since he has undertaken to make all your writings available in translation. Should it be tiresome for you to follow this request yourself, I should count it an honour to enter into correspondence with the publisher as you see fit.

Accept my heartfelt thanks for kindly finding room for 'The Traveller' in the *Horae*. Be assured that I know what an honour this is. I am also very pleased that you think my poem 'To the Ether' worthy of your almanac. Since you permit it, I am sending you the poem to 'those who think they know best'. I have

toned it down and refined it as best I could. I have tried to
introduce a more definite note, insofar as the character of the
poem allowed it. I enclose another poem. It is a reworked and
shortened version of the song to 'Diotima' you already have. I
cherish the hope it might find a place in your almanac in this
form.

You say I should be nearer to you, then you would be able
to make yourself properly understood. Such words from you
mean so much to me!

But will you believe me when I say I cannot afford to let
myself be near you? Really, you animate me too much when I
am with you. I can still clearly remember how your presence
always put me into a pitch of excitement that made it impossible
for me to form any thoughts for the whole of the following
day. While I was before you my heart was almost too small,
and once I had left you I could no longer contain it. Before you
I am like a seedling that has just been planted out. It needs to
be protected from the midday sun. That might make you laugh
but it is the truth.

Hölderlin

50. To Karl Gok

[Frankfurt, ~ 20 September 1797]
[*Sends the letters in which the children thank Karl again for the
presents he sent them. The letters had been lying around for a
while; today they added new ones.*]

The fine autumn days are doing me a power of good. I'm still
living alone with my pupil in the garden. The family has moved
to the city for the fair. The pure, fresh air and the lovely light
that is peculiar to this time of year, and the peaceful earth with
its darker green, with its dying green too, and with the fruits of
its trees gleaming through the leaves, the clouds, the mists, the
greater purity of the night skies – all this is closer to my heart
than any other period of nature. There is a tender, quiet spirit
to this season.

Neuffer did visit me. We spent a few very happy days together. His open-heartedness and cheerful mood are the perfect remedy for the rest of us.

I know how to value, dear Karl, the industry you show in your particular occupation. It's not just *what* we do but *how* we do it, not the substance and the situation but the treatment of the substance and situation that determines the value of human energy. In every human activity there is a perfection, dealing with files included. Of course fish need water and birds need air, and among humans too each has his own element. Only it isn't necessarily the case that the most homogeneous will be the most appropriate. An idealizing mind will do better to create its element in the empirical, the earthly, the limited. If he manages to do this, he, and only he, will be the perfect human being.

51. *To Karl Gok*

Frankfurt, 2 November 1797

My dear Brother,

It means immeasurably much to me to find my being taken up so productively and so sympathetically into a soul such as yours. Nothing calms and soothes me more than a drop of pure, unfeigned love, just as on the contrary people's coldness and hidden desire to dominate always, whatever I do to avoid it, work me up and provoke an excessive tension and unrest in my inner life. Dear Karl, everything we do prospers so well when it happens with a sustained soul and we are enlivened by the quiet, durable fire that more and more I am coming to discern particularly, as their chief characteristic, in ancient works of art of all kinds. But who can maintain a fine bearing if he has to work his way through a crowd where he is pushed and shoved in all directions? And who can keep his heart within the proper confines if the world rains down blows upon him? The more we are attacked by nothingness, which yawns around us like a chasm, or by the thousandfold Thing of human society and activity that devoid of form, soul or love persecutes and disperses us, the more passionate and intense and violent our resistance *must* become. Or is that *not* so? That is precisely what you are now experiencing for yourself, dear Brother. The affliction and neediness from without turn the fullness of your heart into more neediness and affliction. You do not know where to go with your love, and your richness forces you to go begging. Isn't the purest part of us rendered impure in this way, through fate, and aren't we bound to spoil in all innocence? What remedy can there be for this? To be active, to be able to tire oneself out over something or other, helps a good deal. That way we at least have a hint of perfection in our sights which our eyes can feed on from one day to the next. It was with this attitude that I used to read Kant. The man's mind was still remote to me. The whole thing couldn't have been more foreign. But every evening I had overcome new difficulties, which gave me a consciousness of my freedom. And the consciousness of our freedom, of our activity, whatever it exercises itself on, is deeply related to the feeling of a higher, divine freedom that is also the feeling of the highest thing of all, of perfection. And in the object itself, however fragmentary it may be, there is a hint of perfection from the moment any sort of order is brought into it. Otherwise how would many a beautiful feminine soul find a world in a well-tidied room?

The poem 'To the Ether' signed D. in Schiller's new *Almanac* is by me. Perhaps you'll come across it and it will give your heart some fulfilment. – Why don't you go one day to Vaihingen to visit Conz who's a deacon there? You certainly won't regret meeting him and I think he will like you very much as well. Assure him that I hold him in remembrance and thank him in my name for the treasured remembrances he sent me by Neuffer, and for the kind response to my *Hyperion*. Tell him I was just waiting for the second volume to appear before sending him the whole thing and asking him about several points with regard to the little book which are very close to my heart. – I find myself pretty much in opposition to the prevailing taste of

the day but do not intend to leave off from my own obstinate
course in the future, and hope to fight my way through. I am
of one mind with Klopstock:

> The poets who only play,
> They do not know what they or their readers are,
> The proper reader is no child,
> He wants to feel his heart, not play with it.

Heinse, the author of *Ardinghello*, has spoken very encourag-
ingly of *Hyperion* at Dr Sömmerring's.

The other parts of your letter that need answering I'll answer
scrupulously next time and soon. Only I've got so much to
write now. Don't feel you would be under any obligation. That
would be very small-minded of me and you would have to
mean a lot less to me. I shall certainly remain loyal to you. For
we are brothers, even if not in name.

Yours,
Hölderlin

52. *To Karl Gok*

Frankfurt, 12 February, posted 14 March 1798
My dear Brother,
It is a proof to me of your good character that amid all your
affairs you always manage, as I can see, to gain in genuine
inner life. On the other hand the example you set confirms my
favourable opinion of mechanical work: it is not as deadening
as an activity where, in the object and its treatment, there is
more scope for choice. It does not tear one apart as an occupation that engages us in mind and soul does, and leaves us
less passionate, in that passion largely seems to stem from the
uncertainty we find ourselves in when an indefinite object of
attention prevents us from going in any definite direction. If I
only know what actually has to be done I do it perfectly calmly.
But if I have no exact and reliable understanding of the matter

in hand I have no idea what force and how much of it is appropriate and then find myself doing too much for fear of doing too little, or too little for fear of doing too much, i.e. acting out of passion. Dear Karl, it is often more desirable to be occupied merely at a superficial level of our beings than constantly to expose one's entire soul, whether in love or in work, to the destructiveness of reality. But it is hard to convince ourselves of this in the period of youthful awakening, when all our energies strive towards deeds and pleasures, and it is probably quite natural that we willingly sacrifice ourselves, that we give up our initial peace for the fortunes of the world and the uncertain fame of posterity. But we mustn't be too hasty, we mustn't be too quick to swap our beautiful, vital nature, the native delight of our hearts, for conflict and ambition and cares, for unless it is diseased the apple does not fall from the branch until it is ripe.

Dear Karl, I speak like someone who has suffered shipwreck. Such a person is all too likely to advise staying in harbour until the best season for the voyage comes round. I obviously set out too early on, aimed too soon at something great, and shall probably have to pay for it as long as I live. It's unlikely I shall wholly succeed in anything because I did not let my natural disposition mature in peace and quiet, free from presumption and cares.

I'm writing all this more for my own sake, because my heart is full of it. You don't have much need of this sermon.

Shakespeare has taken hold of you entirely – I can well believe it. You too would like to write something of that sort, dear Karl, and I would too. It is no small ambition. You would like to because you would like to have an influence on your nation; I should like to for that reason too, but even more to satisfy my soul, which thirsts for perfection, in the production of such a great work of art.

If you seriously want to have an effect on the German character as a writer, and plough up and sow this vast fallow field, my advice to you would be to do it rather by writing speeches than in poetical works. You would reach your goal more quickly and surely. I have often been surprised that our best minds didn't come on the idea more often of writing a powerful speech, e.g. on the lack of *feeling for nature* in scholars and

civil servants, on religious slavery etc. You are particularly
concerned with political and moral matters in our country,
e.g. guilds, civic rights, communal rights etc. Such subjects are
certainly not too slight, and with your local knowledge they
are just right for you, at least for a start. However, I don't mean
to talk you into or out of anything with all this.

I hope soon to see you and have a talk. If only it can be done
I intend to come home in March. I need peace and quiet, dear
Brother! I'll find it in your company and once I'm with the
family again. Oh Karl, all I want is peace and quiet. Don't think
I'm cowardly or slack. My heart, which has been shaken so
often and so variously for years now, only needs to gather its
strength before I embark once again on a fresh piece of work.

Do you know the root of all my trouble? I want to live for
the art that is my heart's desire, and am forced to shift for a
living in the world, making me often so weary, weary of life.
And why? Because art may feed the masters, but not those
learning their trade. But only to you do I say this kind of thing.
It's weak of me, isn't it, not to wrest for myself like a hero,
against the odds, the freedom I need? But you see, dear Karl,
then I'm at war once again, and that's not good for art either.
But it's too bad. I wouldn't be the first to come to grief who
was born to be a poet. We don't live in a climate for poets. That
is why of ten such plants hardly a single one thrives.

Among my little pieces of work there is not one that was not
interrupted by some deep unhappiness while I was writing it.
You may say I shouldn't pay any attention to what makes me
unhappy, but I say to you I should have to have the kind of
frivolity that would soon lose me all the love of the people
I live among. –

What is going on then in your world of politics? I haven't
been able to find the parliamentary writings yet. I lent them to
someone and can't remember who. Forgive me, dear Brother.
I'll happily make up for it one way or another.

The letters you were asked to get from me must be in safe-
keeping in Nürtingen. I have none here. I know my own heart
and am sure that things had to happen the way they did. So
many days in the best part of my life were spent in misery

because I had to endure disregard and disdain as long as I was not her only suitor. Later I found favour with her and responded in kind, but it was not hard to see that my original, deeper attachment had been extinguished by the unmerited suffering I had put up with. By the end of my third year in Tübingen it was over. The rest was superficial, and I have paid for it enough that I continued to go through the motions during the last two years in Tübingen. I have paid for it more than enough through the irresponsibility that crept into my character because of it and which I only freed myself from again after unspeakably painful experiences. That is the whole truth, dear Karl. If you have to speak about me, deal with it as best you can. I wouldn't want to cause any distress to the good soul for anything.

Your affairs I hope we'll soon be able to have a good talk about together. In any case it pleases me very much that you are turning yourself so rapidly into an accomplished administrator.

The hope is that the Cisrhenanians will very soon be republican in a more vital and real sense. In particular, the military despotism in Mainz, which threatened to stifle every stirring of liberty there, will soon, they say, be reined in.

Goodbye for now, dear Karl.

Ever yours,
Friz

53. To Friedrich Schiller

Frankfurt, 30 June 1798

Do not consider it an immodesty that I am sending you a few poems again; even though I myself do not deem my hopes for your approval to be justified.

However much I am oppressed on many sides, however much my own unbiased judgement robs me of my assurance, I cannot bring myself to separate myself, out of fear of censure, from the man whose singular mind I feel so deeply and whose power would perhaps have taken my courage away long ago were it not just as great a pleasure to know you as it is a source of anguish.

You see right into a person's soul. Therefore it would be pointless and idle not to be candid towards you. You know yourself that every great man deprives those who are not great of their composure, and that only among men who are equal do equilibrium and easiness prevail. For this reason I can admit to you that I am sometimes in a secret struggle with your genius to salvage my freedom from it, and that the fear of being completely ruled by you has often prevented me from approaching you with serenity. But I can never remove myself entirely from your sphere; I should hardly forgive myself such a defection. And it's good that way too. As long as I am in some sort of relationship to you it is not possible for me to become an ordinary person, and even if the transition from the ordinary to the excellent is even worse than ordinariness itself, I, in this case, will choose the worse course.

Your unfeigned admirer,
Hölderlin

54. To Heinrike Breunlin

Frankfurt, 4 July 1798

Dearest Sister,

I have all kinds of things to thank you for: the present you sent, your long letter and all that it contains. After I'd received it and read it I went for a walk and took it with me, wanting to read it again, but I kept it in my pocket because I knew it by heart, and besides was thinking too hard of you and your loyal affection for me to read it again with composure. Dear Sister, the advantage of the various experiences I have had is that I appreciate all the better every sign of sympathy. We are like the herds I have often observed in the fields, the way they move closer together and stand huddled in rain and bad weather. The older and more silent one becomes in the world, the more firmly and gladly one holds on to those who have proved their worth. And it's bound to be that way, for we properly understand and appreciate what we have only when we see how slight many other things are.

Don't mention those trinkets, my dear Rike, they are just to show you I am thinking of you and to express my desire to pay you some greater service. Please accept it for what it is, a harmless pleasure that I treat myself to by wondering which of these things would suit you and so allowing myself to be with you and your family in my thoughts.

You talk of thanks, but the debt of thanks I owe you reaches so far back now. Believe me, someone who lives without hearth and home and often among strangers learns to appreciate it when a friend or his mother or sister welcomes him into their house, and he never forgets it. How many generous and joyful days have I not spent under your roof? – Dear Sister, you yourself can have no idea what a house like yours is worth, where the humane spirit of your dear husband and a heart like yours reign. You are happy, and would feel it even more sharply if you saw how joyless and desolate the world of show and grandeur is, not only for us but for those who live in it and seem to prosper there, when all the while a hidden discontent they do not fully understand themselves gnaws at their souls. The more horses a man sets before his carriage, the more rooms he shuts himself up in, the more servants he has surrounding him, the more he covers himself with gold and silver – the deeper he digs his own grave, where he lies more dead than alive and the others don't notice him any longer, no more than he does them, despite all the fuss they make on both sides. The only person this sorry comedy can delight is the one who looks on and deceives himself. If only I too could stop and stare at the splendour of the world! I'd be happier, and perhaps a perfectly tolerable young man! But the only way you can impress me is by character and by genius, and since these are such rare things in the world I have unfortunately only rarely shown it the proper humility. Well, I'm humbler now, having suffered a bit more, but that's not the right way.

I must break off, the post is going. Give my remembrances to your dear husband. My love to all the children, and to each as it pleases them best. As soon as Miss My-bride-to-be starts scribbling we'll have to set in train a tender correspondence between us. –

All my kind regards to Dr Veiel. I'm delighted at his good taste, and if he's happy into the bargain, even more so.

Yours,
Friz

55. To Karl Gok

Frankfurt, 4 July 1798

You've learnt the habit of putting off writing from me, dear Karl, but I'll set you a good example and write another letter before getting a reply to the one I sent you at about Easter-time. Our dear mother writes saying you're a bit unwell and have a great deal of work. So I can very easily imagine how hard it is to get round to writing a letter. Life is sometimes so disruptive and debilitating that, for all the energy of youth, often one barely has thoughts and patience enough left over for what is necessary, and no period is worse in every respect than a young man's transition to maturity. I think that at no other time in our lives do other people and our own natures cause us so much trouble, and this period really is that of sweat and anger and sleeplessness and anxiety and storminess, the bitterest of our lives, just as the period that follows on May is the most unsettled in the year.

But as with all other things that mature, human beings ferment, and the task of philosophy is simply to ensure that the period of fermentation is as harmless, as tolerable and as brief *as possible*. – Swim through, brave swimmer, and just keep your head above water! Sweet Brother, I have also suffered much, very much, and more than I ever told you or anyone else, because not everything can be told, and even now I still suffer a great deal, and nonetheless I think the best of me has not yet perished. My character Alabanda says in the second volume: 'What lives, is indestructible, *even in its deepest form of subjection remains free*, remains whole, and if you tear it down to its base, and if you smash it to the marrow, yet it remains at bottom unwounded, and its being flits triumphantly from out of your hands etc.' This is true of more or less any human being, and most of all of the truest and best. And Hyperion says: 'Everywhere there remains a joy for us. True pain inspirits. Whoever treads on his misery stands higher. And it is a marvellous thing that only in our sufferings do we fully feel the soul's freedom.' Farewell, dear beloved Brother. Write to me soon. Remember that I am loyal to you, as you are to me! Oh, only remain the person you are, for our country's sake and for mine!

H.

There are letters too from the children.

56. *To Christian Ludwig Neuffer*

Frankfurt, August 1798

I am pleased, my dear Neuffer, that you are content with my bits and pieces. One day, when the fates, whom I love even in unhappiness, will perhaps repay my love with some tranquillity and good spirits, I will make sure you also profit from it. You must know that you, who were the first properly to teach me the joy of true friendship, will and must receive from me everything that men can demand of one another, spirit and action and affectionate devotion. Dear Neuffer, do you honour the times of our shared intimacy as I do? – I believe that people who have loved one another as we have are for that very reason capable of all that is great and beautiful and are bound to achieve it if only they understand one another properly and have the courage to work their way through the dross that hinders them. I know very well I have achieved nothing yet, and perhaps I never shall. But why should that affect my faith in myself? Does it make it a vain illusion? I think not. I shall say I have not understood myself properly if I do not succeed in anything excellent in this world. To understand ourselves, that's what saves us. If we err in ourselves, in our θειον or whatever you want to call it, then all art and labour is in vain. That's why it's so important to stick together and tell each other what is in our minds. If out of petty rivalry etc. we separate and become isolated it's our own greatest loss – the voice of a friend is indispensable if we are to be at one with ourselves again whenever, because of the stupidities of ordinary people and the selfish pride of those who have already achieved something, we are at odds with our own soul, our own best life.

Here are a few more little poems.

I didn't have enough time for what I promised you in my last letter.

Yours,
Hölderlin

57. To Johanna Christiana Gok

Homburg vor der Höhe, 10 October 1798

Dearest Mother,

Your pure good will towards me, which I felt once again in your last letter and which gave me such pleasure, also your partly justified concern for my health, give me grounds to hope that you will not disapprove of the change in my situation which I have been building up to for quite some time.

First of all I must demonstrate to you how stable and appropriate in every respect my present situation is, and when I then go on to name the reasons that inevitably caused me to leave my previous post, despite having stayed put for a long time and with much patience, you will find more cause for contentment than for discontentment in this letter.

Through my work as a writer and by being thrifty with my salary I have in the last one and a half years of my time in Frankfurt got together 500 florins. With five hundred guilders I think one can be quite free of financial worries for at least a

year anywhere in the world, so long as it is not as dear as
Frankfurt. So I had every right to restore the health and energies
I had necessarily forfeited to the strenuous combination of my
official duties and my own work by seeking out a more peaceful
way of life, something which my savings, though not without
considerable effort on my part, had made possible. – In
addition, my friend, the governmental councillor von Sinclair
in Homburg, who had long since been privy to my situation in
Frankfurt, urged me to move over into his house in Homburg,
take board and lodging with him for a small fee, and *get on
with my work and so finally begin to establish for myself a
position in society*. I made many objections to this, among other
things that I risked falling into a state of dependence on him that
would be unfitting between friends. To remove this objection he
found me board and lodging somewhere else where conditions
are extremely pleasant and I live in good health and free from
disturbance and pay 70 florins a year for the rooms, service and
laundry. For lunch, which is really unusually well prepared for
the price, I pay 16 groschen a day. In the evening I have long
been accustomed to drink only tea with a piece of fruit. (As I
have brought far more clothes with me than I need, though
admittedly they were all required in Frankfurt, you can see how
far my savings will get me.)

The members of Sinclair's family are all excellent people who
always treated me with courtesy and kindness on my earlier
visits and, now that I'm actually here, are so generous in their
sympathy and encouragement that I have more reason to keep
myself to myself for the sake of my work and to preserve my
freedom than fear I might lead too solitary a life. My book has
had a certain amount of success at court and the wish has been
expressed to make my acquaintance. The Landgrave's family is
made up of genuinely noble men and women whose attitudes
and way of life set them quite apart from others of their class.
But I take care to keep my distance so as to protect my freedom;
I pay my respects and leave it at that. You understand that
I am only telling you this because you might be pleased to
hear it and it could be useful to me in an emergency. But the
crucial thing is the intelligent, rational, warm companionship

of Sinclair. With such a man every hour brings joy and enrich-
ment for the soul. You can imagine the good influence this is
having on my work and my character. So as not to go on too
long I'll save for another occasion much else that will convince
you how well fitted this place and my present situation are to
my most real needs. It was simply necessary, after all this time,
to adopt a more independent situation to prepare for my future
profession, and judge for yourself whether the place I have
chosen for this purpose could be more suitable. – For all that,
I admit I should very much have liked to remain in my previous
situation a little longer, for one thing because it was terribly
hard to part from my dear pupils, who were doing so well, and
also because I was well aware that any change in my situation,
however necessary and favourable, would upset you. And I
should certainly not have shrunk from the effort it would have
taken to carry on my own work alongside my lessons, although
I must say that I was so involved with the children that it was
simply not possible for me to take my teaching lightly in any
way. The fondness they had for me, and the success of all my
efforts, often cheered me and did make my life easier. But the
discourteous pride, the deliberate, daily belittling of all learning
and culture, the opinions expressed about private tutors – that
they were only servants, that they couldn't expect any special
treatment because they were paid for what they did etc., and
many other casual remarks of that nature let drop in my presence because it's the fashion in Frankfurt – that hurt me, however hard I tried to rise above it, more and more, and sometimes
left me in a state of contained anger that never does body or
soul any good. Believe me, I was patient. If ever you believe a
word of mine, believe this. You will think it exaggerated if I tell
you that nowadays it is simply impossible to hold out for long
in such conditions; but if you could see in what degree *the rich
businessmen in Frankfurt, in particular, are incensed by present
events*, and how they make everyone who depends on them pay
for their resentment, you would be able to understand what I
am saying. – I don't want to speak about the matter any more,
or any more clearly, because I am really very reluctant to speak
ill of people. – It was really these almost daily injuries to my

feelings that made my professional tasks and other occupations unutterably more difficult and would have rendered me quite useless for both had I not sought to counter what I suffered with the most strenuous efforts. However that could only last for a while. The whole of last summer I was almost completely idle once I had finished with the children because most of the time I was too poorly or too tired for anything else. – I am ashamed to talk about myself in this tone, and only do so for your sake, only to convince you of the necessity of a change. – Eventually I had to make the painful decision to part from the dear children, which I had put off for so long and with God knows how much toiling and anxiety. My self-respect, too, prevented me from going on appearing before my friends in such a miserable state. I announced to Herr Gontard that my future development demanded that I make myself independent for a time, I avoided all further explanations, and we parted on polite terms. There are lots of things I'd like to tell you about good little Henry, but I have to banish virtually all thoughts of him from my mind if I am to prevent my feelings from getting the better of me. He is a marvellous boy, full of unusual talents, a boy after my heart in so many respects. He will never forget me, just as I shall never forget him. And I think I have laid good firm foundations in him he will be able to build on in the future. I'm glad I am only three hours away from him so that I can at least find out how he's getting on from time to time. – I must break off here to get the letter to the post in time. Give me the pleasure of one of your kind letters soon. Remember me in Blaubeuren. I mean to write to them very soon. All my love to dear Karl: a long letter will go off to him this week too if possible. How is grandmother? Give her my warmest compliments. I am, as ever, with child-like devotion

Yours,
Friz

My address.
M. Hölderlin, c/o Herr Wagner, glazier in Homburg vor der Höhe.

58. *To Christian Ludwig Neuffer*

Homburg, 12 November 1798

My dearest Neuffer,

I have changed my situation since I last wrote to you and intend to live here in Homburg for a while from my own means. I have been here for just over a month and have spent the time peacefully, at work on my tragedy, with Sinclair for company, enjoying the beautiful autumn days. I was so torn by various sufferings that I probably have the good gods to thank for the blessing of my present calm.

I am very eager to have news of you and to receive your almanac; but I'll almost certainly have to wait unless I come and fetch it from you myself, not because I think you neglectful, but because your letters will only find me here again in 4 weeks' time.

My friend Sinclair, you see, is going to Rastatt on business to do with his court and has suggested that I accompany him, on very favourable conditions. Thanks to Sinclair's generosity I can do this almost without touching my meagre savings and also without significantly interrupting my work, and so it would have been odd of me not to agree.

We are setting off later today or tomorrow.

Perhaps I'll make a trip from Rastatt into Württemberg. If this doesn't prove possible I'll write to you from Rastatt asking you, if you're not prevented by other circumstances, to be in Neuenbürg on a certain date, and I'll come there too so as to see you face to face again. I should love to be able to speak with you again about all the things that interest us both. – Life in poetry is what now occupies my thoughts and senses more than anything else. I feel so keenly how far I still am from arriving at it but all the same my whole soul strives for it, and often it all comes home to me so palpably that I cry like a child when I everywhere feel how my work is lacking in this or that respect and yet I cannot extricate myself from the poetic labyrinth I'm wandering about in. Oh, in my early youth the world frightened my spirit back into itself and I'm still suffering from the effects. True, there is a hospital where poets afflicted as I am may find honourable refuge – philosophy. But I cannot relinquish my first love, the hopes of my youth, and I'd rather die without achieving anything than abandon the sweet land of the Muses, which only chance has cast me from. If you have any good advice, to put me on the right path as quickly as possible, let me know. I lack not so much strength as lightness, not so much ideas as nuances, not so much a main tone as a spectrum of diverse tones, not so much light as shadow, and all this for one reason: I shun the common and ordinary aspects of real life too much. I'm a real pedant, if you like. And yet unless I'm mistaken pedants are usually so cold and loveless, and my heart is always so eager to unite with everybody and everything beneath the moon. I almost think I am pedantic out of sheer love. I'm not shy because I'm afraid that reality might disturb my selfishness but because I'm afraid reality will disturb the intense, ready sympathy with which I commit myself to other things; I am afraid the warm life in me will be chilled by the icy-cold happenings of everyday life, and this fear comes from having always reacted more sensitively than others to anything destructive I encountered, and this sensitivity seems to have its origin in the fact that, relative to the experiences I had to go through, I wasn't of a sufficiently strong constitution, I was not indestructible enough. I can see that. Is being able to see it of any good to me? To this extent, I think: since I am more liable to be destroyed than many other people I must try to extract some advantage from the things that have a destructive effect on me. I mustn't take them for what they are in themselves, but only in as far as they can be of use to my own truest life. I must when I come across them make it a principle to take them as indispensable material without which my innermost will never come to full expression. I must take them up into myself so that when the opportunity arises (as an artist, if that's what I want and am to become) I can place them as shadow next to my light, reproduce them as subordinate tones among which the tone of my soul will spring forth with all the more life. Purity can only be represented in impurity and if you try to render fineness without coarseness it will appear entirely unnatural and incongruous, and this for the good reason that fineness itself, when it occurs, bears the colour of the fate in which it arose; and beauty, when it appears in reality, necessarily assumes a form from the circumstances in which it emerges which is not natural to it and which only becomes its natural form when it is taken together with the very conditions which of necessity gave it the form it has. So for example the character of Brutus is a highly unnatural, nonsensical character unless he is seen amid the circumstances which force his *gentle* spirit to adopt this *stern* form. Nothing fine, then, can be represented without coarseness; and for this reason I shall always tell myself, when I encounter coarseness in the world: you need it just as much as a potter does clay, therefore embrace it and don't reject it or shrink from it. That's my conclusion.

Wanting to ask you for advice and thus to give you a very clear picture of my faults, which of course you're already acquainted with to a point, and at the same time wanting to become more conscious of them myself, I've gone further than I meant to, and so that you can understand my moping properly I'll admit that for some days now my work's been at a standstill, and when that happens I always fall into reasoning. Perhaps these brief thoughts will stimulate you to further reflection about art and artists, and particularly about my main poetic faults and what can be done about them, and perhaps sometime you'll be so kind as to let me know what you think. –

Good wishes, my dear Neuffer! I'll write again as soon as I'm in Rastatt.

                                                        Yours,
                                                        Hölderlin

59. *To Karl Gok*

Rastatt, 28 November 1798

My dear Karl,

We should have become strangers to one another if the similarity of our attitudes and our nature had not made us infinitely and lastingly close, for this time we really have left our friendship without nourishment for longer than at any other period. But the gods, though they do not need a sacrifice, demand it nonetheless as a tribute. And so we too must again begin to make sacrifice from time to time to the divinity between us: the easy, pure sacrifice of speaking to one another about it, of celebrating the god that unites us in the sweet letters that we only exchange so rarely because they come from the heart and not, as so often happens, from the pen. A living flower takes longer to grow than a flower made of taffeta, and a living word must also mature in our hearts before it can appear, and cannot be produced in profusion like the things that one shakes from one's sleeves. It's not that our letters are so extraordinary in their thoughts and wit and in the diversity of their ideas and subjects, but they have something that can be called the sign of all living utterance, which is that they say more than they seem to, because in them a heart stirs that in life in general can never say all that it wants to say. Dear Brother, when will people recognize that the highest power is in its expression also the most modest and that the divine, when it makes itself manifest, can never be without a certain sadness and humility? Of course at the moment of decisive conflict things are rather different! But as you can see that's not what we're talking about. I don't need to tell you how much my heart has been shaken by the changes in my life during the silence between us. That I am living in Homburg, and why, you will have seen from the letter I wrote to our dear mother. Karl, how often I'd have liked to write to you in the last days in Frankfurt, but I concealed my suffering from myself, and there were times when if I had tried to utter it I would have wept out my soul. In Homburg I tried to recover my peace of mind by working constantly, and when

I was tired I spent most of my time with Sinclair. He has acted towards me as a true friend. It was at his suggestion that I accompanied him here. There are all sorts of people here. Only it's a pity that diplomatic *sagesse* keeps everybody's faces expressionless, and their minds too, so that little open social interchange goes on. Nevertheless, despite the prudence common to all, the differences between the French, the Austrians, the Swabians, the Hanoverians and the Saxons and so on are still pretty obvious.

I should very much like to have spoken with you, dear Karl. I did have the plan of at least getting you to come as far as Neuenbürg or Pforzheim to meet there, but the time I had in mind has been marred by bad weather, and this week I mean to go back to Homburg. Next spring, when I've finished what I'm working on, nothing will keep me from following the bidding of my heart and spending a few weeks with you all. That then I'll have a few more miles to walk doesn't matter, especially in the fine days in May. Let the glad, good, pure spirit of life be with us both until then and protect and sustain us! –

The real gain my stay here has brought me is meeting a few young men full of spirit and pure endeavour: *Muhrbeck*, a Pomeranian, a restless soul who is now travelling, drawing inspiration from people and nature for a bold philosophical work he is still jotting down notes for; *Horn*, secretary of the Prussian legation, a man of genuine culture with profound sentiments and great curiosity together with fine manners and conviviality, a thinker with a proper sense of beauty and art; *von Pommer-Esche*, a Swede – all calm and kindness, unpretentious and happy in himself, accomplished in all kinds of disciplines and languages, proud and manly but completely good-natured, figure and countenance intact in their beauty; then also a splendid old man, Councillor *Schenk* from Düsseldorf, an intimate friend of Jacobi's, a pure, cheerful, noble character, lucid and full of ideas – he speaks, often like a very young man, with sheer joyful enthusiasm, especially when talking about his beloved Jacobi, and casts such a friendly eye over us younger ones that together we make up a completely harmonious family.

Let me soon have news of you again, dear Brother. I got R. to tell me a lot about you, and afterwards on his return to Württemberg he also wrote to say he'd visited you as I had asked him to and told me how you were. You'll write to me soon, won't you? Address your letter to M. Hölderlin, c/o Wagner, glazier in Homburg vor der Höhe.

There are hopes here again, more than before, that peace will come soon. I speak to our countryman, Herr Gutscher, secretary of legation, nearly every day. He is a sensible man.

And now good night, dear Karl!

Yours,
Hölderlin

60. To Johanna Christiana Gok

Homburg vor der Höhe, 11 December 1798

Dear Mother,

Your kind letter no longer found me in Rastatt and was sent on to me here. It gave me a great deal of pleasure to see that I am still held in fond memory among my relatives; your kindly thoughtfulness and sympathy especially, dearest Mother, stirred me intensely, and you can imagine how that in itself made me feel drawn towards you. In order to be able to think things over calmly I was obliged to put off my decision about the proposed post as private tutor until the next day, and even then I was unwilling to trust my judgement at first and wanted to let a few more days go by so as to be able to give you an answer that had been properly considered.

Probably the most valid argument I can put forward is that in a year's time I shall hardly have any trouble, should nothing else present itself before then, in finding a similar post, since private tutors who are worth their salt are very hard to come by at present, and many resolve to find some other way of getting by rather than entering into what in our day and age is such a difficult situation and exposing themselves to all the misunderstandings which are now so much a part of this equivocal calling. For a well-defined office, where a man has a mechanical employment set him in advance, is something quite different and can be much more readily executed in tranquillity than educating children, which is something that has no end; and sharing day-to-day life in one household, where, mutually, any pretensions have to be reduced to a minimum if one is to avoid ending up a burden on each other, is so difficult and, as I said, the frame of mind common to almost all those who take on private tutors nowadays is even with the best will in the world and the greatest tact on both sides so hard to cope with that a young man really does best not to venture on this difficult task so long as some other situation is open to him which he doesn't need to be ashamed of and will allow him to make ends meet. But as everything can be learnt, and I feel I now have a fair idea of how to manage a peaceful life as a tutor in most households, I have less cause to fear this position than others who have no experience of it and are less practised and for-bearing – only in such a situation I always forfeit in liveliness of mind what I acquire in reserve and patience. For this reason I think it is my duty to spare myself in this regard for as long as I can without causing distress to others, in order to spend a year with all my living powers devoted to the higher and purer occupations God principally intended me for. – This last remark may surprise you, and you will want to know what these occu-pations are. – From what of my work has come your way up until now you will hardly be able to guess what the business is I most call my own, and yet even in those insignificant pieces I have, from a distance, among those who can hear me, begun to *prepare* the deeper opinion of my heart which I shall perhaps be unable to express fully for a long time yet. At the moment it is not possible to say everything straight out to people because they are too dull and concerned with themselves to abandon the thoughtlessness and irreligiousness they live in like a plague-ridden city and escape to the mountain-tops, where the air is purer and the sun and the stars are closer and we can look down with tranquillity on the turmoil of the world below, that is, where we raise ourselves up to a feeling of the godhead and contemplate all that was and is and will be out of this feeling.

Dearest Mother, you have sometimes written to me on the subject of religion as if you did not know what to make of my religious feeling. Oh, if only I could at one stroke reveal my innermost thoughts to you. – Just let me say this: there is not a living note in your soul which does not find an answering tone in mine. Have faith in me. Do not doubt what is sacred within me and I will open myself to you the more. Oh Mother, there is something between you and me that divides our souls. I don't know what to call it – does one of us have too little respect for the other, or what is it? I say this to you from the bottom of my heart. Even if you cannot put into words all that you are to me it lives in me all the same and on every occasion I have a strange sense that secretly you rule over me and that, with an indelibly faithful attentiveness, my soul is anxious for yours. Can I tell you something? If I have often lacked orientation in my thoughts and drifted around restlessly in the world, it was only because I thought you had no joy in me. But it's that you don't trust yourself, isn't it, you are afraid you will make your sons soft and too headstrong, you are afraid your motherly nature might get the better of you and that your sons would then be left helpless, without direction, and for that reason you have too little confidence in us, and out of love deny yourself the pleasure which is proper to parents when they are older, and prefer to expect less of us so as not to expect too much? –

I wanted to tell you the reasons I had for turning down the post that has been offered me, and I am glad that it has given me the opportunity to speak from the heart again. That is a pleasure we so rarely have in this world that it could easily be forgotten.

I wrote to our dear Karl from Rastatt. Now I won't leave it any longer and write to Blaubeuren too. It troubles me that my dear brother, who deserves to be so happy, does not feel that the situation he is in suits him. Can't you write to me, dearest Mother, and tell me what the unpleasantness is he has to put up with? – It is nice that our dear relatives can find some consolation for the death of the good vicar in the happy state of my dear cousin Karoline. Wish her warmly all the joy she deserves from me. And write to them thanking them sincerely for having thought of me with the job; but I couldn't get away for at least six months and Herr von Gemmingen probably wouldn't want to do without a teacher for his children for so long. If things were different I should have considered myself lucky to enter into relations with Herr von Gemmingen. All my best wishes to dear grandmother and to everybody!

> Yours,
> Friz

All my regards and congratulations to my old friend Gentner.

61. *To Isaak von Sinclair*

> Homburg, 24 December 1798

My dear friend,

The reason I have not written to you for so long is that I would only have put half my mind to it, for until now I have been taken up more than usual by my work, which had become dearer to me because of the interruption. As you well know, I have no trouble abandoning things when you are with me in person, but I take a bit longer about it if presence, which has power over everything, is not there making its agreeable pressure felt.

Thank you very much for your letters. Pommer-Esche's visit gave me enormous pleasure because it was of real benefit to me to see the man again, so pure in his kind, and to take his form and being into me where it will now lodge all the more firmly. Then it also meant much to me to have news of you all again. I have greatly gained in faith and courage since I've been back from Rastatt. You yourself I see more clearly and sharply now that I can think of you together with my new friends, and you know how much it strengthens relationships such as ours if we understand each other and have a clear image of each other in our minds. Once the foundations have been laid, as with us, and one has got a deep, complete feeling of what the other must by his nature remain true to, whatever transformations he might undergo, then love does not need to shy away from judgement, and in this case one can certainly say that faith grows with understanding. And then of course it's true that my soul rejoices all on its own that, despite all the apostles of meagreness, there is more than *one* person in whom nature has expressed herself in her fine abundance and that I can now, besides your own spirit, call others to witness against this doubting heart of mine which sometimes threatens to take sides with the unbelieving mob and deny the god within. Tell them, your friends and mine, that I often think of them, whenever it seems to me that apart from myself and a few solitary beings whom I carry in my heart there is nothing more than my four walls; and tell them that they are to me like a melody in which one seeks refuge when the bad demon threatens to take over. It is the whole truth, all this, but I don't like speaking in such general terms about a few excellent people, and I know very well I would have to write to each of them separately if I wanted to do justice to my feelings.

These past few days I've been reading your Diogenes Laertius. And I've experienced something I've come across before, which is that the transient and changeful nature of human thoughts and systems has struck me as almost more tragic than the destinies which ordinarily we regard as the only real ones; and I think this is natural, for if man is dependent on outside influence even in his most proper and freest activity, in independent thought, and if even here he is always affected by circumstances and by the climate, as is incontrovertibly the case, then where is his dominion? But then it is a good thing, and even the first condition of all life and of all forms of organization, that no force is monarchic in heaven and earth. Absolute monarchy will always cancel itself out, because it has no object; in the strict sense it has never even existed. Everything is interconnected, and suffers as soon as it is active, including the purest thought a human being can have. And properly speaking an *a priori* philosophy, entirely independent of all experience, is just as much a nonsense as a positive revelation where the revealer does the whole thing and he to whom the revelation is made is not even allowed to move in order to receive it, because otherwise he would have contributed something of his own.

Anything made, every product, is the result of the subjective

and the objective, of the individual and the whole, and the fact
that the share the individual has in a given product can never
be completely separated from the share the whole has in it
shows once again how intimately every individual part is bound
up with the whole and that together they make up *one* living
whole which, *individualized through and through as it is, consists of parts which are entirely independent* but *at the same
time intimately and indissolubly interconnected*. Of course,
from any one *finite perspective one of the independent forces
in the whole will be the dominant one*, but it can only be
regarded as temporarily dominant, a matter of degree.

62. *To Karl Gok*

[Homburg, New Year's Eve, 1798]
If your fate doesn't take a turn for the better sooner or later I
give you my most sacred word as a brother that I will be at
your side with all I have and can. In the meantime I beg you,
dear Brother, to look on your situation as cheerfully as possible.
Grant me the satisfaction of having gone through many bitter
experiences not only in my name but in yours too, and grasp
what I have to say to you with a clear, keen mind and believe
that it comes from my love for you: the world will destroy us
utterly if we let every affront penetrate into our hearts, and the
best will quite simply come to grief one way or another unless
they manage, in good time, to react to everything that is done
to them in neediness and paucity of spirit and heart with calm
understanding and not with the goodness of their souls – for
even if hurt the soul remains, as it must, magnanimous, and
does people's paltry insults the honour of taking them seriously.
Believe me, who am certainly not speaking here out of self-
importance but out of a profound sense of my deficiencies based
on many unhappy memories, believe me, calm understanding
is the holy aegis which preserves the heart from poisoned arrows
in the war of the world. And I believe, a fact that comforts me
a good deal, that this calm understanding, more than any other

virtue of the soul, can be acquired by realizing its value and working at it with willingness and perseverance. When I think back over the years half of which I've wasted in sorrow and misguidedness but which you, dear Karl, still have ahead of you, I often feel there are so many things I'd like to write down for you in blood. It is a curious sensation to have fought one's way through with hard effort and only by the skin of one's teeth and to think that others one cares about are not likely to find it any easier. In general we tend to fear fate far less for ourselves than for those who are close to our hearts. –

The bell is just striking twelve, and the year 1799 is beginning. A happy year to you, dearest Brother, and to all the family! And then a great happy new century for Germany and the world!

I'll go to bed on that.

1 January 1799

Today I had put my usual occupations to one side and in my leisure fell into all sorts of thoughts about the interest the Germans currently have in speculative philosophy and in reading matter of a political nature and also, but in smaller measure, in poetry. Perhaps you have read a humorous little essay in the *Allgemeine Zeitung* on Germany's band of poets. This was what first set me off, and since you and I rarely philosophize nowadays there may be some point in writing these thoughts of mine down for you.

The beneficial influence philosophical and political reading matter is having on the development of our nation is beyond dispute, and perhaps the German national character, if, that is, I have derived it correctly out of my very incomplete experience, was more in need of precisely that double influence than of any other. For I believe that the most habitual virtues and flaws of the Germans can be reduced to a rather narrow-minded domestic cosiness. They are always *glebae addicti*, most of them are in one way or another, literally or figuratively, bound to the sod, and if it goes on like this they will end up, like the good-hearted Dutch painter, sinking under the weight of their cherished (moral and physical) acquisitions and inheritances.

Everyone only feels at home where he was born, and only rarely do his interest and ways of thinking give him the ability or inclination to go beyond it. This is the reason for that lack of elasticity, of drive, of a diverse unfolding of the energies, and for the dull, dismissive shyness or the fearful, submissive, blind devotion with which they react to anything that lies outside their own anxiously narrow sphere; the reason too for the lack of a sense of shared honour and shared property, which it is true is very widespread among the modern nations but in my opinion is to be found to an eminent degree among the Germans. And just as one cannot be content shut away in one's room unless one also lives out in the open, so too the individual, particular life cannot subsist without a sense of the universal and an open view onto the world, and at the moment it seems that among the Germans both have perished equally. And it really does show how wrong the apostles of restriction are that among the ancients, where everyone belonged with sense and spirit to the world that surrounded them, there is far more intensity to be found in particular characters and relations than among us Germans for example, and the affected talk of heartless cosmopolitanism and inflated metaphysics can probably not be more truly refuted than by such a noble pair as Thales and Solon, who travelled through Greece, Egypt and Asia together to acquaint themselves with the constitutions and philosophers of the world, and were thus *generalized* in more than one respect but at the same time close friends and more human and even naive in their relations than all the people who seek to persuade us that we should keep our eyes shut and not open our hearts to the world (which always deserves it) if we are to maintain our naturalness.

Now, as the Germans found themselves in this state of anxious narrow-mindedness they could come under no more salutary influence than that of the new philosophy, which takes the universality of interest to an extreme and discovers the infinite striving in the human breast. And even if it does orient itself too one-sidedly towards the great autonomy of human nature, still it is the only possible philosophy *for our time*.

Kant is the Moses of our nation, leading it out of its Egyptian lethargy into the open, lonely wilderness of his speculation and bringing the energetic law down from the holy mountain. Of course they are still dancing round their golden calves and hungering for their fleshpots, and he would probably have to take them out into some quite literal desert for them to relinquish their servitude to the belly and their dead customs and opinions, which have lost all heart and meaning and under which their better, living nature sighs inaudibly, as if in a deep dungeon. In another way, political reading must have just as beneficial an effect, especially if the phenomena of our times are presented with vigour and authority. Man's horizon expands, and if we attend to the affairs of the world daily our interest and involvement in it arises and grows as well, and the sense of the general and the transcendence of our own narrow milieu are certainly encouraged just as much by witnessing the widespread variety of human society and its momentous fates as by the philosophical imperative to generalize our interest and points of view. Just as the soldier feels bolder and more powerful when he is working within an army, and really is, people's energy and liveliness in general increases to the precise degree that the zone of life expands in which they feel themselves to be acting and suffering alongside other people (as long as the sphere doesn't extend so far that the individual loses himself in the whole). For all that, the interest in philosophy and politics, even if it were more general and serious than it is, falls far short of being sufficient for the education of the nation, and it would be a good thing if there were at last an end to the boundless misconceptions that lead to art, and especially poetry, being devalued by those who practise and enjoy it. So much has already been said about the influence of the arts on the education of man, but it always came out as if it wasn't meant to be taken seriously, and that was quite natural, because they didn't reflect on what the true nature of art, and especially poetry, is. They confined themselves to its unassuming external aspect, which is certainly bound up with what it is but is far from making up the whole of its character; they took it to be playful because it appears in the modest form of play, of a game, and so rationally no other effect could be expected of it than that produced by play, that is, diversion, almost the exact opposite of the effect it has when it occurs in its true nature. Then, a person becomes collected, gains focus, and it gives him repose, not empty but living repose, where all the faculties are alert and only seem not to be active because of their intent harmony. It brings people together and joins them, but not as play does, where they are only united in that everybody forgets themselves and the vital particularity of each is held back.

You will forgive me, dear Brother, for writing such a slow and disconnected letter. Few can find the transition from one mood to another more difficult than I; particularly hard is to move from reasoning to poetry and the other way round. Also these last few days I've been so preoccupied by a letter from our dear mother in which she expressed her joy at my religious life and asked me among other things to write a poem for our dear grandmother's 72nd birthday, together with much else in what was an inexpressibly moving letter, that I spent most of the time when I might perhaps have written to you thinking of her and the rest of you dear ones. On the very evening I received the letter I started a poem for our dear grandmother and almost finished it that night. I thought it would give her and mother pleasure if I sent a letter and the poem straight off the next day. But the tones I produced resonated so powerfully within me, the transformations of mind and soul I have undergone since my youth, the past and present of my life, became so pressing as I worked that afterwards I couldn't get to sleep and in the morning had trouble collecting myself again. That's how I am. You will wonder, when you come to see the verses, which are poetically so slight, how they could have had such a curious effect on me. But I have said hardly anything of what I felt as I wrote them. It seems to happen quite often that I proffer my keenest, most vital soul in utterly flat words, so that no one knows what they really mean apart from me.

Now let's see whether I can get a bit further with what I was trying to say before about poetry. I was saying that poetry unites people differently from the way play does; that is, if it is genuine and has a genuine effect, it unites them with all their manifold suffering and happiness and aspiration and hope and

fear, with all their opinions and errors, all their virtues and
ideas, with all about them that is great and small more and
more to form a live, intricately articulated, intense whole, for
this is what poetry itself should be, and the effect is like the
cause. Don't you agree, dear Brother, that the Germans could
do with a panacea of this kind, even after the philosophico-
political cure? Apart from anything else, the disadvantage
intrinsic to a political and philosophical education is that it
may well connect people to the fundamental, incontrovertibly
necessary conditions of law and duty, but how close are we then
to the harmony of humankind? A landscape drawn according to
the optical rules, with foreground, middle distance and background, is a long way from equalling the living work of nature.
But even the best among the Germans are mostly still of the
opinion that if the world were only nice and symmetrical all
would be right with it. O Greece, with your genius, your piety,
what has become of you? Even I, with all my good intentions,
only stumble behind these people, the only humans the world
has known, vainly feeling my way with my thoughts and
actions, and I am often all the more clumsy and muddled in
what I do and say precisely because I stand there in the modern
water like geese with their flat feet and beat my wings helplessly
at the Greek sky. Don't be offended by the comparison. It is
awkward, but true, and between us such things can pass, in any
case it's only really meant for me.

For your encouraging remarks on my little poems and many
other sympathetic and fortifying words in your letter I am very
grateful. We must hold firm together in all our need and our
spirit. Above all let us adopt, with all love and seriousness, the
great words: *homo sum, nihil humani a me alienum puto*. That
does not mean we should be irresponsible, but simply true to
ourselves and clear-sighted and tolerant in our dealings with
the world, and then we must make sure not to let any idle
aspersions of affectation, exaggeration, ambition, oddness etc.
put us off from fighting with all our energies and concentrating
all our rigour and tenderness on bringing all that is human in
us and in others into ever freer and more intimate relation,
whether in figurative representation or in the real world. And

if the realm of darkness irrupts with violence *then* we shall throw our pen under the table and go, in God's name, where the adversity is greatest and we are most needed. Goodbye.

Yours,
Friz

63. To Johanna Christiana Gok

Homburg, January 1799

My dear Mother,

I'm ashamed to have left your lovely letter, which has given me so many hours and moments of pleasure, without an answer for so long. On the very evening I received it I wrote down most of what I enclose for my dear beloved grandmother, and I thanked you in my heart for having reminded me of her birthday, which is sacred to me. The letter to you was to have been written the following day and it would have been a real joy for me if I could have expressed immediately what I felt on receiving yours. But I was prevented from doing so in all kinds of ways. There was probably time enough, but I like to write to you with an untroubled soul. What unsettled me and robbed me of a more tranquil frame of mind was without importance. I say that so as not to worry you. I happened to read some harsh statements which were an assault on my spirits because they went right against my most heartfelt convictions, that was the main thing that disrupted me in the peacefulness of my life. Of course it's not good that I am so fragile and indeed I desire nothing more than a firm, constant mind. The knowledge of my weakness in this respect humbles me more than anything else: for all my honest efforts and consciousness of what would be better and happier I am still as thin-skinned as ever. I have wasted half my youth in sufferings and errors which had this as their one source. Now I think I am more patient and don't take against people, and if I'm not mistaken I am less temperamental in my dealings with others than before, but my inner tranquillity and calm concentration can still be destroyed by impressions that perhaps wouldn't trouble a man of firmer constitution for a moment. Admittedly it is natural that every passing dissonance affects me more deeply now, when I've just escaped hundreds of anxieties and disturbances and am wanting to collect and soothe myself in the harmony of goodness, truth and beauty. I promise you, and myself, to keep on working at it so that I learn to accept on the spur of the moment what I can so easily reconcile when my mind is at rest. I know no greater happiness than to work away modestly and in hope. But that can't happen if one's sensibility is easily hurt. – I also try to strengthen my body with gentle exercise and a routine because I see that sometimes it has to do with that. It's not that I'm not in good health – I'm in better health now than usual and no longer have headaches and stomach pains – but I do find that my nerves are too sensitive. I say all this in particular because you enquire with such tenderness and sympathy how I am. – That you have reacted to what I said about religion with such great joy shows me so clearly that your character only finds repose in the highest sphere. My dear Mother, I can well believe that it must be a relief and cheering for you to think of me as having the best feelings a human soul can have and to be able to hold on to that knowledge amid the doubts and anxieties with which even the best must regard each other, and the more so the closer they are, for in the end we hardly know ourselves and shall never know another person even as well as that. I reserve the right to deliver you a complete profession of faith at more leisure, and I wish I could express my heart's opinion to everyone with the candour and purity I do to you. But the scribes and Pharisees of our time, who have made out of the dear holy Bible a cold prattle that kills heart and spirit, I certainly don't want them as witnesses of my intense, living faith. I know very well how they came to their views, and because God forgives them for giving Christ a worse death than the Jews, making his Word into a letter and him, that lives, into an empty idol, because God forgives them this, I forgive them too. Only I don't care to lay myself and my heart bare where it will be misunderstood, and for that reason keep quiet before professional theologians (that is, those who are not such freely

and in their hearts, but only under duress and because of their
office) just as readily as before those who want to have nothing
to do with it all because for them religion, which after all is the
first and last need of mankind, has been spoilt in childhood by
the dead letter and the terrifying *command** to believe. My
dear Mother, if there are harsh words in these lines they are
certainly not written out of pride or hate but only because I
could find no other way of making myself clear with the necessary brevity. The way things are now, particularly with regard
to religion, this all had to come about, and the state of religion
was almost as it is now when Christ appeared in the world. But
just as winter is followed by spring, so the spiritual death of
man has always been followed by new life, and the holy always
remains holy, whether people respect it or not. And there will
be many who are more religious in their hearts than they are
willing or able to say, and perhaps many of our preachers, who
simply can't find the words, say more, too, in their sermons
than others suspect because the words they use are so ordinary
and have been misused in hundreds of ways. Make do with this
unfeigned expression of my thoughts for the moment, until I
can find an hour when I can write with all my soul. – I quite
agree with you, dear Mother, that it will be good for me in
future to seek out the most modest position I can, and especially
for this reason: that the perhaps unfortunate penchant for
poetry, which from the beginning I always made honest efforts
to oppose by concentrating on occupations thought to be more
serious, is still in me and, to go by all that I have learnt about
myself, will remain so for as long as I live. I cannot say whether
I'm deluding myself or whether it is a true impulse of nature.
But this much I do now know: I have brought acute disquiet
and discontentedness on myself in part by devoting excessive
attention and effort to activities that seem to be less well suited

*Faith can never be bidden, no more than love can. It must be voluntary and
spontaneous. True, Christ says: he that does not believe shall be damned, that
is, as I understand the Bible, severely judged, and that's natural enough, for
the man who is merely good out of a sense of duty and the law can never be
forgiven, because he restricts himself to works, but that doesn't mean that
faith should be imposed on him.

to my nature, such as philosophy. And I did it with a good will because I wanted to avoid the reputation of an empty poet. For a long time I didn't understand why the study of philosophy, which usually rewards the assiduous hard work it requires with tranquillity, only made me more and more restless and even passionate the more completely I surrendered myself to it. And I now explain this to myself as coming from my distancing myself more than was necessary from my proper inclination, and my heart would sigh during this unnatural work for the occupation it loved best like Swiss herdsmen in the army longing for their valleys and their cattle. Don't think this fanciful. For why is it that I am peaceful and good as a child when I'm working undisturbed in sweet leisure at this most innocent of all occupations, which, it is true, and quite rightly, only earns proper respect when it is practised with mastery? Part of the reason why I am a long way from that is perhaps because from boyhood on I never dared work at it as hard as at many other things, which I perhaps devoted myself to in a rather meek, conscientious manner to conform to my circumstances and what people expected. And yet every art requires a man's whole life and everything an apprentice learns must be learnt in relation to his art if he wants to develop his disposition to it and not end up stifling it.

You see, my dear Mother, that I am making you my intimate, and I have no fear of your misunderstanding these honest confessions. There are so few people to whom I can open my heart. Why then shouldn't I exercise my filial right and comfort myself by telling you my deepest concerns? And do not think I have some ulterior motive. I can only write to you with complete truthfulness, and so you will just have to have me as I am. What I really wanted to say was that part of the reason why I should do well to look for a very simple position for the future is that any other would be hard to reconcile with my favourite occupation. There are men, who must have been stronger than I am, that have tried to be men of affairs or scholars in office while remaining poets. But it is always the case that in the end they sacrificed one occupation to the other and that was never good, whether they neglected the job for the sake of their art

or their art for the sake of their job. For if a man sacrificed his
job he was acting dishonourably towards others, and if he
sacrificed his art he was sinning against his god-given, natural
gift, and that is at least as great a sin as sinning against one's
body. Good old Gellert, whom you mention in your kind letter,
would have done better not to become professor in Leipzig. If
his art didn't suffer, his body must have done. So if I do have
to accept a post, as is probably inevitable, I think a living in a
village (right away from the town and the high dignitaries of
the Church) will be the best thing for me. And why not in
the region where you and the family are, rather than among
strangers?

But in any case I prefer to wait a few years yet, and when
I've come to the end of the book I'm writing now and my
money what I'll do is become a private tutor again. The Swedish
secretary of legation von Pommer-Esche, whose acquaintance I
made, as you know, in Rastatt and who recently visited me
here on his way back, offered as he left to arrange a private
tutorship for me in his part of the country (in Swedish Pomerania, in the Wismar region). His father, who if I'm not mistaken
is governor in Stralsund, generally finds posts of that kind for
his acquaintances. I didn't want to refuse outright, so as to have
somewhere to go if need be, especially as he says he will find
me a post where I would accompany a young man to the
university. An increased knowledge of the world (knowledge
of the German people, particularly for someone who wants to
become a German writer, is as vital as knowledge of the soil is
for the gardener) is the only recompense I can hope for from
this laborious employment, and that it is in such a distant,
unfamiliar place, which in any case would not be so noticeable
at a university town, seems to me an advantage rather than a
disadvantage for the few years when I cannot yet count on a
peaceful life near my family. But for the moment I am undecided, and perhaps in the meantime more favourable opportunities of this nature will present themselves. I shall only take up
such a post at all if certain fixed conditions are met to protect
me as far as possible from annoyance and embarrassment. And

if I come to the recognition that such an existence is necessary
for me a while longer, and inevitable, I shall probably summon
up the patience and discretion required. As a curate I would
depend on my vicar, and as I have no experience of this situation
it would probably be no easier, and moreover I should have to
live largely at your expense which I do not want to do. You
have done so much for me already and dear Karl has more need
of your help.

I'm writing all this to you, dear Mother, because I know very
well how much you wish to know where you stand with me,
and if you should find that my life is not an easy one at the
moment you won't take it too much to heart because you know
better than anyone that with our youth what we call happiness
generally tends to fade. I at least prefer not to ask any more of
the world than that I may not find it too difficult to keep true
to my heart and mind in whatever circumstances I have yet to
encounter in life. You and the rest of the family I should in any
case dearly like to see again before I move on from my present
residence which it is true will be a wrench to leave.

I was so pleased with your lovely presents that I could think
of nothing better in my joy than to run to the good people
whose house I live in and announce that I too had got a Christmas present. Thank you very much, and dear grandmother
too. I'm just sorry that my finances no longer allow me, as in
Frankfurt, to give you proof of my feelings for you in this way.
Please give my apologies to my dear sister too, for contenting
myself for now with good intentions. Anyway she knows my
fondness for her and her whole household too well to need any
sign to prove it. The letter you sent me from her was a gift in
itself. I should really have written to her long before now, but
as I was making the journey to Rastatt I hoped to see her in
person, and I've had so much to do since then making up for
lost time that very soon I'm going to have to sit down for a few
days to answer all the letters I owe, and when I do she shall be
among the first.

My best wishes to you, dear Mother. Ask my dear grandmother to take the enclosed page as a small part of the joyful

and earnest feelings with which I celebrated her esteemed birthday in my heart.

Remember me to all the family.

Your loyal son,

Friz

64. *To Johanna Christiana Gok*

Homburg vor der Höhe [, early March 1799]
Dearest Mother,
I can only write you a few words this time. I have so much to do.

I was deeply shaken to hear of the accident which could have had such serious consequences for you and my dear grandmother. May every misfortune pass over you that way!

It is probable that the war that is just breaking out again will not leave Württemberg untouched, although I know from a good source that the French will respect the neutrality of the states of the Empire, of Württemberg too therefore, for as long as possible, because Prussia is using all its influence to ensure it and the French have reason to avoid a war with that power. Should the French be successful there will perhaps be changes in our mother country.

My dear Mother, I beg you with all my truest filial devotion: summon up everything that is noble in your exemplary soul and all the faith that raises us above the earth to look on our times as calmly as possible, and to bear anything untoward that happens to you with the tranquil mind of a Christian. I should lose all my resolve were I to think that the present anxieties might overwhelm your spirits. Remember that I have no father going courageously ahead of me in life, and give me, in the beautiful shape of calm endurance, an example of such courage. I also need it if I am not to become faint-hearted in my own work and cause. If certain possible events occur I shall exert all my energies to prevent anything from happening to you, and not perhaps without effect. But all this is still a long way away. –

65. *To Susette Gontard*

[Homburg, Spring 1799]

That the glory of spring still gives joy to me too, darling, fills me with unutterable gratitude,

66. *To Christian Ludwig Neuffer*

Homburg, 4 June 1799

Dear Neuffer,

You can certainly count on a few contributions from me, and, in accordance with your wishes, I will also let you have some prose pieces. Perhaps I'll also be able to send you a few things by people I know here or am in correspondence with. I wish your second son all the life and all the strength and grace I should wish him if he were my own.

I intend to edit a monthly poetry journal. As I already have most of the material for the first year, at least what of it will be written by me, and given my present mode of life will be able to devote myself entirely to the enterprise, I have hopes of carrying it through. And as I am not yet engaged in a firm contract with anyone, would you please ask Herr Steinkopf whether he wouldn't consider it worth his while to take it on. At least half of the journal will contain actual poetry, the rest made up of essays to do with the history and criticism of art. The first numbers will contain a tragedy, the *Death of Empedocles*, which I have finished apart from the last act and, also by me, lyrical and elegiac poems. The essays will contain: (1) Characteristic traits from the lives of poets ancient and modern, the circumstances they developed in, and especially the artistic character peculiar to each. On Homer, Sappho, Aeschylus, Sophocles, Horace, Rousseau (as author of the *Nouvelle Héloïse*), Shakespeare etc. (2) The setting out of the peculiar beauty of their works, or of individual parts of them. On the *Iliad*, particularly the character of Achilles, on Aeschylus's

Prometheus, on Sophocles's *Antigone* and *Oedipus*, on selected odes by Horace, on the *Héloïse*, on Shakespeare's *Antony and Cleopatra*, on the characters of Brutus and Cassius in his *Julius Caesar*, on *Macbeth* and so on. All these essays will as far as possible be written in a lively manner likely to be of general interest, mostly in the form of letters. (3) Theoretical essays, presented in popular fashion, on declamation, language, on the essence and the different kinds of poetry, and also on the beautiful in general. For all these essays, particularly for the last, I can with good conscience promise new or at least not yet worn-out perspectives, and I think I have a few truths to say that could be useful for art and pleasant to the soul. (4) There will also be reviews of particularly interesting new poetic works. I hope to obtain contributions from Heinse – author of *Ardinghello* – Heydenreich, Bouterwek, Matthisson, Conz, Siegfried Schmid, and also from you if you can spare anything.

The overall tone probably means it would be suitable for the publisher, if he sees fit, to give it the title *Aesthetic Journal for Ladies*. As to its spirit I think I'm justified in saying that it should do more for moral development and genuine recreation than many other publications.

Every month an issue of 4 folio pages, not too closely printed, would appear in octavo format. The publisher could terminate the contract whenever he wanted, only not less than 3 months before a fair.

The question of remuneration I leave to his judgement and sense of fairness. I would only add that I will live entirely for and from the enterprise, and that in any case my frugal existence doesn't require the kind of salary the great men who edited the *Horae* need. I will exert all my courage and industry and all my energies to make this journal viable and commendable, and I will make sure that if possible at least one substantial poetic work, e.g. a tragedy or a novel etc., will appear complete every year.

Should Herr Steinkopf decide to join me in this venture I would gladly promise to set aside the requests I have received for contributions to other journals and deliver at least 4 folio pages a year for his calendar for ladies free of charge.

I would also give him the option of publishing after a certain lapse of time the essays in the journal by me separately, on the conditions that go with the second edition of a book.

I confess it would give me particular pleasure to enter into this relation with Herr Steinkopf, him being your friend and an acquaintance of mine, and even though I must not assume he has the trust in me such a decision requires, still I wanted to let him know of my plan. If he finds it to his advantage it will have been appropriate for me to have made him the proposal, given that I am already in contact with him. If it's not for him then it is no different than if I had not mentioned it. Give him my compliments, and let him have a read of this letter.

Forgive me for making you the middleman. I should not have done so if I could not say of myself that you would find me ready to do anything to be of service to you. In any case I'll send you the promised essays. The prose pieces will probably contain something generally accessible, simple and not too dry, about the lives and characters of Thales and Solon and Plato. I should find it quite difficult to provide a genuinely moral essay for the calendar for ladies without revealing either too much of my deepest feelings and convictions or too little.

Please give me some news and an answer to this letter as soon as ever you can.

Yours,

H.

67. To Karl Gok

Homburg, 4 June 1799

My dear Brother,

Your sympathy and loyalty are a great strength to me, and what you are in yourself, your diligence, the skilful way you have of dividing your mind and energy between your professional affairs and your more general development, your braveness and your modesty, are a constant source of joy. Dear Karl, nothing cheers me more than to be able to say to another human being:

I have faith in you. And though the coarseness and inadequacy
to be found in people often upsets me more than it should, I am
also perhaps happier than others when I encounter goodness,
truthfulness and purity in life, and for that reason I have no
right to accuse nature of anything: it has sharpened my sense
of what is lacking in order to help me recognize excellence with
more and deeper joy. Once I have managed to learn to see and
feel in what is lacking precisely the particular, specific lack, the
lack at that moment, rather than the vague pain it often causes
me, and so also to recognize in better things the particular
beauty, what is characteristically good about them, rather than
remaining content with a general sensation, once I've achieved
this, my mind will be calmer and my work will progress more
steadily. For if we only experience indefinitely what is lacking
we will naturally tend to want to remedy it indefinitely and
so in some cases our energies will be wasted in a vague and
unproductively fatiguing struggle because we don't know
exactly what is lacking and how the lack, the precise lack, is to
be put right and supplied. As long as there are no hitches in my
work it goes very well, but a small mistake that I feel too
keenly to perceive with clarity is sometimes enough to make
me unnecessarily overwrought. And the same is true in my
ordinary life, in my dealings with people, I'm still such a child.
This sensitivity is certainly not a bad thing in itself but in my
case it has not yet developed into a more definite and purposeful
capacity of feeling, and this is probably due among other things
to the fact that I have felt too much inadequacy and not enough
excellence in the conditions and characters I have come across.
– You will find that at the moment those of a more humane
constitution, those spirits whom nature seems to have most
definitely formed for humanity, are always the unhappier ones,
precisely because they are rarer now than in other times and
places. The barbarians around us destroy our best energies
before they can become fully formed and only the resolute and
clear-sighted recognition of this fate can save us, or at least
prevent us from perishing in ignominy. We must seek out perfection, make common cause with it as much as we can, derive
sustenance and wholeness from our sense of it and so gain the

strength to perceive what is crude and askew and malformed not just with pain but as what it is, what constitutes its character and peculiar flaw. In any case, so long as people don't directly encroach on us and disturb us it is not so very hard to live with them in peace. The trouble *lies not so much in their being what they are as in their considering what they are to be the only possible mode, refusing to countenance anything else.* I am against selfishness, despotism and misanthropy, but otherwise I am coming to like people more and more because in all aspects of their activity and characters I see, more and more, the same basic character, the same fate. And indeed, this striving, this giving up of a certain present for something uncertain, different, better and yet better again I see as the original ground of everything the people around me work at and do. Why don't they live like the deer in the forest, content with little, limited to the ground, the food at their feet, where the connection with nature is like that of the baby to its mother's breast? Then there would be no anxiety, no toil, no complaint, little illness, little conflict, there would be no sleepless nights etc. But this would be as unnatural for man as the arts he teaches the animals are to them. To push life onwards, to accelerate nature's endless process of perfection, to complete what he has before him, and to idealize – that will always be the instinct that best characterizes and distinguishes man, and all his arts and works and errors and tribulations stem from it. Why do we have gardens and fields? Because mankind wanted a better world than the one it inherited. Why do we have trade, ships, cities, states, with all their turmoil and their good and bad? Because mankind wanted a better world than the one it inherited. Why do we have science, art, religion? Because mankind wanted a better world than the one it inherited. Even when they chafe against one another in a headstrong way it is because the present is not satisfactory, because they want things different, and so they fling themselves sooner into nature's grave, and accelerate the march of the world.

What is greatest and what is smallest, best and worst in mankind, grows from one root, and all in all everything is good and everybody fulfils in his own way, some more beautifully, some more wildly, his purpose as a human being, namely that of multiplying, quickening, separating, mixing, dividing and uniting the life of nature. It might be thought that this original urge, the urge to idealize or encourage, to rework, develop and perfect nature, no longer animates most people in their occupations nowadays, and that they do what they do out of habit, in imitation, in obedience to convention, out of the necessity into which their forefathers have brought them through industry and invention. But in order to carry on as their forefathers began, along the road of luxury, art, science etc., those that come after have to have precisely the urge in them that inspired their forefathers, in order to learn they need to be constituted as the masters were, but the epigones feel this impulse more faintly and it is only in the hearts and minds of original characters, of independent thinkers, of inventors, that it attains its full vitality. You can see, dear Karl, that I have presented you with the paradox that the artistic and creative impulse with all its modifications and varieties is actually a service human beings render unto nature. But we have long been in agreement that all the meandering rivers of human activity flow into the ocean of nature, just as they begin from it. To show people this path, which they mostly go down blindly, sometimes crossly and reluctantly and all too often in base and vile fashion, to show it to them so that they may go down it with eyes wide open, joyfully and nobly, that is the job of philosophy, art and religion, which themselves proceed from this creative impulse. Philosophy brings the impulse into consciousness, shows it its infinite object in the ideal and so strengthens and clarifies it. Art presents the impulse with its infinite object in a living image, in a higher world of representation. And religion teaches it to sense and believe this higher world precisely where it looks for and wishes to create it, i.e. in nature, both in its own human nature and in the surrounding world, as a latent disposition, as a spirit to be unfolded.

Philosophy and art and religion, the vestals of nature, thus affect man above all, are primarily there for him, and only by giving his concrete activity, which directly affects nature, proper direction and strength and joy do they also have an effect on nature, an effect that is concrete, though indirect. And another effect they have, particularly religion, is that man, to whom nature offers itself as the material of his activity and whom it contains, as a powerful motor, in its infinite system, does not think himself the lord and master of nature and in all his arts and activity preserves a modesty and piety towards its spirit – the same spirit he carries within him and has all about him and which gives him material and energy. For human art and activity, however much it has already achieved and can achieve, cannot produce life, cannot itself create the raw material it transforms and works on; it can develop creative energy, but the energy itself is eternal and not the work of human hands.

Thus for human activity and nature. I wish I could present it to you as it is in my mind and before my eyes too when I look at the people around me, each in his particular world, for it consoles me and gives me peace of mind and reconciles me in particular with the diversity of human occupations, and I get great pleasure from all the industry and feel a deeper sympathy for the doings and sufferings of mankind. It is quite something you are attempting, my dear Brother, if you want to draw up the system of an aesthetic church and to my mind you shouldn't be surprised if the execution of it throws up difficulties which seem almost insurmountable. To set out in philosophical terms the components of the ideal and their internal relations alone would be hard enough, and the philosophical exposition of the *ideal of all human society*, the aesthetic church, may well, if executed in its entirety, be even harder. Just give it your best try – it is best to aim high, and whatever happens you will reap this benefit from it: you will find it easier to gain a clear idea of all other social conditions, both as they are and in potential.

I got so drawn into our favourite realms of thought that I have no time left to say much more about you and about myself.

In any case it is too early yet to tell you anything more definite

about myself and how I intend to live my life in the years to
come and when I might be able to visit you, my dear family.
Oh what good people they are. I cried, tears of joy in my eyes,
when I read your three letters.

To end with I'll copy out a passage from my tragedy, *The
Death of Empedocles*, so that you can see roughly the spirit
and tone of the work I'm devoting my slow love and toil to at
the moment:

> There were times of ecstasy, the soul in me
> Was woken like Endymion by the gods
> And from its child's sleep it opened out
> A living thing and sensed the spirits of life
> That always live in youth – O lovely sun!
> I was not taught by men, my own heart drove me
> Undying in its love for those undying,
> To you, to you, nothing was more like God,
> Your quiet light. And just as you do not
> Hold back your light from life and, unconcerned,
> Discharge your golden fullness, I, with you,
> Was glad to grant my soul's best part to mortals,
> And open, without fear, my heart
> Gave itself like you to the sombre earth
> And all its fates to dedicate all life
> To it in youthful joy until the end.
> I said so often in our quiet hours,
> We made together a covenant of death.
> The trees were swayed then in a different way,
> And the tender sound of streams in the hills came close –
> The joys of all the earth were true, as warm
> And full they ripen out of toil and love:
> You gave them all to me. And often when
> I sat up on the quiet hillside and thought
> In wonder on the wandering fates of man
> Too deeply drawn into your endless changing,
> And sensed that soon my life would start to fade,
> The ether breathed on me as it does on you

> Soothing me and closing the wounds of love,
> And, as cloud gives way to lightning or the sun
> In the upper blue my cares dissolved to air.

Goodbye now, my dear Karl. Write to me as soon as your affairs and the circumstances permit.

Yours,
Hölderlin

68. *To Johanna Christiana Gok*

Homburg, 18 June 1799

Dearest Mother,

If I had nothing else to raise my spirits and fill me with gratitude and faith, a heart such as yours, this kindness and love, would be enough. Believe me, dear, honoured mother, you are holy to me in this pure sympathy of yours, and I would be a man stripped of his senses not to know it and value it. No, the religious spirit that reigns between mother and son will never die out between us! Oh what good people they are, I was moved to say to myself, and wept with joy when I read the three lovely letters from you and from Rike and Karl.

Don't think it impatience and feebleness on my part, which sort so ill with my years and my sex, – if I complained and spoke of desolate hours. It was less my own pain that often prevented me from finding hope in these moments than the sadness that sometimes overcame me in my total solitude when I thought of our present world and of the rare and good people in it and how they suffer precisely because they are better and more excellent. And probably it is *necessary* that I feel this from time to time, for this is what drives me to my purest activity. It is a wonderful thing that no one gets anywhere if he looks on everything with indifference, and at the same time doesn't achieve or further anything either if he despairs, that if he wants to live and be active therefore he has to combine both in his heart, sorrow and hope, joy and pain. And this, I believe, is also what it is to be a Christian. And that is how you meant it too.

How grateful I am to you, too, for your words on my dear departed father. What a good and noble man! Believe me, this is not the first time I have been put in mind of his equanimity of soul, and of how I should like to resemble him. It is not you either, dearest Mother, who have given me this melancholy tendency that I cannot quite pronounce myself free of. I have a pretty clear perspective on my whole life, almost back into my earliest youth, and I know very well at what point my mind took on this disposition. You will perhaps hardly believe it, but I still remember all too clearly. When my second father died, whose love for me is so unforgettable, when, with incomprehensible pain, I felt myself an orphan and saw your daily grief and tears, that was when my soul first altered into this seriousness which has never entirely left me and could only ever grow with the years. But in the depths of my being I also have a serenity, a faith, that often still breaks into true, full joy, only it is not so easy to find words for this as for pain. It gave me great pleasure that you encouraged me to enjoy my youth. I tend to imagine myself a bit younger than I am, and, for all my seriousness and circumspection, probably am often still a little boy, too good-natured sometimes with other people, and the result is always over-sensitivity and distrust. Comfort yourself, dearest Mother, with the thought that I am honest and serious enough to see my faults, and that always leads to more sense.

I have a pleasant piece of news to tell you. I have come to an agreement with the bookseller Steinkopf in Stuttgart to edit a journal of which he will be the publisher. It will appear once a month, most of the essays in it will be by me, the others by writers I shall count it an honour to figure alongside. This will earn me about 500 fl. a year, and so from next year my existence will be assured in a respectable manner for some time. As I have already got quite a long way forward in my work you need not fear, dearest Mother, that this occupation will be too much of a burden for me. In the letter in which he pronounces himself inclined to take it on, Steinkopf has requested that I should first set out for him the commercial conditions and tell him how much I would ask for looking after the journal and supplying my essays. I shall expressly stipulate that I am paid at least a hundred guilders at the beginning of the year and so on every six months until the end, and that way, being provided for for quite a while, I see no reason why I should find myself in the position of having to abuse your kindness. In my next letter I'll give you the definite and more detailed facts about the journal. I take the liberty of accepting the 100 fl. in the way you have judged appropriate, and in my thoughts and deeds I'll never forget it.

You will not find it hard to imagine, dear Mother, how much I want to see you and all the rest of the family again, and if it were not too great a disruption of my affairs and of the few savings I have I'd come up to see you for a few weeks in the autumn. I fear however that for the moment I won't have enough time, and you will not be surprised if in this I keep to my own rules and resolutions as strictly as if I was bound to someone else. If I didn't do this, my present independence would do me more harm than good, and in the end I would find fitting into any sort of order irksome. –

Forgive me for breaking off suddenly, but it is already quite late and I don't like to expose myself to these cool evenings. My health has really become more precious to me having been deprived of it for a while at such an unfortunate time and needing it as I do. All my love and respects to my dear grand-mother. I'll write to my dear sister later this week. I don't want to leave her waiting for a letter any longer.

Yours,
Friz

Hang on to the money for another month or so. If you don't mind I'll write to you for it as soon as I foresee having need of it. At the moment sending cash at least won't be safe.

69. To Johann Friedrich Steinkopf

Homburg vor der Höhe, 18 June 1799
[*Now sets out the idea of the project at greater length. Here among other things he says:*

True popularity dwells less in the everyday nature of the material than in the liveliness and intelligibility of the exposition.

The main aim he proposes is to reconcile the conflicting elements of the ideal, the original-natural, the purely lively on the one hand, and of the real, the cultural, the theoretical, the artificial on the other.] I know very well that the same thing has recently been attempted, and produced a sensation but no fundamental effect; but having looked at this very thoroughly and exactly it appears to me that whether through passion or through ignorance one main point was missing, viz. the proper impartiality: there is the usual exaggeration, the usual reaching for extremes, with incomprehensibility and giving offence to those at the opposite extreme the result. This last experience has however also produced a purer conviction, and I believe that I am not the only one to see things in this way.

So the union and reconciliation of theory with life, of art and taste with genius, of the heart with the understanding, of the real with the ideal, of the cultural (in the broadest sense of the word) with nature – this will be the most general character, the spirit, of the journal.

[*The poetry will not merely be a passionate, rapturous, capricious explosion, and not a forced, cold feat of artifice, but will proceed at once from life and from the ordering understanding, from sentiment and from conviction.*

Essays on poetry in general, on language, declamation, poetic genres, on genius, feeling, imagination etc. on particular poems and their authors] (by giving a sense of the man, his life, his own nature and the nature that surrounded him, they make sure that the poem receives its due as a product of nature).

[*He proposes the title* Iduna, *because he seems to remember a journal's having used that name before. But leaves that up to the publisher.*]

I shall give you news of the success of my efforts to secure a number of collaborators who will serve to recommend the journal in the way you wish as soon as I know where I stand, and at the same time send you the prospectus, which will necessarily depend on this, for you to examine. I can assure you in the meantime that I shall do all I can to approach many different people with all expediency, and not let my good will be put off by any difficulty it might encounter if we turn to men of reputation and expose ourselves to an unsatisfactory response.

Meanwhile I will devote all my time and all my powers to it, and also above all to giving my tragedy the proper pleasurableness and finish, which because of the peculiarity of its subject-matter it can less afford to do without than other works.

[*He intends to deliver 3 folio pages for each monthly issue at 1 carolin each. That makes 36 carolins, and as he needs at least 50 carolins a year, he would ask for the rest to be paid to him as editor.*

At the beginning of next month he will send Neuffer 'Emilie' and a few other poems and some by a young poet whose products are not without talent and felicity.]

70. To Susette Gontard

[Homburg, ~ June 1799]

Every day I have to invoke the absent god again. When I think of great men at the great moments of history, how they caught at the things around them like holy fire and transformed everything dead and wooden, the world's straw, into flame which flew up with them to the heavens; and then of myself, how I often go about like a poor glimmering lamp that would dearly beg a drop of oil to shine into the night a bit longer – then, I tell you, a curious shudder runs through my whole body, and softly I call out to myself the terrible words: more dead than alive.

Do you know the reason for all this? People are frightened of one another, they are afraid that one's genius will consume another's, and so they are willing to grant each other food and drink, but no nourishment for the soul, and they cannot bear it when anything they say or do is taken up in someone else's mind and transformed into flame. The fools! As if anything that people could say to each other were more than firewood, which only becomes fire again when it is caught by the fire of the spirit, just as it issued from life and from fire. And if they will only not begrudge each other mutual nourishment they will both have life and light, and neither will consume the other.

Do you remember our untroubled hours when we were with each other, and we alone? That was triumph! Both so free and proud and alert and open and bright in soul and heart and eye and countenance, and both in such blessed peace with each other. I sensed it and said it then: one could travel the whole world and not find anything to match it. And every day I feel it more keenly.

Yesterday afternoon Muhrbeck came to my room and said, 'The French have been beaten in Italy again.' 'So long as things are right with us,' I said to him, 'things are right enough with the world,' and he fell about my neck and we kissed each other's deeply moved and joyful souls on the lips and our eyes met, full of tears. Then he went. There are still such moments. But can that replace a world? And that's what will make me faithful to you for ever. Many people are excellent in one way or another. But a nature like yours, where everything is joined in intimate, indelible, living union, this is the pearl of time, and whoever has recognized it and seen how its heavenly innate unique happiness is also its deep unhappiness, he is likewise for ever happy and for ever unhappy.

71. *To Christian Ludwig Neuffer*

Homburg vor der Höhe, 3 July 1799

I haven't quite kept my word, my dear friend, and am sending what I promised you a week later than I had intended. I was obliged to go away for a few days when among other things I spoke to our friend Jung, who is in particularly good spirits at the moment. He wants to give me his Ossian for the journal. Some passages would make perfect text to be accompanied by a commentary.

I'm going to take the opportunity, in case it might be of interest to you, to say a few words about the method and manner in which I have written *Emilie*. You can well imagine that given the haste with which I had to set to work I could not express the poetic genre, which I have had in mind for some time, quite as I wanted to and as would be necessary to make palpable the advantages that it probably has, especially with subjects that are not properly heroic. It is not at all the impression of the new that is important to me; but more and more I feel and see how much we are caught between two extremes: having no rules at all, and blind subjection to old forms and the constraint and wrong application that go with it. Do not think, dear Neuffer, that I arbitrarily set and devise myself my own particular form. I examine the feeling that leads me to this or that form and make sure that the one I have chosen doesn't contradict the ideal and in particular the subject which it treats. Of course it is then true that I can be right on a general level but for that reason lose my way in the actual execution, because I simply follow my idea and have no concrete pattern to go by. But there is no alternative: as soon as we deal with any subject that is even a little bit modern it is my conviction that we must abandon the old classical forms, which are so intimately fitted to their subject-matter that they are no good for any other. Now it's true we're accustomed to seeing a love story, for example, *that is no more than that*, being presented in the form of a tragedy, though among the ancients this form, in its inner progression and its heroic dialogue, is quite unsuited to a true

love story. If the heroic dialogue is retained it is always as if
the lovers were quarrelling. If it is abandoned, then the tone
contradicts the fundamental form of tragedy, which of course
is not retained at all strictly but for that very reason loses,
among us moderns, its peculiar poetic value, its meaning. But
then all they want is moving or shattering passages and situations – neither writers nor the public bother much about the
meaning and impression of the whole. And so the strictest of
all poetic forms, *whose whole purpose is to proceed through a
series of harmonious changes without any ornament in almost
exclusively major tones each of which is an independent whole*,
and which in this proud renunciation of all accidentals presents
the ideal of a living whole as briefly and at the same time as
completely and richly as possible, and thus more clearly but
also more seriously than any other known poetic form – the
venerable tragic form has been debased into a means of providing the odd occasion for saying something flashy or tender. But
what headway could they expect to make with it if they did not
choose the subject-matter it was intended for and coupled with
which alone it maintained its life and sense? It had died, like all
other forms when they have lost the living soul for which
they served as the organic frame and out of which they were
originally bodied forth, like, for example, the republican form
in our Free Cities, which is now dead and meaningless because
the people in them are not such that they *need* it, to put it
mildly.

Just as the tragic subjects are made to proceed through a
series of harmonious changes in exclusively major *independent*
tones, and to present with all possible sparing of accidentals a
whole that is full of powerful, meaningful parts, the sentimental
subjects, e.g. love, are wholly suited to proceed through a series
of harmonious changes not in major, proud, firm tones and
with decisive renunciation of accidentals but with *a tender
shying away from accidentals*, and in deep, full, elegiacally
meaningful tones that convey a great deal in the longing and
hope they express, and to present the ideal of a living whole
not with this concerted power of the parts and this irresistible
progress, this rapid concision, but as if on wings, like Psyche

and Cupid, and with *intimate* concision, and the only question is what form this can be managed in with the most ease and naturalness and effect, so that the beautiful spirit of love will have its own poetic figure and mode.

Forgive me if I'm boring you with this uncertain train of thought. I'm living so much on my own that at the moment I often like to spend a leisurely hour conversing with an impartial friend in writing about matters that concern me, and as you can see it makes me chattier than is perhaps agreeable to my correspondent. Admittedly I have said very little to you indeed and had more of a conversation with myself than with you.

It gives me great pleasure that you are devoting yourself to poetry more and more. The age has cast such a heavy burden of impressions on us that only, as I feel more clearly every day, by dint of working hard and long, right into our old age, making ever-renewed serious attempts and experiments can we perhaps in the end produce what nature has primarily destined us for and which in other circumstances would perhaps have matured sooner but hardly with such perfection. If responsibilities which are truly sacred to us both make their claims we shall be making a fine sacrifice to necessity if, at least for a while, we renounce our love for the Muses.

It must have been a happy evening for you when your comedy was performed and you were conscious of yourself, amid the hilarity of the spectators, as the initial moving force behind it. Has it been published and do you think I'll be able to buy it in Frankfurt?

I wish your journal many happy collaborators. Should you be discontented with a number of contributions and prefer to have the gap filled by me, I'd willingly devote you another week, *only in an emergency of course*, otherwise this would be a presumptuous thing for me to say. I'll send you a few more of my poems later with contributions from another young poet. Böhlendorff's, which I enclose, should be of some interest to your readers and you can always make a selection if you see fit.

Be so good and make sure that the intervals which have been left between the iambic stanzas in the manuscript of *Emilie* are printed properly.

Don't take exception to the title; we'll soon have too many prefaces, more prefaces than poems, and if I can as it were replace such a preface with a few words and indicate to the reader that this is only a moment in Emilie's life and that the poet is obliged in general to concentrate all biography as far as possible into a significant moment – why not?

Though I wrote this exercise very quickly I can assure you that I have said very little that lacks dramatic or general poetic purpose.

Good night, dear friend. Remember me to Herr Steinkopf and all my other friends and acquaintances in Stuttgart, and do me a favour and write me something about them too and let me have another letter soon.

Hölderlin

72. To Friedrich Schiller

[Homburg,] 5 July 1799

Only the generosity you have always shown me, esteemed Sir, and the deep devotion towards you, which grows in me day by day, can give me the assurance to burden you with an immodest request, and I should certainly refrain from doing this if I could foresee with certitude that it would cause you displeasure. Perhaps I am blinded by my desire and by the knowledge of how important the satisfaction of this request would be for me. I have therefore every cause to ask for your forgiveness should it really prove a bother to you.

Were I so worthy of your protection that I did not need it I should not ask you for it, or if I needed it so much that I was not worthy of it at all I should not ask you for it either. But I believe I need and am worthy of it just enough to make asking for it excusable.

I have in mind gradually to publish the literary and poetic essays I am in the middle of working on in a humanist journal, and would prefer to wait and see whether I do not at last produce something whose value and success I could be surer of, if only circumstances allowed me the untroubled independence such a thing would require. As it is I am obliged to offer samples which perhaps promise more than they achieve, and in view of my readers cannot do without the authority of a well-established man of reputation if I am to avoid failure, knowing myself and the times as I do.

For this reason I take the liberty of asking you for a few small contributions, if you should not find it below your dignity to give me this public sign of your favour and kindness.

Believe me, esteemed Sir, my admiration for you is too sincere for me not to feel afflicted by this indiscretion. And now that the perilous plea has been uttered I cannot make up for it, as I should like to think I could, by once again expressing, more freely and with less inhibition, the gratitude I felt towards you and could not express when years ago I saw you for the first time, a gratitude which your unforgettable company and every sign of your presence in the world have only made more profound as time goes on.

If there is some goal of merit I might attain in the future, only then shall I be able to thank you properly, for only thanks from someone who has become worthy of you to a higher degree can give you pleasure, and then perhaps I could also justify my immodest request.

Be so kind, even if you should deem my project not worth your emphatic support, as to reply to me nonetheless, however briefly, for if you say nothing I shall take the blame for my indiscretion onto myself, a blame that might well turn out to be more severe than any you would utter against me.

Should you wish, I could send you the manuscript of the first issue for you to inspect.

I am with unfeigned esteem

your

M. Hölderlin

My publisher joins his request to mine.

Allow me to add my address: at the glazier Wagner's in Homburg near Frankfurt.

73. To Johanna Christiana Gok

Homburg, 8 July 1799

Dearest Mother,

Your kind letters are always cause for a sort of celebration when I receive them, and every time I feel as if I was at home, with you, and the motherly love you show me makes you so present, together with the country I know and my dear relatives, so close and true, that being far away is made much easier. You can be quite reassured about my health. For a good while now I've felt perfectly well, and a joyful gratitude for being vouchsafed this, not something we can bestow on ourselves, guides me in my work and in my hours of rest.

You shouldn't have been disquieted by those verses, dearest Mother! It didn't mean any more than how much I want one day to have the peace and quiet to carry out what nature seems to have destined me for. And in general, my dear Mother, I must ask you not to take everything you read of mine as strictly literal in meaning. To express his little world the poet must imitate creation, where not everything is perfect and where God sends rain on good and evil and on the just and the unjust. The poet must often say something untrue and contradictory which then of course resolves itself into *truth* and harmony in the greater whole, where it is said as something *transitory and perishable*. And just as the rainbow only shows its beauty after a storm, so in the poem truth and harmony emerge with even greater beauty and pleasure from falsehood and from error and suffering. – I know and am very grateful, my noble, good mother, that you do all you can to encourage me, and I promise you your blessing shall not be without fruit.

As for the journey you so kindly invite me to make, you will see from the letter to my dear sister how very tempted I am to make use of your kind permission and whether or not it will be possible for me to fulfil this desire.

I have not yet had the opportunity to find out exactly the best way of getting the money to me in complete security, so please wait for my next letter before sending it off. I don't need any more for the moment, even if other things permit me to travel up to see you for a few weeks in the early autumn. Accept my heartfelt thanks again. It was an endless source of joy to hear you say you could now leave off worrying and put your mind to rest in so many regards.

Don't let my indisposition get in the way of any of the joys that at your age you have so fully earned, when you have done so much for us and undergone so many things in life. For I am healthy now, dear attentive mother, and have all the more reason to hope I shall remain so since I shall be able to live for a while in such tranquillity and without any great strain or violent interruption. Pass on my affection to Karl too, when he's there. My best regards to all the family! How much I would like to be part of the joyfulness your dear guests will feel, but the latest preparations for the journal, which I mustn't put off if I am to settle the matter soon, mean that I can't very well get away now.

A thousand respects to my dear grandmother. As ever
your much indebted son,
Hölderlin

74. To Friedrich Wilhelm Joseph Schelling

[Homburg, early July 1799]
My dear friend,
Since we last met I have followed your affairs and your fame with so much loyalty and concern that I think I can allow myself to remind you of my existence again.

If during this time I have given you no sign of life it was mostly because one day I hoped to approach you, who have continued to mean so much to me, in some more important regard or at least having accomplished something that might recall our friendship in a more fitting manner.

Now a request drives me to you sooner than that and even in this form you will not fail to recognize me. I have made use of the solitude in which I have been living here since last year to work without distraction and with all my concentrated and independent powers on something that will perhaps be more mature than what I have written before, and although I have mostly lived for poetry, even so necessity and inclination have not allowed me to stray so far from theoretical concerns that I have not sought to develop my convictions into greater definiteness and completeness and, as far as possible, to put them into application and reaction with the world past and present. For a large part my thoughts and my studies were restricted to what I was mostly working on, poetry, insofar as it is a living art and comes at the same time from genius and experience and reflection and is ideal and systematic and individual. This led me into thoughts about culture and the creative impulse in general, about its ground and its purpose, how far it works ideally and how far actively, and then again how far, as art and creative impulse, it is conscious of its ground and its own essence, beginning from an ideal, and how far it is instinctive, though obeying the laws of its material etc.; and when I came to the end of my investigations I believed I had established the standpoint of so-called humanism in a more solid and comprehensive form than any I had come across before (by attending to the unifying and communal aspects of human natures and the directions they take rather than to what differentiates them, though that too requires just as much attention, it's true). All this material led me to conceive the idea of a humanist journal which would basically be concerned with the practice of poetry, but would also include theoretical approaches, from both historical and philosophical perspectives, and finally would encourage such approaches to subjects other than poetry, from the standpoint of humanism.

Forgive me this laborious preamble, dear friend, but my respect for you prevented me from announcing my project to you *ex abrupto* and I felt I was bound to account in some fashion for what I have been doing, particularly as I might easily fear that what I have produced so far may no longer inspire in you the degree of faith you seemed to have in my philosophical and poetic abilities before, now that I should be able to give you proof of them.

It will be easy for you, who penetrate and encompass human nature with a breadth and skill that are only too rare, to put yourself in my more limited position and with your name and your participation sanction an undertaking whose aim is to *bring people closer together without frivolity or syncretism*. It will do this by treating of and arguing for, though not too strictly, the particular energies and directions and relations in their nature. But while maintaining due respect for each one of these energies, directions and relations it will attempt to make the intimate and necessary connections between them clear and apprehensible, and to show how every one of them only needs to be considered in its excellence and purity in order to see that it is far from contradicting any other, so long as it is also pure, but that each one already contains within itself an openness to reciprocal interaction and harmonious exchange. And likewise the soul within the organic structure, being common to all members and particular to each, leaves not a single one of them in isolation – the soul cannot exist without the organs, nor the organs without the soul, and both, if they do occur separately and so in an aorgic state, will tend to become organic, and already contain the creative impulse within them. As a metaphor I think it makes sense to say that. It was not meant to mean any more than this: spirit that has no substance cannot exist without experience, and experience that has no soul cannot exist without spirit, and they carry within them the necessity of taking on form and constituting themselves through judgement and art, of ordering themselves into an animate, harmoniously changing whole; and finally organic art and the creative impulse it issues from cannot exist either, are not even conceivable, without their inner element, natural disposition and spirit, *and* their outer element, experience and historical learning.

All I wanted was to give you a general idea of the journal's character, to touch on what one might call its spirit. I will try to make the style and tone as accessible as possible.

I didn't think it was quite proper to go into more detail about the plan I have been obliged to draw up or the material I have ready, however much at the same time I was tempted to demonstrate to you, as far as can be done before the thing itself appears, that my project is not ill-founded and frivolous and has perhaps more chance of success than what I have produced before; also that going by what I know and sense of your mind and ways of thinking I shall not be offending against you, not in the general tendency at any rate.

I shall wait for your reply, which I shall attach much hope to, and your thoughts on the matter, before, should you ask me to, going into more length about the spirit and composition of the journal such as I have been able to plan it in my own mind, together with the possible materials for inclusion and those already written.

In any case, friend of my youth, you will forgive me for turning to you with the old familiarity and expressing the wish that with your participation and companionship in this enterprise you might help keep my courage up, which due to my situation and other circumstances has suffered various shocks since we last met – I should be able to admit that to you. For my part, with the greatest possible maturity of my own contributions and the kind participation of the established writers I flatter myself on getting, I will do everything to give the journal the quality it requires for you to be able to answer to your conscience and your public should you, at the least, put your name to it and, if you are able or willing to do no more, contribute once or twice a year. –

The bookseller Steinkopf in Stuttgart, who has shown willingness and understanding towards me in this matter and who perhaps precisely because he is a beginner is seeing to his side of things with great persistency and loyalty, promises to pay every contributor, and I have made it a condition that everyone should be sent *at least* one carolin a folio page. Although I intend to live almost exclusively from and for the journal, nevertheless I thought I should ask no more for myself, seeing that I haven't had much success as a writer so far and my frugal way of life doesn't require any more income than that. But I have left it to his good sense to show his appreciation and, in whatever degree he sees fit, make an exception for the various contributors. – Forgive me for going into that too. But as it is part of it, let the nature of the thing take the blame for not being able to exist without such a pendant.

Be so kind, my dear Schelling, as to at least give me an answer soon, and know that I have always honoured and respected you, and do so more and more.

Yours,

Hölderlin

PS. My publisher makes a point of joining his request to mine. My address is: at the glazier Wagner's in Homburg near Frankfurt.

75. *To Johann Wolfgang Goethe (?)*

[Homburg, July 1799]

I do not know, esteemed Sir, whether you still remember my name well enough to make it unexceptionable to be reading a letter and what is more a plea from me.

Your qualities and your renown would do so much to further the matter I am approaching you about, and the memory of a few unforgettable hours that your good disposition granted me years ago also gives me so much confidence, that I put my request to you not quite without hope of a favourable reply. I have in mind (together with a number of writers) to edit a humanist journal which would be primarily poetic in its fundamental character, both in practice and in theory, which last aim it would pursue by containing essays of a general nature on the ideals shared by all the arts, on what is proper and peculiar to poetic compositions and to poetic speech, but then also addressing various masterpieces by ancient and more recent writers and seeking to show how each of these works is an ideal, systematic, characteristic whole that has issued out of the living soul of the poet and the living world around him and through his art has formed an organization of its own, a nature within nature.

[*But then the discursive essays would also take in art and the creative impulse and the character of the journal in general be that of humanism.*]

I only wanted to describe roughly the spirit and character of the journal, in the hope that at least in its tendency it will not be something you would not countenance.

How important it is for me to win the honour of your support, and how much the project and the public would gain from it – let my very temerity be proof of that. Without it I certainly should not venture to make this request, since a negative answer from you or total silence would carry too much weight for me to be able to remain indifferent. I will do everything I can, through the greatest possible maturity of my own contributions and through the kind sympathy of writers of merit I flatter myself will give the journal the worth it needs,

76. To Heinrike Breunlin

[Homburg, July 1799]

My dear Sister,

I would not forgive myself for having taken so long to thank you for your last, kind letter if in the meantime I hadn't had so many other letters to write which couldn't be put off without causing me difficulties. And it isn't so much that I lacked the time, for an hour or two is easily found, but if I have been busy writing in a tone that between us is foreign (however much it is often a real need for me) it is not easy to find my way back into the mood I like to write to you in and to find words more fit for a brother and sister than those which are appropriate for conversing with people less familiar to us.

For me it is a constant source of joy that the lovely affection we have for one another has not lessened, and that we still mean the same to each other as we always did, and I believe nothing from our youth survives with such persistent liveliness as the love between brothers and sisters and other relatives and am so glad to let myself be guided by it, as a cherished remnant of my past, when I sense that so much in and around me is different now than before. However much my conscience pushes me forward I cannot help often thinking with gratitude, and often with longing, of the days of my youth: in childhood we can still live more by our hearts than by the light of reason, and our sense of the beauty of ourselves and the world is still whole enough for us not to be obliged to derive almost our only satisfaction from hard work at what we have chosen to do.

But when I feel we cannot remain young for ever I often think, and I like the thought, that everything has its time, and at bottom summer is as beautiful as spring, or rather neither one nor the other is completely beautiful – beauty consists more in all seasons and periods of life together in their sequence than in any one on its own. And it is the same with our days. No one day satisfies us entirely, none is wholly beautiful, and each has if not its evil then at least its imperfection, but add them all up and you get a sum of joy and life. –

Dear Rike, I have just read through your letter again and am almost ashamed now at the generalities I have come up with in reply to the kind words that flow from your heart.

If I manage to advance my present occupations enough to be able to take a few weeks off in the autumn, and if I can find a reasonable way of returning where I am now without drawing too much attention to myself in Württemberg, I think I really will follow my heart and come to rest and live once again in the company of you and your dear husband, and with your children and all the rest of the dear family.

If only I could be the bearer of as much joy as I shall receive. But that's silly. We have not changed and shall be seeing one another again, and that is enough. And you will allow me to live in your happy household as if I belonged to it too. – When and where shall I be the one to invite you to stay with me, dear Rike? My own arrangements are ample for me. A couple of nice little rooms, one of which, where I spend most of my time, I've decorated with maps of the four quarters of the globe, a big table of my own in the dining room which also serves as the bedroom, and a chest-of-drawers there too, and here in the study a desk where I keep my money safe and another table with books and papers on it, and another little table by the window, near the trees, where I like being best and get on with my work. And I have chairs too, for a couple of good friends, plenty of clothes brought with me from Frankfurt, cheap but healthy food, a garden with a summer-house the owner lets me use, lovely walks round about, and I pay my bills in a straightforward and orderly way and soon perhaps I'll be my own master with an annual income of 500 florins – I'll tell you more about that next time. That would be enough for the time being. And who knows where my writing will lead me in the future? I might make my fortune. Then I'll set myself up in splendour and invite you to stay.

Forgive me this nonsense, Rike. The way I am means I can only really be spoken about half in jest and half in earnest. But I promise you never to fritter away my days unthinkingly and, so long as it suits my requirements and I am suitable for it, to accept with joy any good situation in society that might present itself, and to establish myself in it. For the moment I think I can wait a bit, since I would have to live without my own home and without an official post of my own anyway, and am not a total burden on our good mother.

It was only very reluctantly, given all the kindness mother showed me during my time at university, that I came to confess to her that despite my expectations I hadn't quite managed to make do this year with what I brought with me from Frankfurt, since I could not foresee my illness and the change in diet it necessitated for almost three months, nor the hard winter and several other expenses. But I have repeatedly and expressly insisted that she make careful note of the 100 florins she intends to send me and also of anything else I may be obliged to ask her for in an emergency, and in this way simply let me have some of my inheritance in advance, should the circumstances require it. And I nevertheless regard it as very generous of our dear mother and of all my beloved family that they favour me with so much confidence, especially as in many respects dear Karl now has greater claims to make on mother's support than I do.

I now enjoy a constant state of health which means I am in good spirits and busier and calmer again, and you won't find it odd, dear Rike, if I admit to you in saying this how much the way I feel and my mental powers depend on my body. But precisely what made my illness so hard to put up with was that it was intrinsically connected with my state of mind, to the extent that the tiniest disagreeable thought would often set it off again whereas the illness itself wore out my poor head and made it fit for nothing. My strength of will and my patience were only enough to prevent me from becoming grumpy and a burden to others. I'm sorry to be talking to you about this again.

The air up here in the hills is a good bit sharper than in Frankfurt or at home. That is the only thing I have against the area and the town itself. The heavens forgive me for it. And the summer is now all the more pleasant.

You can see I'm becoming almost too tender writing to my tender-hearted sister. But there's no harm in that, as long as it's not the only thing I am. I often say to a wild friend I have here: we must be solid and loyal and unrelenting in what we see to be true and good, but to be nothing but iron and steel is not right, especially not for poets.

Every person has something that gives him joy, and who would want to do without it entirely? Mine now is the fine weather, the bright sunshine and the green earth, and I cannot reproach myself for this joy, whatever it is, I have no other now at hand, and even if I did I would never leave off this one or forget it, for it does no one any harm and does not age, and the spirit finds so much meaning in it. And one day, when I'm a grey-haired boy, spring and the morning and the light of evening day by day will make me a little younger until I feel the end and go and sit outside in the open and from there go away – to everlasting youth.

Give my love to your dear children. You were so very right, dear Rike, they would be the best consolers for me if I made a sour face and behaved as if there were nothing but misery and discord and coldness and wrong in the world, as if life were not alive, and as if I and other living beings had no heart and no soul.

Goodbye, dearest! Send my regards to your esteemed husband and tell him he is often in my thoughts and how much I admire him.

Ever your affectionate brother,
Hölderlin

77. *To Friedrich Schiller*

[Homburg, September 1799]

I cannot say enough to thank you, esteemed Sir, for the generosity with which you answered my unseemly request, and I can assure you that the kind words you had for me enrich me as much in real terms as any other help I could wish for. The blessing of a great man is the best help for those who can recognize or sense it, that at least is what I had most need of from you. I have long made the mistake of always wanting to *earn* the right to your company and kind sympathy. For that reason I withdrew from your presence and promised myself that I would only approach you again when I could make more justifiable claims on the attention you honoured me with, and through this false pride I have forfeited the beneficial influence of your instruction and encouragement which I was in less of a position to do without than others because my courage and my convictions are only too easily confused and weakened by the unfavourable effects of everyday life.

The valuable advice you gave me some time ago and repeated in your last letter I have not let go by completely unheeded and I am concentrating everything on developing the precise tone that without being whimsical seemed to lie closest to my natural unaffected disposition. I have made it my maxim to first become proficient in any one kind of writing, and to gain character in it, before I attempt to acquire a flexibility that can only belong to someone who has already achieved a firm standpoint. I thought I could execute the precise tone I wanted to make my own most completely and naturally in the tragic form and have ventured on a tragedy, the *Death of Empedocles*, and this is the work I have been devoting most of my time to during my stay here. – I must admit that I cannot make this confession without feeling slightly ashamed of it, above all to you. To mention just one point, since I have come to a somewhat more thorough recognition of the beauty of the tragic form, the composition of the *Robbers*, in its essentials, and particularly the scene by the Danube as the poem's centre, has revealed itself to me with such grandeur and depth and with such immutable truth that I took this insight as an achievement in itself, and have long wanted to ask your permission to put my thoughts into writing. And that is how you once began, noble master! I have also studied your *Fiesko* and there again it is the inner structure, the whole living shape – which as I see it is the most enduring aspect of the work – that I admired above all, even more than the characters, which while larger than life are so true to it, and the brilliant situations and the magical colourful play of the language. The other plays I still have to attend to, and it will not be easy for me to keep my wits about me when I come to read *Don Carlos*, which for so long was the magical cloud the good god of my youth enveloped me in so that I did not see too early on the pettiness and barbarity of the world that surrounded me.

Forgive me, esteemed Sir, if you should find these utterances, which at least have the virtue of literal truthfulness, not quite seemly. But I should have to say nothing at all to you, or else restrict myself to remarks of a very general nature, which indeed is what I ordinarily do when I write to you, even if occasionally I permit myself to make an exception.

You allow me to tell you something more precise about my situation. It is such that I probably cannot continue in it, without considerable inconvenience, for more than a few months. With my little bit of writing and my life as a private tutor I had put together enough wealth to be able to hope I might live independently at least long enough to get my tragedy to a certain stage of completion. But ill health, which lasted almost all the winter and part of the summer too, forced me for one thing to change my frugal way of life and for another also took up more of my time and energies than my plans allowed for.

who for their part have too many concerns of their own to contribute regularly, even if they are more my equals than your esteemed self and could more readily and acceptably be invited into my company.

78. To Susette Gontard

[Homburg, late August/early September 1799]
Dearest,
Only the uncertainty of my position prevented me from writing before now. The project of the journal which not without good reason I wrote to you about with so much confidence looks to me as if it is going to fail. I had placed so much hope in it as a way of supporting me in my work and allowing me to continue to live close to you. Not only have these hopes and efforts been in vain, but have now ended in many bitter experiences. I had drawn up a viable and modest plan – my publisher wanted things more ambitious: he requested me to secure the collaboration of a host of famous writers he considered to be my friends, and although such a course seemed to me fraught with problems still I was fool enough to let myself be persuaded so as not to appear headstrong, and my old acquiescent heart has got me into frustrations that unfortunately I must write to you about because in all probability my future, and so in a way the life I live for you, depends on it. Not only men whom I was more an admirer of than friend, friends too, darling, even those who could hardly refuse to participate without real ingratitude, have so far left me without response, and I have now been living for a good 8 weeks in this state of hope and expectancy on which my existence more or less depends. What the reason for this turn of events can be, God knows. Are people so very ashamed of being associated with me?
That this cannot well be the case, rationally speaking, is

proved to me by your fine judgement and the judgement of a
few friends who have duly joined me in my venture with true
loyalty, e.g. Jung, in Mainz, whose letter I enclose for you. It
was the *famous*, whose participation was supposed to vouch
for so slight and obscure a thing as me, who offered no help,
and why should they? After all, anybody who makes a name
for himself in the world will seem to detract from their own –
they will then be the uncontested idols no longer. In short, it
seems to me that among these people, whom I can think of as
roughly my equals, there is a bit of professional envy at work.
But knowing this doesn't get me anywhere. I've wasted almost
2 months on preparations for the journal, and probably the
best thing I can do now to avoid being led by the nose any
longer is to write to my publisher asking him if he wouldn't
prefer to take the writings I had intended for the journal on
their own, which even if he did would admittedly fall short of
securing my existence.

And so what I have in mind is to use all the time I have left on
my tragedy, which may take about another three months, and
then I shall have to go home or to a place where I can support
myself by giving lectures, which is not feasible here, or by some
other occupation which will allow me to continue my work.

Forgive me this direct language, dearest. It would only have
been more difficult to tell you what I needed to say, my love, if
I'd let the movement of my heart towards you voice itself, and
it's scarcely possible the way things are with me to preserve the
necessary courage without losing for a few moments the tender
tones of our innermost life. That's precisely the reason why up
till now I haven't written

79. *To Susette Gontard*

[Homburg, ~ November 1799]

Here is *Hyperion*, darling, *our Hyperion*. It is the fruit of the
days when our souls were at one and will give you some joy in
spite of all. Forgive me for letting Diotima die. You remember,

we could never quite agree about that, before. I thought that
the disposition of the whole made it necessary. My darling,
everything that is said about her and about us, all the scattered
remarks about the life of our life, take them as thanks, which
are often all the truer the more ineptly they are expressed. If I
could have formed myself as an artist at your feet, gradually,
in peace and freedom, I'm sure I should have quickly become
what amid the suffering, in its dreams and in broad daylight,
and often in silent despair, my heart longs for.

That we were not to have the happiness we could give each
other is reason enough for all the tears we have wept during
the last years, but to think we shall perhaps both perish in our
prime for want of one another, that is criminal. And that is
what makes me so quiet sometimes, because I have to guard
against thoughts of that kind. Your illness, your letter – however much I seek to blind myself to it, it was again so obvious
to me, unavoidable, that you are always suffering, all the time,
– and all I can do is cry about it! – Tell me, what is better, to
keep quiet what we have in our hearts or to tell it to one
another? I have always played the coward so as to spare you, –
have always pretended to be ready to resign myself to everything
as if I were meant to be a plaything for people and the circumstances and had no solid heart of my own that beats with
loyalty and freedom for what is right and for what it has best
in the world, light of my life, have often denied myself and held
back from my love, which is what I cherish most, sometimes
not even allowed myself to think of you, all to get through life
and this fate of ours as gently as possible, for your sake. – You
too, you who are so peaceful, have always struggled to be calm,
have borne it with heroic strength and kept quiet about what
cannot be altered, have hidden and buried your heart's everlasting decision within yourself, and for that reason things often
go dark around us and we no longer know who we are and
what we have, hardly even know one another. This endless
fighting and contradiction within, it will kill you in the end,
and if no god can assuage it I have no choice but to grieve away
over what has happened to us, or to take nothing into account

but you and look together with you for a way of putting an end to the conflict.

I have already had the thought that we might be able to live from renunciation, as if it might perhaps give us strength if once and for all we said goodbye to hope,

80. *To Johanna Christiana Gok*

Homburg, 16 November 1799

Dearest Mother,

I could well imagine that this time you would be obliged to put off writing for a while, and reconciled myself to it the more readily because I thought of your dear guests and then the journey, which is bound to be good for your health and well-being. How gladly I'd be part of the happy circle in which you are living, and contribute something from my side to the pleasure being with your family gives you. But I think I shall be obeying your own view of things if I postpone my visit at least until our part of the world and the roads generally are rather quieter again. These last days I have been very concerned for our relatives in Löchgau because I guessed that some of the fighting must have occurred at the place itself or very nearby. Now they will be in peace again, at least for a while.

Here we no longer encounter the war except in the papers, and the people of Homburg have earned it: this is the first winter in many years they will spend without foreign boarders and lodgers and without the disruption of war and military charges. I am often amazed that this region, which has been an almost constant scene of war, more or less, is recovering so quickly nevertheless, and that the people are for the most part able to continue to run their households and their lives as usual.

To come to my own affairs, I'm afraid I cannot yet tell you anything more precise about my prospects, and really this displeases me more for your sake than for mine, for if it weren't for the inevitable disadvantage of my present way of life – that it won't immediately satisfy my material needs – I should be content with it for ever. I am deeply conscious that the cause I live for is a noble one and, once it is brought to its proper expressiveness and formal perfection, one that is beneficial to mankind. And with this determination and purpose I live at peace in my occupations, and although I am often reminded (as inevitably happens) that people would perhaps respect me more if they could make out that I held a decent office in society, that's easily borne, because I understand it, and I make up for it in my delight in the truth and beauty of what I have secretly devoted myself to since I was a boy and have returned to from the experiences and lessons of life with all the more resolve. And even if my inner self never attains a clear and full language – and a lot of it depends on luck – at least I know what I have wanted, and I have wanted more than might be supposed from my slight achievements so far and can also hope, from the odd thing I come to hear, that even in inept execution what I do will be taken up and approved by an intuitive soul now and again, and so my existence will definitely not fail to leave some trace on earth.

I make these confessions to you, dear Mother, because it is important to me for my own peace of mind to show myself to you in my present way of life in as sincere and unbiased fashion as I can, the more especially as you have helped me this far with your kind support.

I thank you dearly for what you have sent. Neuffer will probably have kept it back until now because of the unsafe roads. I shall be able to put most of it on one side, and use it partly for the coming journey. It does something to set my mind to rest over all I am costing you that I could not live as a curate either without some help, and that I have at least persevered a reasonable length of time in the, in this regard, more advantageous life of a private tutor.

How it gladdens me that you can in every respect be so content with our Karl. And how much I value his concentrating and applying his energies so manfully in the situation he finds himself in. I honour from the bottom of my heart anyone who makes himself useful to the world in this way, and it only makes me sorry when occasionally I see that in the main people are not so well disposed the other way round, being less inclined to acknowledge someone who because of the nature of his occupation and way of working is in some degree distanced from any particular sphere of activity, and can only survive by having the courage to affirm his own nature, understanding and assuming his fate as others do theirs. And it is the comfort and rule of my life that in the real world no one can be every-thing and is forced to become one particular thing, and, together with the merits of his position and peculiar way of life, bear the disadvantages that necessarily go with it.

Mother, I thank you a thousand times for showing such sympathy for me in this regard even though I have not arrived at anything yet, but you and the rest of the family will surely think it to my credit that I am unable to be indifferent about the judgement you form of me.

I also beg you not to be put off if sometimes in my letters I slip into lengthy reasonings. From what I can gather of the more general moods and opinions of people today, there seems to be developing, as a reaction against the great, violent upheavals of our time, a way of thinking that is very unlikely to animate and awaken the faculties and in fact ends up oppressing and numbing the living soul, without which there can be no joy and no proper value in the world at all. Exagger-ation is never good, and it is no good either when people are frightened of everything that is not already familiar and settled, with the result that they hold all striving towards anything nearer perfection than what we already have to be bad and harmful. Precisely this seems to me the general attitude now-adays, and it is a great weight on my mind because it reaches into the small things in life as well as the greater things, and because no man can free himself from the influence of others, be it harmful or beneficial.

And if on a particular day I am more caught up in feelings of this kind than usual it is only natural that this should show through in my utterances when I come to speak with those close to my heart.

But so as not to go on too long now I will just add that I

hope to be able to say something more certain about the visit I
have been intending for so long, and also about my future
existence, in a month's time.

As always, dearest Mother, I am

your grateful son,

H.

I have just learnt that the French Directory has been dismissed,
the Council of Elders sent to St Cloud and Bonaparte made a
sort of dictator.

81. To Johann Gottfried Ebel

[Homburg, ~ November 1799]

My dear friend,
However much I am obliged to you for your kind promise of
future participation in my literary enterprise the real pleasure
your letter gave me was quite a different one. I felt more strongly
than I can say, as I read it, how much you meant to me from
the first moment, and how much I have done without since I
last saw you.

The more I come to understand and tolerate and love people
in their various sufferings, the more deeply and unforgettably
the outstanding ones among them press themselves into my
mind. And I must confess that I know few people with whom I
can follow my soul with such assuredness as I can whenever I
think of and talk about you, something that happens often. If
only we were closer to one another – for my sake, for you do
not need me, or less than I do you, and I don't know if I would
mean as much to you as I once seemed to. Many experiences,
which given my disposition were almost inevitable, have pretty
much undermined my confidence in all that used to be my chief
source of hope and joy, the ideal image of man and his life and
being; and the ever changing conditions of the world, great
and small, in which I belong frighten me still, now that I am
somewhat freer again, to a degree that I can only admit to you,

because you understand me. Habit is such a powerful goddess that probably no one can abandon her with impunity. The agreement with others that we achieve so easily when we keep to what we already have, this consonance of opinions and customs, only appears to us in its true significance when we have to do without it, and our hearts may well never find the same peace again once we have given up the old ties, for in the end the forging of new ones is something we have little control over, especially as concerns the finer and higher sort. It is true that people who have raised themselves into a new world of rightness and goodness then hold together all the more closely and enduringly.

How much I should have liked to give you a full account of my departure from the household that meant, and still means, so much to both of us. But then I should have had to tell you infinitely more than I can say! I should have preferred to ask you a favour, and should still like to. Our noble friend, whom I have always seen come through her many ordeals in greater affirmation of her best life, even finer and more delicate despite the bitter anomalies of her situation, nonetheless seems to me, if her sadness is not to be the end of her, in great need of a firm, clear word that would secure her inner worth and her own path through life for the future. And it has become virtually impossible for me to communicate with her with the necessary calm. It would be a great service to me, dear Ebel, if you could do this one day. Our own thoughts or a book or whatever else helps to give us direction do some good, but a word from a genuine friend who knows the situation and the person concerned strikes home more truly and has more effect.

Your judgement on Paris affected me deeply. It would have unsettled me less if it had not come from you but someone without such a wide perspective and without your clear unprejudiced eye. I can understand how a powerful fate, capable of shaping so splendidly men and women who are firmly grounded in themselves, simply ends up tearing the weak apart, and I can understand it the more readily when I see that even the greatest owe this greatness not just to their own natures but also to the place in which they had the fortune to come into

active and living relation with their times, but I do not understand why many great and pure forms do so little to help and
heal in general and in particular, and this it is above all that
often makes me so still and humble before the omnipotence
of necessity, which rules over all. If necessity decisively and
constantly outweighs the ability of pure and independent minds
to have an effect then either collectively or individually the end
will be a tragic and fatal one for the people who live in that
time and place. We are fortunate, then, if we still have some
other source of hope. How do you find the new generation,
I wonder, in the world you live in?

82. *To Christian Ludwig Neuffer*

Homburg, 4 December 1799

My dear friend,
First of all let me express to you my sympathy for the death of
your good mother, which I was left to learn from your poem.
You knew the respect I had for this unusual woman, and for
that reason it was almost wrong of you not to write and tell me
about it. But I know very well myself that in many cases it does
a man more good to keep silent than to speak of his suffering
to others.

   You must also be assured that I feel for you in the incon-
venient change in your job, and I regret it all the more since I'd
have liked to see you able to enjoy the success of your poetic
work in peace. It is almost as if no happiness costs more dear
than being a writer, especially a poet. You ask my advice, dear
Neuffer! How I'd like to say something reliable, and how I'd
like to find you a solution myself. But you don't need me to tell
you how much I for my part need advice and the help of a friend.
I confess that little by little I am finding out that nowadays it
is almost impossible to live from writing alone if you don't
want to be too much at the service of others and sacrifice your
reputation for the sake of your livelihood. And for this reason
I am undecided whether sooner or later I should become a

curate or rather a preceptor or private tutor again. I almost think this last alternative the best. And even if some less modest post should present itself I don't know if I would take the opportunity since I should be unwilling to sacrifice either my writing to an office or an office to my writing, and for that reason I should like to choose a post that did not require too much energy and time. If you manage to find something better for yourself I shall be very pleased for you, and I don't know, perhaps with your connections in Stuttgart you can arrange something suitable, for example a journey at the consistory's expense. That would certainly correspond to you and your plans in every respect.

If anything occurs to me that seems to suit you, or if any opportunity shows itself that I find fits in with your wishes, I'll certainly let you know.

About your most recent poems I'll say no more than that they distinguish themselves through the faithful, unadorned representation of the inward or outward life they address. And you know yourself how much that means. Especially 'The Dream' seems to achieve a combination of the ideal-poetic and simplicity. The alterations in the hymn to 'Calm' pleased me particularly in the clarity they maintain alongside their significance. If only I lived closer to you so that we could talk some sense together from time to time about our noble art. For, in confidence, I find more and more that the true recognition of poetic forms greatly aids and facilitates the *expression* of poetic life and spirit, and I am amazed that we wander around so helplessly when I look at the sure, thoroughly purposeful and considered progression of ancient works of art. And I confess only to you that I was a bit angry about the pretty unthinking remarks about poetry you made once last summer (we were talking about *Emilie*). Do not misunderstand me, dear Neuffer! It was not because of *Emilie*, which was dashed off without much thought because I had to and as a favour, it was for the sake of the art that you disparaged in what you said to me. Think me an unfeeling theorist if you like. I know my own mind, and I agree with you entirely when you say our dull aesthetic compendiums are a patchwork of one-sided conceptions you'd like to throw in the fire. Only let the gods give me enough time and equanimity to execute what I see and feel. –

The esteem I have for the progress of your journal and how my own literary affairs stand you can gather, if you like to, from the letter to our friend Steinkopf. I must break off, it's getting late. I hope things will be well with you soon. Console yourself with the Muses and, if it can do any good, with the faithfulness of

your sincere friend,
H.

Please could you send me the 100 florins as a bill as soon as ever possible.

83. *To Johanna Christiana Gok*

Homburg, 29 January [1800]

Dearest Mother,

. . .

I am now *certain* to receive about 400 fl. from my bookseller in quarterly payments. [*Moreover he has arranged things in Stuttgart for Hölderlin to be able to stay there without being obliged to carry out any theological function as soon as the time seems right.*] . . . If therefore I keep my journal going for a few years, which I shall certainly try to do for my reputation's sake, and if I earn a bit more by giving private lessons here or in Stuttgart, I'll be able to reckon with an income that will almost be sufficient. It seems to me sensible, unless I am forced to do otherwise, to interrupt the present form of my occupations and studies as little as possible with a new mode of life and work, as I am only now more or less in harness and after many distractions and troubles have at last gained some steadiness in what I am doing. So the arguments that present themselves to me at the moment are against embarking on such a course, which in any case I should hardly want *you* to carry the burden of. – The point is, if it turned out not to work it would almost be too great an ordeal for the peace of mind that means so much to me and for the patience I have for relations with other people, for, as I say, I sense that I need to grow a bit stronger before I can expose myself to that kind of humiliation, which at least for a time would rid me of the desire and the proper energy to do anything useful in human affairs. And I can admit it to you, dearest Mother: it is precisely on this that my physical and mental wellbeing, if I can put it that way, largely rests. The other reason is that I am now more or less safe for a little while and the thing must be to carry on pursuing a career that whatever happens cannot end so very badly for me, until some definite success results, and now of all times it hardly seems possible to me to combine my present occupations, which require such a concentrated and undivided frame of mind, with a post where I would have to get used to my surroundings and settle into my work all over again.

If you allow me to add that I won't be worse off than many others if in the future I take up a position with somewhat less in the way of funds, then it seems to me well worth the trouble to supplement my income a little in the meantime if it is not quite sufficient, when need arises, especially since if I remain in good health I do not intend in any future position to give up my writing entirely, which though it may never make me rich will not be completely thankless in the end either.

In any case I leave the matter up to you and my dear brother-in-law, having given my opinion as far as the short time allowed it; especially as I am not, as you are, in a position to judge whether the exact circumstances will allow me to secure my existence without taking up a substantial post. If I discount the expenses caused by my ill health last year I find that I can more or less manage with 500 fl., and I could probably earn that much in Stuttgart or here. – You will not blame me for looking on the matter so one-sidedly; as far as higher motives and points of view are concerned, I believe I can claim with a good conscience that in my present occupation I am doing at least as much service and good to people as I would in a parish, even if appearances would seem to suggest the opposite. This is based not just on my own judgement but on the express and earnest gratitude I have received for some of my publications from persons whose opinions command respect.

   In the meantime my departure from here depends above all on the next letter from my bookseller. As it is a matter of expediency you will understand me when I say that whether I stay here or move to Stuttgart hangs on where I find it easier to make a living. In any case I'll carry on here until Easter, because I cannot possibly interrupt my work before then. In about a fortnight I should be able to give you certain news. If Sinclair, who is probably leaving for Swabia later this week to visit a friend in the imperial army, comes to Blaubeuren as he intends to, please don't mention anything to him about my probable departure unless he brings it up himself first. Until I am quite decided myself I prefer not to say anything to him because he doesn't really want me to go and I should like to think the whole matter over and settle it coolly. To quit this place would by the way cost me a great deal, and only the prospect of returning to my beloved homeland and my loved ones, whom I would miss wherever I was, could make it easier. I have got to know good people here, some of them excellent, and enjoy more attention and sympathy than a stranger can expect who has nothing to give but an honest opinion now and then. – There's no need to be anxious about my health, dearest Mother. For a good while now I have enjoyed this most precious possession without interruption and it gives me the more pleasure because I always feared that the bad cramp-like condition might become permanent. This has made me well acquainted with the local doctor, a man who is always cheerful and dependable, someone who for a moment or two at least can make you feel better simply by showing his kind, healthy face. He is your man for all hypochondriacs. – The Gontard you tell me about in your letter who recently died is an uncle of the family I was with. Dear Henry is now in an educational institute in Hanau. The only reason I write so seldom of him is that I can never think of the marvellous boy without sadness. It is a very good thing for him to be out of Frankfurt, where each day corrupted his truly noble character, or at least distorted it. – I have received the money from Neuffer and thank you again for it very much. If I do leave, and if it can be done without inconveniencing you, I would ask for a little bit more, not so much because of the travelling costs, which will not be great, but because I still have a debt to settle with the bookseller in Frankfurt. Thank my dear sister on my behalf for her lovely letter. I would answer it today myself if the same thing weren't happening to me as did to her: my good friend the stove is getting too cold, and so I'd better behave myself, and spare and nurse my thirty-year-old body. The waistcoat will suit me well and keep me warm.

All my love and remembrances. As ever,

your loyal son,

Hölderlin

84. *To Friedrich Emerich*

[Homburg, Spring 1800]

You've reproached me for my silence like a true friend, dear brother, and I beg you once and for all never to misinterpret it. For as long as my interest in my friends and in everything else that touches on me is not less keen than is the case now I shall probably be obliged to appear a bit detached, out of a natural instinct to preserve my sense of self. You wouldn't believe how much trouble I've had with this, and what an old problem it is. Every relationship with other people and other objects immediately takes hold of all my thoughts, so much so that, once I've let some particular interest come to light and be articulated, I then have great difficulty leaving it behind again and moving on to something else. If you write to me, it resonates on and on until by a trick or by violence I manage to devote myself to something else, and if I write to you it's even worse. That's the kind of toiling Swabian I am.

So you have made a courageous start by publishing your poems. With your firmness of mind you've got more right than others to conduct the poetic game a bit like a game of chance for the time being and to cast the dice in the name of genius.

By that I don't at all mean that you haven't used your powers
of reflection too, your artistic sense, which you hardly seem to
do justice to given the faithful and ingenuous way it serves you,
like an honest shield-bearer in battle. I'm sure you will have
been aided by your well-founded judgement and taste, but for
all that you're not completely certain of things. And who is
among our poets, old or young? And who would one thank for
it, given the way matters now stand? We cold Northerners like
to maintain ourselves in doubt and passion, to prevent us from
organizing ourselves into snails' lives out of sheer love of order
and security.

But seriously, Emerich, you must, if some grander career is
not to be yours, make a serious go of poetry. You seem to me
to have in plenty the poetic trinity – a tender sensibility and
vigour and spirit – together with the ethereal element and the
earthly one, to be able to fix this noble life in such a noble art
and to transmit it undamaged to posterity. And that is why I
honour the free, unprejudiced, thorough-going artistic understanding more and more, because I take it to be the holy aegis
that protects the genius from transiency.

I must give you the impression of being a true penitent. But
in my defence I can say that for all the apparent carelessness
with which my works have been written hitherto I went about
them very deliberately and that the fault lies not so much with
me as in the one-sidedness of our modern-day taste if I appear to
be angry and for that reason to have proceeded in a somewhat
revolutionary way. But it was probably good as a beginning,
and as I said you can better make such a beginning than I.
I had the luck to see where I was, and so was able to choose
my subject-matter and arrange it accordingly.

85. To Johanna Christiana Gok

Homburg, 23 May 1800

Dearest Mother,

I was almost quite ready for my departure when I received your letter. Though the news that was the cause of your anxieties had also made me somewhat doubtful about my decision. I enquired in Frankfurt whether the mail-coach was still going and was told it was. I think that in a few weeks' time, at least as far as my journey is concerned, things will be no more difficult than they are now, and as anyway I probably wouldn't be able to move into my lodgings immediately I intend as a compromise to put off my departure until you send me word that my lodgings in Stuttgart are at least fit for me to move into when I arrive. As I am bound to lose some time for my own occupations, it is anyway vital that I begin working again as soon as possible once in Stuttgart.

For the rest, please don't go to any more trouble and cost over the furniture than you absolutely have to. It only recently occurred to me that sooner or later a suitable post abroad might turn up for me, and that seems to me a reason, along with other things, not to settle myself in for a proper long stay. The bookcase is just what I need. If I could always be as sure of my health as I am now, I think I could say I would be able to carry on my work as a writer uninterruptedly enough to live from it. But on the other hand it is no bad thing not to depend on it exclusively, and so I will simply resolve to take on the additional occupations that are open to me in Stuttgart. Having said that, when I listen to the judgements of men and friends on me and what I do, I can't help asking sometimes, in all humility (though it could easily be misinterpreted), why I have to make shift in this way in the workaday world. But so long as I see no other path open to me I'll consider the one I must take the allotted one and adapt to it as best I can.

A few days ago something happened that will give you as much joy as it gave me. A merchant from Frankfurt, whom I

saw just once when I was there, has without saying why made
me the present of a book which is more than a mere courtesy
as its value cannot be much less than 100 fl. I shall pay this
worthy man a visit before long and thank him as he deserves.

Could you be so kind and write to Landauer, asking him to
send me 6 carolins via Herr Kling or whoever else he prefers?*
I wouldn't put you to this bother if I didn't need your credit,
and as you will presumably be writing to Landauer anyway I
thought it better than writing to him directly. The money is
only in case of need.

I wish you could be at peace with me at last. It hurts me more
than I can say always to be causing you trouble and anxiety,
especially as simply being so far away means you cannot wholly
share the little bit of recognition I have so far received in the
world, and so have to remain almost without recompense.

I hope that this time things will not go too badly in our parts.
All my love to my dear sister and to all!

I'm in a hurry because the post's going.

Ever and from my heart,

your grateful son,

Hölderlin

*I'll write to him myself too.

86. To Johanna Christiana Gok

[Stuttgart, end of June 1800]

Dearest Mother,

Thank you very much for your kind letter and the good wishes
it contains. I will endeavour to do everything on my part to
make myself worthy of a rapid and lasting fulfilment of them.

You will not believe with what feelings of gratitude and
respect towards my loved ones I made my way here. The sympathy and encouragement of loyal, well-meaning souls is in the
stage of life I am at now a greater gift than anything one might
otherwise have cause to appreciate.

My lodgings and the welcome I received in my friend's house were all I could wish for.

In general my old acquaintances have been so well disposed towards me that I have every hope of living here in peace and quiet for a time and of being able to do my day's work with less interruption than hitherto.

I consider it a piece of luck already to have had a respectable and pleasing offer of giving lessons in philosophy to a young man who works at the Chancellery, for which I shall be paid one carolin a month.

Otherwise I have had to spend a certain amount to get myself fully established in my living arrangements here. In particular I have reluctantly decided to order myself a desk that also serves as a chest-of-drawers which, as a decent piece of furniture, did seem necessary – Landauer advised it too – because I can't very well maintain order among my papers on the little table, and, as you'll see yourself, can't keep my clothes and linen etc. in the trunk all the time without inconvenience either.

I don't need to pay for the desk immediately, so you won't be bothered with any new expenses for the moment. But if it were possible to help me out with a few carolins more sometime and so secure my position completely I should accept it with heartfelt thanks and probably not pester you again, dearest Mother, for another year. Have patience with me now above all! I shall not be found wanting for industry and good courage and the proper degree of thriftiness, not now or ever.

It really saddens me that for the moment I always have to take more than I can give, when I should like to be nothing but a source of joy to others and especially my family.

Give all my love to my dear sister. Recently I began a little poem to her as I was going along: I'll send it her soon if it can give her a moment's pleasure. The Landauers send you and Rike their respects. It is still my hope that we'll have peace shortly and be freed of the unrest of war.

I have found quite a quantity of clean linen in my trunk, so you mustn't be surprised if you find the dirty washing short of this and that. Please could you mend the trousers and have the short ones dyed. In my next letter I'll let you know how many shirts and so on I still have here, so that you can see what's missing.

Give the dear children a kiss in my name.

Ever your grateful son,

Hölderlin

The bookcase and curtain have turned out exactly as I wished. I've received all my things safely.

87. *To Heinrike Breunlin*

[Stuttgart, September/October 1800]

Dearest Sister,

I don't seem to be keeping the promise I gave you very conscientiously. But if it had been possible I should certainly have written at least once a week since then. The bad year of sickness I've now got through has made me rather slower in my work, and I often have to spend many a good hour thinking things over in an idling sort of way, so cannot afford to be interrupted more often than necessity demands. And because of the novelty of my situation necessity has made itself felt more often than will be the case in future. Also I am gradually feeling more strength again to do what out of love and duty I labour and work on all day long, and so in future can more easily and more frequently find an hour to give up to you.

That you too feel better is one reason why I am more in spirits than usual.

That your heart in its loss begins to feel stronger now *you* have grown stronger again is something I can well understand, dearest Rike.

Only live as peacefully as you can, and bring to mind all that you still have in as favourable and modest a light as possible, and don't let yourself be put off by the fortuitous and rapidly passing moments of sadness that each day holds. You can see yourself how much we mean to one another, for example, and yet if we saw each other every day there would be times now and then when we did not quite get on. So it is with everything. The good things in life often seem unpalatable for the simple reason that they often have, as they must, a rough shell, but because of it we are able to have the kernel in the end.

Give my love to our dear mother; Karl visited me recently before leaving for his new post, which really does seem to be an advantageous one, and he was full of praise and gratitude for the kindness with which she had helped him out of his difficulties. We, her sons, are her great debtors.

Give my love to your dear children. And especially to our esteemed grandmother and, if they are still with you, our other honoured relatives.

You can see, dear Rike, that I am pressed for time again.

Here is my dirty linen, and I take the liberty of asking for a little coffee.

Your loyal brother,
H.

88. *To Heinrike Breunlin*

[Stuttgart, Autumn 1800]

My dear Rike,
I will only write what is absolutely necessary again. If it suits you, my dears, I'll perhaps come and see you later in the week, for a few hours at least, and talk with you at greater length.

Landauer seems very much to want me to stay and has taken steps to find me perhaps a few more lessons, making roughly 3 louis d'or a month. Whether I'll manage as well on that as we all hope is then the question. I've heard nothing from Switzerland as yet. The advice of my family, insofar as it can be impartial and not seek counsel from the heart, will be welcome to me, because I should like to do what is to be done in total agreement. Heaven knows that all I ask is what is *necessary*, and that to necessity I am ready to submit in all its forms. But once, as far as possible, we've recognized what this is, we want

to be as confident and joyful in our minds as we can, in this as
in all other cases.

Only let faith, hope and charity never fade from my heart,
and I will go wherever I must and at the last am sure to say: I
have lived! And if it is not pride or delusion, I think I can say
that little by little, through the ordeals of my life, I have become
more solid and stronger in those respects.

Mrs Landauer sends her regards. She says the bonnets will
probably not cost as much as all that.

My love to everybody.

Your loyal brother,
Friz

89. *To Heinrike Breunlin*

[Stuttgart, ~ mid-October 1800]

Dear Rike,

I am prevented from coming tomorrow; but hope that makes
it all the more likely I'll see you and the family the Sunday after
next.

The beautiful autumn we're having is doing my health a great
deal of good and I feel renewed and alive in the world, and
gradually a new hope that I may do what I have set out to do
among men a while longer revives and increases within me.

You too, dear Rike, are, I hear, firmer on God's ground
again. We are bound to have many more fine days together,
especially when the peace which, so a French officer told me
today, is supposed to have been decided, has at last come.

We have heavy billeting here. At least you and the family are
so far undisturbed by this situation.

My love to our mother and grandmother, and to your
children.

Yours,
H.

90. *To Heinrike Breunlin*

[Stuttgart, October/November 1800]

Dearest Rike,

I thank you and our good mother and grandmother again from my heart for the happy moments I spent amongst you. Such days of rest are our life's reward on earth.

Your letter moved me deeply; but a beneficent calm spread over me at the thought that I am bound together in this way with you, good Sister, and the rest of the family, in what is truest and most holy. This maintains my heart, which in the end only too often loses its voice in too much loneliness and dwindles even from ourselves. And what is all wisdom without this child-like holy voice within us?

I'll make the visit to your friend tomorrow. Today I'm a bit too tired.

May I advise you to go out often into the open this fine autumn, and recover peace and health beneath the lovely blue sky?

I know from my own experience how much this helps, and you will not want for company.

Your dear children are a good for me. How much more so they must be for you. Rarely does one find such happily born and well brought up creatures, & you know yourself what a beautiful and noble purpose it is to govern such a richness and succour their natural growth.

Give them my love, and to our esteemed mother and grandmother.

Your loyal brother,

H.

91. *To Gottlieb Ernst August Mehmel*

[Stuttgart, November/December 1800 (?)]

Please accept my warmest thanks, esteemed Sir, for the sincere efforts with which you are concerned to uphold a better literature, and rest assured that I will take up your kind invitation with the best energies I have.

The rules I commit myself to in so doing correspond so purely and exactly with my own thoughts that I have every reason to hope it will not be too hard for me to obey them. I believe I have grasped their spirit and on the whole have nothing to add to them. If you want to give me a position involving the judgement of poetical works I think I will perhaps be suitable as for several years now my reflections and observations have been almost exclusively devoted to this subject.

The intense study of the Greeks has helped me in this and served instead of the company of friends to save me from becoming too sure of myself or too uncertain in the solitude of my meditations. And the results I have got from this study are rather different from others I am aware of. As you know, there has often been a complete failure to recognize the strictness with which the ancient writers distinguished between the different kinds of poetry, or where this has been acknowledged it is only the externals that have been attended to, and in general their art has been held to be a nicely calculated amusement rather than a sacred propriety with which they *had* to proceed in dealings with the gods. What was most spiritual, for them, had also to be supremely *characteristic*. And likewise its *representation*. Thus the formal strictness and precision of their poetic works, thus the noble forcefulness with which they observed this strictness in subordinate genres, and thus the tact with which they avoided the main characteristic traits in higher genres, precisely because the supremely characteristic contains nothing foreign to it, nothing extraneous, and therefore no trace of coercion. So they presented the gods in human form, but always avoiding actual human proportions; quite naturally, because poetry, which in its whole nature, in its inspiration as in its modesty and sobriety, is a joyous service rendered unto the gods, was never to make men into gods or gods into men, never to commit impure idolatry, but only to bring the gods and humankind closer together. Tragedy shows this *per contrarium*. God and man appear one, then comes a fate that arouses every element of humility and pride in man and in the end leaves behind as human property adoration of the gods on the one hand and a purified soul on the other. It is according to these aesthetic convictions, which follow on from your pronouncements and the words *want*, *ought* and *can* and are probably timely, that I would seek to criticize works of poetry, with unshakeable fairness and attentiveness and sparing as far as possible the writer's person, also bearing in mind,

92. *To Heinrike Breunlin*

[Stuttgart, 11 December 1800]

Dear Rike,

It was wrong of me not to announce the unexpected visitor, and I apologize to you and to him. But the day I should have done it, last Saturday, was so full of happenings that had you seen me and known what was going on in my head you would have found the distractedness which, to be honest, made me quite forget, fairly natural.

My friends pressed me almost unmercifully to stay, various good teaching opportunities were offered me the same day, and besides all this, amid all the errands I had to do, and in inner and outer turmoil, I was to give a final answer to the stranger, who I really became fond of and with whom I then had so much to talk about concerning him and his family and myself and my future situation. I confess, Rike, that I find it easier and easier to reconcile my decision with the feelings of my heart, however much it went against them at first. I have in me such a deep and urgent need of peace and quiet – more than you can guess, or than I want you to. And if I can find this in my future employment I shall be keeping my heart all the fuller in warmth and loyalty towards my relatives and friends, whom I shall never forget. I cannot bear the thought that I too, like so many others, in the critical period of life when even more than in our youth a numbing restlessness gathers round our inward being, that I, to survive, should become so cold and unfeeling and withdrawn. And often I really do feel like ice, and inevitably must if I don't find some quieter place of rest where everything that affects me touches me less nearly, and precisely for that reason upsets me less. For me and, as I believe, for you and the rest of the family too, this is the main argument, and much else being equal it has determined my decision. Of course there is a lot more to be said. I'll explain myself as much as you like when we see one another. – We shall always have each other, my dear Sister, and all my family and friends close to my heart. I should very much like to be able to speak to Karl before I go. Write to him urgently. I haven't had a proper talk with him for a long time. And it would go very much against my heart to have to say goodbye to him in writing. Tell him I'd be pleased if he can find time to come.

I intend to spend at least part of Christmas with you and our dear mother, and to set off from Nürtingen, but dispatching my luggage, or at least the main things I'll need, from here, if mother has no objection. I have very little more expenditure to make here. A pair of boots I think I need, that's all. If our dear mother can come up with a few louis d'or for the journey I'd prefer that to borrowing them here. I have been promised that the travelling expenses will be reimbursed, and probably generously enough to allow me to return whatever money I take with me and use the rest to cover any expenses for a while. Chiefly because of my lessons I'll stay on here until the holidays. – I'll write again by the next post, and not in such a rush as today. Forgive me the haste. Today is Landauer's birthday, and that has meant that I've been interrupted on and off the whole morning and am now expected at table. In Landauer you will find the man to be a brother to you in my place while I'm away. Believe me, what we mean to one another and what all our dear ones mean to me is unalterable.

Yours,

Hölderlin

93. *To Karl Gok*

[Nürtingen, ~ late December 1800]

My dear Karl,

I got your letter on the way here from Stuttgart. Landauer sent it on after me and so it reached me among the various thoughts provoked by leaving Stuttgart and being on the open road with the open world around me. I felt the unending vitality that full of loving trust conducts us through all periods of our existence, sometimes quietly urging, sometimes in its full affirming force, I felt this spirit of youth and wisdom once again just as it must manifest itself if we are to recognize it, and the good and loyal words you wrote to wish me goodbye only served to make this mood yet purer and finer. How much I said to you in reply there and then in my mind as I went on my way. Yes, there is no reason not to say it, I was full of a great sense of comfort for both of us, and this voice of our guardian spirit is still fresh in my mind.

I will write to you again from Stuttgart. I intend to spend a few more days there. Till then make do with these hastily written words and receive into your heart as we part the silent and unutterable joy of *my* heart – and let it endure until it is no longer the solitary joy of a friend and brother but – but what, you ask?

This, dear Karl, that our time is near, that the peace that is forming now will bring us what peace and only peace could bring; for it will bring much that many hope for, but it will also bring what few intimate.

Not that any one form, any one opinion or assertion will triumph, I don't think that has much to do with what peace will give us. What I mean is that selfishness in all its guises will give way to the holy rule of love and kindness, a common spirit will settle over every last thing, and in such a climate, blessed with this new peace, the German heart will open for the first time and silently as the growth of nature unfolds its hidden ramifying powers, this is what I see and believe, and this is what more than anything lets me look forward with good spirits into the second half of my life. – So continue to be glad in

your innocent and modest way of life, my good Karl. You are
preserved, saved up; the storm has passed over you, be glad
that you heard it from a distance in a place of safety and have
kept your soul pure and loving and fearless for the better times
that will come, and believe me, on your safe path you will attain
the higher purpose in life which is meant for you. You can no
more forget it than I can forget you. Let us write often, and try
to visit one another as often as possible too. After all I'm only
three days' journey away from the family. And even if it were
further, Karl, you know how strongly love and faith bind us
together.

Ever yours,
Friz

94. To the family

[Stuttgart, ~ 6 January 1801]

Not a word of all that you said to me in the goodness of your
loyal hearts, my dear ones, shall be in vain, and none of the
kindnesses your love has shown me.

I have arrived here safely, a bit tired, as always happens
when the heart is full and stirred and our thoughts are working
more busily and we nevertheless have to pursue our ordinary
course here on earth. But if only I could always walk on so
between heaven and earth for the rest of my life, equal in
humility and faith, and earn that way the sweet sleep and rest
we hope for.

From now on I will never let discontent gain the upper hand
within me. But pride too shall bend before what is above and
around us. It is certain, I cannot believe it to be otherwise, if I
do what I have to do I too shall fulfil my purpose in life on this
earth as far as humanly possible and be content yet despite the
ordeals of my youth.

I hope to be in as good health at the end of the coming
journey as I am now. Circumstances oblige me to stop here
until Saturday.

Landauer, good friend that he is, intends to accompany me with my other friends as far as Tübingen, which will give me a good start for the rest of the journey. He says you can arrange to have the pieces of furniture collected here whenever you like, straightaway or later.

If he finds a good buyer he says he will dispose of the writing-table.

I shall probably be able to write once more before I leave. It is a real need for me, my dear family, to express to you, as often as I can, what is in my heart.

Believe me, my esteemed Mother, and you my dear, good Sister and Brother, the sincerity, the innocence, the purity of heart that I have experienced in each of you from boyhood, like a voice from the heavens, before I even knew what it was, and that I now recognize and honour as the ground of all that is good and true and close to the gods, – this, this is what would remain unforgettable to me in you, even if I were ever able to forget all the other kindnesses your hearts have blessed me with.

Give my love to all my friends.

Yours,
Hölderlin

95. *To Anton von Gonzenbach*

[Stuttgart, early January 1801]
Allow me, before I can do it in person, to express my sincere thanks for your kind offer of a situation and a function that will be so good and valuable for me. I am bound to respect all you have done to oblige me; I for my part can only promise you good will and attentiveness towards what will be my duties in your house, together with candour and loyalty. And when you say that you attach importance to what it will be my job to achieve, you will certainly also be aware how much value and goodness there is for me in living in the sphere of a family who knows how to be content with itself and exercises daily

the most difficult and loveliest of virtues, that of being happy. Even if I were only an observer amongst you, such an image of peace would be enough for me. I beg you not to take these words as idly spoken.

As in your kindness you have confidence in my capacities as a tutor in general I expect that the particular things I shall have to take account of can wait until we meet and talk.

I hope to set off on [ ] January.

Be so kind as to offer my respects to your esteemed family. I thank your son again and will no doubt often have cause to thank him for having made the separation from my friends and family at home easier by his presence and courtesy and for rendering it so desirable for me to earn the chance to live among a family that he represents so well. In loyalty and truth I am

your obliged

M. Hölderlin

96. To Heinrike Breunlin

[Stuttgart, early January 1801]

My dear Rike,

One last time then from here.

I am ready for my journey. Everything is packed and in order. Yesterday I wrote to Hauptwil, and my only concern is not to let my friends notice any traces of sadness in me.

I shall only be able to enjoy your dear unforgettable words properly once I have the peace and quiet of Hauptwil.

I'll write from Constance, even if only a few words, just so that you will know I'm safe. We two understand each other so well that even the simplest and briefest of words say what is needed and replace the best and deepest utterance of our loyalty to one another.

You know that one is often calm and quiet even though the heart is full. That is how it is with me now. I could not find words for all that I should be saying to you every day and hour,

my dearest, and so it is better for me to give up the attempt and
right up until the end keep to this dry and unmomentous way
of saying goodbye.

Take good care of yourselves, and remain content and joyful in spirit, in the spirit that even in the most painful hours
of parting makes us feel entire the happiness of our related
hearts.

The clear sky can also serve us as a reminder of each other,
if things stay as they are, and be a comfort to us. I shall not
try now to express my thanks for all that you are to me and
all you have done for me but preserve it in my soul, alive
and true.

Goodbye, Sister and friend. Kiss your children for me. Have
your joy in them as I do too. And let our dear mother and our
good brother, since I am far away and your heart is rich and
abundant enough, partake in my name of the love that sweetens
and lightens their life and yours and gives us strength for all
the good in life.

Yours ever,

Friz

97. To Johanna Christiana Gok

Hauptwil, near Constance, 24 January 1801

Dear Mother,

Please accept the good news I am able to give you of my
situation here as a first form of thanks for all the kind and loyal
care you have shown me, especially during the time I spent at
home.

I can really say, and I have been convinced of this throughout
the 10 days I have been here, that the large family I am living
with consists of people among whom one can only live in
contentment, with the soul at rest – there is so much cheerful
innocence among the children and such common sense, such
fine goodness, among the older members. The master of the

house in particular I hold to be a good and admirable man who seems especially knowledgeable and wide in experience for someone of his class, while preserving a simplicity that interests me greatly. He brings to bear a quiet, undemanding, but very real presence on his children (of whom the oldest is married and also lives in the house).

On this occasion I won't go into any further descriptions; suffice it to say that as things are I am contented and my work is on a good footing and going well, and I hope that in years to come people will be as contented with me as they are now, and you, who are dearest to me, will always hear good report of me and one day be able to stop worrying about me at last. I am also in the best of health. How pleased I shall be to hear something from you again soon and feel the nearness of your love. You are so good to me. I am very glad that last year I lived not far from you all for a proper length of time. I had become so estranged from other people and with you I felt once again, and perhaps for the first time with any clarity, that with you, for as long as I live, there remains a refuge for my heart and a lasting joy that no one can take from me. Next time I will write to my dear sister and to Karl separately. The letter I sent from Constance you will probably have received by now. I shall be able to settle at least part of what I owe you with my next letter. Herr Gonzenbach has already instructed me to name my travelling expenses, and as soon as the opportunity arises I shall present him with what I have worked out.

I am obliged to end here. I am expected and the letter must be off by this evening.

Maintain your love for me, dear Mother, and make the most of the peaceful times that will now come. And it is proper for you to spend the years of maturity you now enjoy more in pleasure and calm and serenity than you have done till now. You have done so much for us! And you know yourself that not everyone is blessed in having such a mother, such a daughter and such grandchildren before her eyes every day.

And your absent sons are devoted enough to you to live in such a way as withstands your strictest judgement.

Give my regards to my venerable grandmother.

Ever your loyal son,

Hölderlin

My address is: c/o Herr Anton Gonzenbach in Hauptwil, near Constance.

I have successfully delivered Fräulein Schwab's letter. They had warm memories of her there.

98. *To Heinrike Breunlin*

Hauptwil, near St Gallen, 23 February 1801

My dear Sister,

I am writing to you and the rest of the dear family on the day when among us here all is full of the news of the negotiated peace, and knowing me as you do I do not need to tell you what my feelings are. And this morning, when the head of the household greeted me with the news, I hardly knew what to say. But the clear blue of the sky and the pure sunlight on the Alps close by were all the more welcome to my eyes at that moment since otherwise I should not have known where to look in my joy.

I think all will now be well in the world. Whether I consider the recent or the distant past, everything seems to be leading up to an exceptional period, days of beautiful humanity, days of certain, fearless goodness and ways of thinking that are lucid and holy and exalted and simple all at once.

This and the grandeur of nature in these parts wonderfully lifts and fills my soul. You would be as struck as I am by these shining eternal mountains, and if the God of glory has a throne on earth it is above these splendid peaks.

I can only stand there like a child and wonder and rejoice in silence when I'm out on the nearest hill and down from the ether come the heights stepping closer and closer into the friendly valley whose slopes are thick with the evergreen of fir woods and whose floor is seamed through with lakes and streams, & that's where I live, in a garden, where under my window willows and poplars stand by a clear water I love to listen to at night when all is quiet and beneath the serene starry sky I write and think.

You see, Rike, I look on my stay here as a man who has gone through a good deal in his youth and is now content and untroubled enough to give thanks from the bottom of his heart for what is there. And the more at peace I am, the more brightly and animatedly the memories of you dear ones far away quicken within me, and yes, I shall say it, since I feel it so vividly, should yet happier days be in store for me you and all we love will only be more unforgettable. In the meantime I shall rely on living with a good conscience and doing my duty; for the rest, let God decide. And if the only happiness the future held for me were to be able to see you and mother and our brother and your children again from time to time, and be a guest at your table, that would be enough.

That mother in her kindness intends to dispense me once again from repaying what I owe her goes against our agreement. She must at least allow me to thank her in some other way than in these words, which come so easily.

Keep in good health and please persuade our dear mother and grandmother to go out for a walk in the country from time to time in the spring, so that it becomes a habit. I have great faith in this and believe it makes for a long life and strengthens the mind.

Give Karl my apologies for not having written yet. But he knows as well as I do that we are always close and belong to one another for ever. Still, all that is good and sacred must be celebrated, and for that reason our correspondence should never remain interrupted for too long. But then the letters to you are meant for him as well, as for all the dear family.

Goodbye, and write again soon.

Yours,

H.

99. *To Christian Landauer*

[Hauptwil, February 1801]

My dear Landauer,

I wanted to leave writing to you until I had collected myself here and looked around a bit, and I think I can say that I hope to hold my own in the present situation.

The contact with you and the other friends has brought me real gains, something I always lacked and will try to make the most of. With you I learnt for the first time a proper peace, the peace that comes from relying on the ground of people's hearts after having got to know them by genuine signs. And then one is also more firmly and truly attached to life and to those that matter.

I can make good use of this with the people I'm living among now. They are, in my coolest judgement, exactly what I hoped for, the kind of well-founded people who take an interest in things outside their sphere just to the degree that their hearts are not weakened by it and their sympathy and sociableness remain unforced and true.

That is precisely the reason I will never forget you all, and during the best hours I spend in company here I am reminded of you.

Really I should like to send each of you a personal greeting and say to each how true it is that a lovely echo of our time together in Stuttgart stays with me, and particularly during the journey was my accompaniment morning and evening.

I am still greatly struck by the Alps which are a few hours distant from here; nothing has ever made such an impression on me before. I stand before them and they are like a wondrous legend from the heroic youth of our mother earth and remind me of the old creative chaos as they look down in their calm and above their snow in the brighter blue the sun and the stars shine down day and night.

And now, at the beginning of spring, you can well imagine the good all the elements are doing me and how I feed my eyes on the hills and streams and lakes round here, this being the first spring in three years I can enjoy with a free soul and open senses.

My dear friend, I have long harboured delusions which have been a burden to me and to others and a disgrace in the eyes of the Lord of life and my guardian spirit. I always thought that in order to live at peace with the world, to love other people and to look on the holiness of nature with true eyes, I had to submit, and in order to be something to anyone else give up my own freedom. At last I feel the truth: only where the strength is whole can love be. This truth has come upon me unawares in moments when I looked around me completely pure and free again. The more certain a person is in himself and the more collected in the best of his life, and the more easily he raises himself up out of subordinate moods into the true individual one again, the brighter and more encompassing his eye will be, and he will have a heart for everything that is easy and difficult and great and dear to him in the world.

I would of course have begun by speaking of the peace but the first pages of this letter were written I think a fortnight ago. What pleases me most about it is that with it the over-important role political alliances and misalliances have played is over and a good beginning has been made towards the simplicity that is proper to them. In the end it's true, the less people know and experience of the state, whatever form it takes, the freer they are.

It is everywhere a necessary evil to have compulsory laws and their executors. With the end of war and revolution I think that inner Boreas, the spirit of envy, will also cease, and let us hope a lovelier form of sociability than the merely solid and bourgeois will unfold!

Forgive me, dear Landauer, if I'm boring you going on like this in my thoughts. But to you I can surely speak as if I were speaking to myself.

Make sure you keep me in good remembrance with the ladies if you want to do me a service. You'll laugh at me, but I must thank you especially for the golden hours of music. The genial tones repose within me and will often stir again whenever I'm at peace with myself and it's quiet round about.

Remember me to all the friends. I think they know and feel that I'm true to them. With each in turn I hold conversations; no one that was dear to me has faded from my mind's eye. Goodbye.

Yours,

H.

100. *To Christian Landauer*

[Hauptwil, ~ March 1801]

I have just received your second letter, my good and loyal friend, and in your gentle rebuke I feel keenly what you are to me and always will be.

I haven't yet worked out when the post goes from here. Altogether my head has been a bit confused over the last few weeks.

Oh you know it, you understand me perfectly when I say that the longer I have kept it from myself the more suddenly it comes over me, this, that I have a heart but can't see what for, have no one to talk to here, no one I can wholly open myself to.

Tell me, is it a blessing or a curse, this loneliness which is part of my nature and which, however carefully I seek out situations meant in every respect to help me out, I am all the more irresistibly driven back into? – If only I could spend a day with you all, reach you my hands. – My dear friend, if you go to Frankfurt, think of me. Will you? I hope I shall always be worthy of my friends.

Yours,

H.

101. *To Karl Gok*

[Hauptwil, ~ March 1801]

My dear Karl,

I feel we no longer love one another as before and have not done for a long time, and this is my fault. *I was the first to introduce the cold tone*. At the beginning of my time in Homburg, do you remember the letters you wrote me then? But an unbelief in eternal love took hold of me. And I was to slip into the terrible superstitious error of believing in what is indeed a *sign* of the soul and of love, but if taken to be more than that is the death of them. Believe me when I tell you I struggled until I was almost dead with exhaustion to keep hold of the higher life where I could see it and believe in it – I underwent sufferings which, so it seems, are more overwhelming than anything a man can withstand with all his powers of endurance. – I mean every word of this. – And finally, my heart torn at from every side but still holding firm, I had to go and let my thoughts get caught up in bad doubts over a question whose answer is so straightforward when our minds are clear: what is more important, temporality or eternal life? Only too great a lack of esteem for all that has to be could have led me into an even greater error, which was, to a disproportionate degree and with a quite superstitious seriousness, to have regard for and attach importance to all things external, to everything that does not lie in the domain of the heart. But I carried on until I had learnt the truth. And having learnt it I tore myself from my mistakes to say this: that all is lost if unity and holy, general love are lost, which make the love of a brother so easy. There is only one quarrel in the world: what is more important, the whole or the particular? And whenever it is put to the test this quarrel cancels itself out in action, since the person who acts truly out of a sense of the whole is of his own accord more ordained to peace and more disposed to attend to the particular because his human sense, precisely what most belongs to him, becomes just as unlikely to let him fall into pure generality as into egoism or whatever you want to call it.

A Deo principium. Whoever understands this and keeps to it, by the life of life, he is free and strong and full of joy, and the opposite is always a chimera and as such melts into nothing.

So let that hold for us too in this renewal of friendship which is anything but empty ceremony or whim: *a Deo principium.*

I still think the way we used to, but now apply it more concretely. All is an infinite unity, but in this totality there is one supreme unifying *unity* which *in itself is not an I*, and this, to us, is God.

I speak as if I wanted to prove something to someone who did not believe, and my heart is always so full of the life of those who love what is holy. Tell me what this means. You can see into my heart. Is there still unbelief? Unbelief in a lovely understanding where one does speak, and with all the clarity that comes from joy, but where one takes the friendship of the other as a fact and rejoices in him in every syllable, but without being insistent? Yes, it is unbelief, but not in the other's heart, which belongs to the whole and so also to me. As if the two of us didn't have to love each other, just as we love something higher which in order to be expressed and honoured needs two brothers and more, needs brothers and sisters, a whole world of human beings. Brother of mine! The good do not abandon one another. They cannot as long as they are good and the whole in which they are comprised is good. Only often the means are missing for the different parts to communicate, very often among us human beings the signs and words are still missing. And so you see we have to remind one another, make up for what has been neglected, by speaking, by speaking out to say what we are to each other and what for. The misuse of words, falsifying them or not keeping them, is very wrong, but so certainly is not using them enough. And with this letter I do not mean any more than that we should begin again, as if from the start. In the future, whenever we feel how cold our words are when we speak, the more we will try to put our souls and our loyalty to one another into them, the more all that is good will come to life within us. And then the moments when we finally succeed in coming out with something proper and right, when as brother to brother, as man to man, as human soul to human soul we are present in living witness to something sacred and joyful, those moments will be worth all our hopes and any measure of success.

Here in this innocence of life, here under the silver Alps, I shall at last breathe more easily and freely again. I am chiefly occupied in studying religion. You, with your youthful energy and solitude, with that glorious feeling on which, as on a rock, everything divine is founded, the feeling of carrying out your duty, you will also stand truly beside me. A single word spoken from the untrammelled soul is so much, and you know how much. Above all I ask you, you above all, to tell me your heart's opinion on anything that touches on the subject, and to listen to what I have to say to you as a brother so as to be able to say, with the authority only a brother can have: this or that was not for me. Firm faith, inviolable honesty and pure, free openness, let us live by them!

What would life be without flowers like these? But bound together in such truth, in a bond that reaches to the heavens, we also see with the eyes of a higher being, and in the clear element that the spirit receives and creates we move with much more lightness and power and find then our place in the world. And those that are not yet born, they will feel it in times to come too.

These golden hopes are still with me, my dear Karl, as they are also with you.

Goodbye. And write soon. You will feel a sense of joy already. I know, and you must know it too: in the coming years we shall mean a great deal to one another.

Your brother
Hölderlin

102. *To Friedrich Schiller*

Nürtingen, near Stuttgart, 2 June 1801

For a long time I have held hopes of finding the occasion to remind you of my existence again, honoured Sir, and I just wanted to bring to completion the work on some papers before showing them to you. You must almost have given me up, and I thought it would be not unpleasant for you to see that I have not quite been overwhelmed by the pressure of circumstances and that to an extent at least I live and try to develop further in a manner worthy of your old generosity towards me. But now I am obliged to write sooner than I originally intended. My wish one day to live near you, in Jena, has become a virtual necessity and as I have weighed up the pros and cons the only thing left for me to do is to apply for your authorization of this course, since I can do nothing without your approval.

My experience so far has shown me that it is not possible for me to sustain a completely independent existence while working with complete independence.

For that reason, with only rare interruptions, I have mostly lived as a tutor, and though on the whole I have done what was required of me I have repeatedly had to suffer the dissatisfaction of others when I have been inept, or their oppressive compassion if for once I seemed to be having some success. In such situations I very often thanked you from the bottom of my heart for having given me by your companionship a joy that no unhappy hour has yet been able to extinguish in me. But nevertheless my patience gradually turned into something of a passion, and I always found myself, when in doubt, taking the course that was more likely to lead to my sacrificing the true aims of my life to the needs of others. Now I am aware, and am quite lucid about it, that it is not impossible to come to terms with being prevented from living out one's personal vocation, but false resignation is just as liable to come to a bad end as too great a rashness. This is particularly apparent to me now, when, unless something else turns up, in a few weeks I shall be obliged to go and act as a curate to some parish priest in the country. It is not that I do not acknowledge the possible worth and particular joys this sphere may have. But I can see that the type of work and the whole style that have now become part and parcel of this kind of post contrast so greatly with my way of expressing myself that the contradiction would end up making me lose all facility of communication.

For years almost my sole preoccupation has been with Greek

literature. Once I had embarked on this study it was not possible for me to stop until it had given me back the freedom which at the beginning it can so easily take away, and I believe I am in a position to be of particular use to younger people who are interested by freeing them from servitude to the Greek letter and helping them understand that the great clarity these writers have is a consequence of their abundance of spirit.

I have also been prompted to form particular ideas about the necessary equivalence of supreme principles and pure methods that are necessarily different, which put into full context and presented with proper definition might be apt to shed some light on the cultural sphere and on those areas that are excluded from it.

I beg you, esteemed Sir, to read these self-laudatory words which the circumstances force from me with your customary kindness, and above all not to think that in telling you about myself so directly and at such length I might have forgotten the modesty proper towards someone greater than myself.

I only wanted to put to you candidly the reasons that convince me that it would make quite good sense for me to go to Jena and try to devote the larger part of my time to giving lectures there, which, as I understand it, I am permitted to do.

I do not really expect a large number of people to attend, but as many as usually come to lectures of this kind. I hope also that I should not be getting in the way of anybody else.

Should you advise against it, that will help me settle into some other course, and I shall see how to keep myself going.

You will not disdain to brighten up my life and its development a little by taking an interest in it, because after all I am not otherwise so vain as to seek to give it a significance it does not have.

You are the joy of a whole nation, probably something you rarely see. Perhaps it might not seem completely without value for you then to see a new pleasure in life unfold in one who honours you unconditionally, and to know yourself the origin of it.

I should forget a lot, a very great deal, the moment I were to see you again and greet you with the awe I felt when I met you for the first time.

Yours truly,
Hölderlin

103. To Immanuel Niethammer

Nürtingen, near Stuttgart, 23 June 1801

My esteemed friend,

I have plucked up the courage to break the silence that has established itself between us since you found it necessary to stop writing to me. I hesitate to remind you of myself again, for the reason that drives me to do so is so out of the ordinary that it might surprise you. But I am confident that you will not hold the pleasure I have in communicating with you against me, and the more so when I think of the sympathy with which you watched over me in days gone by, and of the friendship I used to enjoy.

The need to write to you has become irrefutable, for I have now reached the point where I require your advice, which you never refused me when I asked for it in the past.

The last few years I have lived in conditions which were not appropriate to my life-plan and in which I only rarely felt the happiness of being content with my state.

I did not want to enter a clerical office, and now, at the age of 31, it makes me uncomfortable to consider the prospect of becoming a curate and having to depend on a vicar. Work as a tutor, which presented itself as a possibility and which I have indeed practised, appeared to me to be worthwhile only for the reason that everyday life with the children entrusted to my care made it possible to nurture their intellectual development from within and, through the daily instruction I gave them, to awaken in them the consciousness that one day they would have to continue along the path of education alone. But the changeful conditions in which the life of a private tutor unfolds did not correspond to either my nature or my life-plan, and so it was always my endeavour to follow this with a period of independence in which it was possible to employ myself according to my own lights. And so I lived for almost two years in Homburg in the company of my friend Sinclair, and there was able to work entirely in my own way and pursue literary studies.

Recently I have returned home to Swabia from Switzerland, where I spent a not very happy time as a tutor. And here an old project which I had all but abandoned has lodged itself in my mind again, so firmly that every day I reflect on how it might best be realized. In my life I have only too often had the experience of seeing my plans and desires, however closely they corresponded to my nature, far exceed reality and end up squashed by the circumstances which fate had ordained my life to adopt. I want to change my situation and am resolved not to continue any longer my present life as a freelance writer. I have in mind to go to Jena and should like to make myself useful there by giving lectures in the field of Greek literature, which in the past few years has formed the greater part of my occupations. I should like to show young people who are interested what the characters of the great works are and explain to them what sort of spirit was capable of organizing the material and releasing the poetic life in it. Such an activity now suits my purpose entirely, and I expect from it a turn for the better in my life.

What I intend will not have anything to do with the kind of questions a mere etymological or linguistic erudition might raise. I also hope not to clash with Counsellor Schütz and Professor Tennemann, as I have heard that both these gentlemen give lectures on subjects in Greek literature.

I have already written to Counsellor Schiller and put to him the grounds which prompt me to change the situation of my life. I know you are friendly with him and so I hope it is not presumptuous of me to ask you to have a talk with him about my plan, including whether it is possible to assure my existence and give my activities stability in a position at the university.

It would be a great help to me if you could make some comment on this important decision soon. Your advice, whatever it is, will be dear to me in any case.

Be assured that the memory of your friendship is always a comfort to me, and let me tell you that the expectation of soon living near you again fills me with joy.

Ever yours,

Fr. Hölderlin

Fondest good wishes to Schelling.

104. *To the family*

[Stuttgart, ~ October/November 1801]

My dear family,

This time I have so much to thank you for that it would be better to say nothing at all than the little I should confine myself to now. Know that to be certain of hearts like yours, to have been convinced of your sympathy and loyalty on so many occasions and to grow in that conviction – this is a happiness in my life that is worth speaking about and more so than many other things I have to do without and do without willingly. And if my situation should change, I ask you to look at it from the best point of view. I should have an existence free from anxiety together with an occupation which has become a habit with me, and with any luck I shall find good people. I must enter into the life of dependence in one form or another, and educating children is an especially happy business now, because it is so innocent.

Yours,

Friz

105. *To Karl Gok*

Nürtingen, 4 December 1801

My dear Karl,

I come to take my leave. But let us not complain – in cases like this I always prefer to keep the mind content and in honour of God pass over sadness to focus on what is good.

This much I can confess: that in all my life I have never been so firmly rooted to my home country, never in my life have I valued being with my friends and relations so much, and felt so great a reluctance to leave them.

But I have the sense that it is better for me to be out of the country, and you, dear Karl, know very well yourself that for the one as for the other, to stay put or to travel abroad, we need God's protection if we are to survive. For you, it is above all keeping busy that maintains you in your way of life. Otherwise things would become too narrow for you. What I need, essentially, is to manage to do what I have set out to achieve. Otherwise I would be swept away into distraction.

The main thing is that the old love between us two brothers should not fail. It is a sacred happiness when despite different ways of life human beings are held together by bonds such as the one between us. That is the greater meaning that everywhere spurs us on and saves us. And men in particular do not need to resemble one another in their souls for there to be love between them. But without this openness of heart there can be no happiness for them. O Karl, forgive me, so that things can be pure between us.

Goodbye then. Things will go well for you at home since you are so well founded in what you do. Think of me sometimes.

Yours,
Hölderlin

106. *To Casimir Ulrich Böhlendorff*

Nürtingen, near Stuttgart, 4 December 1801

My dear Böhlendorff,

Your kind words and your presence in them gave me much pleasure.

Your *Fernando* has done me a great deal of good, I breathe more easily. The progress of my friends seems to me such a good sign. We share the same fate. If one of us advances then the other will not be far behind.

Dear Böhlendorff, you have gained so much in precision and supple efficiency and lost nothing in warmth; on the contrary, like a good blade, the elasticity of your mind has proven to be all the stronger in the school of constraint. This is what I congratulate you for above all. Nothing is harder for us to learn than the free use of what we are born with. And it is my belief that clarity of exposition is originally as natural to us as heavenly fire is to the Greeks. For precisely that reason the Greeks are more likely to be *surpassed* in fine passion, which is what you have managed to keep, than in the presence of spirit and faculty for exposition we find in Homer.

It sounds paradoxical. But I put it to you again, for you to verify and make use of as you wish: in the process of civilization what we are actually born with, the national, will always become less and less of an advantage. For that reason the Greeks are not such masters of sacred pathos, because it was native to them; on the other hand they are exceptional in their faculty for exposition, from Homer onwards, because this extraordinary man had the feeling necessary to capture the *Junonian sobriety* of the occident for his Apollonian realm, and so truly to appropriate the foreign.

With us it is the other way round. That is also why it is so dangerous to derive our aesthetic rules from the sole source of Greek excellence. I have laboured at this for a long time and know now that apart from what must be the supreme thing with the Greeks and with us, that is, living craft and proportion, we cannot properly have anything in common with them.

But what is our own has to be learnt just as much as what is foreign. For this reason the Greeks are indispensable to us. Only it is precisely in what is proper to us, in the national, that we shall never match them because as I said, the *free* use of what is our *own* is hardest of all.

And it seems to me that your good genius has prompted you to give the dramatic form a more epic treatment. Taken as a whole, it is a *genuine* modern tragedy. For that is the tragic with us, to go away from the kingdom of the living in total silence packed up in some kind of container, not to pay for the flames we have been unable to control by being consumed in fire.

And in truth our innermost soul is moved as much by one as by the other. It is not such an imposing fate, but a deeper one, and a noble soul accompanies with fear and pity someone dying in that way too, and holds the spirit up amid the fury. Jupiter in his splendour will always be the last thought when a mortal perishes – whether he dies according to ancient destiny or according to ours – if the poet has presented this death as he should and as you clearly intended to and on the whole and particularly in several masterly touches have done:

> A narrow path leads to a sombre valley,
> Where treachery has forced him into refuge

and other places. – You are on the right path, keep to it. But I want to study your *Fernando* properly and take it to heart, and then perhaps say something more interesting to you about it. It can never be enough!

As to myself and what has happened to me up until now, how far I have remained and become worthy of you and my friends, and what I am working on and, such as it is, will soon produce, I'll tell you all about that in my next letter which will come to you from the vicinity of your Spain, that is from Bordeaux, where I set off next week to be a private tutor and preacher in a German Protestant household. I shall have to keep a hold of my wits in France, in Paris; and I look forward too to seeing the sea, and the sun of Provence.

O my friend, the world lies more brightly before me than usual, and is more serious. Yes, it pleases me the way things are, pleases me like in summer when 'with a calm hand the holy father of old shakes lightning like blessings from the ruddy clouds'. For among all that I can see of God this sign has become my chosen one. Before, I could shout for joy about a new truth, a better conception of what is above and around us; now I fear that I might end up like old Tantalus who got more of the gods than he could stomach.

But I do what I can as well as I can, and think, when I see that I on my path must go where all the others go too, that it is god-forsaken and madness to look for a path out of all danger – there exists no plant to remedy death.

And so, goodbye, dear Böhlendorff, for the time being. I am now full of parting. It's a long time since I have cried. But when I decided I had to leave my country, perhaps for ever, the tears came, and they were bitter. For what do I have in the world that is dearer to me? But they have no use for me. I will always be German and cannot do otherwise, even if the needs of my heart should drive me to Tahiti for nourishment.

Send greetings to Muhrbeck. How is he? He will be preserved, I'm sure. We shall not lose him. Forgive me the ingratitude. I had recognized you, I saw you, but through tinted glasses. There is so much I have to say to you, my good friends! It must be the same with you. Where will you live in future, my Böhlendorff? But those are just worries. If you write to me, address the letter to Landauer, merchant in Stuttgart. He will make sure it gets to me. Send me your address too.

Yours,

H.

107. *To Johanna Christiana Gok*

Lyons, 9 January 1802

My dear Mother,

You will be surprised to receive a letter from me in Lyons at this stage. I was obliged to stop in Strasburg longer than I expected for my passport, and the long journey here from Strasburg was made even longer by flooding and other unavoidable circumstances that held me up.

The journey so far has been hard and eventful but it has also given me many pure moments of joy. I cannot help admitting I thought of you sometimes and also of him who is a source of courage to me and has preserved me up until now and will continue to accompany me.

I know, a solitary occupation tends to make it harder to come to terms with the wide world; I think though that God and an honest heart help us to get by, and modesty towards other people.

I am still tired, dear Mother, from the long cold journey, and things are so lively here now that only by holding in intimate remembrance those who know us and can be said to be fond of us can we find our bearings again.

Tomorrow I set off for Bordeaux and should get there quickly as the roads are better now and the rivers are no longer in flood.

I forgot to say that it was the authorities in Strasburg who advised me, as a foreigner, to take the route via Lyons. So I shall not see Paris. And I am content that way.

I look forward to starting my proper job soon.

I will write you and the rest of the dear family a lot more from Bordeaux, when things are calmer.

Give my love to everyone.

Karl will be in Nürtingen by now. Think of me sometimes when in the evenings you are all sitting together. Ask my dear sister to remember the best hours we had together and to mention their uncle to the children sometimes.

I cannot thank you enough for all the kindness and support and sympathy.

I hope you are well.

Your loyal son,

Hölderlin

108. *To Johanna Christiana Gok*

Bordeaux, 28 January 1802

I'm here at last, dear Mother, have had a good welcoming, am in good health and will not forget the thanks I owe the Lord of life and death. – I can only write a few words for the moment; I arrived this morning, and my attention is too much taken up with my new situation for me to be able to tell you with the necessary calm some of the interesting things about the journey I now have behind me. Moreover, so much has happened to me that I can scarcely begin to talk about it yet.

These last few days I have been walking in nothing but fine spring weather, but not long before, high up in the snowy hills of the fearful Auvergne, in storms and wilderness, the nights icy-cold and a loaded pistol beside me in the rough beds – I prayed a prayer then that was the best of my whole life and that I shall never forget.

I am preserved – give thanks, as I do.

My dears, once I was out of danger I greeted you like someone reborn and reproached myself immediately for not having made special mention of my dear grandmother in the last letter from Lyons, I spoke to you, dear Mother, saw my sister before me, and in my head, full of joy, began to write Karl a hopeful, solemn letter.

I am now hardened through and through, initiated as you could wish. I think I shall remain so, in the main. Fearing nothing and enduring a good deal. What good a safe refreshing sleep will do me. My accommodation is almost too grand. I would be happy with secure simplicity. My work will I hope go well. I want to devote myself to it entirely, and make a good start. Take care of yourselves. With all my heart and sincerity,

Yours,

H.

PS. My letter has been delayed a few days. I have begun to get acquainted and to assume my duties, and could not have made a better start. 'You will be happy here', the Consul said to me when he received me. I think he was right.

109. To Johanna Christiana Gok

Bordeaux, Good Friday 1802

My dear Mother,

Do not misunderstand me if I express more the necessary composure at the loss of our now blessed grandmother than the grief which the love in our hearts feels. I find that without a certain firmness of mind it is difficult to get by; I do not want to give counsel to my family but for my part I must preserve and maintain my soul, which has already undergone so many ordeals, and the good and tender words that, as you know, come off my tongue so easily, I must be sparing with them for now, it is not right for me to upset you and myself even more. The new and pure life, which, as I believe, the departed enjoy after death and which is also the reward for those who, like our dear grandmother, lived their life in holy simplicity, this youth in heaven which is now hers, which for so long her soul longed for, this peace and joy after suffering, will also be your reward, dear Mother, dear Sister; and probably a noble death, a safe passage from life into life, awaits my brother and me also as, I believe, it does all those we hold dear.

In the meantime may a true and constant spirit be with us, and heaven on high grant that we not be idle, and be measured in what we do, and carry out the role we have chosen with felicity.

Things here could hardly be better. And I hope gradually to

come to deserve all that my situation gives me and when one day I come home again not to be completely unworthy of the truly excellent people I am obliged to in this place.

Think of me often, my dear ones, but do not let it disrupt your own concerns. For my brother I wish that he may continue to prosper in his sphere, in his affairs, as he has done up till now.

The little children will be giving you a great deal of pleasure, and you are fortunate to be surrounded in that way, by living images of hope, as I am by my pupils. Send my love to my friends, and tell them I'm sorry not to have written: being so far away and having so much to do has prompted me to be economical with letters for the moment. What we are to one another remains unchanged.

Yours truly,

H.

110. *To Casimir Ulrich Böhlendorff*

[Nürtingen, ~ November 1802]

My dear friend,

I have not written to you for a long time, have since been in France and seen the sad solitary earth, the shepherds of southern France and individual beauties, men and women, who grew up in the fear of patriotic doubt and of hunger.

The violent element, the fire of the sky, and the quiet of the people, their life in the open and their straitenedness and contentment, stirred me continually, and as one says of heroes I can probably say of myself: that Apollo has struck me.

In the regions that border on the Vendée the wild, warlike quality interested me, the purely male, where the life-light is immediate in the eyes and limbs and which, feeling death, feels a kind of virtuosity and satisfies its thirst for knowledge.

The athleticism of people in the south, in the ruins of the ancient spirit, made me better acquainted with the true essence of the Greeks; I got to know their nature and their wisdom, their bodies, the way they grew up in their climate and the rules by which they protected their exuberance from the violence of the element.

This determined their popularity, their manner of receiving foreign natures and of communicating with them, this is the source of their peculiar individuality which appears alive in as much as supreme understanding in the Greek sense is the power of reflection, and we may grasp this if we learn to grasp the heroic body of the Greeks; this is tenderness, like our own popularity.

Seeing the antiquities left me with an impression that has helped me understand not only the Greeks themselves but all that is highest in art, which even where movement and the phenomenalization of concepts and of every aspect of serious meaning is at its height still keeps every part in place, entire and true to itself, so that surety, in this sense, is the supreme kind of sign.

After many shocks and commotions of soul I needed to find a firm footing, for a while, and I am now living in my home town.

Nature in these parts also stirs me more powerfully the more I study it. Storms, not just in their greatest manifestation, but seen as power and figure, among the other forms of the sky, the effect of the light, shaping nationally and as principle and destiny, so that something is holy to us, the intensity of its coming and going, the characteristicness of the woods and the coincidence in one region of different characters of nature, so that all the holy places of the earth are together in one place, and the philosophic light at my window, they are now my joy. May I keep in mind how I have come to where I am now!

My dear friend, I think that we will not annotate the poets up to our time, but that song will take on a quite different character and that we've had little success because since the Greeks we are the first to sing nationally and naturally again, with actual originality.

Make sure you write to me soon. I need your pure tones. Psyche among friends, the formation of thoughts in conversations and letters, is vital for artists. Otherwise we have none

for ourselves; but they belong to the holy image we are shaping.
Take good care of yourself.

Yours,

H.

111. *To Friedrich Wilmans*

Nürtingen, near Stuttgart, 28 September 1803
Excellent and highly esteemed Sir,
I am very grateful to you for having taken such a kind interest
in the translation of the Sophocles tragedies.

As I have not yet heard anything from my friend Schelling,
who had undertaken to approach the theatre in Weimar, I
prefer to follow the safer course of taking advantage of your
kind offer.

I am quite happy with the first volume's not appearing until
the spring book fair, especially as I have plenty of material to
preface the tragedies with an introduction which I shall probably be able to complete later in the autumn.

Greek art is foreign to us because of the national convenience
and bias it has always relied on, and I hope to present it to the
public in a more lively manner than usual by bringing out
further the oriental element it has denied and correcting its
artistic bias wherever it occurs.

I shall always be grateful to you for having sent your kind
letter when you did because you have given me an opportunity
to express myself at a point when I can write more out of a
sense of nature and more for my own country than usual.

I remain, Sir, with true esteem,
your most obedient servant
Friedrich Hölderlin

112. *To Friedrich Wilmans*

Nürtingen, near Stuttgart, 8 December 1803

Esteemed Sir,

Forgive me for the delay in sending the manuscripts of the Sophocles tragedies. I wanted, as I had a better view of the whole, to change a few things in the translation and the notes. The language in the *Antigone* did not seem lively enough. The notes did not express sufficiently my convictions about Greek art or the meaning of the plays. Even now I am still not satisfied with them. If you think it appropriate, I should like to send you a specially written introduction to the tragedies of Sophocles in the next six months or whenever else might be suitable.

I'll look out some short poems for an almanac from among my papers straight after sending off this manuscript. I have a few things you might like.

I haven't yet written to Schelling. But will do later this week.

If you should find it awkward to send the edition of these tragedies to Goethe or the Weimar theatre, be so kind as to let me know. As I am personally acquainted with Herr von Goethe it will not be out of place for me to send it myself.

Later this winter I also intend to send you single lyric poems of some length, 3 or 4 folio pages, each poem to be printed separately because they will deal directly with our country and the times.

I have been very glad of your kind encouragement. To have come into contact with you is for me a truly fortunate turn of events.

Your devoted servant,

Friedrich Hölderlin

113. *To Friedrich Wilmans*

Nürtingen, near Stuttgart, [late] December 1803

Esteemed Sir,

Thank you for having taken the trouble of sending me a sample of the print of the Sophocles tragedies. I think that with letters like these it is easier for the eyes to find the meaning, since with over-pointed letters one is easily tempted just to look at the type.

The physical beauty of the printing does not seem to lose anything because of it, not to me at least. It makes the lines stand more firmly balanced.

I am in the middle of going through a few Night Poems for your almanac. But I wanted to reply to your letter directly to prevent any sense of frustration from coming into our relationship.

It is a joy to sacrifice oneself to the reader and to enter with him into the narrow limits of our still child-like culture.

In my view love poems are always a weary flight, for we are still no further forward now, despite the difference of materials. The high and pure rejoicing of poems on our times is another thing altogether.

The prophetic quality of the *Messias* and of certain odes is an exception.

I am very eager to know how you will react to the sample of several longer lyric poems. I hope to send them to you in January; and if your judgement of this experiment is the same as mine it will probably be possible for them to appear in time for the spring book fair.

The introduction to the tragedies of Sophocles I intend to write separately, at the latest in time for the autumn fair; it will then be for you to decide, esteemed Sir, whether you want to make use of it or not.

I hope to send you soon an answer from Schelling.

I will try to find some subscribers in Stuttgart for the edition of the *Views* you have been so kind to send me a prospectus of.

I am acquainted with a number of people there who might buy such works and could recommend them to others.

With all my regards, dear friend, and until a further sign of my devotion,

Hölderlin

114. To Leo von Seckendorf

Nürtingen, 12 March 1804

My dear friend,

I recently tried to visit you, but could not find your house. So I am fulfilling the duty that necessitated this visit in writing, and send you the prospectus of some picturesque views of the Rhine; possibly you could subscribe, and find other subscribers. The Prince has already shown an interest. I am eager to see how they will turn out – whether they will be pure and simple reproductions of nature, so that on both sides nothing extraneous and uncharacteristic is included and the earth achieves a good balance with the sky, and such that the light, which defines the particular proportions of this balance, is not oblique and deceptively attractive. A great deal probably depends on the angle within the work of art and on the frame surrounding it.

The antiquities in Paris in particular have given me a genuine interest in art, so that I should like to study it more.

I would also ask you to take an interest in a translation of mine of the tragedies of Sophocles which has been accepted by the same publisher, Herr Wilmans in Frankfurt, and will come out at Easter.

Fable, the poetic view of history, and the architectonics of the sky preoccupy me above all at the moment, especially the national and its difference from the Greek.

I have gained a general sense of the various fates of the heroes, knights and princes – how they serve fate or relate to it in a more ambiguous manner.

I really should like to see you in Stuttgart sometime and have conversation with you. I truly value having as learned and humane a man as you among us. I have written as much to Herr von Sinclair.

I think there is a lot more I have to say to you. The study of our country, of its conditions and estates, is unending and at a very early stage.

That the good time may not become empty of spirit, and that we may find ourselves and one another again!

I think of the days of simplicity and quiet that may come. If the enemies of our mother country trouble us, a courage has been preserved, to defend against this other that does not quite belong to us. With humble regards,

Hölderlin

115. *To Friedrich Wilmans*

Nürtingen, near Stuttgart, 2 April 1804

Esteemed friend,

I have gone through the printer's errors in the *Oedipus*.

I almost preferred the raw print, probably because in this typography the traits which mark the solid aspect of the letters hold their own so well in relation to the modifying traits, and this was even more noticeable in the raw print than in the filed version. The inventor is often bashful towards his public, and his mannered courtesies then cause him to lose all trace of individuality, especially the solidity characteristic of this typography. That being said, refining the typography in this way is more of an apparent loss than a real one.

Once it is better known perhaps you will use the raw form of the first printing and leave it as it is, or give it a touch with the file.

I say this to show you how well I understand the quality of your work. And this over-severe use of the file only detracts from the solidity at first sight; if one sits with the pages set straight before one, or at a pure angle to them, the more solid traits appear clearly.

I only await the copies to send to Herr von Goethe and Herr von Schiller and to a few others who might be interested.

I should like to send a special copy to the Princess of Homburg. I do not know if you want to select special paper for it.

I am certain I have written in the direction of eccentric enthusiasm and thus reached Greek simplicity; I hope to continue to stick to this principle, even if that means exposing more boldly what was forbidden to the original poet, precisely by going in the direction of eccentric enthusiasm.

I look forward to sending you something very soon on which I place a particular value at the moment.

It is my wish that the ideas and points of contact which have brought this book about may come into contact as quickly as possible.

Goodbye for the time being, my dear Wilmans.

Your friend,

Hölderlin

116–20. *Five letters from Tübingen to Johanna Christiana Gok, 1807–28*

My esteemed Mother,
That I am allowed to take this opportunity of writing to you is far from disagreeable to me. After all, it is the compliments of my being, so dependent on you, and the attempts to open my devoted soul to your continuing kindness that I should like to assure you of in the contents of these letters, which are certainly not written without devotion. Do not take exception to my breaking off so soon. I am

your most obedient son

Hölderlin

My esteemed Mother,
Here I am writing to you again. The repetition of what one has written is not always an unnecessary state of affairs. It is founded in the nature of the matter that if one is exhorting

oneself to good and saying something serious to oneself it will not be taken amiss if one says the same as before and does not always come up with something out of the ordinary. I will content myself with that. I present my compliments to you in all obedience and am

your obedient son

Hölderlin

My esteemed Mother,
My letter-writing will not always mean a great deal to you as I have to say what I say, as far as possible, in few words, and as I now have no other way of saying. I take the liberty of asking you to look after me, as usual, with all your kindness, and not to doubt the good sentiments due to you. I am

your obedient son

Hölderlin

My esteemed Mother,
Forgive me if in its devotion to you my soul should look for words to seek to demonstrate its thoroughness and devotedness. I do not think my conceptions of you are very far wrong in respect of your virtuousness and kindness. But I should like to know in what ways I must exert myself to be worthy of that kindness, that virtuousness. As Providence has brought me thus far, I hope perhaps to continue my life without dangers and utter doubt. I am

your most obedient son

Hölderlin

Forgive me, dearest Mother, if I should be unable to make myself quite understood to you.

I repeat with all politeness what I have been able to have the honour of saying to you. Speaking as a scholar, I beg God in his goodness to help you in everything, and to help me.

Look after me. Time is literal and all-merciful.

I remain

your most obedient son

Friedrich Hölderlin

PART 2

ESSAYS

Translated by Jeremy Adler

'I was slumbering, my Callias . . .'[1]

I was slumbering, my Callias! And my slumber was sweet. Gracious twilight rested upon my spirit as upon the souls in Plato's first Elysium.[2] But the genius of Maionia[3] awoke me. Half in a rage he stepped before me, and my innermost being trembled at his call.

In sweet intoxication, I lay upon the coast of our archipelago, and my eye feasted upon him as he smiled at me so kindly and still, and the rose-coloured mist so benignly veiled the distance above him where you live, and further our heroes. Soft and sweet as the stroking hand of my Glycera,[4] the early morning air touched my cheek. I played with the gracious creature in childish dreams. –

Exhausted by glowing fantasies, I finally reached for my Homer.

By chance I found the place[5] where, following the day of battle, the cunning son of Laertes, and Diomedes the wild, walk after midnight through blood and weapons into the enemy camp, where the Thracians, exhausted from the day's work, are lying in a deep sleep, far from the fires of their watchmen. Diomedes rages all around like a furious lion among the sleepers. Meanwhile, Ulysses ties up the excellent horses as a joyful booty. And clears away the bodies that Diomedes' sword had slain, so that the horses do not shy, and whispers to his wild companion that it is time to go. Diomedes is still pondering some bold act. He wishes either to raise aloft a chariot standing beside him, full of sundry weapons, and carry it off, or to dispatch further Thracians to join the thirteen already struck by his sword. But Athene steps before him and exhorts him to return.

And now the joy of victory after the extraordinarily reckless deed! How they leap from their steeds at the friendly welcome from their brothers-in-arms, with sweet speech and a shake of the hands! and then to throw themselves into the cooling sea, to wash away the sweat, and strengthen their tired limbs, and now to sit down to the meal, made young again and in good spirits, and to their guardian Athene from their cups to pour sweet wine as a child-like sacrifice. O my Callias! that triumphant feeling of strength and bravery!

This was also prepared for you, a voice said to me, and I would have wished to hide my glowing face in the earth, so powerfully did shame take hold of me before our heroes and those of Homeros! I have now made up my mind, let it cost what it may.[6]

You should see how I forced my heart's stern exhortation to wear artificially cheerful colours, to make it more bearable for me, and so as to be able to smile upon this thought as a good idea, and forget it!

'There is a natural state . . .'[7]

There is a natural state of the imagination, which, though it has in common with that anarchy of ideas organized by the intellect a lawlessness, must nevertheless, with respect to the law by which it should be ordered, be distinguished from it.

By this natural state of the imagination, by this lawlessness, I mean the moral kind; and by this law, the law of freedom.

There, the imagination is considered as such, here, in relation to the appetite.

In that anarchy of ideas where the imagination is considered theoretically, a unity of the manifold, an order of perceptions, was indeed possible, but accidental.

In this natural state of the imagination where it is considered in connection with the appetite, moral lawfulness is indeed possible, but accidental.

There is a side to the empirical appetite, the analogue to that which is called nature, which is at its most striking where necessity and freedom, the limited and the unlimited, the sensuous and the sacred, appear to unite, a natural innocence, one would like to say a morality of the instinct, and the imagination which is in tune with it is heavenly.

However, as such this natural state also depends on natural causes.

It is pure good fortune to be thus attuned.

If the law of freedom did not exist, under which both the appetite and the imagination stand, there would never be a fixed state, which would be like the one just indicated, at least it would not be up to us, to hold it fast. Its opposite would also occur without us being able to prevent it.

But the law of freedom rules, without any regard for the assistance of nature. Whether or not nature is conducive to exercising the law, it rules. Indeed, it presupposes resistance in nature, otherwise it would not rule. The first time that the law of freedom expresses itself to us, it appears to punish. The origin of all our virtue arises through evil. Morality can therefore never be entrusted to nature. For even if morality did not cease to be morality as soon as the grounds for the determination of action lie in nature and not in freedom, then the legality, which could be produced through nature alone, could only be a very uncertain thing, changeable according to time and circumstance. Just as natural causes would be differently determined, this legality would[8]

On the Concept of Punishment[9]

It seems that the Nemesis of the ancients was not just represented as a daughter of the night because she is so terrible, but because of her mysterious origin.

It is the necessary fate of all enemies of principle, that with all their claims they end up in a circle. (Proof)

In the present case they would say: 'Punishment is the suffering of lawful resistance and the consequence of wicked acts. Wicked acts are those, namely, which are followed by punishment. And punishment follows where there are wicked acts.' They could not possibly name an independent criterion for a wicked act. For, if they are to be consistent, according to them the result must determine the value of an act. If they wish to avoid this, they have to argue from principle. If they do not do so and if they decide the value of an act by its results, then the results – morally considered – are based in nothing higher, and the lawfulness of the resistance is no more than a word, punishment is simply punishment, and if the mechanism or chance or arbitrariness, what you will, inflicts something unpleasant on me, then I know that I have acted wickedly, I have nothing more to ask, what happens happens lawfully, because it happens.

Now it certainly does seem as if something like this were the case where the original concept of punishment occurs, in moral consciousness. For there, namely, the moral law presents itself negatively, and, being infinite, cannot present itself in any other way. In the fact, however, the law is active will. For a law is not active, it is only imagined activity. This active will must be directed against another activity of the will. We ought not to want something: that is its immediate voice within us. We must therefore want something that the moral law opposes. But what the moral law is we neither knew earlier, before it opposed our will, nor do we know it now that it opposes us, we simply suffer its resistance as a result of the fact that we wanted something that is opposed to the moral law, and according to this result we decide the value of our will; because we suffered resistance we consider our will to be wicked, we cannot, it seems, further examine the lawfulness of the resistance, and if this is the case, we only recognize it from the fact that we suffer; it does not differ from any other suffering, and with the same right as I deduce a wicked will from what I call the resistance of the moral law, I deduce a wicked will from any other resistance that is suffered. All suffering is punishment.

There is, however, a difference between a ground of knowing and a real ground.* It is not at all the same thing if I once say: I recognize the law by its resistance, and then: I recognize the law on account of its resistance. Whoever treats the resistance of the law as its real ground is forced to perform the above circle. For them the law does not take place at all if they do not experience its resistance, their will is only contrary to the law because they experience it as contrary to law, if they suffer no punishment then they are not wicked. Punishment is what follows wickedness. And wickedness is what is followed by punishment.

But then there does not seem to be much to be gained from the distinction between the ground of knowing and the real ground. If the resistance of the law to my will is punishment and I can only know the law from the punishment, the question arises, firstly, can I know the law from the punishment? and secondly, can I be punished for transgressing a law that I did not know?

To this it may be answered that, insofar as one considers oneself punished, one necessarily presupposes the transgression of the law in oneself, and that in the punishment, insofar as one judges it a punishment, necessarily the[10]

*Ideal without punishment no law
real without law no punishment

Being Judgement Possibility[11]

Being – expresses the connection of subject and object.

Where subject and object are absolutely, not only partly, united, namely so united that no division can be executed without damaging the essence of that which is to be separated, there and nowhere else one can speak of a *being as such*, as is the case with intellectual intuition.[12]

But this being should not be confused with identity.[13] When I say: I am I, then the subject (I) and the object (I) are not united such that no separation can be executed without damaging the essence of that which is to be separated; on the contrary, the I is only possible by virtue of this separation of the I from the I. How can I say: I! without self-consciousness? But how is self-consciousness possible? By opposing me to myself, separating me from myself, but notwithstanding this separation recognizing myself in the opposition as one and the same. But to what extent the same? I can, I must ask this; for it is opposed to itself in another respect. Therefore identity is not a union of object and subject that takes place absolutely, therefore identity does not = absolute being.

Judgement is, in the highest and strictest sense, the primal separation[14] of the object and the subject that are most intimately united in intellectual intuition, that separation, by which object and subject first become possible, the original division. The concept of division itself contains the concept of a reciprocal relationship between object and subject, and the necessary premiss of a whole of which object and subject are the parts. 'I am I' is the most apposite example of this concept of an original division, as a *theoretical* division, since in the practical original division *I* is opposed to the *Not-I*, not to *itself*.

Reality and possibility are different, like mediate and immediate consciousness. If I think of an object as possible, then I am only repeating the prior consciousness by force of which it is real. There is for us no conceivable possibility that would not be a reality. Hence the concept of possibility does not apply at all to the objects of reason, because they never appear in consciousness as that which they ought to be, but only the concept of necessity. The concept of possibility applies to the objects of the understanding, that of reality to the objects of perception and observation.

Hermocrates to Cephalus[15]

So you seriously believe that the ideal of knowledge can be represented in a particular time in a particular system?

You even believe that the ideal has already been realized and that all that is missing from Jupiter Olympius is the pedestal?[16]

Perhaps! It depends especially on how the latter is taken.

But would it not be a curious thing if this of all forms of mortal striving were privileged in this way, if here of all places the perfection that everyone seeks and nobody finds existed?

I have always believed that for its knowledge as for its actions mankind needed an infinite progress, an unbounded time, in order to approach the boundless ideal; I called the opinion that science could be completed or was completed at a particular time scientistic quietism; there will always be error, whether it contents itself with an individually determined boundary or simply denies a boundary that is in fact there, even though it ought not to be.

That was of course possible under certain conditions, which at the proper time you should rigorously avail yourself of. In the meantime, let me ask whether the hyperbole really unites with its asymptote, whether the transition from[17]

Fragment of Philosophical Letters[18]

Must hold, and this and nothing else he means and must mean when he talks of a deity, if he speaks from his heart and not from a servile memory or from the standpoint of his profession. The proof lies in few words. Neither from himself alone, nor solely from the objects surrounding him, can man experience that there is more than machinery, that there is a spirit, a god, in the world, but he can in a more lively relation, raised above need, which he maintains to that which surrounds him.

And everyone would, according to this, have his own god, insofar as everyone has his own sphere in which he is active and which he experiences, and only insofar as several people have a common sphere, in which they are active and suffer humanly, that is, risen above need, only insofar do they have a common deity; and if there is a sphere in which all live simultaneously and to which they feel they maintain a relation beyond need, then, but only insofar, do they all have a common deity.

But one must not forget here that a human being can indeed also put himself in the place of another, can make the sphere of the other his own sphere, that therefore, naturally, the one cannot find it so difficult to approve the way of feeling and the representation of the divine which develops from the particular relations which he maintains to the world – unless that representation has emerged from a fanatical, an arrogant or a slavish life, from which, then, an equally needy, fanatical representation of the spirit that governs this life always develops, so that this spirit always bears the shape of a tyrant or of a slave. But even in a limited life man can live infinitely, and even the limited representation of a deity that emerges for him from his life can be an infinite one.   Elaboration.

So, just as someone can approve of the limited but pure way of life of another, he can also approve of the limited but pure mode of representation which the other holds of the divine. It is, on the contrary, a desire of human beings, as long as they are not hurt and angered, not dejected and not outraged and involved in a just or unjust struggle, to make, just as in many other matters, their different kinds of representation of the divine join one another, and thus to give the limitedness which every single kind of representation has, and must have, its freedom, in that it is contained in a harmonious whole of kinds of representation, and, at the same time, precisely because in every particular kind of representation lies also the meaning of the particular way of life which everyone has, to give the necessary limitedness of this way of life its freedom, in that it is contained in a harmonious whole of ways of life.

You ask me, why – even if man, according to his nature, rises above need and thus finds himself in a more manifold and more intimate relation to his world, even if, as *far* as he rises above physical and moral need, he always lives a higher human life, so that there is a higher, more than mechanical *connection*, a higher *fate* between him and his world, even if really this higher connection is most holy to him, since in it he feels himself and his world, and everything he possesses and is, as being united – why he has to *represent* the connection between himself and his world, why he has to form an idea or an image of his fate, which, strictly speaking, can neither really be thought, nor is available to the senses?

You ask me this, and all I can say by way of an answer is that man also rises above need to the extent that he can, and wants to, *remember* his fate and be *grateful* for his life, that he also *feels* more thoroughly his more thorough connection with the element in which he moves, that, by rising above need in his activity and the experiences linked to it, he also experiences a more infinite, more thorough satisfaction than the satisfaction of needs – if his activity is of the right kind, not too far-looking *for him*, for his powers and his skill, if he is not too restless, too indeterminate, on the other hand not too anxious, too restricted, too moderate. If, however, man sets about it in the right way, then there is for him, in every sphere peculiar to him, a life beyond need, a higher life, and therefore a more infinite satisfaction, that goes beyond the satisfaction of need. Now, just as every satisfaction is a momentary standstill of *real life*, so is such a more infinite satisfaction too, only with *this* big difference, that the satisfaction of need is followed by a *negative* one, as, for example, the animals usually sleep when they have eaten, a more infinite satisfaction, however, by a standstill of *real life*, too, but that this one life takes place in the spirit, and that man's power repeats the real life which granted him the satisfaction, in the spirit, until the perfection and imperfection peculiar to this spiritual repetition drive him back into real life. I am saying, that more infinite connection that goes beyond need, that higher fate, which man experiences in his element, is also felt by him more infinitely, satisfies him more infinitely, and out of this satisfaction emerges the spiritual life, where he, as it were, repeats his real life. But insofar as there is, in his real life, a higher, more infinite connection between him and his element, this connection can be repeated neither in mere *thought*, nor in mere *memory*, for mere thought, noble as it is, can nonetheless repeat only the *necessary connection*, only the inviolable, universally valid, indispensable laws of life, and in precisely the degree in which it ventures beyond this realm peculiar to it and dares to think the more intimate connection of life, it also denies its own peculiar character, which consists of being capable to be understood and proven without any particular examples. Those more infinite, more than necessary relations in life can, admittedly, also be thought, but not *merely* thought; thought does not exhaust them, and if there are higher laws, which govern that more infinite connection of life, if there are unwritten divine laws, of which Antigone speaks when she has buried her brother despite the strict public order not to do so – and there must be such laws if that higher connection is not a fantasy – I am saying, if there are such laws, then they are, insofar as they are understood and represented *merely* separately and not in life, insufficient, firstly because in precisely the degree in which the connection of life becomes more infinite, the activity and its element, the procedure and the sphere in which it is observed, thus the law and the particular world in which it is exercised, are connected with each other more infinitely, and precisely for this reason the law, even if it was universally valid for civilized people, could nonetheless never be thought without a particular case, never in abstraction, if one did not want to deprive it of its peculiarity, its intimate connection with the sphere in which it is exercised. And then the laws of that more than infinite connection in which man can find himself with his sphere are, after all, always merely the conditions which make that connection possible, and not the connection itself.

Hence, this higher connection cannot be repeated in thoughts alone. Thus, one can speak of the duties of love and friendship and kinship, of the duties of hospitality, of the duty to be magnanimous towards one's enemies, one can speak of that which does, and that which does not, befit this or that way of life, this or that estate, this or that age or gender, and we have really turned the more delicate, more infinite relations in life partly into an arrogant morality, partly into a vain etiquette or an empty rule of taste, and with our iron concepts we believe ourselves to be more enlightened than the ancients, who considered those tender relationships as religious ones, that is, as relationships which are to be considered not so much in themselves, as with regard to the *spirit* that governs the sphere in which those relationships take place. To what extent were they *right*? They were right for this reason, that, as we have already seen, to precisely the degree that the relationships rise above the physically and morally necessary ones, the procedure and its element are also more indivisibly bound together, the individual form and manner of certain fundamental experiences can be thought absolutely.

And this is precisely the higher enlightenment that we, for the most part, lack. Those more tender and more infinite

relationships must, thus, be considered with regard to the spirit
that governs the sphere in which they take place. This spirit,
however, this more infinite connection, itself[19]

That is, they are of the kind where the people who live in
them can, in this respect, admittedly exist without one another,
isolated, and that these legal relationships become positive only
through their disturbance, that is, that this disturbance is not
an omission, but an act of violence, and is likewise prevented
and limited again through violence and coercion, that, therefore, the laws of these relationships are also negative in themselves, and positive only on condition that they have been
broken; whilst those freer relationships, as long as they are
what they are and exist undisturbed,[20]

Hints for the continuation

Difference between religious relationships and intellectual
moral legal relationships on the one hand, and on the other
hand, physical mechanical historical relationships, so that the
religious relationships possess in their parts on the one hand
the personality, the independence, the reciprocal limitation, the
negative, equal being-next-to-one-another of the intellectual
relationships, on the other hand the intimate connection, the
implication of the one in the other, the inseparability in their
parts, which characterize the parts of a physical relationship,
so that the religious relationships, in their representation, are
neither intellectual nor historical, but intellectual-historical,
that is, Mythical, both as far as their subject-matter and as
far as their presentation is concerned. Thus, in respect of the
subject-matter they will contain neither merely ideas or concepts or characters, nor mere events, facts, nor both separately,
but both in one, and, to be precise, in such a way that, where
the personal parts have more weight and are the main sections,
the inner content, the representation, the outer content will be
more historical (epic myth), and where the event is the main
section, the inner content, the outer content will be more personal (dramatic myth), only one must not forget that both the

personal and the historical parts are always only subordinate sections, in relation to the true main section, to the *God of the myth*.*

Likewise the presentation of the myth. Its parts will, on the one hand, be put together in a way that through their thorough reciprocal fitting limitation none of them stands out *too* much and each obtains a certain degree of independence precisely through that, and in this respect the presentation will have an intellectual character, on the other hand, they will, in that every part goes a little further than is necessary, precisely through that obtain that inseparability which is otherwise peculiar only to the parts of a physical mechanical relationship.

Thus, all religion would in its essence be poetic.

(In addition, one could speak here about the unification of several people into one religion, where everyone honours his own god and all honour a common one in poetic representations, where everyone celebrates his own higher life and all celebrate a common higher life, the celebration of life, in a mythical way. Furthermore, one could speak of founders of religions, and of priests, what they are from this point of view; those, the founders of religions (if they are not the fathers of a family, which passes on their business and their fate), if they[21]

*The lyrical-mythic is yet to be determined.

Seven Maxims[22]

There are degrees of enthusiasm. Beginning with merriness, which is probably the lowest, right up to the enthusiasm of a general, who in the midst of battle in his clarity mightily maintains his genius, there is an infinite ladder. To ascend and descend this ladder, is the vocation and bliss of the poet.

There are inversions of words within a period. Greater and more effective, then, must be the inversion of the periods themselves. The logical position of the periods, where the ground (the ground period) is followed by the becoming, the becoming by the goal, the goal by the purpose, and the subordinate clauses are always simply attached at the end of the main clauses to which they most closely relate – is certainly useful to the poet only on the rarest occasions.

That is the measure of enthusiasm, that is given to every individual, that the one still maintains his consciousness to the necessary degree in a greater, the other only in a weaker fire. There where sobriety leaves you, there is the limit of your enthusiasm. The great poet is never removed from himself, he may elevate his self as high as he wishes. One can also *fall* to the heights, just as into the depths. The latter is prevented by the elastic spirit, the former by the gravity that resides in sober reflection. But feeling is surely the poet's best sobriety and reflection, if it is right and warm and clear and forceful. It is a rein and a spur to the spirit. Through warmth it drives the spirit further, through tenderness and rightness and clarity it determines its limit and holds it, so it does not lose itself; and hence the feeling is at once both understanding and will. If, however, it is too tender and soft, it becomes deadly, a gnawing worm. If the spirit limits itself, the feeling feels its immediate limit too fearfully, grows too warm, loses its clarity, and drives the spirit into the unlimited with incomprehensible unease; if the spirit is freer, and if it immediately elevates itself above rules and matter, the feeling fears the danger that the spirit might lose itself as anxiously, as before it feared the limitation, it becomes frosty and dull, and weakens the spirit, so that it sinks and falters, and wears itself out with superfluous doubts. If his feeling is already so sick, the poet can do nothing better than, since he knows it, in no case, to allow himself to be immediately frightened by it, and only to heed it thus far, that he continues slightly more restrainedly, and employs his understanding as easily as possible, in order to correct his feeling immediately, be it limiting or liberating, and, when he has several times helped himself through in this way, return to his feeling its natural certainty and consistency. Altogether he must accustom himself not to wish to achieve the whole that he intends in the individual moments, and to suffer that which is momentarily incomplete; his desire must be, that he surpasses himself from one moment to the next, *to the degree and in the manner that the object demands it*, until finally the main tone of the whole profits. But under no circumstances should he think that he can only surpass himself in a *crescendo* from weakness to strength, he will thus become untruthful, and over-strain himself; he must feel that he gains in lightness that which he loses in significance, that stillness replaces intensity, and thoughtfulness replaces verve in a beautiful way, and thus in the continuance of his work there will not be a necessary tone that does not to a certain extent surpass the one before, and the dominant tone will only be dominant because the whole is composed in this and in no other way.

Only that is the truest truth, in which even error, because it is placed within the whole of a system, in its time and in its place, becomes truth. This is the light that illuminates itself and also the night. This is also the highest poetry, in which even the unpoetic, because it is said at the right time and in the right place in the whole of the work of art, becomes poetic. But for this a ready understanding is most necessary. How can you employ the thing in the right place if you are still shyly tarrying over it and do not know how much is in it, how much or how little to make of it. That is eternal bliss, is the joy of the gods, that one sets every individual thing into the place in the whole where it belongs; hence without understanding, or without thoroughly organized feeling, no excellence, no life.

Must a person lose in the dexterity of his powers and of his senses what he gains in the universality of his spirit? After all, neither is anything without the other!

Out of joy you must understand purity as such, understand people and other creatures, grasp 'everything essential and typical' about them, and recognize every relation in sequence, and go on repeating their components in their context until once again the living intuition emerges *more objectively* from your thoughts, out of joy, before need arises; the understanding which only arises out of need is always one-sided and crooked.

Love, however, gladly makes gentle discoveries (if the soul and the senses have not grown shy and opaque from a hard fate and monastic morality) and wishes not to miss anything, and where it finds so-called errors or mistakes (parts that momentarily diverge from the tone of the whole because of their nature, or because of their position and movement) it feels and observes the whole all the more inwardly. Hence all cognition should begin with the study of beauty. For he has gained much who can understand life without mourning. Incidentally, enthusiasm and passion are also good, piety, that does not wish to touch, to understand, life, and then despair, when life itself emerges from its infinity. The deep feeling of mortality, of change, of one's temporal limitations inflames a person, so that he attempts much, it exercises all his powers, and does not allow him to succumb to laziness, and one struggles after chimeras for so long until finally something true and real can be found again to understand and with which to occupy oneself.

In good ages one rarely finds enthusiasts. But when a man lacks great and pure subjects, he creates some phantom or other out of this and that, and closes his eyes so that he can interest himself in it, and live for it.

Everything depends on the excellent not excluding the inferior, and the more beautiful not excluding the barbaric too much from amongst themselves, but not mixing too much either, *but certainly and without passion recognizing the distance between them and the others, and working and suffering out of this understanding.* If they isolate themselves too much, they lose their effectivity, and they go under in their solitude. If they mix too much, no proper effectivity is possible either, for they either speak and act towards the others as if towards their equals, and overlook the point where these have a fault and where they must initially be taken hold of, or they model themselves too much on them, and imitate the bad habits which they should purify. In both cases they remain ineffective and must die away, because they either always express themselves into their time without any echo, and remain alone notwithstanding all their struggles and appeals, or they too servilely take up the alien, the more common into themselves, and are stifled by it.

The wise, however, who only distinguish with the mind, only in general fashion, quickly return to pure being, and succumb to a yet greater indifference because they believe they have distinguished sufficiently, and treat the non-opposition, to which they have returned, as the eternal one. They have duped their nature with the lowest degree of reality, with the shadow of reality, of the ideal opposition and distinction, and it avenges itself by[24] receive its due as a product of nature. Learned reviews and biographies, and all speculation, which only belongs to polemic, lie outside our remit.

Bonhomie, not cold frivolity, light clear order, brevity of the whole – not affectedly mischievous saltos and curios.

The Standpoint from which we should consider Antiquity[26]

We dream of education, piety etc. and have none at all, it is adopted – we dream of originality and independence, we think we are saying something new, and all this is simply a reaction, as it were a mild revenge on the servility with which we act towards antiquity. There really seems to be little choice other than to be crushed by what we have adopted, and by the positive, or else, with a violent presumption, to set oneself as a living force against everything learned, given and positive.[27] The hardest part in this appears to be that antiquity seems to be entirely opposed to our own original drive, which aims to fashion the unformed, to perfect the original and the natural, so that the human being born to art naturally and everywhere prefers to take what is rough, untutored, child-like, rather than a shaped material, in which he who wishes to create form will find the ground already prepared. And the universal reason for the demise of all peoples, namely that their originality, their own living nature, succumbed beneath the positive forms, the luxury that their fathers produced,* also appears to be our own fate, only to a greater degree, inasmuch as an almost infinite antiquity, which we know either through education or through experience, influences and oppresses us.** On the other hand, nothing seems more advantageous than precisely the circumstances in which we find ourselves. *For there is a difference between whether the creative drive works blindly or consciously, whether it knows whence it came and whither it strives, for the only error in a human being is that the creative drive loses its way, takes an unworthy and completely wrong turn, or at least misses its proper place, or, if it has found this,* *stops half way, with the means that should lead to the end.**** *That this may to a high degree happen less,***** is secured by this means, that we know whence and whither this creative drive to formation goes, that we know the essential directions by which it approaches its goal, that the detours and false paths which it can take are not unknown to us, that we consider everything that has emerged before us and around us from this drive* as having emerged from the original communal ground, from which it always emerges with its products, that we recognize the essential directions that it took before us and around us, and also its strayings around us, and then, from the same ground that we regard as alive and equal everywhere, as the origin of every creative drive, we place our own direction, which is determined by the preceding pure and impure directions, which we do not repeat***** out of insight, so that in the ORIGINAL GROUND OF ALL THE WORKS AND DEEDS OF HUMANITY we FEEL ONE AND UNITED WITH ALL, BE IT GREAT OR SMALL, but in the particular direction, which we take,******[28]

*Examples presented in a lively manner.
**Expand.
***Lively examples
****To keep in view above all.
*****We do not repeat the pure directions, because
******our particular direction *action*. Reaction against the positive animation of the dead by means of *real reciprocal relation*

Note on Homer[29]

NB. In the letters on Homer first characters, then situations, then the action, which in the drama of the characters is there for the sake of the character and of the main character, since from *the alternation of tones*[30]

'*I am pleased . . .*' (On Achilles)[31]

I am pleased that you mentioned Achilles. He is my favourite among the heroes, so strong and gentle, the most perfectly achieved and the most transient blossom of the heroic world, '*born for so brief a time*' according to Homer,[32] precisely because he is so beautiful. I am tempted to think that the ancient poet only lets him appear so little in the action, and lets the others make so much noise, whilst his hero sits in his tent, to profane him as little as possible in the tumult before Troy. He had enough to tell of Ulysses. The latter is a sack full of change that takes a long time to count, but you are through with the gold much quicker.

'But most of all I love . . .' (On Achilles)

But most of all I love and admire the poet of all poets because of his Achilles. It is unique, with what love and with what spirit he observed and preserved and elevated him. Take the old men Agamemnon and Ulysses and Nestor with their wisdom and folly, take the noisy Diomedes, the blindly raging Ajax, and compare them to the genius, the omnipotent, melancholically tender son of the gods, Achilles, to this *enfant gâté*[33] of Nature, and how the poet placed him, the youth full of the strength of a lion and spirit and grace, in the middle, between precocity and harshness, and you will find a wonder of art in Achilles' character. The youth stands in the most beautiful contrast with Hector, the noble faithful pious man, who is a hero completely out of duty and fine conscience, whereas the former is everything out of a rich and beautiful nature. They are just as contrary as they are related, and for that very reason it is all the more tragic when finally Achilles appears as Hector's mortal enemy. The friendly Patroclus lovingly joins Achilles and really suits his defiant friend.

One also sees how highly Homer respected the hero of his heart. One has often wondered why Homer, who wishes to sing the wrath of Achilles, hardly lets him appear at all. He did not wish to profane the son of the gods in the tumult before Troy.

The ideal being could not appear every day. And Homer could really not have sung him more magnificently and tenderly than by allowing him to step back (because the youth in his genial nature, as an infinite being, feels infinitely hurt by Agamemnon, who was proud of his rank), so that every loss of the

Greeks, beginning with the day when the only one is missed in the army, recalls his superiority over the splendid crowd of masters and servants, and the rare moments when the poet allows him to appear before us are illuminated all the more by his absence. These are then drawn with wonderful force and the youth appears alternately lamenting and avenging, inexpressibly touching and then terrible again, one after the other, until in the end, when his suffering and his anger have reached their highest point, after a terrible outburst the thunderstorm dies down, and shortly before his death, which he knows in advance, the son of the gods reconciles himself with everyone, even with old Priam.

This final scene is heavenly, after everything that went before.

A Word on the Iliad[34]

One is sometimes undecided in oneself about the merits of different people, and almost embarrassed, like children when you ask them who they love most among the people who are near to them, each one has his own qualities and at the same time his own faults; the one commends himself to us by completely fulfilling that, wherein he lives, in that he has formed his nature and his reason for a more limited situation which is nonetheless appropriate to human nature; we call him a natural human being, because he and his simple sphere are a harmonious whole, but in comparison with others he appears to lack energy and then again profound feeling and spirit; another interests us more because of the size and strength and perseverance of his powers and convictions, through courage and self-sacrifice, but he strikes us as too nervous, too dissatisfied, too forceful, too one-sided in some cases, too much in conflict with the world; yet another wins us over because of the greater harmony of his inner forces, through the completeness and integrity and soul with which he absorbs impressions, through the meaning which for that very reason an object, the world that surrounds him, both in its details and as a whole, can have for him, which meaning is then apparent in his utterances on this object; and just as insignificance hurts us more than anything else, so that person will be particularly welcome to us who treats us and that, wherein we live, as truly significant, as long as he can make his way of seeing and feeling accessible enough and wholly comprehensible to us; but we are not seldom tempted to think that this person, in feeling the spirit of the whole, takes too little notice of individual things, that, when

others cannot see the wood for the trees, he forgets the trees
for the wood, that for all his soul he is rather uncomprehending,
and for that reason also incomprehensible to others.

Then we tell ourselves again, that no man in his outer life
can be everything at once, that to have a being and a consciousness in the world one has to determine on something, that
inclination and circumstances determine one person to this and
the next to another peculiarity, that this peculiarity no doubt
then appears most, but that other qualities, which we miss, are
not therefore completely absent in a true character and only lie
more in the background, that these qualities we miss[35]

On the Different Modes of Poetic Composition[36]

One is sometimes undecided in oneself about the merits of different people. Everyone has his qualities and at the same time his own faults. The one pleases us thanks to the simplicity and appropriateness and uninhibitedness with which he continues in the particular direction to which he has devoted himself. The moments of his life follow one another uninterruptedly and easily, with him everything has its place and its time; nothing varies, nothing is unsettled, and because he keeps to what is ordinary, he is rarely exposed to great effort or to great doubts. Certain, clear, ever constant and moderate and appropriate to the place and to the moment and wholly in the present, he is never unwelcome either, provided that we are not too tense and high-spirited, he leaves us as we are, we get on easily with him; he doesn't actually advance us much, doesn't actually interest us deeply either; but then we do not always wish for this and especially when we are greatly moved we do not at first have a more genuine need than such company, than such an object, in which we most readily recover an equanimity, a peace and clarity.

We call the character described in this manner eminently *natural*, and are at least as correct in our homage as one of the seven wise men who in his own language and his own mode of understanding maintained that everything comes from water.[37] For if in the moral world nature, as it really seems, in her progress always begins with the simplest relationships and forms of life, then those straightforward characters are not without reason to be called the original, the most natural.[38]

has communicated, so everyone who wishes to express his opinion on the matter, must first explain himself in firm concepts and words.

So it is in this instance.

The natural tone, which especially is proper to the epic poem, can easily be noted just from its externals.

In a single passage from Homer one can remark the very point that can be noted about this tone as a whole. (Just as in general with a good poem a passage can represent the whole work, so it is with this tone and this poem.) I here choose the speech of Phoenix, in which he seeks to move the raging Achilles to make peace with Agamemnon, and to help the Achaeans again in their battle against the Trojans:

and, godlike Achilleus, I made you all that you are now,
and loved you out of my heart, for you would not go with another
out to any feast, nor taste any food within your own halls
until I had set you on my knees, and cut little pieces
from the meat, and given you all you wished, and held the wine for
    you.
And many times you soaked the shirt that was on my body
with wine you would spit up in the troublesomeness of your
    childhood.
So I have suffered much through you, and have had much trouble,
thinking always how the gods would not bring to birth any
    children
of my own; so that it was you, godlike Achilleus, I made
my own child, so that some day you might keep hard affliction from
    me.
Then, Achilleus, beat down your great anger. It is not
yours to have a pitiless heart. The very immortals
can be moved; their virtue and honour and strength are greater than
    ours are.[39]

The expansive, constant, really true tone strikes the eye.

And so the epic poem also keeps to the real as a whole. It is, if one (simply) considers it in its peculiarity, a character painting, and only when seen from this standpoint throughout the

Iliad, too, interests us and can be explained properly from every side.* In a character painting all the other merits of the natural tone, too, are at their essential points. This *visible* sensuous unity, the fact that everything chiefly originates in the hero and leads back to him, that beginning and catastrophe and end are tied to him, that every character and situation in all their variety, everything that is said and everything that happens, is directed like the points in a line towards the moment when he appears with his greatest individuality, *this* unity is, as one can easily recognize, only possible in a work whose actual purpose resides in the representation of characters, and so where the main source lies in the main character.

So from this point there also follows the calm moderation which is so peculiar to the natural tone, which shows the characters so within their limitations, and gently modulates their variety. The artist in the mode of writing poetry of which we are speaking is not so moderate because he considers this method to be the only poetic one, he does not for example avoid the extremes and contrasts because he does not wish to use them at all, he well knows that in the right place there are poetically true extremes and contrasts of characters, of events, of thoughts, of passions, of images, of feelings, he excludes them only insofar as they do not belong to the present work; he had to select a fixed standpoint, and this is now the individual, the character of his hero, as he has by nature and education attained his own definite existence, his reality. But it is precisely this individuality of character that necessarily gets lost in extremes. If Homer had not removed his inflammable Achilles so tenderly carefully from the fray, we would hardly be able to distinguish the son of the gods from the element that surrounds him, and only where we find him peacefully in his tent, as he delights his heart with his lyre and sings the men's victorious deeds, while his Patroclus sits opposite him and

---

*And if the incidents and circumstances wherein the characters represent themselves are developed so extensively, it is above all because they appear this way to the people who experience them, without being much altered or driven out of their ordinary mood or manner.[40]

silently waits until he ends his song, only here do we have the youth properly before our eyes.[41]

Thus, to maintain the individuality of the character represented, which is what he is now most concerned with, the epic poet is so thoroughly moderate.

And if the circumstances, in which the epic characters find themselves, are represented so exactly and extensively, it is, again, not because the poet attributes all poetic worth to this circumstantiality. In another example he would avoid it up to a certain degree; but here, where his standpoint is the individuality, reality, particular being of his characters, the surrounding world must also appear from this standpoint. And that the surrounding objects appear from this standpoint with that same exactitude can be observed in ourselves, whenever we in our own most ordinary mood, without disturbance, become aware of the circumstances in which we ourselves live.

I would like to add quite a few points to this if I were not afraid of straying too far. Still I will add that this detail in the circumstances represented is simply a reflection of the characters, insofar as they are individual, at all, and are not yet more closely defined. The surroundings can be accommodated to the character in yet another way. In the *Iliad* Achilles' individuality, which admittedly is made for this, eventually communicates itself more or less to all things and people that surround him, and not just to the circumstances, but also to the characters. In the contests which are mounted to honour the dead Patroclus, in more or less noticeable a fashion the other heroes of the Greek army almost all take on his colouring, and in the end old Priam in all his suffering seems to rejuvenate before the hero, who yet was his enemy.

But one can easily see that this last already goes beyond the natural tone, as it was considered and described up until now, in its *pure* peculiarity.

In this alone, however, it positively affects us, through its extensiveness, its constant change, its reality.

The Ground of the Empedocles[42]

The tragic ode begins in the highest fire, the pure spirit, pure intimacy has overstepped its mark, for it did not hold with sufficient measure those relations in life which are necessarily, that is, which are as it were in any case inclined towards contact, and are, through the whole mood of intimacy, excessively inclined towards it, namely consciousness, reflection or physical sensuality, and so, through an excess of intimacy, that strife began, which the tragic ode simulates right at the start, in order to represent purity itself. It then proceeds through a natural act from the extreme of differentiation and of need into the extreme of the non-differentiation of purity, the metaphysical, that seems not to recognize any need, from whence it falls into a pure sensuality, into a more modest intimacy, for the originally higher more divine bolder intimacy appeared to it as an extreme, and it can no longer fall into that degree of excessive intimacy with which it began upon its opening tone, for it has, as it were, experienced where this led, it must pass over from the extremes of differentiation and non-differentiation into that still awareness and feeling, where it must necessarily of course experience the struggle of the one, more strenuous awareness, that is, its original tone and its own character, as an opposite, and must pass over into it, if it is not in this modesty to end tragically, but because it experiences it as an opposite, the idealic, which unites these two opposites, emerges more purely, the original tone is found again and with awareness, and so from thence it passes over again through moderate freer reflection or feeling more certainly, freer, more thoroughly (i.e. out of the experience and knowledge of heterogeneity) back into the original tone.

General Ground

It is the deepest intimacy that expresses itself in a tragic dramatic poem. The tragic ode, too, represents the intimate in the most positive differentiations, in real opposites, but these opposites are, after all, more present simply in the form and as the immediate language of feeling. The tragic poem conceals the intimacy in the representation even more, expresses it in stronger differentiations, because it expresses a deeper intimacy, a more infinite divinity. Feeling no longer expresses itself immediately, it is no longer the poet and his own experience which appears, even if every poem, the tragic one too, must emerge out of poetic life and reality, out of the poet's own world and soul, because otherwise the real truth would everywhere be missing, and nothing at all can be understood and brought to life if we cannot translate our own character and our own experience into an alien analogical subject. Even in the tragic dramatic poem, therefore, the divine that expresses itself is that which the poet feels and experiences in his own world, even the tragic dramatic poem is for him a picture of that which is alive, which is and was present to him in his life; but as this image of intimacy everywhere denies, and must deny, its ultimate ground, it must everywhere approach the symbolic; the more infinite the intimacy is, the more inexpressible, the more near to the *nefas*,[43] the more strictly and coldly the image must differentiate between man and his element as it is felt, in order to hold the feeling fast within its limits, the less the image is able to express the feeling immediately, it must deny it both according to the form and according to the subject-matter, the subject-matter must be a bolder, more alien metaphor and example of it, the form must wear more the character of opposition and division. Another world, alien events, alien characters, but like every bolder metaphor, fitting all the more intimately to the basic subject-matter, and only heterogeneous

in the outer form, for if this intimate relation of the metaphor
with the subject-matter, the characteristic intimacy, which is
the very ground of the image, were not visible, then its remote-
ness, its alien form, would not be explicable. The alien forms
must be all the more alive, the more alien they are, and the less
the visible subject of the poem resembles the subject which
forms the ground, the character and the world of the poet, the
less may the spirit, the divine, as the poet has experienced it in
his world, deny its presence in the artificial alien subject. But
even in this alien artificial subject, the intimate, the divine, can
and may not express itself other than by a degree of differentiation which is all the greater, the more intimate the feeling is
which forms the ground. Hence (1) tragedy according to its
subject and form is dramatic, that is (a) it contains a third
subject, different and more alien to the poet's own character and
his own world, which he chose, because he found it analogous
enough to put his total feeling into it and, as if in a vessel, to
preserve it there, and indeed all the more certainly, the more
alien this subject is in its analogy, for the most intimate feeling
is exposed to transience in precisely that degree in which it does
not deny the true temporal and sensual relations (and it is
therefore a lyrical law, indeed, to deny the physical and intellectual connection, even if the intimacy there is in itself less deep,
that is, easier to hold). For precisely this reason, the tragic poet,
because he expresses the deepest intimacy, wholly denies his
person, his subjectivity, and also the object which is present to
him, he translates them into alien personalities, alien objectivity
(and even where the total feeling which forms the ground most
clearly betrays itself, in the main character, who sets the tone
of the drama, and in the main situation, where the object of the
drama, fate, most clearly expresses its secret, where it most
assumes the form of homogeneity against its hero (which most
powerfully takes hold of him), even there[44]

and bad outcome which the false attempts at the restoration of
pure intimacy have in the mind, is not treated once more by the
suffering *self-actingly* through a new appropriate inappropriate
attempt, but is made by another in anticipation, which takes

the same path, but stands a step higher or lower, so that the spirit, attacked by false attempts at improvement, is not only disturbed by its own self-activity, but is altered even more by the anticipation of an alien and equally false one, and prejudiced to an even more violent reaction.

Ground of the Empedocles

Nature and art[45] are, in pure life, only opposed harmoniously. Art is the blossom, the perfection of nature, nature only becomes divine through the connection with heterogeneous but harmonious art; when each is wholly that which it can be, and one combines with the other, replaces the weakness of the other, which it must necessarily have, to be wholly that which it can be as something particular, then perfection is there, and the divine is in the middle between the two. More organic, more artificial man is the blossom of nature; more aorgic[46] nature, if it is purely felt by a purely organized man, purely formed and educated in his way, gives him the feeling of perfection. But this life is only in feeling and not available to knowledge. If it is to become cognizable, then it must represent itself by dividing itself in that excess of intimacy where the opposites reverse, so that the organic, which gave itself over too much to nature, and forgot its own nature and consciousness, passes over into the extreme of self-activity and art and reflection, whereas nature, at least in its effects on a reflecting man, passes over into the extreme of the aorgic, the incomprehensible, the unfeelable, the unlimited, until through the progress of the opposed reciprocal effects the two which were originally united meet, as at the start, only that now nature has become more organic through man, who forms and cultivates, through the creative drive and the creative powers in general, whilst man has become more aorgic, more universal, more infinite. This feeling belongs, perhaps, to the highest that can be felt, when the two opposites, the more universalized spiritual lively artificial pure aorgic man and the handsome form of nature, meet. This feeling belongs perhaps to the highest that man can experience, for the present harmony reminds him of the former reverse pure relation, and he doubly feels himself and nature, and their union is more infinite.

In the middle lies the struggle, and the death of the individual, that moment where the organic lays down its selfhood, its particular existence, that had become an extreme, and the aorgic lays down its universality, not as at the start in an ideal mixture, but in a real highest struggle, in that the particular at its extreme must actively and increasingly universalize itself towards the extreme of the aorgic, must increasingly tear itself from its centre, and the aorgic must increasingly concentrate itself towards the extreme of the particular and increasingly gain a centre and become the most particular and increasingly gain a centre and become the most particular of all, *where, then the organic which has become aorgic seems to find itself again and seems to return to itself, in that it supports itself upon the individuality of the aorgic, and the object, the aorgic, seems to find itself, in that, at the selfsame moment where it assumes individuality, it also finds the organic at the greatest extreme of the aorgic, so that in this moment,* IN THIS BIRTH OF THE GREATEST ENMITY THE GREATEST RECONCILIATION SEEMS TO BE REAL. *But the individuality of this moment is only a product of the greatest strife, its universality only a product of the greatest strife*; thus, just as reconciliation appears to be there, and the organic now works towards this moment in its own way, and the aorgic in its own way, so, upon the impressions of the organic, the individuality that emerged from the aorgical and that is contained in the moment becomes more aorgic again, upon the impressions of the aorgic the universality that emerged from the organic and that is contained in the moment becomes more particular again, so that the unifying moment, like a phantom, dissolves ever more, and by reacting aorgically against the organic it removes itself from the latter even more, but thereby and by its death reconciles and unites the warring extremes out of which it emerged more beautifully than in its own life, in that the union is now not in a single individual and is therefore not too intimate, in that the divine no longer appears physically, in that the happy deceit of the union ceases in precisely that degree, in which it was too individual and unique, so that the two extremes, of which the one, the organic, must be frightened away by the passing moment and thereby be elevated into a purer universality, the aorgic, as it passes over into the latter, must become an object of more calm contemplation for the organic, and the intimacy of the past moment now emerges more universally more controlled more differentiatingly, more clearly.

Thus Empedocles is a son of his sky and of his time, of his homeland, a son of the mighty oppositions of nature and art in which the world appeared before his eyes. A man, in whom these oppositions unite *so* intimately, that they become *one* within him, that they reverse and lay down their original differentiating form, that that, which counts as more subjective in his world and is more present in particularity, namely differentiation, thought, comparison, forming, educating, organization and being organized, is in *himself* more objective, so that he, to put it as strongly as possible, is more differentiating, thinking, comparing, forming, educating, organizing and organized, *when he is less conscious and insofar as he is less conscious of himself*, that with him and for him the speechless gains speech, and with him and for him the universal, the more unconscious, gains the form of consciousness and particularity, whilst that, however, which for others in his world counts as more objective, and is present in a more universal form, the less differentiating, and differentiable, the more unthinking, more incomparable, unformable, ineducable, unorganized and disorganizing, is more subjective in him and for him, so that he is more undifferentiated and more undifferentiating more unthinking in his effect, more incomparable more unformable and ineducable, more aorgic and more *dis*organic, when he is more conscious, and when and insofar as he is more conscious of himself, that in him and for him what speaks becomes unspeakable or not to be spoken, that in him and for him the more particular and more conscious takes on the form of the unconscious and universal, that thus in him these two opposites become one, because in him they reverse their differentiating form and also unite insofar as they are different in their original feeling – a man like this can only arise out of the deepest opposition of nature and art, and just as (ideally) the excess of intimacy emerges from intimacy, so *this real excess of intimacy* emerges out of enmity and out of the greatest strife, where the aorgic only takes on the modest form of the particular, and seems to reconcile itself with the over-aorgic, the organic only takes on the modest form of the universal, and so seems to reconcile itself with the over-organic and over-alive, because both at the greatest extreme penetrate and touch each other most deeply, and herewith in their outer form must take on the shape, the semblance of the opposite.

Thus Empedocles, as we said, is the result of his period, and his character refers back to it, just as he emerged from the same. His fate manifests itself in him, as in a momentary union, which must, however, dissolve, in order to become more.

He seems all in all to be born to be a poet, seems, therefore, in his subjective more active nature already to possess that unusual tendency to universality, which under different circumstances, or through understanding and avoidance of its excessive influence, becomes that peaceful contemplation, that completeness and thorough definition of consciousness, with which the poet looks at a *whole*, and likewise there seems to reside in his objective nature, in his passivity, that happy gift which, even without conscientious and conscious ordering and thinking and forming and educating, is inclined towards ordering and thinking and forming and educating, that educability of the senses and of the character, which in lively manner takes up everything of that kind easily and quickly in its totality, and which gives artificial activity more to say than to do. But this faculty was not to have effect and to remain within its own specific sphere, he was not to take effect according to his nature and measure, in his peculiar limitation and purity, and to allow this mood, through its free expression, to become the more universal mood, that which was simultaneously the destiny of his people; the fate of his time, the powerful extremes in which he grew up did not demand song, where purity can, still, be readily grasped in an ideal representation which lies between the figure of fate and of the primal, if the time has not too far removed itself therefrom; nor did the fate of his time demand a real deed, which admittedly takes effect and helps immediately, but also more one-sidedly, and all the more, the less it *exposes* the whole man, it demanded a *sacrifice*, where the whole man really and visibly becomes that, wherein the fate of his time seems to dissolve, where the extremes really and visibly seem to unite in one, but precisely for that reason are too intimately united, and for that reason the individual perishes and must perish in an idealic act, because the premature physical union that emerged out of need and strife manifested itself in him, and resolved the problem of fate, which can, however, never resolve visibly and individually, because otherwise the universal would be lost in the individual, and (what is still worse than all the great movements of fate, and is the only thing that is impossible) the life of a world would die out in a single detail; on the other hand, if this detail, as a premature result of fate, dissolves[47] because it was too intimate and real and visible, the problem of fate, though materially it dissolves in the same way, formally dissolves in a different way, in that precisely that excess of intimacy which originally emerged by good fortune, but only as an ideal and as an attempt, has now, through the greatest strife, become real, and to that extent and precisely for that reason really annuls itself[48] in those degrees, forces and tools in which the original excess of intimacy, the cause of all strife, annulled itself, so that the force of the intimate excess really disperses, and riper true pure universal intimacy remains.

Thus Empedocles was to become a victim of his time. *The problems of the fate in which he grew up were to appear to be resolved in him, and this resolution was to prove an apparent temporary one, as more or less with all tragic persons*, who in their characters and expressions are all more or less attempts to resolve the problem of fate, and all annul and transcend and preserve themselves insofar and in that degree, in which they are not universally valid, if their role, their character and its utterances do not otherwise automatically manifest themselves as something transient and momentary, so that the one, who

apparently resolves fate most completely, also manifests himself
most in his transience and in the progress of his various efforts
most strikingly as a sacrifice.

How is this now the case with Empedocles?

The mightier the fate, the oppositions of art and nature, the
more it lay within them to individualize themselves ever more,
to gain a fixed point, a hold, and a time like that takes hold of
every individual for so long, challenges each to a solution, until
it finds someone in whom its unknown want and its secret
tendency manifest themselves more visibly as achieved, and
only from there, then, can the newly discovered dissolution
pass over into the universal.

Thus the time individualizes itself in Empedocles, and the
more it individualizes itself in him, the more brilliantly and
really and visibly the mystery seems to be resolved in him, the
more necessary his destruction becomes.

(1) As such, the lively, all-assaying artistic spirit of his people
will in itself have reproduced itself more aorgically, more
boldly, more limitlessly inventively in him, just as from the
other side the blazing skies and the lush Sicilian land will have
manifested themselves in a more felt, more speaking manner
both for him and in him, and once he was assailed from both
sides, the one, the more active force of his nature, will have
strengthened the other as a counter-effect, just as his artistic
spirit will have nurtured itself and developed out of the feeling
part of his character. – (2) Among the hyper-political, ever-
arguing and calculating Agrigentians, among the advancing and
self-renewing social forms of his town, a character such as his,
which always strove to invent a complete whole, will have been
only too readily inclined to become a reforming spirit; similarly
the anarchic freedom, with which everyone pursued his own
originality, without bothering about the peculiarity of the
others, together with his own rich, self-sufficient nature and
bristling energy, will have made him, more than others, more
unsocial, more solitary, more proud and peculiar, and these
two sides of his character, too, will have reciprocally elevated
and exaggerated each other. (3) A freethinking boldness, which
increasingly opposes itself to the unknown which lies beyond

human consciousness and action, the more intimately man originally found himself united with it in feeling and was driven by
a natural instinct to preserve himself from loss of self and total
self-oblivion against the too powerful, too deep and friendly
influence of the element, this freethinking boldness, this negative philosophizing, this not-thinking of the unknown, which
is so natural among a high-spirited people, will have made
Empedocles – since he was in no way made for negations – go
one step further, and he will have tried to become the master
of the unknown, he will have wanted to assure himself of it, his
spirit will have striven towards servility to such an extent that
he will have attempted to encompass the overpowering natural
world, to understand it through and through, and to become
conscious of it, as he could be conscious and certain of himself,
he had to struggle for identity with it, and so his spirit had to
take on aorgic form in the highest sense, had to tear itself away
from itself and its own centre, and always penetrate its object
so excessively that he lost himself in it, as in an abyss, where
thereupon, however, the whole life of the object will have
taken hold of his deserted self, which had but been made more
infinitely receptive by the boundless activity of his spirit, the
object's life will have become an individuality in him, will
have given him his particularity, and will have modelled this
particularity after itself more thoroughly in precisely that degree
in which he spiritually actively gave himself over to the object,
and so the object appeared in him in subjective form, as he had
taken on the objective form of the object. He was the universal,
the unknown, and the object was the particular. And so the
conflict between more unconscious nature and art, thinking,
structuring, the shaping and educating human character seemed
to be resolved, they seemed combined into one in the greatest
extremes, up to the very point that they exchanged their reciprocally differentiating forms. This was the magic with which
Empedocles appeared in his world. Nature, who ruled his freethinking contemporaries with her power and attractions all the
more strongly, the more ungratefully they abstracted from her,
here appeared with all her melodies in the spirit and voice of
this man and did it so intimately and warmly and personally,

as if his heart were hers, and the spirit of the element dwelt in human form amongst the mortals. This gave him his grace, his fearfulness, his divinity, and every heart that was moved by the storm of fate flew to him, as did the spirits which erred leaderless and unsteadily hither and thither in the mysterious night of the times; and the more humanly, the more according to their own being he associated with them, the more, with this soul, he made their cause his own, all the more, when it had once appeared in his divine form and was then returned to them again in a manner more their own, was he adored. This basic tone of his character displayed itself in all his relationships. They all adopted it. Thus he lived in his greatest independence, in the relationship which, even without the more objective and more historical relations, mapped out his path for him, so that the external circumstances, which led him the same way (as essential and indispensable as they are for bringing to light and into action what might perhaps have remained only a thought in him), nevertheless, despite all the conflict in which he appears to stand with them subsequently, still meet his freest mood and soul, which is no surprise, since this very mood is also the innermost spirit of the circumstances, since all the extremes in these circumstances originated from this very spirit and returned towards it once again. In his most independent relationship the problem of his time resolves itself in the first and the last problem. Just as from here this apparent solution begins to annul itself, and thus ends.

In this independent relationship, in that greatest intimacy which forms the basic tone of his character, he lives with the elements, whilst in this respect the world around him lives in the very greatest opposition, on the one hand in that freethinking not-thinking, non-recognition of what is alive, and on the other in the greatest servitude towards the influence of nature. In this relationship he lives (1) in general, as a feeling person, (2) as a philosopher and poet, (3) as a solitary, who cultivates his gardens. But by this he would not yet be a dramatic character. Hence, he must resolve fate not simply in universal relationships, and by his independent character, he must do so in particular relationships, upon the most particular occasion, in the most particular of tasks. But he has with his people, too, just such an intimate relationship as with the life of the elements. He was not capable of the violent negative spirit of innovation, which only through opposition strives against that defiant anarchic life which will suffer no influence, no art; he had to go a step further; so as to order what is alive, he had to strive to seize it with his innermost being, he had to try with his spirit to master the human element, every inclination and drive, their soul, and the incomprehensible, the unconscious and the instinctive within them, and precisely through that, his will, his consciousness, his spirit, had to lose itself and become objective, in that he went beyond the ordinary and human limits of knowledge and activity, and he had to find that which he wished to give, whilst, however, the objective resounded within him all the more purely and deeply, the more open his character became by virtue of the fact that the spiritually active man had surrendered himself, and this in the particular as in the universal.

Thus he behaved with the same proud enthusiastic submissiveness as a religious reformer, as a political being, and in every action he performed for their sake and against them, and in appearance the whole fate was resolved by the very expression of this exchange of object and subject. But in what can this expression reside? Which is the expression that, in a relationship like this, can satisfy the party who disbelieves from the start? And everything depends on this expression, because that which unites must perish, because it appeared too visibly and physically, and it can only do so by expressing itself in some most particular point and case. They must see the unity that exists between them and the man, but how can they? By virtue of the fact that he obeys them to the very utmost? And in what? In a point where they are in the most doubt about the union of the extremes in which they live. Now, if these extremes consist in the strife of art and nature, he must reconcile nature with art before their eyes at precisely that point, where nature is at its uttermost remove from art. – From this point, the fable unrolls.

He does it with love and disgust,* he gives proof, now they believe everything is completed. He recognizes them by it. The deception, in which he had lived, as if he were one with them, now ends. He withdraws, and they grow cold towards him. His antagonist uses this, effects the banishment. His antagonist, as great as Empedocles in his natural talents, seeks to solve the problems of the time in another, in a more negative way. Born to be a hero, he is not so much inclined to unite the extremes, as to subdue them, and to attach their reciprocal action to something lasting and firm, which is placed between them, and keeps each within its limit by making each one its own. His virtue is reason, his goddess necessity. He is fate itself, only with the difference that in him the opposing forces are attached to a consciousness, to a point of separation, which confronts them clearly and certainly, which attaches them to a (negative) ideality and gives them a direction. As, in the case of Empedocles, art and nature unite at the extreme point of conflict by this, that the active in excess becomes objective, and the lost subjectivity is replaced by the deep influence of the object; so, in his antagonist, art and nature unite by this, that an excess of objectivity and of being-outside-oneself and of reality (in such a climate, in such a tumult of passions and alternation of originality, in such an imperious fear of the unknown), in a brave, open character, must take the place of the active and forming and educating, whereas the subjective, rather, assumes the passive shape of suffering, of enduring, of firmness, of certainty, and if the extremes take on the shape of rest and of the organic, either through the skill in enduring the same, or from outside, then the subjectively active, that which organizes, must become the element, and here, too, the subjective and the objective must exchange their shape, and become one in one.

*for the fear of becoming positive must, naturally, be his greatest, out of the feeling that the more truly he expresses the intimate, the more surely he will perish.

The declining fatherland, nature and man, insofar as they stand in a particular reciprocal relationship, and constitute a *particular* world that has become ideal, and a connection between things, and insofar dissolve, that out of that world and of the remaining race and the remaining forces of nature, which are the other, the real principle, a new world, a new, but also particular reciprocal relationship should form, just as the decline emerged from a pure, but particular world. For the world of all worlds, the all in all, which always *is*, only *manifests* itself in all time – or in the decline or in the moment, or, more genetically, in the becoming of the moment, and in the beginning of time and world; and this decline and beginning is like the language expression sign representation of a living, but particular whole, which precisely becomes that whole in its effects, and specifically in this way, that, as is the case with language, from the one side little or nothing living and existent seems to reside in it, whilst, from the other, everything does. In living existence, one kind of relation and *kind of substance* predominates; although all others can be discerned in it, in the transition the possibility of all relations predominates, but the particular one is to be extracted, to be drawn from it, so that through it as infinity the finite effect emerges.

This decline or transition of the fatherland (in this sense) experiences itself in the limbs of the existing world thus, that in the very moment and in that degree in which what exists dissolves, that which newly emerges, the youthful and possible, is also felt. For how could the dissolution be felt without union? If, therefore, that which exists is to be felt in its dissolution and is felt, then *the unexhausted* and the *inexhaustible* from among the *relations* and *forces* must be felt *in the process*, and it, the dissolution, must be felt more through these than vice versa, for nothing comes out of nothingness, and this taken by degrees means as much as: that which passes over into negation, and insofar as it departs from reality, and is not yet something possible, can have no effect.

But *the possible* which steps into *reality*, as *reality dissolves*, this has a real effect, and it effects both the sensation of the dissolution and the memory of that which is dissolved.

Hence the thoroughly original character of all truly tragic language, the everlastingly creative quality . . .[50] the emergence of individuality out of the infinite, and the emergence of the finite-infinite or individual-eternal out of both, the comprehending, quickening, not of that which has become incomprehensible and fatal, but of the incomprehensibleness, the fatalness of the dissolution, and of the struggle of death itself, by the harmonious, comprehensible and alive. In this, it is not the first, raw pain of the dissolution, which in its depth is *still too* unknown to the sufferer and observer, that expresses itself; there, the newly emergent, the idealic, is undefined, more an object of fear, whereas by contrast the dissolution as such, *seems* existent, more real, and the real or that which is dissolving is contained in necessity in the state between being and not-being.

The new life is now real, that which should dissolve, and has dissolved, possible (ideally *old*), the dissolution is necessary and possesses its peculiar character between being and not-being. In the state between being and not-being, however, the possible everywhere becomes real, and the real becomes ideal, and in the free imitation of art this is a terrible, but divine dream. The dissolution, therefore, as necessary, from the viewpoint of idealic memory, as such becomes an idealic object of the newly developed life, a look back along the path, which had to be travelled, from the beginning of the dissolution up to the point where out of the new life, a memory of the dissolved, and, out of that, as explanation and union of the gap and the contrast which sets in between the new and the past, the memory of the dissolution can follow. This idealic dissolution is fearless. The beginning- and end-point has already been set, found, secured, for that reason this dissolution is also more secure, more unimpedable, bolder, and it manifests itself as that which it actually is, as a reproductive act, by which life passes through all its points, and in order to attain the whole sum, it does not linger over any one, and dissolves itself at each, in order to recreate itself in the next; only that the dissolution becomes more ideal to that degree in which it advances beyond its starting-point, whilst the creation becomes more real to the same degree, until finally out of the sum of these sensations of declining and emerging that are infinitely undergone in a single moment, a whole feeling of life, and from this the only excluded thing, that which had dissolved at the start, emerges in the memory (through the necessity of an object in its most complete state), and after this memory of the dissolved, of the individual, is united with the infinite feeling of life by the memory of the dissolution, and the gap between them is filled out, then out of this union and comparison of the past individual, and the infinite present, the actual new state, the next step, which should follow the past, emerges.

Hence, in the memory of the dissolution the latter, since its two ends are fixed, entirely becomes the secure unimpedable bold act, which it actually is.

But this idealic dissolution is distinguished from the real one by virtue, again, of passing from the infinitely-present to the finitely-past, so that: (1) at each of its points dissolution and creation, (2) each point in its dissolution and creation and every other, (3) every point in its dissolution and creation and the total feeling of dissolution and creation are infinitely more enmeshed with each other, and everything interpenetrates, touches and concerns each other more infinitely in pain and joy, strife and peace, movement and rest, form and un-form, and so effects a heavenly fire instead of an earthly one.

Finally, and again because, conversely, the idealic dissolution passes from the infinitely-present to the finitely-past, the idealic dissolution is distinguished from the real by this, that it can be defined more consistently throughout, that it is not led (in anxious unrest) to draw together several essential points of dissolution and creation into one, nor become anxiously side-tracked into the inessential, which hinders the dreaded dissolution and thus also creation, that is, actually, into something deadly, nor does it one-sidedly and anxiously limit itself, with utmost extremity, to a single point of dissolution and creation, and so to what is actually dead, but, rather, it takes its own precise, straight, free path and is at every point of the dissolution and creation wholly that which it can be at that point, but only at that point, and is hence wholly individual, and naturally therefore does not force onto this point anything improper, distracting, which would in itself and at this point be insignificant, but instead, it freely and completely passes through the single point in all its relations to the other points in the dissolution and creation, which lie beyond the first two points *capable* of dissolution and creation, namely the opposed infinitely-new and the finitely-old, the real-total and the ideal-particular.

Finally, the idealic dissolution is distinguished from the so-called real (because, inversely, the former passes from the infinite to the finite, *after it has passed from the finite to the infinite*) by this, that the dissolution must appear as merely a real nothing out of ignorance of its end- and starting-points, so that everything existent, that is, particular, appears as all, and a sensual idealism, an Epicureanism, appears, as Horace, who probably only introduced this point of view dramatically, tellingly represented it in his *Prudens futuri temporis exitum*[51] etc. – thus the idealic dissolution is finally distinguished from the so-called real by this, that the latter appears to be a real nothing, the former, because it is a becoming of the ideally-individual into the infinitely-real, and of the infinitely-real into the individually-ideal, gains content and harmony to precisely the degree that it is conceived as a transition from what exists into the existent, just as the existent gains in spirit to precisely the degree, that it is conceived as having come about out of the transition, or as coming about at the transition, so that the dissolution of the ideally-individual does not appear as a weakening and death, but as a revival, as growth, and the

dissolution of the infinitely-new does not appear as an annihil-
ating force, but as love, and both together appear as a (transcendental) creative act, whose character it is to combine
ideally-individual and really-infinite, whose product is therefore
the really-infinite combined with the ideally-individual, where
the infinitely-real takes on the form of the individually-ideal,
and the latter takes on the life of the infinitely-real, and both
unite in a mythical state, where, with the opposition of the
infinitely-real and the finitely-ideal, the transition itself stops,
too, so far that the latter gains in rest what the former won
in life, a state which is not to be confused with the lyrical
infinitely-real, as little as in its emergence during the transition
it is to be confused with the epically representable individually-
ideal, for in both cases it combines the spirit of the one with
the comprehensibility sensuousness of the other. In both cases
it is tragic, that is, in both cases it combines infinitely-real with
finitely-ideal, and both cases differ only in degree, for during
the transition, too, spirit and sign, in other words the material
of the transition with the latter and the latter with the former
(the transcendental with the isolated) are, like living organs
with an organic soul, harmoniously opposed and one.

Out of this tragic union of the infinitely-new and the finitely-
old a new individuality develops, in that the infinitely-new,
since it took on the form of the finitely-old, now individualizes
itself in its own form.

The newly-individual now strives to isolate itself and to
writhe free of infinity to precisely the degree that from the
second point of view the isolated, individually-old strives to
generalize itself and to dissolve into the infinite feeling of life.
*The moment where the period of the individually-new ends, is
where the infinitely-new* acts *as dissolving*, as an *unknown*
power towards the individually-old, just as in the former period
the new acted as an unknown power towards the infinitely-old,
and these two periods are opposed to one another, namely the
first as mastery of the individual over the infinite, of the one
over the whole, to the second as the mastery of the infinite over
the individual, of the whole over the one. The end of this second
period and the beginning of the third resides in that moment,

where the infinitely-new acts as a feeling of life (as an I) towards
the individually-old as an object (the Not-I),[52]

After these oppositions, the tragic union of the characters; and
after this, the opposition of the characters to the reciprocal and
vice versa. After these, the tragic union of both.

'When the poet is once in command of the spirit . . .'[53]

When the poet is once in command of the spirit, when he has
felt and appropriated the common soul, that is common to all
and peculiar to each,[54] has held it fast, assured himself of it,
when further he is certain of the free movement, the harmonious
alternation and onward striving, with which the spirit tends to
reproduce itself in itself and in others, certain of the beautiful
progressus planned in the ideal of the spirit and its poetic
deductive mode, when he has understood that a necessary conflict arises between the most original demand of the spirit,
which aims at the community and united simultaneity of all
parts, and between the other demand, that commands it to
depart from itself and to reproduce itself in itself and in others
in a beautiful progress and alternation, when this conflict
always holds him fast and draws him on, on the way to realization, when further he has understood that firstly this community and affinity of all the parts, this spiritual import, could
not be felt at all if they were not, by degrees, different according
to their sensuous import, even when discounting the harmonious alternation, even when the spiritual form (the being simultaneous and together) is identical, that further this harmonious
alternation, that striving onwards, could, again, not be felt and
would be a light and empty play of shadows, if the alternating
parts, even given the difference of their *sensuous* import, would
not stay the same according to their *sensuous* form in the
alternation and striving onwards, when he has understood that
that conflict between spiritual import (between the affinity of
all the parts) *and spiritual form* (the alternation of all the parts),
between the tarrying and the striving of the spirit, *dissolves by*

this means, that in the striving of the spirit, in the alternation of the spiritual form, the *form of the subject-matter remains identical in all the parts* and that it replaces the very same amount as must be lost in the harmonious alternation of the original affinity and unity of the parts, that it constitutes the objective *import* in contrast to the spiritual form and gives the latter its complete meaning, that on the other hand the *material alternation* of the *subject* that accompanies the eternal aspect of the *spiritual* import, the variety of the same, satisfies the demands of the spirit which it makes *in its progress* and which are *held up by the demand for unity and eternity in every moment*, that this very material alternation constitutes the objective form, the shape, in contrast to the spiritual import; when he has understood that on the other hand *the conflict* between the *material alternation* and the *material identity* is dissolved *by this means*, that the loss of material identity,[i] of passionate progress fleeing from interruption, is replaced by the

---

[i] material identity? This must originally be that in the subject-matter, before the material alternation, which in the spirit the unity is prior to the idealic alternation, it must be the sensuous point of contact for all the parts. For the subject-matter, like the spirit, must be *adopted* and *held fast* by the poet, out of free interest, *when* once it is present in its entire structure, *when* the impression which it made on the poet, the first pleasure, that could also be accidental, has been examined and found to be receptive for the treatment of the spirit and effective, appropriate to the purpose that the spirit reproduce itself in itself and in others, *when* it is felt again after this examination and has been called forth again in all its parts, and is apprehended in an as yet unspoken, felt effect. And this effect is actually the identity of the subject-matter, because all parts concentrate within it. Yet it remains indeterminate, the subject-matter is still undeveloped. It must be clearly spoken in all its parts, and by this very means weakened in the liveliness of its total impression. It must be so, for in the unspoken effect the subject-matter is present to the poet, but not to others, furthermore the spirit has not yet really reproduced this [it has been conjectured that 'this' (*diß*) is a slip of the pen for 'itself' (*sich*), which gives a better sense: translator] in the unspoken effect, which only allows it to recognize the capacity that lies for this in the subject-matter, and gives it a striving to realize the reproduction. The subject must therefore be distributed, the total impression must be suspended, and the identity must become a striving from one point to another, where the total impression then surely comes about when the starting-point and the mid-point and the end-point enter into the most intimate relationship, so that at the conclusion the end-point returns to the starting-point and the latter to the mid-point.

ever-onwards-resounding all-compensating *spiritual import*,
and the loss of material variety, which arises from the quicker
striving towards the main point and impression, from this
material identity, is replaced by the ever-alternating idealic spiritual form; when he has understood how, conversely, the very
conflict between the spiritual calm import and the spiritual
alternating form, as much as they are irreconcilable, as well as
the conflict between the material *alternation* and the material
identical striving towards the main moment, as much as they
are irreconcilable, make the one as the other *capable of being
felt*, when finally he has understood how the conflict between
the spiritual import and the idealic form on the one hand, and
between the material alternation and the identical striving on
the other hand unite at the points of repose and in the main
moments and as much as they cannot be reconciled in the same,
precisely here and for that very reason become capable of being
felt and actually are felt, when he has understood this, then
everything depends for him on the receptivity of the subject-
matter to the idealic import and to the idealic form. If he is
certain and in command of both of these, the receptiveness of
the subject-matter, and the spirit, at the capital moment he
cannot go wrong.

How must the subject now be constituted that is optimally
receptive for the idealic, for its import, for the metaphor and
for its form, the transition?

The subject is either a series of events, or views, realities, to
be described, to be painted, subjectively or objectively, or it is
a series of endeavours, ideas, thoughts, or passions, necessities,
to be indicated subjectively or objectively, or a series of fantasies, possibilities, to be formed subjectively or objectively.[ii]
In each of these three cases it must be capable of an idealic
treatment, if, that is, there is a real ground to the events or the

---

[ii] If the feeling is the meaning, then the representation is figurative, and the
spiritual treatment shows itself episodically.
If the intellectual intuition is the meaning, then the expression, the material, is
passionate, the spiritual treatment shows itself more in the style.
If the meaning is a more actual purpose, then the expression is sensuous, the
free treatment metaphorical.

views that are to be narrated, described, or to the thoughts and
passions that are to be drawn, or to the fantasies that are to be
formed, if the events or views emerge from true endeavours,
the thoughts and passions from a true matter, the fantasies
from a beautiful feeling. This ground of the poem, its meaning,
should form the transition between the expression, what is
represented, the sensuous subject, that which is actually uttered
in the poem, and between the spirit, the idealic treatment. The
meaning of the poem can be twofold, as also the spirit, the
idealic, as also the subject, the representation, are twofold,
namely insofar as this is understood as practical or theoretical.
Theoretically these words express nothing other than the poetic
procedure, as it can be observed in every genuinely poetic transaction, guided by genius and by judgement; practically the
words designate the appropriateness of each particular poetic
sphere of influence to the poetic procedure, the possibility that
resides in the element of realizing that procedure, so that one
can say that in every element objectively and really the idealic
faces the idealic, the living faces the living, the individual faces
the individual, and the only question is what is to be understood
by this sphere of influence. It is that in which and through
which each poetic transaction and procedure realizes itself, the
vehicle of the spirit, by means of which it reproduces itself in
itself and in others. *In* itself the sphere of influence is greater
than the poetic spirit, but not *for* itself. Insofar as it is considered
in relation to the world, it is greater; insofar as it is held fast
and appropriated by the poet, it is subordinate. According to
its tendency, according to the import of its striving, it is opposed
to the poetic transaction, and the poet is all too easily led astray
by his subject, in that the latter, being taken out of its context
in the living world, resists poetic limitation, in that it does not
wish to serve as a mere vehicle for the spirit; in that, even if it
is properly chosen, its most immediate, its first progress with
respect to the spirit is antithesis and spur, with respect to the
poetic, fulfilment, so that its second progress must be partly
unfulfilled, partly fulfilled. Etc.

But it must become apparent how notwithstanding this conflict, in which the poetic spirit stands in its transaction with

every specific element and sphere of influence, the latter nonetheless favours the former, and how that conflict dissolves, how
in the element which the poet chooses as his vehicle, there
nonetheless resides a receptivity for the poetic transaction, and
how he realizes all the demands, the whole poetic procedure in
its metaphoric, in its hyperbolic,[55] and its character[56] in himself in reciprocal relations with the element, albeit this resists
in its initial tendency, and is directly opposed, yet unites with
the spirit at the mid-point.

Between the expression (the representation) and the free idealic
treatment there lies the grounding and meaning of the poem.
This is what gives the poem its seriousness, its firmness, its
truth, this secures the poem against the free idealic treatment's
becoming an empty manner, and the representation a vanity.
This is the spiritually sensuous, the formally material quality
of the poem; and if the idealic treatment in its metaphor, its
transition, its episodes is more unifying, whereas the expression,
the representation in its characters, its passion, its individu-
alities is more divisive, the meaning stands between the two, it
is characterized by the fact that it is everywhere opposed to
itself: that it divides everything united, instead of the spirit's
reconciling everything that is formally opposed, fixes everything
that is free, generalizes everything particular, because according
to the meaning what is treated is not simply an individual
whole, nor a whole united into a whole in connection with
its own harmonious opposition, but a whole as such and the
connection with the harmonious opposition is also possible
because of an opposition to the individual tendency, in the
import, but not in the form; that the meaning unifies by opposition, by the meeting of extremes, in that these are reconcilable
not according to the import, but in the direction and the degree
of their opposition, so that it *reconciles* even *the most contradictory*, and is thoroughly hyperbolic, that the meaning does
not progress through formal opposition, where, however, the
one is related to the other in terms of import, but through
opposition in import, where however the one is the same as the
other in terms of form, so that the naive and the heroic and the

idealic[57] tendency contradict one another, in the object of their tendency, but are reconcilable in the form of their conflict and striving, and united according to the law of activity, thus united in the most general of all, in life.

It is precisely by this means, by this hyperbolic procedure, according to which the idealic, the harmoniously opposed and united, is considered not just as this, as a beautiful life, but also as life as such, so also as capable of another condition, namely not a harmoniously opposed one but a directly opposed one, an extreme, such that this new condition is only reconcilable with the previous one through the idea of life as such – it is precisely by this means that the poet gives the idealic a beginning, a direction, a meaning. The idealic in this form is the subjective ground of the poem, from which one starts, to which one returns, and since the inner idealic life can be understood in different moods, can be considered as life as such, as generalizable, as fixable, as divisible, so there are also different kinds of subjective grounding; either the idealic mood is understood as a feeling, in which case it is the subjective ground of the poem, the chief mood of the poet in the entire transaction, and precisely because it is held fast as a feeling it is through this grounding considered as something *generalizable* – or the idealic mood is fixed as a striving, in which case it becomes the chief mood of the poet in the entire transaction, and the fact that it is fixed as a striving ensures that through the grounding it is considered as something *fulfillable*, or the idealic mood is fixed as an intellectual intuition,[58] in which case this is the basic mood of the poet in the entire transaction, and the very fact that it is held fast as this ensures that it is considered as something *realizable*. And so the subjective grounding requires and defines an objective one, and prepares it. Thus in the first case the subject-matter is understood as general *first*, in the second as fulfilling, in the third as occurring.

Once the free idealic poetic life is fixed in this way, and once, depending on how it was fixed, it has been given its meaningfulness, as generalizable, as fulfillable, as realizable, once it is, in this way, through the idea of life as such, connected with its direct opposite, and taken hyperbolically, an important point is still lacking in the procedure of the poetic spirit, by means of which it gives its transaction not the mood, not the tone, nor the meaning and direction, but reality.

For, *considered as pure poetic* life, the poetic life remains *according to its import* thoroughly united with itself, as something *connected with its harmonious oppositions* by virtue of the harmonious as such and the temporal lack, and it is only opposed in the alternation of forms, only in the manner not in the ground of its striving onwards, it is only more hovering or more lingering or more rapid, only more sustained or more relaxed or more taut, more curved or more directed or more thrown, only more or less interrupted by chance; *considered* as life defined and grounded by the poetic reflection through the idea of life as such and through the lack in the unity, it begins with an idealically characteristic mood, in this case it is no longer simply something connected with its harmonious oppositions, it is present as such in a particular form, and advances in the alternation of moods, where the succeeding one is each time defined by the preceding one, and is opposed to it in import, that is to say opposed according to the organs in which it is grasped, and insofar more individual, more general, fuller, so that the different moods are only connected in that in which purity finds its opposition, namely in the manner of the striving, connected as life as such, so that the purely poetic life can no longer be found, for in each of the alternating moods it is in a particular form, that is to say connected with what is directly opposed to it, so no longer pure, in the whole it is only present as something that strives onwards and according to the law of striving only as life as such, and from this standpoint there is certainly a conflict of individual (material), general (formal) and the pure.

The pure, grasped in each specific mood, conflicts with the organ in which it is grasped, it conflicts with the purity of the next organ, it conflicts with the alternation.

The general as a particular organ (form), as a characteristic mood, conflicts with the pure that it grasps in this mood, as a striving onwards in the whole it conflicts with the pure that is grasped in it, as a characteristic mood it conflicts with the adjacent mood.

The individual conflicts with the pure that it grasps, it conflicts with the adjacent form, being individual it conflicts with the generality of the alternation.

The procedure of the poetic spirit in its transaction therefore cannot possibly end here. If it is the true method, something else must also be discoverable in it, and it must be demonstrated that the procedure that gives the poem its meaning is solely the transition from the pure to this thing which must be discovered, and back from this to the pure. (The mediatory link between the spirit and the sign.)

If then that which is directly opposed to the spirit, the organ in which it is contained and through which all opposition is possible, could be considered and grasped not only as that *through* which the harmoniously united is formally opposed but through which it is also formally united, if it could be considered and grasped not only as that through which the various harmonious moods are materially opposed and formally united but through which they are also materially united and formally opposed, if it could be considered and grasped not just as that which is, as a unifier, simply formal life as such, and, as something particular and material, not unifying, only opposing and dividing, if it could be considered as something material, as unifying, *if the organ of the spirit could be considered as that which, in order to make the harmoniously opposed possible*, must be RECEPTIVE *both for the one and for the other harmoniously opposed*, that therefore, insofar as it is a formal opposition for the purely poetic life, it must also be a formal union, that, insofar as it is a material opposition for the particular poetic life and its moods, it must also be materially unifying, that that which limits and defines is not negative, that it is also positive, that, although in what is harmoniously united it is opposed to one as the other when these are considered separately, thinking them both together it is the unification of them both, then that act of the spirit which with regard to the meaning only had a thoroughgoing conflict as its result will be just as unifying as it was oppositional.

But how can the act be grasped in this quality? As possible and as necessary? Not simply *through life as such*, for then the act would be possible and necessary insofar as it is considered simply as materially opposing and formally unifying, directly defining life. Nor simply through the *unity* as such, for then the act would be possible and necessary insofar as it is considered simply as formally opposing. But in the concept of the *unity* of the *One*, such that, among the harmoniously united, *one* as well as *the other* is *present in the point of opposition and union*, and that IN THIS POINT THE SPIRIT is FEELABLE IN ITS INFINITY, which through the opposition manifested itself as finite, that the pure, which in itself conflicted with the organ, is *present* to *itself* in this very organ and only by that means *is a living thing*, that, where it is present in different moods, the one immediately following the basic mood is only *the lengthened point*, which leads thither, namely to the *mid-point*, where the harmoniously opposed moods meet, that therefore just in the very strongest contrast, in the contrast between the first idealic and the second artificially reflected mood, in the *most material* opposition (which lies between the harmoniously united spirit and life, meeting in the mid-point, and present in the mid-point), that just in this, the most material opposition, which is opposed to itself (*in relation to the point of union towards which it strives*), in the conflicting *progressive acts* of the spirit, if they only *emerge from the reciprocal character of the harmoniously opposed moods*, that just there the most infinite represents itself at its most feelable, most negative-positive and hyperbolically, so that through this contrast between the representation of the infinite in the conflicting striving towards the point and its meeting in the point the simultaneous intimacy and differentiation of the harmoniously opposed living feeling lying at the ground is replaced and at the same time is represented more clearly by the free consciousness, and in a more developed shape, more generally, as an own world according to its form, as a world in the world, and so as the voice of the eternal to the eternal.

The poetic spirit in the procedure which it observes in its transaction can therefore not content itself in a harmoniously

opposed life, nor with the understanding and fixing of it by
means of hyperbolic opposition; if it has reached that stage, if
its transaction lacks neither harmonious unity nor meaning
and energy, neither harmonious spirit as such nor harmonious
alternation, then it is necessary, if the One is not (insofar as it
can be considered in itself) to cancel itself out as an undifferentiated entity and become an *empty* infinity, or if it is not to
lose its identity in an alternation of antitheses, be these as
harmonious as possible, and so not be anything whole or one
any more, but break up into an infinity of isolated moments (as
it were, an atomic series), – I say: then it is necessary that the
poetic spirit in its unity and harmonious progress gives itself an
infinite point of view, a unity in its transaction, where in the
harmonious progress and alternation everything goes forwards
and backwards, and by means of its *thorough characteristic
relation* to this unity gains not only an objective connection,
for the observer, but also a felt and feelable connection and
identity in the alternation of contrasts, and it is its final task to
have in the harmonious alternation a thread, a memory, so
that the spirit never remains present to itself in the individual
moment, and again in an individual moment, but continuously
in one moment as in the next, and in the various moods, as it
is wholly present to itself, IN THE INFINITE UNITY, which is
now the dividing point of the One as One, but then again the
unifying point of the One as the opposed, and in the end
both at once, so that in it the harmoniously opposed is neither
opposed as a unity, nor united as an opposition, but as both in
One, as a united opposition felt undividedly and invented as
something felt. This sense is actually poetic character, neither
genius nor art, poetic individuality, and to this alone is granted
the identity of enthusiasm, to this is granted the perfection of
genius and art, the manifestation of the infinite, the divine
moment.

Poetic individuality is therefore never simply the opposition
of the One and never merely relation; unification of the opposed
and the alternating, the opposed and the united is indivisible
within it. If this is the case, it can, in its purity and subjective
wholeness, as original sense, in the acts of uniting and opposing

with which it works in harmoniously opposed life, be passive, but in its last act, where the harmoniously opposed as something harmonious and opposed, and the One as a reciprocal relation are conceived in it as One, in this act it cannot and must not at all be conceived by itself or become its own object if it is not to be, instead of an infinitely united and living unity, a dead and deadening unity, something become infinitely positive;[59] for if unity and opposition are indivisibly connected and one in it, poetic individuality can appear to reflection neither as an opposable unity, nor as a unitable opposition, it can therefore not appear at all, or only in the character of a positive nothing, of an infinite stasis, and it is the hyperbole of all hyperboles, the boldest and final essay of the poetic spirit, if ever in its procedure it undertakes it, to grasp the original poetic individuality, the poetic I, an essay by means of which it would cancel out this individuality and its pure object, the One, and alive, the harmonious reciprocally effective life, and yet it must do so, since it should and must be everything that it is in its transaction with *freedom*, in that it creates its own world, and instinct naturally belongs to the actual world in which it exists; since therefore the poetic spirit should be everything with freedom, it must also assure itself of this, its individuality. But since the poetic spirit cannot recognize its individuality through itself and in itself, an external object is necessary, and namely one by which pure individuality, among several special neither purely opposing nor purely relating but poetic characters which it can assume, is determined to assume any one, so that therefore, both through pure individuality and through the other characters, the individuality now selected and its character as determined by the subject-matter now selected is knowable and is to be held fast with freedom.

(Within subjective nature the I can only know itself as an opposite, or as relating, but not, within subjective nature, as a poetic I in a threefold quality, for as it manifests itself within subjective nature, and is distinguished from itself, and distinguished in and by itself, only the known with the knowing and the knowledge of both taken together can ever constitute the threefold nature of the poetic I, and neither as a known understood by the knower (nor as a knower understood by the knower), nor as a known and knower understood by knowledge, nor as knowledge understood by the knower, in none of these three separately conceived qualities is it invented as a pure poetic I in its threefold nature, as opposing the harmoniously opposed, as (formally) uniting the harmoniously opposed, as comprehending in one the harmoniously opposed, the opposition and the union, on the contrary, it remains in real contradiction with and for itself.[iii] – Thus only insofar as it is not distinguished by itself and in and through itself, if it is made

[iii] It is simply not comprehensible to itself as a knowing subject in its real conflict as something *posited* as materially opposed thus (for a third but not for itself) as something formally uniting (as known), as something *positing* as opposed, thus (for a third) *formally* united; as something opposed, formally uniting, as something opposing, formally united in knowledge, opposed in the materially united and opposed, thus[60]

Namely insofar as the I in its subjective nature distinguishes itself from itself and posits itself as an opposing unity in the harmoniously opposed, insofar as this is harmonious, or as a unifying unity in the harmoniously opposed, insofar as this is opposed, it must either deny the reality of the opposition, of the difference, in which it knows itself, and declare the act of distinguishing within subjective nature to be either an illusion and arbitrary, which it produces for itself as a unity in order to know its identity, in which case the identity itself, that is known from it, is an illusion, it does not know itself, is not a unity, or it treats the distinction from itself as (dogmatically) real, that namely the I behaves as a distinguisher or as a unifier according to whether, in its subjective nature, it finds before it something to be distinguished or something to be unified; thus it posits itself as contingent as a distinguisher and as a unifier, and because this should take place in its subjective nature, from which it cannot abstract without cancelling itself out, as absolutely contingent in its acts, so that it knows *itself, its* act, neither as an opposer nor as a unifier. In this case yet again it cannot know itself as identical because the different acts in which it is present are not *its* acts, it cannot even posit itself as contained in these acts, for these acts do not depend on it, it is not the I which differs from itself, but it is its nature, in which it behaves in this way as a driven thing.

However, even if the I wanted to posit itself as identical with the harmoniously opposed side of its nature (to cut with its sword the eternal knot, the contradiction between art and genius, between freedom and organic necessity), it would not help; for if the difference between opposing and unifying is not real, then neither the I in its harmoniously opposed life nor the harmoniously opposed life in the I are knowable as a unity; if the difference is real, then again neither the I in the harmoniously opposed is knowable as a unity through itself, definitely distinguishable by means of a third, and if this third, insofar as it was elected with freedom, thus also does not cancel out pure individuality in its influences and determinations, but can be observed by it, where pure individuality also observes itself as something determined by choice, something empirically individualized and characterized, only then is it possible that the I appears in the harmoniously opposed life as a unity, and conversely, that the harmoniously opposed appears as a unity in the I and becomes an object in beautiful individuality.)

(a) But how is that possible? In general?

(b) If it becomes possible in such a way that the I knows itself and acts in poetic individuality, what consequence results from this for poetic representation? (The I recognizes in the threefold subjective and objective essays the striving for pure unity.)

(a) If man in this solitude, in this life with himself, this contradictory *middle state* between a natural connection with a world that is also naturally present and between the higher connection with a world that is also naturally present but has been elected *freely* as his sphere and recognized in advance, one that in all its influences does not determine him against his will, if he has lived in this middle state between childhood and mature humanity, between mechanically beautiful and humanly beautiful life, life beautiful with freedom, and has known and experienced this middle state, how he must remain in thorough contradiction with himself, in the necessary conflict of (1) the striving for pure selfhood and identity, (2) the striving for

---

for it is driven, nor is the harmoniously opposed knowable as a unity in its I, for this, as a driven thing, is not knowable as a unity.

Everything depends on the fact that the I does not just remain in a reciprocal relation with its subjective nature, from which it cannot abstract without cancelling itself out, but that it *SHOULD FREELY CHOOSE* an *OBJECT FROM WHICH, IF IT SO WISHES*, it can *ABSTRACT, to be absolutely, APPROPRIATELY DETERMINED by it and TO DETERMINE it.*

Herein resides the possibility, that the I may become knowable in the harmoniously opposed life as a unity, and the harmoniously opposed as a unity in the I in a pure (poetic) individuality. Pure subjective life only attains to free individuality, to unity and identity within itself, by the choice of its object.

significance and differentiation, (3) the striving for harmony, and that in this conflict every one of those strivings must cancel itself out and show itself to be unrealizable, that he must therefore resign himself, relapse into childhood or wear himself out in fruitless self-contradictions if he remains in this state, then there is *one* thing which draws him out of this sorry dilemma, and the problem of how to be free, like a youth, and to live in the world like a child, with the independence of a cultivated human being and the accommodation of an ordinary person, resolves itself in following the rule:

Put yourself *through free choice* in harmonious opposition with an outer sphere, just as you in yourself are in *harmonious* opposition, by nature, but unrecognizably, as long as you remain in yourself.

For here, in following this rule, there is an important distinction from the course of action in the former state.

In the former state, namely in that of solitude,[61] harmoniously opposed nature could not become a recognizable unity because the I, without cancelling itself out, could posit and recognize itself neither as an active unity, without cancelling out the reality of differentiation, that is, the reality *of knowing*, nor as a suffering unity, without cancelling out the reality of unity, its criterion of identity, namely activity; and that the I, in that it strives to know its unity in the harmoniously opposed, and the harmoniously opposed in its unity, must posit itself thus absolutely and dogmatically as an active unity, or as suffering unity, comes about because in order to know itself through itself, it can only replace the natural intimate relation in which it stands to itself, and by means of which distinguishing is made more difficult for it, with an unnatural (self-cancelling) distinction, because it is by nature so very much One in its difference with itself that the difference necessary for knowledge, which it gives itself through freedom, is only possible in extremes, that is, in striving, in intellectual essays, which realized *in this way* would cancel themselves out, because in order to *know* its unity in the (subjective) harmoniously opposed, and the (subjective) harmoniously opposed in its unity, the I must necessarily abstract from itself, insofar it is posited in the

(subjective) harmoniously opposed, and reflect on itself, insofar
as it is not posited in the (subjective) harmoniously opposed,
and vice versa, but since it cannot make this abstraction from
its being in the (subjective) harmoniously opposed, and this
reflection on its non-being in it, without cancelling itself and
the harmoniously opposed, without cancelling the subjective
harmonious and opposed and the unity, so the essays, which
it nonetheless makes in this way, must be essays of the kind
that, were they realized in this way, would also cancel themselves out.

This is therefore the difference between the state of solitude
(the intimation of his essence) and the new state, where the
human being puts himself in harmonious opposition with an
external sphere through free choice, that, *just because he is not
so intimately connected with this sphere, he can abstract from
it and from himself, insofar he is posited in it*, and can *reflect
upon himself*, insofar he is not posited in it, this is the reason
why he departs from himself, this is the rule for his manner of
proceeding in the external world. In this way he fulfils his
destiny, which is – knowledge of the harmoniously opposed in
himself, in his unity and individuality, and again knowledge of
his identity, his unity and individuality in the harmoniously
opposed. This is the true freedom of his being, and if he does
not attach too much to this external harmoniously opposed
sphere, does not become identical with it, as he is with himself,
so that he can never abstract from it, nor is too attached to
himself, and can abstract too little from himself as an independent person, if he neither reflects too much on himself, nor
reflects too much on his sphere and his time, he is then on the
right path of his destiny. The childhood of ordinary life, where
he was identical with the world and could not abstract from it
at all, where he was without freedom and therefore without
knowledge of himself in the harmoniously opposed and of the
harmoniously opposed in himself, and considered in himself
was without resolution, independence, any actual identity in
pure life, this time he will regard as the time of desires, where
man strives to know himself in the harmoniously opposed and
the latter in himself as a unity, by giving himself wholly to

objective life; where, however, the impossibility of a knowable identity in the harmoniously opposed manifests itself
objectively, as it was already manifested subjectively. For since
he does not know himself at all in his subjective nature in this
state, and is only objective life in the objective, he can only
strive to know the unity in the harmoniously opposed by proceeding in his sphere, from which he can no more abstract than
the subjective man can from his subjective sphere, in the same
way as the latter does in his. He is posited in it as in the
harmoniously opposed. He must strive to know himself, seek
to distinguish himself from himself in this sphere, in that he
makes himself into an opposer insofar as the sphere is harmonious, and into a unifier insofar as the sphere is opposed. But if
he strives to know himself in this difference, he must either
deny to himself the reality of the conflict in which he finds
himself with himself, and treat this conflicting procedure as an
illusion and as arbitrary, which only expresses itself in order
that he recognize his identity in the harmoniously opposed
(but then this identity of his too is an illusion, as something
recognized), or he treats the distinction as real, namely by
behaving as a unifier and a distinguisher, depending on whether
he finds something to distinguish or to unite in his objective
sphere, thereby making himself contingent as a unifier and a
distinguisher, and because this should take place in his objective
sphere, from which he cannot abstract without cancelling himself out, absolutely contingent, so that neither as a unifier nor
as an opposer does he *himself* know *his act*. In this case he
again cannot know himself as identical, because the various
acts in which he finds himself are not his acts. He cannot know
himself at all, he is not something distinguishable, it is his
sphere in which he acts mechanically in this way. But even if he
wished to posit himself as identical with his sphere, to dissolve
in highest intimacy the conflict of life and personality which he
always strives, and must strive, to unify and to recognize in
One, then it does not help, insofar as he conducts himself in his
sphere such that he cannot abstract from it, because he can
only know himself in extremes of antitheses of distinguishing

and uniting for the very reason that he dwells too intimately in his sphere.

Thus in a too subjective condition, as in too objective a one, the human being seeks to achieve his destiny in vain, which consists in knowing himself to be contained as a unity in the divine-harmoniously opposed, as well as, conversely, knowing the Divine, the One, the harmoniously opposed to be contained as a unity in himself. *For this is only possible in a beautiful holy, divine feeling*, in a feeling which is beautiful for the reason that it is, and can only be, neither only pleasant and happy, nor only sublime and strong, nor only unified and calm, but everything at once, in a feeling which is holy because it is, and can only be, neither only selflessly devoted to its object, nor only selflessly resting on its inner ground, nor only selflessly hovering between its inner ground and its object, but everything at once, in a feeling which is divine because it is neither only consciousness, only reflection (subjective or objective), with loss of inner and outer life, nor only striving (subjectively or objectively defined), with loss of inner or outer harmony, nor only harmony, as in intellectual intuition and its mythical, figurative subject-object, with loss of consciousness and of unity, but because it is all this at once, and can only be, in a feeling which is transcendental and can only be so because in the unity and the reciprocal relation of the aforementioned qualities it is neither too pleasant and sensual, nor too energetic and wild, nor too intimate and enthusiastic, neither too selflessly, i.e. too self-forgetfully devoted to its object, nor too selflessly, i.e. too arbitrarily resting on its inner ground, nor too selfless, i.e. too undecidedly and emptily and uncertainly hovering between its inner ground and its object, neither too reflected, too conscious of itself, too sharp and for that very reason unconscious of its inner and outer ground; nor too moved, too occupied in its inner and outer ground, for that very reason unconscious of the harmony between inner and outer, nor too harmonious, for that very reason too unconscious of itself and of the inner and outer ground, for that very reason too uncertain, and less receptive towards the actual infinite, which is defined by it as a *definite* real infinity, as located in the external and capable of only a lesser duration. In short, because it is present in a threefold quality, and can only be so, this feeling is less exposed to one-sidedness in any one of its three qualities. On the contrary, all the powers originally awake from it which those qualities more definitely and more knowably, but also more isolatedly, possess, just as those powers and their qualities and expressions concentrate themselves in turn in the feeling, and gain in it and through reciprocal connection, living, independently existing determinacy, as its organs, and freedom, as belonging to it and not limited to themselves in their limitation, and completeness, as comprised in its totality; these three qualities may express themselves as tendencies to know the harmoniously opposed in the living unity or vice versa, in a more subjective or a more objective state. For precisely these various states emerge from this feeling as from the union of the same.

S⁶²

Hint for Representation and Language⁶³

Is not language like the knowledge which was discussed earlier, and of which it was said that it contained the unified as a unity and vice versa? and that it had a threefold character etc.

Must not for the one as for the other the most beautiful moment lie at the point where the actual *expression*, the most spiritual language, the liveliest consciousness, where the transition from a determined infinity to the more general one lies?

Does not the fixed point lie just here that determines the relations of the sequence of the design as well as the character and degree of the local colours and of the illumination?

Will not all judgement of language be reduced to verifying according to THE MOST CERTAIN AND AS FAR AS POSSIBLE INFALLIBLE CHARACTERISTICS *whether it is the language of a genuine, beautifully described emotion?*

Just as knowledge anticipates language, language remembers knowledge.

Knowledge anticipates language, after it (1) was still unre-

flected pure feeling of life, of the determined infinity within
which it is contained, (2) after it had repeated itself in the
dissonances of inner reflecting and striving and composing, and
now, after these vain essays to find itself inwardly again and to
reproduce itself, after these secret anticipations which must also
have their time, goes beyond itself, and finds itself again in the
whole of infinity, i.e. is in command of and conscious of its
entire inner and outer life through the subjectless pure mood,
as it were through the echo of the original living feeling which
it gained and could gain through the total effect of all inner
essays, through this higher divine receptivity. In this very
moment, in which the original living feeling, which has been
purified into a pure mood receptive towards an infinity, finds
itself as an infinite in the infinite, as a spiritual whole in the
living whole, it is in this moment that one can say that the
language is anticipated, and if, as in the original feeling, a
reflection occurs, it is no longer dissolving and generalizing,
distributing and representing, to the point of mere mood, it
gives the heart everything back that it took from it, it is an
enlivening art as before it was a spiritualizing art, and with
one magic blow after another it calls forth the lost life more
beautifully, until it feels as whole again as it originally felt. And
if it is the progress and destiny of life as such to fashion itself
from the original simplicity into the highest form, where for
that very reason the infinite life is present to the human being,
and where as the most abstract entity he absorbs everything
all the more intimately, to bring back then from this highest
opposition and union of the living and spiritual, of the formal
and the material subject-object, the life to the spiritual, the form
to the living, the love and the heart to the human being and the
thanks to his world again, and finally after fulfilled anticipation,
and hope, when namely that highest point of cultivation, the
highest form in the highest life was present in the *expression*,
and not just in itself as at the beginning of the actual expression,
nor in the striving, as in the continuation of this expression,
where the expression calls forth life from the spirit and the
spirit from life, but where it has found the original life in its
highest form, where *spirit and life is the same on both sides*,

and knows its discovery, the infinite in the infinite, after this final and third completion, which is not just original simplicity, of heart and life, where the human being feels himself naturally *as* in a limited infinity, nor just achieved simplicity of the spirit, where that very feeling, purified into a pure formal mood, absorbs the entire infinity of life (and is ideal), but spirit revived again out of infinite life, not happiness, not ideal, but achieved work and creation, and can only be found in the expression, and outside the expression can only be hoped for in the ideal that emerged from the expression's determined original feeling, as finally after this third completion, where the determined infinity is called forth so far into life, the infinite one is spiritualized so far, that the one is equal to the other in spirit and life, as after this third completion the determined is enlivened more and more, the infinite is more and more spiritualized, until the original feeling ends as life in just the way that *in the expression* it began as spirit, and the higher infinity from which the feeling took its life spiritualizes itself just as much as it was present in the expression as a living entity, – thus if this seems to be the course and the destiny of mankind as such, then the same is the course and the destiny of all and every poetry, and as at the stage of education where the human being emerged from original childhood and struggled upwards in opposing attempts to the highest form, to the pure echo of the first life, and *thus* feels himself as an infinite spirit in infinite life, as the human being only really begins life at this stage of education and anticipates his activity and his destiny, so the poet anticipates, at the stage where he also has struggled from an original feeling through opposed essays upwards to the tone, to the highest pure form of the same feeling and sees himself wholly engaged in his whole inner and outer life with that tone, at this stage he anticipates his language, and with that the actual completion for the present and at the same time for all poetry.

It has already been said that on that level a new reflection sets in, which gives the heart everything back that it took from it, which is an enlivening art for the spirit of the poet and of his future poem, as it was a spiritualizing art for the original feeling of the poet and of his poem. *The product of this creative*

reflection is language. For in that the poet feels himself engaged
in his entire inner and outer life with the pure tone of his
original feeling, and looks around in his world, the latter is just
as new and unknown to him, the sum of all his experiences, his
knowledge, his observation, his thinking, art and nature as it
manifests itself in him and outside of him, everything is as if
for the first time, for that very reason not understood, undeter-
mined, dissolved in nothing but substance and life, present to
him, and it is above all important that he treats nothing as
given at this moment, does not assume anything positive, that
nature and art, as he has got to know them and sees them, do
not *speak* before a language is there *for him*, i.e. before what is
now unknown and unnamed in his world becomes known and
named for him precisely by having compared it and found it to
conform with his mood, *for* if any language of nature or art
existed for him in a definite form before his reflection on the
infinite substance and the infinite form, then *to this extent* he
would not be within his sphere of influence, he would depart
from his creation, and the language of nature or art, every
modus exprimendi[64] of the one or the other would be, from the
first, insofar as it was not *his* language, not a product that had
emerged out of his life and his spirit, but as a language of art,
as soon as it is present to me in a particular form, already
an act determining the creative reflection of the artist, which
consisted in his taking from his own world, from the sum of
his outer and inner life, which is more or less also my own, in
taking from this world the subject-matter to denote the tones
of his spirit and to call forth from his mood the life which
underlies it with this related sign, in, therefore, insofar as he
names me this sign, his borrowing the subject-matter from my
world, occasioning me to translate this subject-matter into the
sign, where there is then the following important difference
between me as a definite and him as defining instance, that
he, in that he makes himself comprehensible and intelligible,
progresses from the lifeless, immaterial and therefore less
opposable and more unconscious mood by explaining it (1) in
the infinity of its consonance through a relative totality in both
form and matter of a related subject, and through an ideally

alternating world, (2) in its definition and actual finitude
through the representation and listing of its own subject-matter,
(3) in its tendency, its generality in the particular, through the
contrast of its own subject-matter with the infinite subject-
matter, (4) in its measure, in the beautiful definition and unity
and firmness of its infinite consonance, in its infinite identity and
individuality, and carriage, in the poetic prose of an all-limiting
moment, whereto and wherein every named part relates and
unites negatively and for that reason expressly and sensuously,
namely the infinite form with the infinite subject-matter by this
means, that *through that moment* the infinite form assumes a
structure, the alternation of the weaker and the stronger, the
infinite subject-matter assumes a euphony, an alternation of
the brighter and quieter, and that both unite negatively in the
slowness and rapidity and finally in the cessation of motion,
ever through the moment and through the underlying activity,
the *infinite beautiful* reflection, which in its continuous limitation is at the same time continuously relating and unifying.

Feeling speaks in a poem idealically – passion naively – the imagination energetically.

Thus the idealic in a poem acts on feeling (by means of passion), the naive on passion (by means of imagination), the energetic[66] on the imagination (by means of feeling)

naive poem.
Basic tone.
  Passion. etc.   by means of imagination.
Language.
  Feeling Passion Imagination Feeling Passion Imagination
      Feeling.
  By means of imagination.
Effect.
  Passion Imagination Feeling Passion Imagination Feeling
      Passion.

energetic poem.
Basic tone.
  Imagination. etc.   by means of feeling.
Language.
  Passion Imagination Feeling Passion Imagination Feeling
      Passion.
  chiefly by means of feeling.
Effect.
  Imagination Feeling Passion Imagination Feeling Passion
      Imagination.

Idealic poem.

Basic tone.

Feeling etc.   by means of passion.

Language.

Imagination Feeling Passion Imagination Feeling Passion Imagination.

chiefly by means of passion.

Effect.

Feeling Passion Imagination Feeling Passion Imagination Feeling.

?

Imagination Passion Feeling Imagination Passion Feeling Imagination.

by means of Feeling.

Feeling Imagination Passion Feeling Imagination Passion Feeling.

Style of the Diotima song.[67]

'The expression, the characteristic . . .'[68]

The expression, the characteristic sensuous individual normal quality of a poem, is always constant to itself, and if each of the different parts is different in itself, then the first in every part is like the first of the others, the second in every part is like the second of the others, the third of every part is like the third of the others. The style, the[69]

The lyric, in appearance idealic poem, is in its meaning naive. It is a continuous metaphor[71] of *one* feeling.

The epic, in appearance naive poem, is in its meaning heroic. It is a metaphor of great endeavours.

The tragic, in appearance heroic poem, is in its meaning idealic. It is the metaphor of an intellectual intuition.

The lyric poem is in its *basic mood* the *more sensual*, in that this mood contains a unity, which expresses itself most easily, and for that very reason in its external appearance it strives not so much for reality and cheer and grace, it avoids sensuous connections and representations so much (because the pure basic tone wishes to incline that very way), such that in its formations and in their composition it tends to be miraculous and supersensory; and its heroic energetic dissonances, in which it loses neither its reality, its living quality, as in an idealic image, nor its tendency to elevation, as in the more immediate expression, these energetic heroic dissonances, that unite elevation and life, are the dissolution of the contradiction in which it becomes caught, when on the one side it cannot and does not wish to fall into sensuousness and, on the other, to deny its basic tone, the intimate life. If, however, its basic tone is more heroic, richer in import, as is e.g. the basic tone of a Pindaric ode, the one for Diagoras the Fencer,[72] if it thus has less to lose in ideality, then the lyric poem begins naively, if the basic tone is more idealic, more related to the artistic character, the figurative tone, if it thus has less intimacy to lose, the lyric poem begins heroically, if the basic tone is most intimate, if it can lose in import, but yet more in elevation and purity of import, the lyric poem begins idealically.

In the lyric poem, the emphasis falls on the more immediate language of the feelings, on the most intimate; the lingering, the attitude, on the heroic; and the tendency, on the idealic.

The epic, in external appearance *naive poem* is in its *basic mood* the more *pathetic*, the more heroic, aorgic;[73] it therefore strives in its execution, its artistic character, not so much for energy and movement and life as for precision and repose and plasticity. The opposition between its basic mood and its artistic character, its actual and its figurative, metaphoric tone, resolves itself in the realm of the ideal, where on the one side it does not lose so much life, as in its narrowly confining artistic character, nor as much moderation as in the more immediate expression of its basic tone. If its basic tone, which may well vary in mood, is more idealic, if it has less life to lose, but its disposition tends more towards organization, wholeness, then the poem can begin with its basic tone, the heroic, $\mu\eta\nu\iota\nu$ $\alpha\epsilon\iota\delta\epsilon$ $\theta\epsilon\alpha$,[74] and be heroic-epic. If, however, the energetic basic tone has a less idealic disposition, but more affinity with the artistic character, which is the naive one, then the poem opens idealically; but if the basic tone possesses its own character so much that for this reason it must lose in disposition towards the ideal, but even more towards naivety, the poem will begin naively. If that which unites and mediates the basic tone and the artistic character of the poem is the spirit of the poem, and this must be maintained most of all, and this spirit in an epic poem is the idealic, then the epic poem must linger on it most of all, whereas the most emphasis is on the basic tone, which is here the energetic one, and the tendency is on the naive, which is the artistic character, and everything concentrates therein, and must therein distinguish and individualize itself.

The tragic, in its *external appearance heroic poem* is, according to its *basic tone, idealic,* and all works of this kind must be based on *one* intellectual intuition, which can be no other than that unity with all that lives, which, though it is not felt by a more limited nature, and can only be vaguely apprehended in its highest aspirations, can be recognized by the spirit and emerges from the impossibility of an absolute division and isolation and can most easily be expressed by saying that the real separation, and with it everything really material transient, and also the connection and with it everything really spiritual permanent, the objective as such, and also the subjective as such, are only a condition of the primally-one, in which it dwells because it must depart from itself, on account of the stasis which cannot occur in it because the nature of the union in it must not remain always the same, according to the matter, because the parts of the One must not remain always in the same closer and further relation, so that all encounters all, and each receives its entire right, its entire measure of life, and in the continuation each part becomes equal to the whole in its completeness, and by contrast the whole in the continuation becomes equal to the parts in definition, the whole gaining content, the parts intimacy, the whole gaining life, the parts liveliness, the whole in the continuation feeling itself more, the parts fulfilling themselves more; for it is an eternal law, that the whole which is rich in import in its unity does not feel itself with the definition and liveliness, not in that sensuous unity, in which its parts feel themselves, they also being a whole, only more loosely connected, so that one can say, if the liveliness, definition, unity of the parts, where their wholeness is felt, exceeds *their* limits, and turns into suffering and the most absolute decision and isolation *possible*, only then does the whole feel itself *in these parts* as lively and definite as they feel themselves in a calmer but also moved condition in their more limited wholeness (as e.g. the lyric (more individual) mood is, where the individual world strives to dissolve itself in its most complete life and purest unity, and at the point where it individualizes, in that part where its parts run together, appears to pass away, in the most intimate feeling, as only there the individual world is felt in its wholeness, as only where feeler and felt wish to separate the more individual unity is present at its most lively and definite, and resounds). The feelability of the whole therefore progresses in the very same degree and relation as the division in the parts and in its centre progresses, in which the parts and the whole are most feelable. The unity present in the intellectual intuition embodies itself in the very same degree in which it departs from itself, in which the division of its parts takes place, which only separate themselves, because they feel themselves to be too unified, when in the whole they are closer to the centre, or because they do not feel themselves to be united enough according to their completeness, if they are secondary parts, lying further from the centre, or, according to their liveliness, if they are neither secondary parts, in the given sense, nor essential parts, in the given sense, but because they are not yet actualized, because they are still only divisible parts. And here, in the excess of the spirit in unity, and in its striving for materiality, in the striving of the divisible more infinite more aorgic, in which everything more organic must be contained, because everything more definitely and more necessarily present necessitates a more definite, more unnecessarily present, in this striving of the divisible more infinite for division, which communicates itself in the condition of the highest unity of everything organic to every part contained within it, in this necessary *arbitrariness of Zeus*[75] actually lies the ideal beginning of the real division.

From here it continues up to the point where the parts are at their utmost tension, where they oppose each other most strongly. From this conflict it returns into itself, namely to that point where the parts, at least the originally most intimate, annul themselves in their particularity, as *these* parts, in this place of the whole, and a new unity emerges. The transition from the first to the second is probably that point of highest tension in the conflict. And the exit to that point is distinct from the return in that the former is more ideal, the latter more real, that in the former the motif is ideally determinative, reflected, more from the whole than individual, etc., in the latter emerging from passion and the individuals.

This basic tone is less lively than the lyric, more individual one. Therefore it is also, since it is more universal and the most universal,

If in the basic tone of the tragic poem there is more disposition for reflection and emotion for its middle character, but less disposition for representation, less earthly element, as it is natural that a poem whose meaning is more profound, and whose attitude and tension and power to move are stronger and more tender, does not so readily and so easily show itself in its most expressive utterance, as when the meaning and the motives lie closer to the expression, are more sensuous, then it properly begins with the idealic basic tone,[76]

If the intellectual intuition is more subjective, and if the division chiefly proceeds from the concentrating parts, as in the *Antigone*, then the style is lyric, but if it proceeds more from the secondary parts and is more objective, then it is epic, and if it proceeds from the highest divisible, from Zeus as in the *Oedipus*, then it is tragic.

In every poetic kind, the epic, tragic and lyric, a basic tone with a *richer subject* will express itself in the naive, a *more intense, more emotional* one in the idealic, and the more *spirited* in the energetic style; for if in the more spirited basic tone the division occurs from the infinite, it must first influence the concentrating parts or the centre, it must communicate itself to these, and insofar as the division has been accepted, it cannot express itself formatively, not by reproducing its own wholeness, it can only react, and this is the energetic beginning. It is only through this division that the contrasting main part reacts, which was also affected by the original division, but which as the more receptive part did not reproduce it so quickly, and reacted only now; through the action and reaction of the main parts, the secondary parts, which were also moved by the original division, but only to the point that they strove to change, are now moved to the point of real expression, by this expression the main parts etc., until the original divider has attained its complete expression.

If, however, the division proceeds from the centre, this occurs either through the more receptive main part; for then this reproduces itself in the idealic formation, the division separates[77]

'Does the idealic catastrophe . . .'[78]

Does the idealic catastrophe,[79] by the natural opening tone's becoming its opposite, not resolve itself into the heroic?

Does the natural catastrophe, by the heroic opening tone's becoming its opposite, not resolve itself into the idealic?

Does the heroic catastrophe, by the idealic opening tone's becoming its opposite, not resolve itself into the natural?

Yes, for the epic poem. The tragic poem goes a tone further, the lyric poem uses this tone as an opposite and in this way returns, in every style, to its opening tone, or: the epic poem stops with its initial opposition, the tragic poem with the tone of its catastrophe, the lyric poem with itself, so that the lyric end [is a naive-idealic one, the tragic a naive-heroic, the epic an idealic-heroic.][80]

the lyric				
naive		heroic		idealic
	X		X	
idealic		naive		heroic

the tragic				
idealic		naive		heroic
	X		X	
heroic		idealic		naive

the epic				
heroic		idealic		naive
	X		X	
naive		heroic		idealic

Lyric.[81]
naive *Idealic*, heroic *Naive*, idealic *Heroic* – heroic *Idealic*,
idealic *Naive*, naive *Heroic*, heroic *Idealic*

Tragic.
idealic *Heroic*, naive *Idealic*, heroic *Naive* – naive *Heroic*,
heroic *Idealic*, idealic *Naive*, naive *Heroic*

Epic.
heroic *Naive*, idealic *Heroic*, naive *Idealic* – idealic *Naive*, naive
Heroic, heroic *Idealic*, idealic *Naive*

Poetological Tables[82]

	L.		T.		N.
naive	Idealic	idealic	Heroic	heroic	Naive
heroic	Naive	naive	Idealic	idealic	Heroic
idealic	Heroic	heroic	Naive	naive	Idealic
heroic	Idealic	naive	Heroic	idealic	Naive
idealic	Naive	heroic	Idealic	naive	Heroic
naive	Heroic	idealic	Naive	heroic	Idealic
heroic	Idealic.	naive	Heroic.	idealic	Naive.

Aj.[83]

or the other way round

heroic	Idealic
idealic	Naive
naive	Heroic
heroic	Naive
idealic	Heroic
naive	Idealic
heroic	Naive.

Ant.

	id.	na.	her.	id. /	naive	her.	id.
	naive	her.	id.	na. /	her.	id.	na.
⟨	her.	id.	n.	h. /	id.	n.	her.
	id.	n.	he.	id. /	n.	h.	id.
	na.	her.	id.	n. /	her.	id.	n.
	her.	id.	n.	h. /	id.	n.	h.
	id.	n.	h.	id. /	n.	h.	id.

	her.	id.	na.	h. /	id.	n.	h.
	id.	n.	h.	id. /	na.	h.	id.
⟨	n.	h.	id.	n. /	h.	id.	n.
	h.	id.	n.	h. /	id.	n.	h.
	id.	n.	h.	id. /	n.	h.	id.
	n.	h.	id.	n. /	h.	id.	n.
	h.	id.	n.	h. /	id.	n.	h.

	n.	h.	id.	n.	h.	id.	n.
	h.	id.	n.	h.	id.	n.	h.
	id.	n.	h.	id.	n.	h.	id.
⟨	n.	h.	id.	n.	h.	id.	n.
	h.	id.	n.	h.	id.	n.	h.
	i.	n.	h.	id.	n.	h.	id.
	n.	h.	id.	n.	h.	id.	n.[84]

1	2	3	4	5	6	7
hinh	inhi	nhin	hinh	inhi	nhin	hinh.
1	2	3	4	5	6	7
hinhinh	inhinhi	nhinhin	hinhinh	inhinhi	nhinhi	hinh.[85]

'The tragic poet . . .'[86]

The tragic poet does well to study the lyric poet, the lyric poet the epic, and the epic poet the tragic. For in the tragic lies the completion of the epic, in the lyric the completion of the tragic, in the epic the completion of the lyric. For even if the completion of each is a mixed expression of them all, one of the three aspects is always the most conspicuous in each.

Review of Siegfried Schmid's Play The Heroine[87]

This work stands out considerably from the usual run of productions of this sort, so injurious to art and humanity and lacking in authenticity, and because on the one hand the taste for the comic obviously and disproportionately inclines towards caricature, and on the other for this very reason an unjust prejudice against everything comic seems to be spreading, it ought to be a maxim to make special efforts to further genuine writings of this kind.

The characters and situations in this play, along with the whole plot, are, as they ought to be in this domain of poetry, a true but *poetically grasped* and *artistically presented* copy of so-called ordinary life, that is, life that stands in a weaker and more distant relation to the whole and for that very reason will be infinitely significant when it is comprehended poetically, but to a high degree insignificant in itself.

And it is precisely this contrast that the comic writer deals with and which he gives us an aesthetically true view of. With a divining mind and a well-disposed heart he seizes both the common and the uncommon characters and situations of his plot: how some, being too little occupied and fixed by their object, everywhere tend to attach more importance to things than they *really* contain; how others, being too tightly bound to the reality of the same sphere, strive to wriggle free of it with violence and cunning and so to destroy the conditions of such a significantly insignificant sphere; and how both go wrong because the narrow sphere cannot in itself be quite sufficient for them and yet they are too caught up in it, and as a consequence are fantasies both.

Whether the writer grasps this more clearly or more obscurely, and whether he recognizes that with a subject of this kind, as with every subject he might choose, he will always be tearing a fragment of life out of its living context and selecting it for his treatment, this is precisely what makes him an artist and what contains the ground for the presentation of his poem. For with this presentation everything tends towards solving and eliminating the contrast of excess and one-sidedness in which every subject will appear outside its living context. The writer tries to arrive at this first by representing the contrast in pure antitheses, sufficiently evenly and sharply; then by adequately grounding and motivating it, and finally by putting all parts of the subject into as thorough a relation as possible – in all these ways the writer seeks to give the subject, which because of its isolation lurches between extremes, the development which will permit it to appear in the purest and best particular relation to the whole, he seeks not so much to elevate it or to make it concrete as to turn it into a natural truth. And precisely where his subject is drawn most from reality, as in the idyll and comedy and elegy, he will above all have to make up for his theft by giving it an aspect of aesthetic truth, by presenting it in its most natural relation to the whole, not by making it even more concrete. For this is the business only of the great epic poem, which actually starts from the most supersensual poetic material and for that very reason has the longest way to travel to bring its ethereal true object back into contact with the rest of life and close to the senses; therefore the present reviewer believes that the representation and language of the *Iliad* gain quite a different meaning if we feel that it is sung much more in honour of Jupiter the Father than of Achilles or anyone else.

The present reviewer believes he may be forgiven for this digression because the uncertainty and prejudice about the points that have been mentioned are to all appearances still powerful enough and far from negligible, and because it will no doubt be found more tolerable if he says a word out of turn, but with good intentions, than if he chose the best opportunity to make his obstinacy prevail.

This reviewer also thinks that in what has been said thus far, insofar as it is applicable to comedy, he has happened upon the point of view which must have principally guided the author of this play; and to what extent the writer has proceeded consistently is clear to the reviewer above all from the fact that the small inconsistencies in the poem are so noticeable.

So for example in most of the scenes the conversations between the soldiers are sometimes carried on in too uninterrupted a manner. Or is it not the case that the speeches should be interrupted all the more rapidly or heavily, the more extravagantly they *have* to tend towards the common or the uncommon? But with a great deal of felicity and out of a proper feeling of its appropriateness, use is also made of the iambic line in these conversations, such that one does not feel it precisely because it belongs there, and precisely so that word for word a sharper contrast becomes sensible in the coarser speeches. In this as in much else, the author has the authority of the ancient comedians, e.g. of Terence,[88] on his side, and in those days people did after all have pretty good taste.

Particularly worthy of mention are the masterly characters who are placed between opposed roles in a mediating, complementary function, such as that of *Klapp*, of the *boy* in the woods, together with the *simple-minded mistress of the inn*.

And for many fine deviations from the main subject, well conducted and in keeping with the nature of the play and its characters, one can feel particularly grateful and take pleasure in the fact that these passages do not leave us with less than they seem to promise.

All the more so since in comedies what we call the intrigue of the play is for the most part nothing more than a feigned prudishness on the part of the Muses, intended to attract us all, and since the impropriety dissolves into nothing, leaving only purity behind, it is regrettable that the author made so much of this part of the play. As far as the characters go, they are, to a high degree, unerringly conceived. They are true and perfectly suited to comedy, narrow-minded creatures who for that very reason try to exercise every cunning. But their affectations, though correctly conceived, did seem to the reviewer to be portrayed with disproportionate severity.

The author is, however, to be forgiven for this, as for the most part it is the custom with modern poetry, here too, as in the rhymes of a lyric poem, to wear heavy weights on the soles of the feet instead of the wings of Mercury[89] and to make the complications of comedy even worse than they are in the more serious domain of life itself.

But as the difficulty the writer creates for himself here is in any case only felt by those who also and equally feel how great a sacrifice he is making, as moreover the artist's life among us is brief enough, it is perhaps no bad advice to the German poet who by nature is more in touch with the ancients not to let himself be put off any longer by his more complicated neighbours, so that here too more and more simplicity and more *appropriate* ease can be introduced.

(trans. CL)

'The meaning of tragedies . . .'[90]

The meaning of tragedies can most easily be understood in a paradox. For everything primal, because all potential is justly and equally divided, does not in fact manifest itself in its primal strength, but actually in its weakness, so that really and essentially the light of life and the manifestation of weakness are part of every whole. Now, in the tragic, the sign in itself is insignificant, ineffective, but the primal is straight out. For actually, the primal can only appear in its weakness, but insofar as the sign in itself is postulated as insignificant = 0, the primal, the hidden ground of every nature, can represent itself. If nature actually represents itself in its weakest gift, then the sign when it represents itself in its strongest gift is = 0.

Notes on the Oedipus[91]

I.

It would be good, to secure our poets too a proper position in society, if we also, whilst taking account of the differences in the times and conditions, were to elevate poetry to the $\mu\eta\chi\alpha\nu\eta$[92] of the ancients.

Other works of art too, when compared with the Greek, lack certainty; at least, until now they have been judged more according to the impressions they make than according to their calculable law, or by other procedures through which beauty is produced. But modern poetry particularly lacks a school and appropriate craft, so that its procedures may be calculated and taught, and, when learnt, always be repeated reliably in practice. Among men, one must above all bear in mind that every thing is *something*, i.e. that it is cognizable in the medium (*moyen*[93]) of its appearance, and that the manner in which it is defined can be determined and taught. For this and for higher reasons poetry requires especially certain and characteristic principles and checks.

To these belongs, firstly, the calculable law.

Next, one must observe how the content differs from this law, and by what means; how the particular content relates to the general calculation within a continuum which, though endless, is yet determined throughout; and how the development and the intended statement, the living sense which cannot be computed, may be related to the calculable law.

In tragedy, the law, the calculation, the manner in which the whole man, a system of feelings, develops under the influence of the element, and the way in which ideas and feelings and reflections emerge in different orders, but always according to a fixed rule, is more by counterpoise than by pure succession.

For the tragic *transport*[94] is essentially empty, and the most unbounded of all.

Hence the rhythmic succession of ideas wherein the *transport* manifests itself demands a counter-rhythmic interruption, a pure word, *that which in metrics is called a caesura*, in order to confront the speeding alternation of ideas at its climax, so that not the alternation of the idea, but the idea itself appears.

By this means the succession of the calculation and the rhythm is divided, and its two halves so relate to each other that they appear to be weighted equally.

Now if the rhythm of ideas is so constituted that, with eccentric rapidity, the *first* tend to be torn along by the *later* ones, the caesura or counter-rhythmical pause must lie *from the front*, so that the first half is, as it were, shielded from the second; then, precisely because the second half is initially faster, and seems to weigh more heavily, as a result of the caesura's counter-action the balance will tend to incline from the end towards the beginning.

If the rhythm of ideas is so constituted that the *following* are, rather, compressed by the *initial* ones, the caesura will come to lie more towards the end, because it is the end which must, as it were, be shielded from the beginning; then, the balance will incline more towards the end, since the first half extends further, and consequently the balance sets in later. So much on the calculable law.

The first of the tragic laws here indicated is that of the Oedipus.

The *Antigone* follows the second law here mentioned.

In both plays, it is the speeches of Tiresias which constitute the caesura.

He steps into the path of fate as the guardian of the natural power which tragically removes man from his orbit of life, the very mid-point of his inner life, to another world, and tears him off into the eccentric orbit of the dead.

2.

The *intelligibility* of the whole principally depends on considering the scene where Oedipus *interprets the oracle too infinitely*,
and is tempted to the *nefas*.[95]

For the oracle says:

> We have been commanded clearly, by Phoebus, the king,
> To drive out the land's disgrace, which is nourished
> By this ground, and not to feed incurable disease.[96]

That could mean: judge strictly, in a general way, hold a pure
court, maintain good civil order in the state. But thereupon,
Oedipus immediately speaks like a priest:

> By what cleansing? etc.[97]

And turns to the *particular*,

> And for which man does he mean this fate?[98]

And *thus* leads Creon's *thoughts* to the terrible word:

> To us, O king, Laius was formerly the master
> In this land, before you steered the town.[99]

Thus the oracle is connected with the story of Laius' death,
which does not necessarily belong here at all. However, in
the scene which immediately follows, the mind of Oedipus,
knowing all, in an angry intimation, really gives expression to
the *nefas*, by suspiciously interpreting the general command-
ment as particular, by relating it to the murderer of Laius, and,
finally, by also treating the sinful deed as infinite.

> Whoever of you the son of Labdacos,
> Laius, did know, and through whom he died,
> To him I say, that he all should tell to me etc.[100]

> And this man makes me
> Curse whoever he may be here in this land
> Of which I hold the power and the thrones,
> Neither invite him in, nor speak to him;
> Do not admit him to sacred vows, and not
> To the offerings.[101]

> Clearly
> The Pythian oracle of the God
> Shows me this.[102]

Hence, in the ensuing dialogue with Tiresias, the wonderful angry curiosity; because knowledge, when it has broken through its limits, as if intoxicated in its own magnificent and harmonious form, which can yet remain, at first, provokes itself to know more than it can bear or grasp.

Hence, afterwards, in the scene with Creon, the suspicion: because an ungovernable thought, which is weighed down with sad secrets, becomes unsure, and the faithful and certain spirit suffers in angry immoderation that delights in destruction and only follows the tearing rapacity of time.

Hence in the centre of the play, in the speeches with Jocasta the sad calm, the simplicity, the pitiable, naive mistake of the powerful man: it is here that he tells Jocasta of his supposed birthplace and of Polybus, whom he fears he will kill, because he is his father; and of Merope, whom he wishes to flee so as not to marry her, because she is his mother, according to Tiresias' words, whereas the latter really told him that he was Laius' murderer and that the latter was his father. For in Oedipus' argument with Tiresias, which has already been touched on, Tiresias tells him:

> The man you've long
> Been hunting, threatening and proclaiming *the murder*
> *Of Laius*, is here; a stranger, as people say,
> He dwells with us; yet soon as a native
> He'll be known, as a Theban, and will not
> Like his fate.[103]

. . .

He'll be known, indeed, dwelling with his children,
As a brother and a father, and of the wife who
Bore him, son and husband, *in one bed with*
His father, and his murderer.[104]

Hence then, at the beginning of the second half, in the scene
with the Corinthian messenger, where he is tempted back to
life again, the despairing struggle to find himself; and also the
degrading, almost shameless attempt to gain control of himself,
his foolishly wild search for consciousness.

JOCASTA
For upwards Oedipus bends his courage
In manifold torment, not, like a man,
Thoughtfully, interpreting new from old.[105]

OEDIPUS
O dearest you, my wife's, Jocasta's head!
Why did you call me out here from the houses?[106]

OEDIPUS
The old man, as it seems, withered through sickness.
MESSENGER
And through sufficient measure of great age.[107]

One should note how Oedipus' spirit is here uplifted by the
good words: the following speeches can therefore be interpreted
in terms of a nobler motive. Here Oedipus, who now is precisely
not carrying his load with Herculean shoulders, in great weakness, in an effort to gain control of himself, casts aside his regal
cares:

Well then! Who now, my wife, would once again
Interrogate the prophesying hearth, or the birds
Screeching from above? According to their signs
I was to kill my father, who slumbers

Dead beneath the earth; but here
Am I, and my spear is clean, unless differently
In a dream he fell through me; thus may he
Have died, through me. With him he also took
Today's visionary oracles, and now he lies
In Hades, Polybus, no longer valid.[108]

Eventually his speeches are mainly ruled by his insane searching after a consciousness.

MESSENGER
Well you show, child, that what you do, you know not.
OEDIPUS
What, by the holy gods, old man, *say something*![109]

OEDIPUS
What's that you say? Did Polybus not plant me?
MESSENGER
Almost as much as one of us.
OEDIPUS
How so? A father who is like No-one?
MESSENGER
A father, simply. Polybus not; nor I.
OEDIPUS
But why, then, did he call me his child?[110]

MESSENGER
I release you since your toes are tied.
OEDIPUS
Mighty disgrace I brought out from the swaddles.
MESSENGER
So that you have your name after this matter.
OEDIPUS
That, O gods! that, by mother, father, speak![111]

JOCASTA
By the gods, no! If you care for your life,
Do not enquire. My sickness is complete.

OEDIPUS

Have good courage! If I came from three mothers,
Three times a slave, it would not make you worse.[112]

OEDIPUS

Let break, what must. I'll know my family,
Even if it's base, I'll yet discover it.
She is quite right, since women will think big,
To be ashamed about my humble birth.
I, though, thinking myself a son of gifted
Fortune, do not wish to be dishonoured.
For this is my mother. And small and large,
Surrounded was I by co-begotten moons.
And thus produced, thus will I not go,
Without seeking out, wholly, what I am.[113]

It is precisely this all-searching, all-interpreting quality that in
the end causes his spirit to succumb to the rough and simple
language of his servants.

Because such men live in violent circumstances, their language too, almost like the Furies, will speak in a more violent
configuration.

3.

The representation of the tragic depends primarily on this: that
the fearful enormity of God and man uniting, and the power of
nature becoming boundlessly one with man's innermost being
in rage, thereby comprehends itself, that the infinite unification
purifies itself through infinite separation. Της φυσεως γραμματευς ην τον καλαμον αποβρεχων εννουν.[114]

For this reason the ever-oppositional dialogue; for this reason
the chorus as antithesis to the latter. For this reason the over-
chaste, over-mechanical and factually ending interlocking of
the various parts; both in the dialogue and between the chorus
and the dialogue and between the great sections or episodes
which consist of chorus and dialogue. Everything is speech
against speech, which mutually cancel each other out.

Hence in the choruses of the *Oedipus*, the lamenting and peaceful and religious elements, the pious lie (*If I am a sooth-sayer*, etc.[115]), and the sympathy to the point of complete exhaustion towards a dialogue which, in its angry sensitivity, will tear apart the souls of these very listeners. And hence, in the various scenes, the fearfully ceremonial forms, the drama like a trial for heresy: it is a language for a world where, in a leisurely age, and amid plague, confusion of the mind and a universally awakened spirit of prophecy, God and man *communicate in the all-forgetting form of unfaithfulness*. This happens so that no gap occurs in the course of the world, and so that *the memory of the heavenly ones does not die out*. Divine unfaithfulness is retained best of all.

At a moment like this man forgets both himself and the God and, in a sacred manner, of course, turns himself round like a traitor. – For at the most extreme edge of suffering, nothing exists besides the conditions of time or space.

Man forgets himself there because he is wholly in the moment; and God, because he is nothing else than time. And both are unfaithful: time, because at such a moment it reverses categorically – beginning and end simply cannot be connected; and man, because at this moment he must follow the categorical reversal, and therefore simply cannot be in the following what he was at the beginning.

Thus stands Haemon in the *Antigone*. And thus Oedipus himself at the centre of the tragedy of *Oedipus*.

Notes on the Antigone[116]

The rule, the calculable law of the *Antigone*, relates to that of the *Oedipus* like ＿＿／ to ＼＿＿, so that the balance inclines more from the beginning towards the end, than from the end towards the beginning.

The rule is one of the various successions in which idea and feeling and reflection develop, according to poetic logic. For just as philosophy always treats only one faculty of the soul, so that the representation of this *one* faculty makes a whole, and the mere connection between the *parts* of this faculty is called logic: so poetry treats the various faculties of a human being, so that the representation of these different faculties makes a whole, and the connection between *the more independent parts* of the different faculties can be called the rhythm, taken in a higher sense, or the calculable law.

But if this rhythm of ideas is so constituted that in the rapidity of enthusiasm the *former* are more torn along by the *later ones*, the caesura (a), or the *counter-rhythmical interruption*, must lie *from the front*, so that the first half is, as it were, shielded from the second; and then, precisely because the second half is initially more rapid and seems to weigh more heavily, as a result of the caesura's counter-action the balance will tend to incline from the end (b) towards the beginning (c).

$$\text{c} \underset{}{\overset{\text{a}}{\diagdown\!\_\_\_}} \text{b}$$

If, however, the rhythm of ideas is so constituted that *the following* are, rather, compressed *by the initial ones*, the caesura (a) will come to lie more towards the end, because it is the end which must, as it were, be shielded from the beginning; and then the balance will incline more towards the end (b), since the first half (c) extends further, but the balance sets in later.

$$c \underline{\qquad \diagup} b$$

2.

What, dared you such a law as this to break?

Because *my* Zeus accounted it to me not;
Nor here at home the justice of the death-gods etc.[117]

The boldest moment in the course of a day or in a work of art is where the spirit of time and nature, the heavenly by which man is overwhelmed and the object in which he is interested, come to oppose each other most wildly; because the object of sense only extends so far, as a first half, but the *spirit awakens most mightily where the second half begins*. At this moment, a man must *take hold of himself more firmly than ever*, which is why he then stands with his character at its most open.

The tragically mediocre feebleness of the time,[118] whose object does not, after all, really interest the heart, follows the tearing spirit of time most immoderately; the latter then appears wild and does not, like a spirit by day, spare mankind, but on the contrary acts mercilessly, as the spirit of ever-living and unwritten wilderness and of the world of the dead.

CREON
Yet, like good the bad should not be taken.
ANTIGONE
Who knows, below there may well be a different rite.[119]

The lovable, the sensible in adversity. Dreamily naive. This is the essential language of Sophocles, since Aeschylus and

Euripides know more how to objectify suffering and anger than
human reason passing through the midst of the unthinkable.

> CREON
> If I remain faithful to my origin, do I lie?
> HAEMON
> But you aren't, *if you don't honour the name of God.*[120]

Instead of: if you tread the honour of the Gods. It was probably
necessary to change the sacred expression here, since it is significant at the centre, as a serious and independent word,
around which all else is objectified and transfigured.

Admittedly, the manner in which time reverses at the centre
is not really alterable; similarly, the manner in which a character
categorically follows categorical time, and the move from the
Greek to the Hesperian;[121] however, the sacred name under
which the highest is felt or occurs can be altered. The speech
refers to Creon's oath.

> You'll not much longer
> Brood in the jealous sun.[122]

Just as the sun becomes relative physically, so, on earth,
among men, the sun can really become relative in the moral
sphere.

> I have heard, that like the desert has become etc.[123]

Probably the highest trait in Antigone. The sublime mockery
surpasses all her other utterances, insofar as sacred madness is
the loftiest human phenomenon and is here more soul than
language; and indeed it is necessary to speak of beauty in the
superlative in this way, because her attitude also depends partly
on the superlative of human spirit and of heroic virtuosity.

To the soul, working in secret, it is a great aid that, at the
highest point of consciousness, it avoids consciousness; and
before the manifest god overwhelms it, it opposes him with a

bold, often even with a blasphemous word, and so preserves
the sacred and living possibility of the spirit.

In high consciousness the soul then always compares itself
with objects which have no consciousness, but which in their
fate take on the form of consciousness. Such an object is a land
grown barren, which in its original lush fertility has too greatly
intensified the effects of the sun and becomes dry for that
reason. The fate of Phrygian Niobe; as it is everywhere the fate
of innocent nature, which everywhere in its virtuosity passes
over into the all-too-organic, to just the degree that man
approaches the aorgic,[124] in more heroic circumstances and
motions of the affects. And Niobe is then quite properly the
image of the early genius.

> She counted for the Father of Time
> The hourly strokes of gold.[125]

Instead of: administered for Zeus the goldenly-streaming
becoming. To bring it closer to our mode of understanding. In
more particular or vaguer contexts one probably has to say
Zeus. *In serious* contexts preferably: Father of Time or: Father
of the Earth, because it is his character, contrary to the eternal
tendency, to reverse *the striving out of this world into the other*
into *a striving out of another world into this one*. For we
must everywhere represent the myth more *demonstrably*. The
goldenly-streaming becoming probably means the rays of light,
which also belong to Zeus insofar as time, which is meant here,
is more calculable through such rays. But this is always the case
if time is counted in suffering, because then the heart feels
the passing of time much more, in sympathy, and therefore
understands the simple passage of the hours, whilst reason does
not infer the future from the present.

But because this firmest constancy in the face of advancing
time, this heroic hermit-like existence, really is the highest form
of consciousness, it therefore motivates the following chorus,
which is truly universal, and is the essential point of view from
which the whole must be understood.

For, as a contrast to the over-intimate quality of the previous scene, the chorus expresses the greatest degree of impartiality towards the two opposing forms of character which inspire the actions of the various people in the drama.

Firstly, that which characterizes the antitheos,[126] where some-one behaves as if he were acting *against* God, but according to God's intent, and without the law recognizes the spirit of the Almighty. Then, the pious fear of fate, and with that, the honouring of God as one lawfully given. This is the spirit of the two antitheses that are impartially placed against one another in the chorus. In the first sense acting more as Antigone. In the second as Creon. Both, insofar as they are opposed, not as national and anti-national, and thereby as formed, like Ajax and Ulysses,[127] nor like Oedipus opposed to the Greek country people, and the original ancient character, as a free-thinker against faithful simplicity; but equally balanced against one another, and only differentiated in terms of time, so that one principle mainly loses *because it begins*, and the other *wins because it follows*. In this respect, the strange chorus here under discussion fits most appropriately to the whole, and its cold impartiality is warmth, just because it is so peculiarly appropriate.

3.

Tragic representation, as is suggested in the 'Notes on the *Oedipus*', depends on this: that the immediate God who has become wholly One with man (for the God of an apostle is, rather, mediated, being highest reason in the highest spirit), that *infinite* inspiration, sacredly separating itself, comprehends itself *infinitely*, which is to say in opposites, in a consciousness which cancels out consciousness, and the God, in the form of death, is present.

Hence, as the 'Notes on the *Oedipus*' have already indicated, the form of a dialogue, and the chorus as contrast to it; hence the dangerous structure in the scenes, which, in the more Greek manner, necessarily concludes factually in the sense that the *word* becomes *factual* more *mediately*, overwhelming the more physical body; according to our own age or way of thinking, it becomes factual more immediately, overwhelming the more spiritual body. The *Greek tragic word is deadly-factual*, because the body which it overwhelms really kills. But now, because we live under the more essential Zeus, who not only *pauses* between this earth and the wild world of the dead, but, on his way into the other world, *more decidedly forces down to earth* the natural process which is eternally hostile to man; and because this greatly changes our essential and national ideas, and our literature must be national, so that its subjects are chosen according to our view of the world, and its ideas are national, because of this, the Greek ideas alter, insofar as the Greeks' main aim is to grasp themselves, since this was their weakness, whereas the main aim in the modes of understanding for our own age is to hit upon something successfully, to have a fate, since fatelessness, δυσμορον,[128] is our weakness. For this reason, the Greek has more skill and athletic virtues, and, as paradoxical as the heroes of the *Iliad* may appear to us, he must possess this as an essential *distinction* and serious virtue. With us, this tends to be more subordinate to that which is fitting. And so also the Greek modes of understanding and poetic forms tend to be more subordinated to our national ones.

And so, *the deadly-factual, the real murder through words, is to be considered more as essentially Greek, which form of art is subordinated to a more national form of art*. A national one, as may well be demonstrated, may be more a killing-factual, than a deadly-factual word; it would not actually end with murder or death, because this is where the tragic must be grasped, but end more in the manner of the *Oedipus at Colonus*, so that *the word* from an inspired mouth is terrible, and kills, but not in a Greek, palpable way, with an athletic and sculptural spirit, where the word overwhelms the body, so that the latter kills.

So, more Greek or more Hesperian, tragic representation depends on a more violent or uncontrollable dialogue and choruses, more halting or interpreting in the case of the dialogue, they give the infinite strife direction or force, being the *suffering organs* of the divinely struggling body, which are really needed because even in his tragically infinite form the god cannot communicate himself to the body with absolute immediacy but must be comprehensibly *grasped*, or appropriated in a lively manner; above all however, tragic representation consists in the factual word, which is a continuum rather than an utterance, and goes fatefully from the beginning to the end; in the nature of the action, in the arrangement of the persons in relation to one another, and in the form of reason which develops in the terrible leisure of a tragic age and which, just as it represented itself in opposites at its wild conception, so afterwards, in a humane age, is accepted as a secure belief, born of divine fate.

The nature of the action in the *Antigone* is that in a revolt, where, insofar as it is a national matter, everything depends on the fact that everyone, being overwhelmed by the infinite reversal, and thoroughly moved, apprehends himself in the infinite form in which he is moved. For national reversal is the reversal of every mode of understanding and form. But a total reversal in these, like any total reversal without any check, is not granted to man as a creature endowed with perception. And in a national reversal, where the whole shape of things changes, and nature and necessity, which always remain, tend to a new shape, whether going over into wilderness or into a new form, in a change like this, all mere necessities are biased in favour of the change; whence, in the eventuality of such change, even a neutral man (and not only one who is moved *against* the national form), can, by a spiritual violence of the time, be forced to be patriotic and present in an infinite form, in the religious, political and moral form of his fatherland. ($\pi \varrho o \varphi \alpha \nu \eta \theta \iota\ \theta \varepsilon o \varsigma$.[129]) And serious observations of this kind are necessary for an understanding of Greek art, as of all true works of art. Now, the essential mode of procedure in a revolt (which is, of course, only one kind of national reversal, and has an even more definite character) has just been suggested.

If a phenomenon like this is tragic it occurs by reaction, and the intrinsically formless is kindled by that which is excessively formal. What is characteristic here is therefore this, that the persons living through a fate *of this kind* are not, as in the *Oedipus*, in the shape of ideas, engaged in a dispute about truth, not fighting for their reason; and not like one who fights for life or property or honour, like the persons in the *Ajax*; but, rather, that they oppose each other as persons in the narrower sense, as persons of rank, and formalize.

The arrangement of these persons in relation to each other is, as in the *Antigone*, to be compared to a contest between runners, where the one who first runs out of breath and jostles against his opponent has lost, while the struggle in the *Oedipus* may be compared to a boxing match, that in the *Ajax* to a fencing bout.

The form of reason which here shapes itself tragically is political, and specifically republican, because the balance between Creon and Antigone, the formal and the anti-formal, is too equal. This becomes especially clear at the end, where Creon is almost mistreated by his servants.

Sophocles is right. This is the fate of his age and the form of his native land. One can, indeed, idealize, e.g. pick the best moment; but the national modes of understanding, at least with respect to their subordination, must not be altered by the poet, who represents the world on a smaller scale. For us, a form like this is just usable, because the infinite, like the spirit of states and of the world, cannot in any case be *grasped* otherwise than from a clumsy standpoint. The native forms of our poets are nonetheless to be preferred, where there are such, because they do not just exist to explain the spirit of the age, but to hold on to it and to feel it, once it has been understood and learnt.

On the Fable of the Ancients[130]

Their principles
The shape of the same
System
Relation. Movability.

Different forms which these, despite the necessity of their formation, suffer as principles.

Sense and content of the same.

Mythological content.
Heroic
Purely human.

Sense of such fables in general.

Higher morals.

Infinity of wisdom.

Connection between humans and spirits.[131]
Nature; as it takes effect, history.

Pindar Fragments[132]

Unfaithfulness of Wisdom

O child, you whose spirit most hangs
On the skin of the wild, crag-loving beasts
Of Pontus, may you befriend every town,
Praising the present
Goodly,
And think otherwise in another age.[133]

Capacity of the solitary school for the world. The innocence of
pure knowing as the soul of intelligence. For intelligence is
the art of remaining faithful under various circumstances; and
knowing, of being certain in reason, notwithstanding positive
errors. If reason be exercised intensely, it will attain its strength
even in diffuseness; insofar as reason easily recognizes what is
alien by means of its own polished acuity and is therefore not
easily confused in uncertain situations.

Thus Jason, a pupil of the Centaur, steps before Pelias:

I believe that I possess
Chiron's teaching. From the grotto, namely, I come,
From Cariclo and Philyra, where the
Centaur's daughters nurtured me,
The sacred ones; twenty years, indeed,
I dwelt, and never a foul deed
Nor such a word did I address
To them, and have now come home
To restore the rule of my father.[134]

Of Truth

> Beginning of great virtue, Queen Truth,
> May you not trip up
> My thinking on harsh falsehood.[135]

Fear of truth from taking pleasure in it. For the first living understanding of truth in a living sense is, like all pure feeling, exposed to confusion; so that one does not err through one's own fault, nor through a disturbance, but because of the higher object, for which, relatively, the mind is too weak.

Of Rest

> The public realm, once a citizen
> In quiet weather has grasped it,
> He should explore
> Of great-manly rest the sacred light,
> And the uproar in his breast,
> From the depths, fight off, with its gales; for it
>   brings poverty,
> And is inimical to teachers of children.[136]

Before the laws, of great-manly rest the sacred light, can be explored someone, a law-giver or a prince, in the *more rapacious* or *more steady* fate of a fatherland and according to the way in which the receptivity of the people is constituted, must grasp the character of that fate, the *more kingly* or *more total* element in the affairs of men, at an untouched time, *more usurpatorially*, as with the Greek sons of Nature, or *with more experience*, as with men of learning. Then, the laws become the means to hold fast to that fate in its untouched state. What holds for a prince originally, holds good as imitation for the more essential citizen.

Of the Dolphin

> He who in the waveless depths of the sea by flutes
> Was moved, so lovingly, by the song.[137]

The song of nature, in the weather of the Muses, when the clouds hang like flakes over blossoms, and over the melting of golden flowers. At this time every creature gives its own note, its loyalty, the way it hangs together in itself. Then only the difference between species makes a division in nature, so that everything is therefore more song and pure voice than accent of need or on the other hand language.

It is the waveless sea, where the quick fish feels the pipe of the Tritons, the echo of growth in the soft plants of the water.

The Highest

> The Law,
> Of everyone the King, mortals and
> Immortals; which is just why
> It mightily maintains
> The rightest right with the very highest hand.[138]

The immediate, strictly speaking, is impossible for mortals, as it is for immortals; the God must distinguish different worlds, according to his nature, since heavenly goodness, for its own sake, must be sacred, unalloyed. Man, as a knowing creature, must also distinguish different worlds, because knowledge is only possible through opposition. For this reason the immediate is, strictly speaking, impossible for mortals, as for immortals.

Strict mediacy, however, is the law.

And for this reason it mightily maintains the rightest right with the very highest hand.

Cultivation, insofar as it is the form in which man and God meet, the law of church and state and the inherited statutes (the sanctity of the god, and for man the possibility of knowledge, of an explanation), these maintain mightily the rightest right with the very highest hand. More strictly than art, they hold fast the living affairs in which, in time, a people has encountered itself and continues to. 'King' here means the superlative, which is only the sign for the highest ground of knowing, not for the highest power.

Age

> Whoever rightly and sacredly
> Passes his life,
> Sweetly nourishing his heart,
> Long life making,
> Him Hope shall accompany, who
> Most of all for mortals
> Their flexible opinion rules.[139]

One of the most beautiful images of life, the way in which guiltless custom preserves the living heart, from which hope comes; that then gives simplicity a florescence, with its manifold trials, making sense flexible and so life long, with its hastening leisure.

The Infinite

> Whether I of Right the wall,
> The high one, or of crooked deception
> Will ascend, and so me myself
> Circumscribing, will live
> Myself out; about this
> Have I equivocal a
> Mind, exactly to say.[140]

One of the wise man's jokes, and the puzzle should almost not be solved. For the wavering and struggling between right and intelligence only resolves itself in a continuous relation. 'I have an equivocal mind exactly to say.' That I may then find out the connection between right and intelligence, which must not be ascribed to them themselves but to a third, through which they hang together infinitely (exactly) – that's why I have an equivocal mind.

The Sanctuaries

At first did
They the well-advising Themis,
The heavenly ones, on golden steeds, beside
The ocean salt,
The Times, to the ladder,
To the holy one, lead, of Olympus, to
The shining return,
The rescuer's ancient daughter,
Of Zeus, to be,
But she
To the golden-bound, the goodly one,
To the shining-fructified places of rest gave birth.[141]

How man posits himself, a son of Themis, when, out of a sense
for the perfect, his spirit, on earth and in heaven, found no rest,
until meeting in fate, on the tracks of ancient cultivation, God
and man recognize one another again, and in the remembrance
of original need man is happy *where he can hold himself*.

Themis, the order-loving one, did to the *sanctuaries of mankind*, the still places of rest, give birth, which nothing alien
can harm, because in them the working and life of nature
concentrated itself, and a presentiment around them, as if in
remembrance, experiences exactly what they themselves did
once experience.

The Life-Giver

The man-conquering: after
The centaurs learnt
The power
Of the honey-sweet wine, suddenly they thrust
The white milk with their hands, the table away,
        spontaneously,
And drinking out of silver horns
Intoxicated themselves.[142]

The concept of the centaur is probably that of the spirit of a river, insofar as the latter forms a course and a boundary, with violence, on the originally pathless and upwards growing earth.

His image therefore occurs at places in nature where the shore is rich in rocks and grottoes, *especially at places where originally the river had to leave the mountain chain and had to tear diagonally through its direction.*

Hence centaurs are also originally teachers of natural philosophy, because nature can best be examined from this point of view.

In regions such as this the river had originally to wander about aimlessly before it could tear out a course. By this means there formed, as beside ponds, damp meadows and caves in the earth for suckling creatures, and meanwhile the centaur was a wild herdsman, like the Odyssean Cyclops. The waters longingly sought their direction. But the more firmly the dry land took shape upon the banks and secured its direction by means of the firmly rooting trees, by bushes and grapevines, the more the river also, which took its motion from the shape of the bank, had to gain its direction until, forced on from its source, it broke through at a point where the mountains that enclosed it were most loosely connected.

Thus the centaurs *learnt the power of the honey-sweet wine*, they took their motion and direction from the firmly formed banks, so rich in trees, and hurled *the white milk and the table away with their hands*, the fashioned wave drove away the calm of the pond, the way of life on the banks also changed, the attack of the wood with the storms and the secure princes of the forest aroused the leisurely life on the heath, the stagnating waters were so long repulsed from the steeper shore *until they grew arms*, and so with a direction of their own, *drinking* spontaneously *from silver horns*, made a path for themselves, took on a destiny.

The songs of Ossian especially are true centaur-songs, sung with the spirit of the river, and as if by the Greek Chiron, who also taught Achilles to play the lyre.

Appendix

The Oldest Programme for a System of German Idealism[1]

an ethics. Since the whole of metaphysics will in future go over into morals (for which Kant only gave an *example* with his two practical postulates, but *exhausted* nothing), this ethics will be nothing less than a complete system of all ideas or, which is the same thing, of all practical postulates. The first idea is of course the idea of *myself* as an absolutely free being. With this free, self-conscious being a whole *world* immediately steps forth – out of nothingness – the only true and conceivable *creation ex nihilo*. – Here I will descend to the fields of physics; the question is this: how must a world be constituted for a moral being? I would like to give our physics, which is slowly and with difficulty moving forward by experiments, wings once again.

Thus – if philosophy provides the ideas, experience the data, we can finally achieve the grand physics I expect from future ages. It does not seem that contemporary physics can satisfy a creative mind such as ours is, or ought to be.

From Nature I come to *Man's actions*. First the idea of humanity – I want to show that there is no idea of the *State* because the State is a *mechanical* thing, just as there is no idea of a *machine*. Only that which is the object of *freedom* can be called an *idea*. We must therefore also go beyond the State. – For every State has to treat free human beings as mechanical cogs; and it should not do that; thus it must *stop*. You can see from this that all ideas, of eternal peace and so forth, are only the *subordinate* ideas of a higher idea. At the same time I here wish to lay down the principles of a *history of mankind*, and strip the whole miserable mess made up of State, constitution, government, legislation – right down to the skin. Finally, there come the ideas of a moral world, Godhead, immortality – the overturning of all superstition, false belief, and the persecution of the priestcraft that lately feigns reason, by means of reason itself. – The absolute freedom of all spirits, that contain the intellectual world within themselves and cannot seek God or immortality *outside themselves*.

Finally the idea that unites them all, the idea of *beauty*, taking the word in a higher, Platonic sense. I am now convinced that the highest act of reason, that in which reason contains all ideas, is an aesthetic act, and that *truth and goodness are only united in beauty*. – Indeed the philosopher must possess as much aesthetic power as the poet. People without aesthetic sense are intellectual pedants. The philosophy of the spirit is an aesthetic philosophy. You cannot be clever about anything, you can't even think cleverly about history – without aesthetic sense. Here it should become manifest what people actually lack who can understand no ideas – and admit frankly enough that they do not understand anything, as soon as matters go beyond tables and indices.

By this means, Poesy regains a higher dignity, and in the end becomes again what it was in the beginning: *the educator of humanity*; for there will be no more philosophy, no history, Poesy alone will survive all other arts and sciences.

At the same time we often hear that the masses must have a *sensible religion*. Not just the masses but the philosopher needs this too. Monotheism of reason and the heart, polytheism of art and the imagination, that is what we need!

First I will here speak of an idea which as far as I know has never entered anyone's head before – we must have a new mythology, but this mythology must stand in the service of ideas, it must be a mythology of *reason*.

Unless we make ideas aesthetic, that is to say mythological, they have no interest for the *people*, and conversely, unless mythology is rational the philosopher will be ashamed of it. In the end the enlightened and the unenlightened must join hands, mythology must become philosophical to make the people rational, and philosophy must become mythological to connect philosophers to the senses. Then eternal unity will reign amongst us. Never again the look of disdain, never the blind trembling of the people before its wise men and priests. Then finally we can expect the *equal* education of *all* powers, of the individual and of all individuals. No power will be suppressed any more, then the universal freedom and equality of all spirits will reign! – A higher spirit sent from heaven must found this religion amongst us, it will be the last, the greatest task of humanity.

Notes

Two different styles of annotation have been used for the letters and essays, to satisfy the demands imposed by two very different kinds of text. As the letters, by their private nature, require frequent annotation, it was thought best not to clutter the text with numerals; the note on each letter is intended as a kind of running commentary. Due to the complexity of the essays, which may often prompt the reader to turn to a commentary for support, notes have been signalled in the text.

NOTES TO THE LETTERS

The number at the end of the notes to each letter is that in Adolf Beck's Stuttgart edition (vol. 6 of *Sämtliche Werke*, Friedrich Beissner and Adolf Beck (eds.), 1943–85). Though not the most recent edition of the letters, it was the founding work and has the fullest commentary; my notes mostly follow Beck's. I have also consulted the Frankfurt edition, edited by D. E. Sattler and others from 1975 onwards; the two volumes containing the correspondence are 18 and 19 (published in 1993 and 2007). Reference is sometimes made to Friedrich Hölderlin, *Selected Poems and Fragments*, translated by Michael Hamburger, edited by Jeremy Adler (Penguin, 1998 and 2007), abbreviated to *Selected Poems*.

Many of Hölderlin's letters have only survived as drafts which may or may not tally with what was actually sent. Many have also been passed down in transcripts made in the nineteenth century, sometimes partly in digest form, where the copier has made only a précis of what seemed to him unimportant passages. In the rare instances where such letters have been included in the present selection, the digests are given in italics and in square brackets (Letters 35, 50, 69, 75 and 83).

Where a date-line is given in square brackets it is missing in Hölderlin's manuscript, though for the sake of elegance these brackets have been removed in the Notes and List of Letters. Where dates are approximate this is indicated by a tilde (~). In early letters to his family Hölderlin signed with the short form of his Christian name – his spelling has been retained: Friz (pronounced 'Fritz'). Later he sometimes used the academic title he acquired in autumn 1790, that of *Magister*, abbreviated to M.

There is frequent mention of money in the letters. It is almost impossible to arrive at equivalents for the sums involved, but writing to his mother on 29 January 1800 Hölderlin reckons, probably with a good deal of optimism, that he could live for a year on 500 florins. A florin he sometimes calls a *Gulden*, which I have translated as guilder, and he abbreviates it to fl. A florin was made up of 60 *Kreuzer* (cr.). A carolin was worth 11 florins, as was a Napoleonic louis d'or. A thaler (dollar) was worth about 1½ florins and was made up of 24 groschen (groats): the less familiar, foreign names have been kept.

1. To Johanna Christiana Gok. Maulbronn, June 1788 (extract)

Excerpted from a long letter giving an account of a journey to Speyer in the Rhineland, the first journey Hölderlin made outside Württemberg. (B23)

2. To Immanuel Nast. Maulbronn, 6 September 1788

The last of fourteen letters to Nast. **Elsner:** Johann Christoph Friedrich (1770–1806) and **Bilfinger:** Christian Ludwig (1770–1850), both at school with Hölderlin. An early poem is dedicated to Bilfinger, who after abandoning his theological training for the law pursued a successful career as a diplomat. **Landbek:** Johann Jonathan Christian (born 1763), soon gave up painting. **Hiemer:** Franz Karl (1768–1822), minor painter, actor and writer, did a well-known portrait of Hölderlin in 1792. **I finished something:** could be the poem 'Am Tage der Freundschaftsfeier'/'On the Day of the Celebrating of Friendship', or perhaps the so-called Marbach quarto, in which Hölderlin made fair copies of most of his poems just before leaving Maulbronn, or his translation of the first two books of Homer's *Iliad*. (B24)

3. To Christian Ludwig Neuffer. Nürtingen, December 1789

unpleasantnesses: Hölderlin was unhappy at the Stift and thinking of switching to law. **granted leave to travel:** by the authorities at the Stift.

hymn to Columbus: lost, though much later Hölderlin returned to the theme: see 'Kolomb'/'Colombo' in *Selected Poems*, pp. 304/305. **collection of old German legends**: *History of the Countess Thekla von Thurn, or Scenes from the Thirty Years War* (Frankfurt and Leipzig, 1789), not by Bürger, but by Benedikte Naubert. **Gustavus**: Gustavus Adolphus, King of Sweden from 1611 till his death in 1632, was the subject of several poems by Hölderlin at this time. He took part in the Thirty Years War on the Protestant side. **Stäudlin**: Gotthold Friedrich (1758–96), the 'beloved predecessor', Swabian man of letters who edited various literary journals and published some of Hölderlin's earliest poems. Hölderlin knew him from 1789, dedicated a poem to him and was introduced by him to Matthisson and Schiller. Banished from Württemberg in 1793 for openly supporting the French Revolution, he drowned himself. **M. Hoffman**: Carl Theophil (born 1768), an acquaintance at the Stift. **guardroom**: *Ritterstube*, one of the heated rooms at the Stift, shared with about ten other students. (B28)

4. To Maria Eleonora Heinrike Hölderlin. Tübingen, mid-November 1790

Hegel and **Schelling**: see List of Correspondents. **repetitor**: gifted students at the Stift could stay on to teach once their studies were over and were known as 'repetitors'. **Breyer**: Karl Friedrich Wilhelm (1771–1818), later became a historian influenced by Schelling, who was a cousin of his. **Karl**: Hölderlin's half-brother Karl Gok, then fourteen. (B36)

5. To Johanna Christiana Gok. Tübingen, ~ 14 February 1791

Reflects Hölderlin's reading of Leibniz, Wolff, Kant (the 'fierce opponent'), and his theological preoccupations in the Stift. It is uncertain what of **Spinoza**'s he knew, but he read and made excerpts from Friedrich Heinrich Jacobi's *On the Doctrine of Spinoza* (1785). (B41)

6. To Johanna Christiana Gok. Tübingen, ~ June 1791

knight errant: Hölderlin had made a journey to Switzerland in the spring. In 1789 he had broken off an engagement to Louise Nast. **wine money**: instead of drinking wine at table, students at the Stift could choose to receive an equivalent amount of cash. (B45)

7. To *Christian Ludwig Neuffer. Tübingen, 28 November 1791*

Written after a visit earlier in the autumn to his friends Neuffer and Rudolf **Magenau** (1767–1846) who had both left the Stift in September. **My girl**: Elise Lebret. **love and friendship**: variation on Goethe, *Iphigenie auf Tauris*, 665–6, quoted by Hölderlin more than once. **Jean-Jacques**: i.e. Jean-Jacques Rousseau (1712–78). **Uhland**: Ludwig Joseph (1722–1803), superintendent (high-ranking minister) at the Stift. *Saltus dithyrambicus*: (Latin) 'dithyrambic leap'. **Swabian Almanac**: it contained several poems by Hölderlin. (B47)

8. To *Heinrike Hölderlin. Tübingen, early March 1792*

Christlieb: Wilhelm Christian Gottfried (born 1772). **Karl**: Hölderlin's half-brother Karl Gok (see List of Correspondents). **Kamerer**: Clemens Christoph (1766–1826), later mayor of Reutlingen, and a family friend. **statutes**: under pressure from Duke Karl Eugen of Württemberg, the statutes governing life in the Stift were being reformed, the main intention being to suppress the liberal instincts released under the influence of the French Revolution. **Prince Wilhelm**: Friedrich Wilhelm Karl of Württemberg (1754–1816), succeeded his (Catholic) father in 1797. **Georgii**: Eberhard Friedrich (1757–1830), a member of the consistory or ecclesiastical authority governing the Stift. (B49)

9. To *Heinrike Hölderlin. Tübingen, June 1792*

The news in the *Schwäbische Merkur*, edited by Christian Gottfried **Elben**, was indeed wrong. **Luckner**: Nikolaus von, by birth a German, guillotined 1794. **Lafayette**: Marie-Joseph (1757–1834), famous for his role in the American War of Independence, soon to defect to the Austrians. **Fräulein Stäudlin**: probably Lotte, one of the sisters of Gottfried Stäudlin. (B51)

10. To *Christian Ludwig Neuffer. Tübingen, July 1793*

Stäudlin: see note to Letter 3 (to Neuffer, December 1789). **Ilissos**: river near Athens, setting for Plato's *Phaedrus*. **Hyperion**: Hölderlin's only novel, published in its final version in two volumes in 1797 and 1799. **if posterity**: this florid sentence repeats almost verbatim words of Neuffer's. **my hymn**: 'Dem Genius der Kühnheit'/'To the Genius of Boldness'. **Matthisson**: Friedrich (1761–1831), poet. **Hesiod**: Greek poet active about 700 BC, his main works are the *Theogony* (an epic relating the doings of the gods) and *Works and Days* (a didactic poem). (B60)

11. *To Karl Gok. Tübingen, September 1793*

new acquaintance: perhaps Matthisson (see notes to last letter). **something else:** Schiller's *Don Carlos* (1787). (B65)

12. *To Johanna Christiana Gok. Waltershausen, 3 January 1794*

Waltershausen, within striking distance of Jena and Weimar, belonging to the family of Charlotte von Kalb (1761–1843), a friend of Schiller's, married to Major Heinrich von Kalb (1752–1806). Hölderlin was responsible for the education of her eldest son Fritz (1784–1852). **Neckar:** the river of Hölderlin's home, flowing through Tübingen, Nürtingen and Stuttgart. **Schubart:** Ludwig Albrecht (1765–1811), son of the poet Christian Friedrich Daniel Schubart (1739–91), whom Hölderlin visited in 1789. **Jäger:** Karl Christoph Friedrich (1773–1828). **Prof. Ammon:** Christoph Friedrich (1766–1850), Kantian theologian. **Blaubeuren:** where Hölderlin's sister moved on her marriage. **Löchgau:** Hölderlin had family there. (B71)

13. *To Johanna Christiana Gok. Waltershausen, 23 January 1794*

concerns about the war: the French, who had occupied Belgium and the left bank of the Rhine in 1793, did not cross the Rhine again during 1794. **Troll:** unidentified. **Kleinmann:** probably Samuel Christoph Friedrich (1771–1854), later vicar of Bönnigheim. (B73)

14. *To Friedrich Schiller. Waltershausen, ~ 20 March 1794*

In a moment: refers to Hölderlin's first meeting with Schiller, in Ludwigsburg in September 1793. **any authority:** a deleted extension at the end of this sentence makes the Kantian provenance of Hölderlin's ideas particularly clear: 'and will then be receptive to an example of selfishness denied, and so to the negative principle of morality *in concreto*'. As in Letter 29 (to Ebel, 2 September 1795), to which this can be usefully compared, the other main influence is Rousseau. **some verses:** the poem 'Das Schicksal'/'Fate', which Schiller did publish in his magazine *Thalia*. **M. Hölderlin**: Hölderlin signs with his title, *Magister*, a sign of his insecurity. (B76)

15. To Karl Gok. Waltershausen, 21 May 1794

working on something now: his novel, *Hyperion*. **Thalia**: Schiller's magazine published Hölderlin's *Fragment of Hyperion* and the poems 'Das Schicksal'/'Fate', 'Dem Genius der Kühnheit'/'To the Genius of Boldness' and 'Griechenland'/'Greece' in this period. **Urania**: edited by J. L. Ewald, contained a different version of 'Greece'. **Flora**: a magazine edited by the publisher Cotta (who was to publish *Hyperion*), did not contain anything by Hölderlin until 1801. **Kant**: Immanuel (1724–1804), whose critical philosophy Hölderlin had been reading since the Stift. **Hiemer**: see note to Letter 2 (to Nast, 6 September 1788). (B80)

16. To Christian Ludwig Neuffer. Waltershausen, early July 1794

blow: Neuffer's fiancée Rosine Stäudlin lost her father on 21 May 1794. **Herder's Tithonus and Aurora**: appeared in 1792. **Catiline**: Neuffer's translation of Sallust was eventually published in 1819. **Kant's aesthetics**: *Critique of Judgement* (1790). **my poem to boldness**: 'To the Genius of Boldness' appeared in Schiller's *Neue Thalia* in 1795. **Fräulein Hegel**: Hegel's sister Christiane. **Hesler**: Ernst Friedrich (1771–1822), together with Hölderlin at the Stift and then in Jena, by which time he had published three plays (see next letter). (B83)

17. To G. W. F. Hegel. Waltershausen, 10 July 1794

'Kingdom of God!': for the new world of divine immanence the friends hoped for; Hegel uses the same words in a letter to Schelling in January 1795 (not included in this volume). **lakes and Alps**: Hegel had a job as private tutor in Bern. **Frau von Berlepsch**: Emilie von Berlepsch (1757–1830), wrote verse (*Sommerstunden*, 1794). **Baggesen**: Jens Immanuel (1764–1826), Danish writer. **Mögling**: Friedrich Heinrich Wolfgang (1771–1813), at the Stift; see Letter 49 (to Schiller, August 1797). **enclosed sheet**: not known what this is. (B84)

18. To Karl Gok. Waltershausen, 21 August 1794

Reflects Hölderlin's reading of Kant and Fichte and his work on *Hyperion*. **Robespierre**: guillotined on 28 July 1794. (B86)

19. To Christian Ludwig Neuffer. Waltershausen,
10 October 1794

in the *Thalia*: see the next letter. The poem 'Fate' appeared in the same issue. **another project ... death of Socrates**: never carried out. **Reinhard's *Almanac* and the *Academy* and Conz's *Museum***: none of these journals contained poems by Hölderlin. **an essay on *aesthetic ideas***: apparently not written. **Conz**: Carl Philipp (1762–1827), repetitor at the Stift from 1789 to 1791 and a Hellenist, he had a strong influence on Hölderlin there, kept in contact with him, and was one of the first to try to collect and publish his work; see Letter 51 (to his brother Karl, 2 November 1797). **'Grace and Dignity'**: Schiller's treatise 'Über Anmut und Würde' on the relations between aesthetics and ethics was published in 1793. **my poem to the genius of youth**: this was reworked into 'Der Gott der Jugend'/'The God of Youth' and appeared in Schiller's *Muses' Almanac* in 1796. **Gotthold**: Stäudlin (see Letter 3 to Neuffer, December 1789). **Hiller**: Christian Friedrich (1769–1817), with Hölderlin in Maulbronn and Tübingen, they made a journey to Switzerland together in 1791. (B88)

20. To Christian Ludwig Neuffer. Jena, November 1794

Wieland: Christoph Martin (1733–1813), novelist, dramatist and poet, his collected works had just been published. **Fichte**: Johann Gottlieb (1762–1814), post-Kantian philosopher, had just become professor of philosophy at Jena and was in the ascendant. Hölderlin had already read him and immediately began to attend his lectures. **Meyer**: Johann Heinrich (1760–1832), a painter in the classical manner summoned to Weimar by Goethe. **Professors' Club**: a circle, mostly of academics, which met once a week; Goethe sometimes went, and students could too. ***Goethe*** and **Niethammer**: see List of Correspondents. (B89)

21. To Johanna Christiana Gok. Jena, 17 November 1794

Friemar: birthplace of Hölderlin's grandfather on his mother's side, Johann Andreas Heyn. **were it not for the thought**: a thought prompted by Fichte. **Coadjutor Dalberg**: Karl Theodor von Dalberg (1744–1817), governor of Erfurt and coadjutor (first assistant and named successor) to the Elector of Mainz, becoming elector himself in 1802; friend of Schiller's. **Fichte's ... lectures**: Fichte was giving (in his words) 'a sort of introduction to transcendental philosophy'. **Paulus**: Heinrich Eberhard Gottlob (1761–1851), from Swabia, professor of oriental languages and of exegesis at Jena, later in Würzburg and Heidelberg. (B90)

22. To Johanna Christiana Gok. Jena, 16 January 1795

a vice: masturbation, generally considered so at the time. **a piece of work**: *Hyperion*. **Herder**: see note to next letter. (B92)

23. To Christian Ludwig Neuffer. Jena, 19 January 1795

Herder: Johann Gottfried (1744–1803), was an important forerunner of the Romantics and stimulator of all kinds of thinking, including Hölderlin's. His *Ideas for a Philosophy of the History of Mankind* was published in four parts, 1784–91. **Wilhelm Meister**: the first volume of Goethe's novel *Wilhelm Meister's Apprenticeship* appeared at Christmas 1794. **part of your *Aeneid***: part of Book 7; Neuffer had finished a translation of Virgil's *Aeneid* by 1790 but destroyed it, began again, and eventually published a complete version in 1816. **the Nisus and Euryalus episode**: Neuffer's version of this (from Book 9 of the *Aeneid*) was published in 1794. Hölderlin later translated part of the same episode himself. **Voss**: Johann Heinrich (1751–1826), famous for his great translations of Homer, published a complete *Aeneid* in 1799. **Woltmann**: Karl Ludwig (1770–1817). **Bürger**: Gottfried August (1747–94), among other things author of the ballad 'Lenore' (1773), which influenced Coleridge's 'Rime of the Ancient Mariner'. **my Tübingen affairs**: refers to Hölderlin's difficult relationship with Elise Lebret. **a friend in the house**: Wilhelmine Marianne Kirms (born 1772). As a companion of Charlotte von Kalb she lived with her in Waltershausen when Hölderlin was there, having escaped from an unhappy marriage (her husband later died). In July 1795 she gave birth to a daughter, Luise Agnese, who died fourteen months later of smallpox. Hölderlin may have been the father. (B93)

24. To G. W. F. Hegel. Jena, 26 January 1795
(letter damaged)

Basis of a Total Theory of Knowledge: Fichte's main work (*Grundlage der gesamten Wissenschaftslehre*) which began appearing in summer 1794, as did his *Lectures on the Vocation of the Scholar*. (B94)

25. To Karl Gok. Jena, 13 April 1795

a human being should always act ... a valid law for everyone: Kant's 'categorical imperative' (in the *Critique of Practical Reason*), but Hölderlin makes it more personal by calling it the 'sacred unalterable law of [one's] being'. **'There is in human beings ... have no consciousness'**: not a quotation from Fichte, but a summary of his thinking in the third part of the *Wissenschaftslehre*. **Philosophical Journal**: see Letter 34 (to Niethammer, 24 February 1796). **Cotta**: Johann Friedrich (1764–1832), published the 'little work', *Hyperion*, in 1797 and 1799. (B97)

26. To Christian Ludwig Neuffer. Jena, 28 April 1795

Heydenreich: Karl Heinrich (1764–1801), professor of philosophy at Leipzig. **Göschen**: Georg Joachim (1752–1828), publisher, of Goethe and Schiller among others. **a house in a garden**: Hölderlin had moved and was sharing a house with his new friend Sinclair (see List of Correspondents). **Heyne**: Christian Gottlob (1729–1812), professor of classical philology at Göttingen and founder of modern textual criticism, he had responded favourably to extracts from Neuffer's Virgil. **Ovid's Phaethon**: *Metamorphoses*, Book 2.1–366; Schiller turned it down, and Hölderlin later felt the task had been a waste of his time. **Miss Lebret**: Elise (see note to Letter 23, to Neuffer, 19 January 1795). (B99)

27. To Christian Ludwig Neuffer. Jena, 8 May 1795

Neuffer's fiancée Rosine Stäudlin died of consumption on 25 April 1795. (B100)

28. To Friedrich Schiller. Nürtingen, 23 July 1795

Hölderlin had left Jena at the end of May 1795, exactly why is not clear, and was living at home with his mother. **the first piece of work:**

his translation of the Phaethon episode from Ovid's *Metamorphoses*.
(B102)

29. To Johann Gottfried Ebel. Nürtingen, 2 September 1795

the rest of my journey: having met Ebel in Heidelberg on his way back
from Jena, Hölderlin continued home to Nürtingen. (**rational in the
strict sense**): Hölderlin means in Kant's sense. **Rousseau:** Hölderlin is
quoting from Rousseau's novel *Julie ou la Nouvelle Héloïse* (1761),
Part 5, Letter 3: 'the first and most important form of education is to
render the child apt to be brought up.' **Livy:** the Roman historian
(59 BC–AD 17). **Plutarch:** Greek philosopher and biographer (before
AD 50–after 120), his *Parallel Lives* was a favourite eighteenth-century
source for teaching about the classical world and was recommended
by Rousseau. **a young scholar:** Hölderlin is thinking of Hegel. **M. Fr.
Hölderlin:** as in Letter 14 (to Schiller, 20 March 1794), which also
sets out a programme of education, Hölderlin uses his academic title,
Magister. (B103)

30. To Friedrich Schiller. Nürtingen, 4 September 1795

contributions: probably the poems 'Der Gott der Jugend'/'The God of
Youth' and 'An die Natur'/'To Nature' of which Schiller took only
the first for his *Muses' Almanac* for 1796. **res nullius**: term from
Roman law – 'nobody's thing', common property. **the idea of an
infinite progress in philosophy:** see Appendix, 'The Oldest Programme
for a System of German Idealism', which grew out of conversations
held between Hölderlin and Schelling at about this time; and Letter
34 (to Niethammer, 24 February 1796). **'warm themselves on ice'**:
quotation from Goethe's novel *Wilhelm Meister's Apprenticeship*
(1795). (B104)

31. To Johann Gottfried Ebel. Nürtingen, 9 November 1795

Sinclair: see List of Correspondents. **this invisible church militant:** the
idea of a 'spiritual economy' in and through which a life 'full of divine
meaning' ('Der Archipelagus'/'The Archipelago', *Selected Poems*,
pp. 110/111) could come about. **an apostle:** Paul – see 1 Thessalonians
4:15 and the end of the next letter. (B106)

32. To G. W. F. Hegel. Stuttgart, 25 November 1795

repetitorship: at the Stift in Tübingen – the best former students were eligible to become such tutors. **my former foolishness:** his relationship with Elise Lebret. **the Tübingen gravediggers:** the dogmatic theologians they had been taught by. **Renz:** Karl Christoph (1770–1829), at the top of the class that included Hegel and Hölderlin, and highly regarded by them and Schelling, he did become a repetitor in 1797, then spent a quiet life as a parish priest. (B107)

33. To Johann Gottfried Ebel. Nürtingen, 7 December 1795

your kind invitation: to take up the house-tutorship with the Gontards. Hölderlin did not leave for Frankfurt until after Christmas. (B109)

34. To Friedrich Immanuel Niethammer. Frankfurt, 24 February 1796

Hölderlin had been in Frankfurt as private tutor in the Gontard household since the beginning of the year. **the essays:** the *New Letters on the Aesthetic Education of Man* Hölderlin talks about later in this letter. This title indicates a revision of and challenge to Schiller, whose *On the Aesthetic Education of Man* had been published in 1795, also as a series of letters. See Hölderlin's 'Fragment of Philosophical Letters', which corresponds to what he says here. **Reinhold:** Karl Leonhard (1758–1823), Fichte's predecessor as professor of philosophy in Jena, popularizer of Kant. **Schelling:** he had just published his own *Philosophical Letters on Dogmatism and Critical Philosophy* in Niethammer's journal; these *Letters* are probably what Hölderlin means by 'a better path' at the end of this paragraph, whereas Schelling's former 'less good' path was that taken by his treatise *Of the I as a Principle of Philosophy or On the Absolute in Human Knowledge* (1795). (B117)

35. To Karl Gok. Frankfurt, 20 March 1796 (fragment)

The end of the letter only survives in digest. **aesthetics:** the thinking here, in which beauty appears as 'the pure ideal of all thought and action', is close to that in 'The Oldest Programme for a System of German Idealism'. *cacumina rerum:* (Latin) 'the summits of things'. (B119)

36. *To Karl Gok. Frankfurt, 2 June 1796*

'Love and pleasure are the wings of great doings': from Goethe's classical play *Iphigenia in Tauris* (1787). Hölderlin wrote the same words into Hegel's album on 12 February 1791. **true thoroughness**: the thoughts of this paragraph are Kantian; see in particular *Critique of Judgement*, § 76. **Natural Right**: *Basis of Natural Right according to Principles of the Theory of Knowledge* (1796). **book**: *Hyperion*. (B121)

37. *To Christian Ludwig Neuffer. Frankfurt, June/July 1796*

a being in the world: Susette Gontard. **10th June**: almost certainly a slip for 10th July. **Hamburg**: where Susette Gontard's family came from. In fact they went no further than Kassel. (B123)

38. *To Friedrich Schiller. Kassel, 24 July 1796*

Hölderlin, Susette Gontard, her children and mother-in-law and the governess Marie Rätzer, fleeing the French revolutionary army, arrived in Kassel on 13 or 14 July and stayed there. **a short contribution**: four poems, including one to Susette Gontard, which arrived too late to get into Schiller's almanac. **in flight**: French troops occupied Frankfurt on 14 July. (B124)

39. *To Karl Gok. Kassel, 6 August 1796*

great events: French troops had entered Stuttgart on 18 July and overrun most of Swabia, but Nürtingen, where Hölderlin's mother was, was not much affected. **Greek thunderbolts**: an allusion to the second Persian war (480–479 BC). **General Saint-Cyr**: Laurent Gouvion (1764–1830), general in the French army. **Condé's monstrous lot**: the Prince de Condé, who had fled France in 1789, fought with an army of mercenaries notorious for their brutality. **Heinse**: Wilhelm (1749–1803), author of the novels *Ardinghello und die glückseligen Inseln* (*Ardinghello and the Isles of the Blest*) (1787) and *Hildegard von Hohenthal* (1795–6) and librarian to the Elector of Mainz, came to Kassel in flight from the French armies. He was a friend of the Gontard family and Hölderlin dedicated his elegy 'Brod und Wein'/ 'Bread and Wine' (*Selected Poems*, pp. 150/151) to him. **Landgrave**: the title of certain German princes. **statues in the museum**: the Museum Fridericianum in Kassel contained many copies of classical statues and some original pieces. Heinse, an expert, would have been a good guide. (B125)

40. To Karl Gok. Frankfurt, 13 October 1796

German Boeotia: after the mountainous region in Greece the ancient Athenians regarded as uncultivated. **spa town:** Bad Driburg, where they spent about a month. **Arminius:** chief of a Teutonic tribe who drove the Roman governor Varus out of south Germany in AD 9, the subject of *Hermanns Schlacht* (*Arminius' Battle*) (1767), a drama by F. G. Klopstock (1724–1803). **the woods near Hardt:** see the poem 'Der Winkel von Hahrdt'/'The Nook at Hardt' (*Selected Poems*, pp. 172/173). **the proposal I made:** Hölderlin had (rashly) offered to help pay for Karl to go to university in Jena, but their mother was against it. **cassimere:** 'a thin fine twilled woollen cloth used for men's clothes' (*Oxford English Dictionary*). (B126)

41. To G. W. F. Hegel. Frankfurt, 24 October 1796

Hölderlin arranged a private tutorship with the Gogel family in Frankfurt which Hegel took up in January 1797. (B127)

42. To G. W. F. Hegel. Frankfurt, 20 November 1796

(B128)

43. To Friedrich Schiller. Frankfurt, 20 November 1796

total silence: Schiller had not replied to Hölderlin's letters since the departure from Jena in May 1795, but he answered this one immediately. (B129)

44. To Johann Gottfried Ebel. Frankfurt, 10 January 1797

Written in response to a disillusioned letter from Paris, where Ebel had gone in 1796 out of enthusiasm for the French Revolution. **fermentation and dissolution:** Hölderlin took up the thought of this sentence in his essay-fragment 'The declining fatherland . . .'. It was how he saw his times. **one good soul in particular:** Margarete Gontard (1769–1814), Susette Gontard's sister-in-law. **Henry:** the Gontards' son and Hölderlin's pupil. **someone else who might suit you:** Ebel must have been looking for a tutor on someone's behalf. (B132)

45. To Christian Ludwig Neuffer. Frankfurt, 16 February 1797

a poem to her: this poem, one of several with the title 'Diotima', is not included in *Selected Poems*. '**Whom the gods love receives great joy and great sorrow**': probably a quotation from an early, lost version of *Hyperion*. (B136)

46. To Friedrich Schiller. Frankfurt, 20 June 1797

This letter, and the next four, were written from the Gontards' summer residence outside Frankfurt. **why it is harder to bring nature to its proper expression**: compare these thoughts to the essay-fragment 'The Standpoint from which we should consider Antiquity'. **positively**: like Hegel, Hölderlin uses the word 'positive' to designate the nominal, the given, the merely formal. An opposite relation would be a dialectic, or in Hölderlin's language a 'living' one. **the enclosed poems**: 'An den Aether'/'To the Ether' and 'Der Wanderer'/'The Traveller', and perhaps 'Die Eichbäume'/'The Oaktrees' too. The first appeared in the *Muses' Almanac* for 1798, the other two in the *Horae*. (B139)

47. To Christian Ludwig Neuffer. Frankfurt, 10 July 1797

Lang's almanac: Neuffer had asked whether he might send it in to the *Taschenbuch für häusliche und gesellschaftliche Freuden* (*Album for domestic and social Delight*), edited by Carl Lang in 1797. (B140)

48. To Karl Gok. Frankfurt, August 1797

a tragedy: first mention of Hölderlin's unfinished play, *The Death of Empedocles*. '**The Traveller**': 'Der Wanderer'; see *Selected Poems*, pp. 136/137. (B142)

49. To Friedrich Schiller. Frankfurt, August 1797

your letter: now lost, but the next paragraph must be a response to its contents. **the new translation of *Kabale und Liebe***: Schiller's second play – *The Minister*, translated by M. G. Lewis (London, 1797), that's 'Monk' Lewis. '**those who think they know best**': 'An die klugen Ratgeber' – neither this nor 'Diotima' were accepted. (B144)

50. To Karl Gok. Frankfurt, ~ 20 September 1797

This letter has only survived in a copy, partly in digest. (B145)

51. To Karl Gok. Frankfurt, 2 November 1797

The poets who only play: quoted (from memory) from Klopstock's *Die deutsche Gelehrtenrepublik* (*The Intellectual Republic of Germany*, 1774). **Dr Sömmerring:** Samuel Thomas (1755–1830), a famous anatomist with connections to Goethe and the Humboldt brothers, professor of anatomy, surgery and physiology at the University of Mainz from 1784, in Frankfurt since 1792, where he was a friend of the Gontard family. (B147)

52. To Karl Gok. Frankfurt, 12 February, posted 14 March 1798

parliamentary writings: among Hölderlin's books at his death was *Über das Petitionsrecht der Wirtembergischen Landstände* (*On the Right of Petition of the Estates of Württemberg*, 1797), which may have belonged to Karl. This and whatever else he had he perhaps lent to Hegel, who began writing a political pamphlet on Württemberg at this time. **The letters:** Elise Lebret had apparently requested that her letters to Hölderlin be returned – what follows refers to her. **unspeakably painful experiences:** perhaps refers to the unverified but possible story recounted in the notes to Letter 23 (to Neuffer, 19 January 1795). **Cisrhenanians:** the inhabitants of the left bank of the Rhine, occupied by the French. Early in 1798 towns in these areas, starting with Mainz, began to acquire their own republican administrations. (B152)

53. To Friedrich Schiller. Frankfurt, 30 June 1798

Possibly June in the date-line is a slip of the pen for July; Schiller noted receipt of the letter on 6 August. **a few poems:** 'Dem Sonnengott'/ 'To the Sun-God', 'Vanini', 'Der Mensch'/'Man', 'Sokrates und Alcibiades'/'Socrates and Alcibiades', 'An unsre grossen Dichter'/ 'To Our Great Poets', of which only the last two, the shortest poems, were included in Schiller's *Muses' Almanac* for 1799 (for the last three, see *Selected Poems*, pp. 16–25). Schiller did not reply to this letter. (B159)

54. To Heinrike Breunlin. Frankfurt, 4 July 1798

your dear husband: Hölderlin's sister had married Christian Matthäus Theodor Breunlin in October 1792. **Miss My-bride-to-be:** Hölderlin's jocular name for his niece; his sister had two children. **Dr Veiel:** Johann Gottlob (born 1772), having studied law became mayor of Blaubeuren. The remark on his 'good taste' refers to his future wife. (B161)

55. To Karl Gok. Frankfurt, 4 July 1798

human beings ferment: one of Hölderlin's favourite metaphors of transition, with the implication of clarification to come; used in *Hyperion* and elsewhere. **My character Alabanda:** what follows is from an earlier version of *Hyperion* than the published one. **And Hyperion says:** in a letter to Diotima, same wording as in the published novel. (B162)

56. To Christian Ludwig Neuffer. Frankfurt, August 1798

my bits and pieces: poems sent to Neuffer earlier in the summer for his *Taschenbuch für Frauenzimmer von Bildung* for 1799. Together with the 'little poems' mentioned at the end of this letter, they make up eighteen short odes, all but two of which are translated in *Selected Poems*, pp. 6–17 ('An die Parzen'/'To the Fates' to 'Sonnenuntergang'/'Sunset'). θειον: (Greek) 'divine element', probably borrowed from Plato. **what I promised:** he had promised a longer poem. (B163)

57. To Johanna Christiana Gok. Homburg, 10 October 1798

Hölderlin left the Gontard household at the end of September in more heated circumstances than this letter suggests. Homburg vor der Höhe was only an hour or two from Frankfurt. **My book has had a certain amount of success at court:** *Hyperion* and its author made a deep impression on Auguste of Hesse-Homburg in particular. Later Hölderlin dedicated his translations of Sophocles to her (see notes to Letter 115). She was the daughter of the Landgrave (Prince) Friedrich V of Hesse-Homburg, dedicatee of 'Patmos'. At the time, their residence was being used to billet French military staff. (B165)

58. To Christian Ludwig Neuffer. Homburg,
12 November 1798

my tragedy: *Der Tod des Empedokles/The Death of Empedocles*, which Hölderlin worked on throughout his time in Homburg but never finished. **your almanac:** see notes to Letter 56 (to Neuffer, August 1798). **Rastatt:** Hölderlin spent about two weeks in Rastatt, where since December 1797 a congress had been negotiating territorial and other consequences of French invasion. **Neuenbürg:** on the edge of the Black Forest, roughly half-way between Rastatt and Stuttgart. **Life in poetry:** these thoughts are at the centre of Hölderlin's preoccupations in Homburg. (B167)

59. To Karl Gok. Rastatt, 28 November 1798

Muhrbeck: Friedrich (1775–1827), taught philosophy at Greifswald, where his father was a professor. A friend of Böhlendorff's (see list of correpondents) – with him he spent much of 1799 in Homburg with Hölderlin and Sinclair. *Horn*: Fritz (1772–1844), like Muhrbeck attached to the revolutionary groups in Jena. Met Hölderlin again in 1802 in Regensburg. *von Pommer-Esche*: Johann Arnold Joachim (1774–1814), secretary of the legation from Swedish Pomerania. **Councillor** *Schenk*: Johann Heinrich (1748–1813). **Jacobi:** Friedrich Heinrich (1743–1819), man of letters and non-systematic philosopher. **Gutscher:** Jakob Friedrich (1760–1834), not part of the official legation from Württemberg but of a delegation representing the estates. (B169)

60. To Johanna Christiana Gok. Homburg,
11 December 1798

the proposed post: with the von Gemmingen family in Heilbronn, north of Stuttgart. **Gentner:** Karl Christian Friedrich (1767–1824), had been at the Stift. (B170)

61. To Isaak von Sinclair. Homburg, 24 December 1798
(fragment)

This letter is close to the Homburg essays in tone and subject. Sinclair was still in Rastatt. **Diogenes Laertius:** wrote in the third century AD his *Lives and Opinions of the Famous Philosophers*, Hölderlin's main source for *Empedocles*. **the transient and changeful nature of**

human thoughts and systems: compare Keats to J. H. Reynolds, 3 May 1818: 'a mighty providence subdues the mightiest Minds to the service of the time being, whether it be in human Knowledge or Religion'. (B171)

62. *To Karl Gok. Homburg, New Year's Eve/1 January* 1799

glebae addicti: properly, *glebae adscripti* (Latin), 'bound to the sod', a legal term for the status of certain peasants. **Thales and Solon**: the linking of these two fifth-century Greeks, the natural philosopher and the legislator, derives from Diogenes Laertius; in fact they were unconnected. **So much has already been said about the influence of the arts on the education of man**: especially by Schiller in *On the Aesthetic Education of Man*; the remarks on 'play' in the next sentence seem to be directed at thoughts in this work. **the verses**: 'Meiner verehrungswürdigen Grossmutter'/'To my honoured grandmother'. *homo sum . . . alienum puto*: (Latin) 'I am human and think nothing human foreign to me', from the Roman playwright Terence's *The Self-Tormentor*. (B172)

63. *To Johanna Christiana Gok. Homburg, January* 1799

Gellert: Christian Fürchtegott (1715–69), a popular writer of didactic poems, became professor of moral philosophy in 1745. **the book I'm writing now**: *Empedocles*. (B173)

64. *To Johanna Christiana Gok. Homburg, early March* 1799

the war: the war of the Second Coalition began formally on 12 March 1799. **changes**: as Hölderlin knew from Sinclair, and was perhaps more nearly involved in (see end of letter), groupings of revolutionary republicans in Württemberg had hopes of founding a Swabian republic with the help of the French. (B175)

65. *To Susette Gontard. Homburg, Spring* 1799

The beginning of a draft. Hölderlin's actual letters to Susette Gontard are lost. The four extant fragments are drafts which may contain precisely what Hölderlin did not dare say. (B176)

66. To Christian Ludwig Neuffer. Homburg, 4 June 1799

a few contributions: for Neuffer's *Taschenbuch für Frauenzimmer von Bildung* for 1800, his 'second son'. **a monthly poetry journal**: Hölderlin later considered calling the journal *Iduna* – it was a project which didn't in the end come off. **Steinkopf**: see List of Correspondents. **On the *Iliad*, particularly the character of Achilles**: see the essay-fragments on Achilles ('I am pleased . . .' and 'But most of all I love . . .'), 'A Word on the *Iliad*', and 'On the different Modes of Poetic Composition' in this volume. **Bouterwek**: Friedrich (1766–1828), professor of philosophy and aesthetics in Göttingen, author of the novel *Graf Donamar* (1791–3), which was an influence on *Hyperion*. **Siegfried Schmid**: (1774–1859), a friend of Sinclair's in Jena, known to Hölderlin since autumn 1797, the elegy 'Stutgard'/ 'Stuttgart' (*Selected Poems*, pp. 142/143) is dedicated to him and he also received, in his words, 'splendid letters' from Hölderlin, which have not survived. **the *Horae***: Schiller's journal *Die Horen*, which had recently stopped appearing. **the promised essays**: not written. (B178)

67. To Karl Gok. Homburg, 4 June 1799

The thoughts in this letter, which should possibly be dated 14 June 1799, give an idea of what Hölderlin had in mind for his journal and are close to some of the theoretical prose he did write in Homburg, especially to 'The Standpoint from which we should consider Antiquity'. **a passage from my tragedy**: from the second version of *Empedocles*, lines 397–430. (B179)

68. To Johanna Christiana Gok. Homburg, 18 June 1799

my second father: Johann Christoph Gok died in 1779 when Hölderlin was almost nine. (B180)

69. To Johann Friedrich Steinkopf. Homburg vor der Höhe, 18 June 1799 (copy and digest)

project: to edit the 'monthly poetry journal' announced in Letter 66 (to Neuffer, 4 June 1799). Steinkopf was to be the publisher. **popularity**: Hölderlin is no doubt responding to a request made by Steinkopf. **the same thing has recently been attempted**: by the brothers August Wilhelm and Friedrich Schlegel in their journal *Athenäum*, which began appearing in 1798. The criticisms which follow apply to them.

Hölderlin himself is aiming for more balance. **its due as a product of nature**: the same words are used in the prospectus (see below). *Iduna*: in Norse myth the keeper of the magic apples that preserved the youth of the gods. She was a goddess, married to Bragi, god of poetry. Hölderlin may have known of this myth from a dialogue by Herder, *Iduna or the Apple of Youth*, published in Schiller's *Horae* in 1796. There does not appear to be an earlier journal with this title. **prospectus**: see the fragment of this that survives – 'From a Draft of the Journal Plan'. Its rejection of 'affectedly mischievous saltos and curios' is again a jab at the Schlegels. **my tragedy**: *Empedocles*, which was to appear in the journal. *'Emilie'*: see notes to Letter 71 (to Neuffer, 3 July 1799). *a young poet*: probably Emerich (see List of Correspondents). (B181)

70. To Susette Gontard. Homburg, ~ June 1799 (draft)

firewood: behind this word lies the Greek υλη, which means wood, firewood, but also matter. The combination of matter and spirit (through and in poetry) is a focus of the essay 'When the poet is once in command of the spirit . . .'. With the general thought of this passage compare Keats to J. H. Reynolds, 19 February 1818:

> Man should not dispute or assert but whisper results to his neighbour, and thus by every germ of Spirit sucking the Sap from the mould ethereal every human might become great, and Humanity instead of being a wide heath of Furze and Briars with here and there a remote Oak or Pine, would become a grand democracy of Forest Trees.

'The French have been beaten in Italy again': the French suffered three defeats in Italy that year, at Cassano (27 April), by the Trebbia (17–19 June) and at Novi (15 August), setbacks for the republican cause. (B182)

71. To Christian Ludwig Neuffer. Homburg, 3 July 1799

what I promised: the idyll *Emilie vor ihrem Brauttag/Emilie before her bridal day* which Hölderlin had written at Steinkopf's request. **Jung**: Franz Wilhelm (1757–1833), a radical democrat and friend of Sinclair's; his translation of Ossian, which Hölderlin had read and approved of in manuscript, appeared in 1808. He lived in Mainz. **the strictest of all poetic forms**: Hölderlin's reflections on tragedy continued in several of the Homburg essays, in *Empedocles*, and in his later work on Sophocles. **another young poet**: this might be Friedrich Joseph Emerich, whose poems Hölderlin took an interest in; see Letter 84 to him (Spring 1800) and List of Correspondents. **Böhlendorff**: see List of Correspondents. (B183)

72. To Friedrich Schiller. Homburg, 5 July 1799

Schiller replied on 24 August, sending no contribution and advising Hölderlin 'as a sincere friend' against launching a periodical at all. (B184)

73. To Johanna Christiana Gok. Homburg, 8 July 1799

those verses: 'An die Parzen'/'To the Fates', which appeared in Neuffer's *Taschenbuch für Frauenzimmer von Bildung* for 1799. It begins 'One summer only grant me . . .'. **God sends rain**: Matthew 5:45, 'for he maketh his sun to rise on the evil and on the good, and sendeth rain on the just and on the unjust'. (B185)

74. To Friedrich Wilhelm Joseph Schelling. Homburg, early July 1799

Probably not the actual letter Hölderlin sent to Schelling but a draft. Perhaps the first contact with him since their meeting in April 1796. Since then Schelling had become a professor in Jena and made a name for himself with two major publications. In his reply Schelling agreed to contribute, but begged him not to use the term 'humanism'. The tone and subject-matter of this letter are close to the essays. A recently discovered letter to Ebel, dated 6 July 1799, has much the same contents (often verbatim) and is not included here for that reason. *ex abrupto*: (Latin) without preamble. **aorgic**: a word probably of Hölderlin's own devising, meaning 'natural', 'tied to the elements', 'shapeless'. (B186)

75. To Johann Wolfgang Goethe (?). Homburg, July 1799 (incomplete draft)

Survives only as a copy and part-digest. Beck doubts whether any such letter was actually sent, and possibly the draft is not addressed to Goethe at all, though much makes it likely. (B187)

76. To Heinrike Breunlin. Homburg, July 1799

without drawing too much attention to myself: once within the borders of Württemberg, without an identifiable job, Hölderlin became exposed to pressure from the ecclesiastical authorities to become a clergyman. **a wild friend**: Sinclair. (B188)

77. To Friedrich Schiller. Homburg, September 1799
(incomplete draft)

the generosity: in the letter this replies to Schiller had declined to contribute to the journal and warned Hölderlin off the whole project. **Robbers**: *Die Räuber* (1781), Schiller's first play. **Fiesko**: Schiller's second play (1783). **Don Carlos**: Schiller's fourth play (1787). (B194)

78. To Susette Gontard. Homburg, late August/early
September 1799 (incomplete draft)

a place where I can support myself by giving lectures: Hölderlin is thinking of Jena. (B195)

79. To Susette Gontard. Homburg, ~ November 1799
(incomplete draft)

Hyperion: the second volume had just appeared. **that you are always suffering**: Susette Gontard had written: 'without you my life is withering away and slowly dying'. (B198)

80. To Johanna Christiana Gok. Homburg,
16 November 1799

Bonaparte made a sort of dictator: on 9 November (18 Brumaire in the revolutionary calendar) Napoleon assumed total power in France. Though the words 'a sort of dictator' sound negative, Hölderlin may either be distancing himself from the term or using it in the Roman sense of a consul assuming total powers to bridge a crisis. (B199)

81. To Johann Gottfried Ebel. Homburg, ~ November 1799
(incomplete draft)

Ebel was still in Paris; see Letter 44 to him (10 January 1797). (B201)

82. *To Christian Ludwig Neuffer. Homburg,*
4 December 1799

The last letter to Neuffer. **your most recent poems:** in Neuffer's *Taschenbuch für Frauenzimmer von Bildung* for 1800, which he had just sent and which also contained several poems by Hölderlin. **the sure, thoroughly purposeful and considered progression of ancient works of art:** the same thought recurs in the 'Notes on the *Oedipus*'. (B202)

83. *To Johanna Christiana Gok. Homburg, 29 January 1800*

Survives as a copy and part-digest. Hölderlin's mother had written urging him to take up a post of some kind in Württemberg, perhaps a teaching post. He was in any case considering moving to Stuttgart, which he eventually did in June. **with somewhat less in the way of funds:** Hölderlin is thinking of tapping into his inheritance from his father, which was held in trust by his mother. **Dear Henry:** Susette Gontard's son and Hölderlin's pupil in Frankfurt. (B204)

84. *To Friedrich Emerich. Homburg, Spring 1800* (draft)

publishing your poems: these seem to have been published in 1799. They were reviewed in summer 1800. **We cold Northerners:** anticipates thoughts in Letter 106 (the first letter to Böhlendorff, 4 December 1801). **a true penitent:** seems to refer to Hölderlin's advocacy of 'artistic sense' over 'genius'. **if I appear to be angry:** i.e. in making the criticisms in this letter. (B206)

85. *To Johanna Christiana Gok. Homburg, 23 May 1800*

the news: the French, under Moreau, had again crossed the Rhine on 25 April 1800 and advanced through Württemberg as far as Ulm. **my lodgings:** at Landauer's (see List of Correspondents). **abroad:** i.e. outside Württemberg, though Hölderlin's next job was in fact in Switzerland. **additional occupations:** private lessons. **Herr Kling:** a draper, business friend of Landauer's. (B207)

86. *To Johanna Christiana Gok. Stuttgart, end of June 1800*

Hölderlin had left Homburg in June 1800, gone first to his mother's in Nürtingen (where since the death of her husband in March his sister and her children also lived) for about ten days, then to Landauer's in

Stuttgart. **a little poem**: only notes for a poem to Hölderlin's sister exist. **peace**: this did not come until the Peace of Lunéville in February 1801. (B208)

87. *To Heinrike Breunlin. Stuttgart, September/October 1800*

in its loss: Hölderlin's brother-in-law had died on 2 March. (B214)

88. *To Heinrike Breunlin. Stuttgart, Autumn 1800*

Hölderlin was forced to begin searching for another source of income, including looking out for another post as house-tutor. **nothing from Switzerland**: this refers not to Hauptwil, but to another post he turned down in favour of Hauptwil in December. **faith, hope and charity**: cf. 1 Corinthians 13:13. (B215)

89. *To Heinrike Breunlin. Stuttgart, ~ mid-October 1800*

the peace: it came, briefly, with the Peace of Lunéville in February 1801. (B216)

90. *To Heinrike Breunlin. Stuttgart, October/November 1800*

(B217)

91. *To Gottlieb Ernst August Mehmel. Stuttgart, November/ December 1800 (?)* (incomplete draft)

This letter was previously thought to be to Schütz (see the note to Letter 103, to Niethammer, 23 June 1801). **your kind invitation**: Hölderlin had been asked to work as a reviewer for the *Erlanger Literatur-Zeitung*, edited by Mehmel and Johann Georg Meusel, who issued guidelines for reviews. **The intense study of the Greeks**: while in Homburg Hölderlin did a word-for-word translation of most of Pindar's Olympian and Pythian odes, and made a particular study of tragedy. ***per contrarium***: (Latin) through its opposite, 'negatively'. **the words *want, ought* and *can***: together with other phrases at the end here, pick up terms in the editors' guidelines. (B203)

92. To Heinrike Breunlin. Stuttgart, 11 December 1800

the unexpected visitor: Emanuel von Gonzenbach, son of Anton von Gonzenbach (see List of Correspondents), who was in Stuttgart looking for a tutor for his younger sisters. **Landauer's birthday**: Hölderlin wrote a poem for the occasion, 'To Landauer'. (B219)

93. To Karl Gok. Nürtingen, ~ late December 1800

common spirit: (*Gemeingeist*) could be translated by 'public spirit' but it has religious as well as political connotations: in a late variant to 'Der Einzige'/'The Only One' Hölderlin uses the word for Dionysus. (B222)

94. To the family. Stuttgart, ~ 6 January 1801

(B223)

95. To Anton von Gonzenbach. Stuttgart, early January 1801 (draft)

your son: see notes to Letter 92 (to Heinrike Breunlin, 11 December 1800). (B224)

96. To Heinrike Breunlin. Stuttgart, early January 1801

(B225)

97. To Johanna Christiana Gok. Hauptwil, 24 January 1801

Hölderlin came to Hauptwil, near St Gallen in Switzerland, in mid-January to take up his third post as tutor in the house of Anton von Gonzenbach (see List of Correspondents). (B227)

98. To Heinrike Breunlin. Hauptwil, 23 February 1801

the negotiated peace: the Peace of Lunéville, agreed on 9 February 1801. Hölderlin's response was the poem 'Friedensfeier'/'Celebration of Peace' (*Selected Poems*, pp. 208/209). **these splendid peaks**: see the beginning of 'Heimkunft'/'Homecoming', and 'Unter den Alpen gesungen'/'Sung beneath the Alps' (*Selected Poems*, pp. 158/159 and 76/77). (B228)

99. To Christian Landauer. Hauptwil, February 1801

Boreas: the north wind. (B229)

100. To Christian Landauer. Hauptwil, ~ March 1801

(B230)

101. To Karl Gok. Hauptwil, ~ March 1801

a *sign* **of the soul:** perhaps by 'sign' Hölderlin means physical presence, external aspect. In his poetic thinking in the Homburg essays 'sign' is related to 'ground': the ground expresses itself in a sign which is always different, even opposed to it. *A Deo principium*: 'the beginning is from God'. (B231)

102. To Friedrich Schiller. Nürtingen, 2 June 1801

Hölderlin had left Hauptwil in mid-April, precisely why is not known, and was at his mother's again. This is his last letter to Schiller, who did not reply. **the great clarity these writers have is a consequence of their abundance of spirit:** this anticipates the thoughts of Letter 106 (to Böhlendorff, 4 December 1801). (B232)

103. To Immanuel Niethammer. Nürtingen, 23 June 1801

silence: probably they had not been in touch since Hölderlin's last letter, of 24 February 1796, Letter 34. **Schütz:** Christian Gottfried (1747–1832), editor of the *Allgemeine Literatur-Zeitung* and professor of rhetoric and poetry at Jena. **Tennemann:** Wilhelm Gottlieb (1761–1819), professor of philosophy at Jena, specializing in Greek philosophy. (B233)

104. To the family. Stuttgart, ~ October/November 1801

Probably written on a short visit to Landauer's, who had news of a tutoring job in Bordeaux. (B234)

105. To Karl Gok. Nürtingen, 4 December 1801

(B235)

106. To Casimir Ulrich Böhlendorff. Nürtingen, 4 December 1801

Your *Fernando*: the play *Fernando oder die Kunstweihe. Eine dramatische Idylle* (1802), which Böhlendorff had just sent. **what we are born with**: the word Hölderlin uses is *das Nationelle*. In his new understanding, the Greeks and the Germans, the ancients and the moderns, are born with opposing origins or natures, and for that reason imitation of the Greeks in the neoclassical sense is wrongheaded. As epitomized in their burial rites, the Greeks are fiery (associated by Hölderlin with passion, the sky, formlessness) whereas the moderns are earthy (associated with clarity, sobriety, form). The aim of culture, though, is a balance, to be achieved by the moderns in a way diametrically opposed to the Greeks, by tending towards fire. Homer achieved this balance by appropriating 'occidental' plasticity, and Hölderlin praises Böhlendorff for combining 'precision' and 'warmth' in his play. *Junonian sobriety*: Juno, famous for her stately beauty, represents here plastic form. **Apollonian realm**: Apollo was among other things the sun-god ('heavenly fire'). **living craft and proportion**: the balance. The word here translated by 'craft', *Geschick*, can also mean propriety, in the sense of the 'sacred propriety with which they [the Greeks] *had* to proceed in dealings with the gods' (Letter 91 to Mehmel, November/December 1800?). **the Greeks are indispensable to us**: because they allow us to experience in the foreign clarity of their art our own original nature. **fear and pity**: according to Aristotle's *Poetics* the emotions through which tragedy produces catharsis. **Jupiter**: the supreme god, made palpable by tragedy. **preacher**: Hölderlin was dispensed from preaching duties, but was apparently ready to take them on. **'with a calm hand . . . ruddy clouds'**: freely citing Goethe's poem 'Grenzen der Menschheit'/'Limits of humankind'. **this sign**: i.e. lightning. **Tantalus**: who in Greek mythology was allowed to eat with the gods but proved unworthy and was cast into the underworld to suffer for ever. (B236)

107. To Johanna Christiana Gok. Lyons, 9 January 1802

Hölderlin arrived in Strasburg from Nürtingen on 15 December where he had to wait two weeks before being allowed to continue. Possibly he chose the unusual route via Lyons himself, knowing that Napoleon was due there, and he may well have seen him. (B237)

108. *To Johanna Christiana Gok. Bordeaux,*
28 January 1802

Most of the 350-odd miles from Lyons to Bordeaux Hölderlin covered on foot. His new job was in the household of the wine-merchant (also consul for Hamburg) Daniel Christoph Meyer (1751–1818) where he had four or five girls to teach. (B238)

109. *To Johanna Christiana Gok. Bordeaux,*
Good Friday 1802

Good Friday: 16 April. **our now blessed grandmother:** she had died on 14 February 1802. (B239)

110. *To Casimir Ulrich Böhlendorff. Nürtingen,*
~ November 1802

On 10 May 1802 Hölderlin had obtained a passport in Bordeaux for the return journey to Germany, which he made via Paris and Strasburg, arriving in Stuttgart some time between mid-June and the beginning of July in a bad state. Both the journey and the reasons for leaving Bordeaux are mysterious. The thinking in the first letter to Böhlendorff (Letter 106), the tension between formlessness and form, is evident here too in the descriptions, but it has become less theoretical and more a matter of lived experience, a threat. **virtuosity:** the second section of the 'Notes on the *Antigone*' also speaks of Antigone's 'virtuosity' as she faces death. **popularity:** (*Popularität*) possibly glossed in the following phrase ('their manner of receiving foreign natures and of communicating with them'), or else meaning 'what defines them as a people'. **the antiquities:** in Paris (see Letter 114 to Seckendorf, 12 March 1804), where Napoleon had brought trophies from Italy and Egypt. **the coincidence in one region ... in one place:** see 'Vom Abgrund nemlich . . .'/'For from the abyss . . .': 'And there I am / All things at once' (*Selected Poems*, pp. 312/313). The landscape around Nürtingen is transitional, mixing northern and southern vegetation. (B240)

111. *To Friedrich Wilmans. Nürtingen, 28 September 1803*

the translation of the Sophocles tragedies: Hölderlin's translations of *Oedipus the King* and *Antigone* were published by Wilmans in 1804. He intended to do more. **Schelling:** Hölderlin had visited him in June 1803 when Schelling was appalled by his appearance. **the theatre in**

Weimar: directed by Goethe. How seriously Schelling intended this proposal is uncertain – there is no evidence he made any approach. **an introduction:** mentioned in the next two letters too, but sadly never written. **the oriental element:** 'heavenly fire' as opposed to the 'occidental', modern element (see Letter 106 to Böhlendorff, 4 December 1801). **artistic bias:** Hölderlin's odd word is *Kunstfehler*, the process through which the Greeks corrected their inborn tendency towards fire, which Hölderlin now thinks of as having been overdone, at least from a modern perspective. The first letter to Böhlendorff (Letter 106) provides a sort of commentary. (B241)

112. To Friedrich Wilmans. Nürtingen, 8 December 1803

lively enough: i.e. it did not bring out the 'oriental element' enough (see previous letter). **short poems for an almanac:** Wilmans had asked for poems for an annual he was editing. Hölderlin sent the 'Night Poems' mentioned in the next letter. **single lyric poems of some length:** (some of) the hymns, mentioned again in the following two letters to Wilmans; see especially 'Friedensfeier'/'Celebration of Peace' with its prefatory note (*Selected Poems*, pp. 208/209). (B242)

113. To Friedrich Wilmans. Nürtingen, late December 1803

letters like these: Hölderlin's Sophocles was printed in Roman type rather than Gothic script. **Night Poems:** 'Nachtgesänge', nine poems which belong together: 'Chiron', 'Tränen'/'Tears', 'An die Hoffnung'/ 'To Hope', 'Vulkan'/'Vulcan', 'Blödigkeit'/'Timidness', 'Ganymed'/ 'Ganymede', 'Hälfte des Lebens'/'Half of Life', 'Lebensalter'/'Ages of Life', 'Der Winkel von Hahrdt'/'The Nook at Hardt' (all in *Selected Poems*). They appeared in Wilmans' annual in 1804. **the Messias and . . . certain odes:** by Klopstock, who had died earlier that year. *Views: Picturesque Views of the Rhine from Mainz to Düsseldorf*, published by Wilmans. See next letter. (B243)

114. To Leo von Seckendorf. Nürtingen, 12 March 1804

antiquities in Paris: which Hölderlin saw on his way back from Bordeaux. **Fable:** probably meaning myth; see the essay 'On the Fable of the Ancients'. **enemies of our mother country:** probably Hölderlin is thinking of the Elector of Württemberg and his conservative supporters at the court, who were adopting a more and more absolutist stance at this time. (B244)

115. To Friedrich Wilmans. Nürtingen, 2 April 1804

the raw print: Hölderlin is writing this letter having just received and gone through the final book-form of his Sophocles translations – Wilmans had forewarned him of the many printer's errors. By 'raw print' he means the 'sample' he thanks Wilmans for in Letter 113, presumably a sort of galley proof. This appears to have been in a rougher form. The references to the 'file' probably have no basis in typographical practice, but refer metaphorically to a process of refinement and tidying-up. **Princess of Homburg**: Princess Auguste of Hesse-Homburg (1776–1871); the Sophocles translations included the printed dedication:

> To Princess Auguste of Homburg. You encouraged me years ago with a kind letter and I have owed you a reply ever since. Now, as a poet, here too, has to do something else that is necessary or pleasant, I have chosen this occupation because it is bound in laws which, though foreign, are solid and historical. Otherwise it is my intention, if time allows, to sing of the forebears of our princes and their seats and the angels of the sacred country.

Hölderlin met her in Homburg thanks to Sinclair, and she made a collection of his poems written out in her own hand. **in the direction of eccentric enthusiasm**: Letter 106 (to Böhlendorff, 4 December 1801) offers a framework for understanding this difficult sentence: 'eccentric enthusiasm' is another term for the native Greek tendency, as opposed to occidental 'sobriety'. In his work as translator of Sophocles, which he hoped to continue, Hölderlin has brought out 'what was forbidden to the original poet' by going towards this Greek pole and away from his native pole, which is the direction he had explained to Böhlendorff that modern writers had to go in. Hölderlin wrote '*gegen die exzentrische Begeisterung*', which could mean '*against* eccentric enthusiasm', but it is hard to make any sense of the words if they are taken in this way. (B245)

Letters from Tübingen, 1807–28

The sixty-six letters or notes Hölderlin wrote at his guardian Zimmer's prompting, almost all to his mother (who died in 1828), cannot be dated accurately. (B263, B270, B298, B299, B307)

NOTES TO THE ESSAYS

In the first instance, these translations of Hölderlin's essays were based on the text established by Friedrich Beissner in his critical edition of Hölderlin's works, the Stuttgart edition (vol. 4 of *Sämtliche Werke*, 1961), and in the later one jointly edited by Friedrich Beissner and Jochen Schmidt, the Insel edition (*Werke und Briefe*, 2 vols., Frankfurt, 1969). The major revisions to the earlier readings by Wolfram Groddeck and D. E. Sattler in the Frankfurt edition (*Entwürfe zur Poetik*, 1979; *Empedokles I/II*, 1985; *Pindar*, 1987; *Frühe Aufsätze und Übersetzungen*, 1991) and by Michael Knaupp and Michael Franz in the Munich edition (*Sämtliche Werke und Briefe*, 3 vols., 1992–3) were then worked into the text.

A word on the textual problems may be in order. The fragmentary state of many of Hölderlin's manuscripts makes the editing extremely difficult. The texts established in the Stuttgart edition were long regarded as standard. However, the Frankfurt edition substantially revised the texts, emphasizing the essays' fragmentary character, newly reconstructing them from the manuscripts and at key points proposing a different ordering of their paragraphs, notably for the essays previously known as 'Judgement and Being' ('Being Judgement Possibility') and 'On Religion' ('Fragment of Philosophical Letters'). The disagreement between these two main critical editions is carried over into the two principal 'reading editions': Knaupp largely follows Sattler, and Schmidt (in *Sämtliche Werke und Briefe*, 3 vols., Frankfurt, 1992–4) follows Beissner, except in the case of the essays 'The Ground of the *Empedocles*' and 'The declining fatherland...' which are freshly edited in the context of the *Empedocles* material by Katharina Grätz. The most recent editor of Hölderlin's essays, Johann Kreuzer, generally follows Knaupp in his edition (*Theoretische Schriften*, 1998).

The most obvious effect of these editorial differences is in the essay titles. Hölderlin himself gave titles to only a few of the essays. Beissner, often following earlier editors, supplied them where they were lacking, and for a long time the essays were known under these unauthorized titles. Sattler then undid Beissner's work by proposing different ones, sometimes based on new information and usually adopting Hölderlin's opening words. These titles (along with some variants suggested by Knaupp/Franz!) have gradually established themselves, and since the old forms have no authority in Hölderlin, Sattler's are mostly given here, though the perhaps more familiar titles are placed in the Notes to aid identification. Where a title is not Hölderlin's own this is indicated (by the words 'Title supplied'), except when it simply takes the opening words.

In textual terms the present edition is a compromise: what seemed in each case to be the best or most likely reading of the manuscripts has been adopted (the Frankfurt edition provides facsimiles), with Knaupp's edition serving as a dependable arbiter, although some of Beissner's solutions have been retained. The ordering of the essays follows the chronology proposed in Knaupp's edition. Chronological questions aside, this sequence affords a very coherent approach to Hölderlin's ideas, even if it does not resolve all the questions of dating. The notes are largely based on those in the German editions.

Footnotes printed in the text are Hölderlin's own – they often have the status of additions or reminders rather than annotations, but in order not to occlude the fragmentary, provisional nature of these essays they have not been integrated into the text as they arguably could be. For the same reason, and insofar as it is compatible with the shift from handwriting into print, the form of the essays as they are preserved in the manuscripts has been respected – almost no attempt has been made to rationalize discrepancies or to add punctuation. Where Hölderlin underlines, the translation uses italics. Where he double or triple-underlines, the English appears in small capitals. Occasionally Hölderlin wrote a word in Roman script for emphasis – this has also been given as italics.

Finally, a word should be said about our translation of Hölderlin's word 'idealisch': since in his usage it is more the adjective of 'idea' than of 'ideal', we have coined the English 'idealic' to signal the difference.

'I was slumbering, my Callias . . .'/'*Ich schlummerte, mein Kallias . . .*'

Beissner: To Callias (An Kallias)

1.   Beissner first published this text in 1944, treating it as an essay for Hölderlin's planned journal, *Iduna*. However, in 1966 Maria Cornelissen argued that it belongs with Hölderlin's novel, *Hyperion*, a view accepted by Sattler and Knaupp in their editions. Knaupp considers it could have been written as early as 1792 and points out that it already contains many of *Hyperion*'s major themes. Schmidt, while noting the links to *Hyperion*, includes it with the essays and puts it not later than 1794.

The name Callias occurs in Plato's *Protagoras* and in other dialogues. It was adopted by Schiller as a title for a treatise on aesthetics which is preserved in draft in the form of letters to his friend Körner, written in January–March 1793. It also occurs in Wieland's novel *Agathon* (1794), which Hölderlin read soon after its publication.

2. Plato's doctrine of the pre-existence of the soul as described by Socrates in the *Phaedo*, 110b–111c, 114c.

3. The town traditionally regarded as Homer's birthplace, Smyrna, lies in Lydia, formerly inhabited by the Maionians.

4. **Glycera**: a feminine Greek name, meaning 'sweet one', which also occurs in Wieland's *Agathon*.

5. Homer, *Iliad*, Book 10.469ff.

6. In the manuscript, the text is here interrupted with a quotation from Rousseau's *Julie ou la Nouvelle Héloïse* (1761), which can be read as a self-criticism: '*Votre lettre vous dément par son style enjoué; et vous n'auriez pas tant d'esprit si vous étiez moins tranquille*' ('Your letter gives you away by its playful style; and you would not be so witty if you were less calm', Part 1, Letter 9).

'There is a natural state . . .'/'*Es giebt einen Naturzustand . . .*'

Beissner: On the Law of Freedom (Über das Gesetz der Freiheit)

7. This early essay was probably written at Waltershausen in the second half of 1794. The ideas reflect contemporary empirical psychology and the debate between Schiller and Kant on the nature of freedom.

8. The rest of the manuscript is probably lost.

On the Concept of Punishment/*Über den Begriff der Strafe*

9. This early essay was probably written in Jena in January 1795. The text is fragmentary and it is possible that it was never completed. The theme concerns the possibility of establishing the principles of law and of a philosophy of law. It was probably influenced by Fichte's interest in founding law in morality.

10. The rest of the manuscript is probably lost.

Being Judgement Possibility/*Seyn Urtheil Möglichkeit*

Title supplied
Beissner: Judgement and Being (Urtheil und Seyn)
Knaupp: Being, Judgement, Modality (Seyn, Urtheil, Modalität)

11. This essay was probably written in Jena. Beissner dates it to early 1795, Sattler places it after 5 April 1795 and Knaupp gives between mid-April and the end of May 1795. The text, written on both sides of a single sheet, was first discovered around 1960 and was first published by Beissner. The order of the paragraphs and hence also of the title words has since been challenged. Whereas Beissner treated the text as beginning with judgement and reality (paragraphs 4 and 5), Sattler argued for the present form, a revision accepted by Knaupp.

    The essay presents a philosophical programme, centring on Hölderlin's concept of 'intellectual intuition' (see following note); compare Letter 30 (to Schiller, 4 September 1795) and Letter 34 (to Niethammer, 24 February 1796). The concept recurs in the essays 'When the poet is once in command of the spirit . . .' and 'The lyric, in appearance idealic poem . . .'. The arguments need to be considered in relation to Hölderlin's ongoing debate with the positions taken by Fichte and Schelling.

12. **intellectual intuition**: spiritual vision, the highest form of knowledge in Neoplatonic epistemology. Kant disputed its possibility; Fichte treated it as the highest act of the I; and Schelling regarded it as an act by which the I constitutes itself. For Hölderlin, it is the highest insight, the view 'that everything is one' ('dass Alles eins ist').

13. Hölderlin here appears to criticize Schelling. Both he and Fichte derive the law of identity (I = I) from self-consciousness, but it is chiefly Schelling who treats self-consciousness as absolute being, regarding identity as the absolute being of the I.

14. Hölderlin here uses an etymological pun, deriving *Urteil* (judgement) from *Ur-Teilung* (original division). This stems from Fichte, who appears to have used it in his Jena lectures in the winter semester of 1794–5, many of which Hölderlin attended.

Hermocrates to Cephalus/*Hermokrates an Cephalus*

15. According to Beissner, this essay was written in early 1795, but Knaupp now places it after March that year. It was inspired by the discussion of Fichte's *Wissenschaftslehre* (*Theory of Knowledge*, 1794–5) by Friedrich Niethammer, Hölderlin's philosophical mentor (see List of Correspondents). Niethammer questioned Fichte's attempt to provide an absolute foundation for knowledge. The same position is here taken by Hermocrates.

    The names Hermocrates and Cephalus are from Plato's

Timaeus. Cephalus (= head) recalls Niethammer's nickname, 'das Köpfchen' ('little head').

16. The image is that of a sculpture of Jupiter on a pedestal.

17. The manuscript breaks off here.

Fragment of Philosophical Letters/
Fragment philosophischer Briefe

Title supplied

Beissner: On Religion (Über Religion)

18. Beissner treated this fragmentary essay as a late piece. Groddeck and Sattler suppose a hypothetical dating of 1796/7. Knaupp proposes February/March 1796. The Frankfurt edition reconstitutes the manuscript, and with a couple of qualifications Knaupp accepts this reading. It would follow from this that what survives is not an essay on religion, but may represent fragments of the 'philosophical letters' Hölderlin announced to Niethammer in a letter of 24 February 1796 (Letter 34). The essay anticipates key concepts in the essay attributed to Hegel, Schelling and Hölderlin, 'The Oldest Programme for a System of German Idealism' (see Appendix).

   The translation follows Knaupp. In Beissner's original ordering of the paragraphs the text begins with the present fifth paragraph and the paragraphs that follow, and then takes the four paragraphs here printed first before closing with the final section, 'Hints for the continuation'. At the bottom of the third page of the manuscript, beneath a line, stands the end of a sentence which must have begun on the missing page. Beissner includes it in the main text. It is given here:

   > and as he grasps it more clearly or more vaguely in an image, the character of which expresses the character of the peculiar life which everyone in his own way can, and does, live infinitely.

   This seems to refer to an unidentified author Hölderlin is commenting on, as perhaps also at the beginning of the essay.

19. Gap of a page in manuscript.

20. The sentence breaks off.

21. The manuscript breaks off here, perhaps due to loss.

Seven Maxims/*Sieben Maximen*

Title supplied
Beissner: Reflection (Reflexion)
Knaupp: Frankfurt Aphorisms

22. This fair copy was made in or around 1799. The aphorisms were probably written earlier. They may have been inspired by those of Novalis and Friedrich Schlegel printed in the *Athenaeum* (May and June, 1798). It is possible that Hölderlin collected them in connection with his plans for his journal, *Iduna*.

'The wise, however . . .'/'*Die Weisen aber . . .*'

23. This fragmentary essay opening occurs among the papers to do with *Empedocles* and appears to have been written before the drama. The Frankfurt edition proposes the hypothetical dating of April 1799.

24. The text breaks off here.

From a Draft of the Journal Plan/*Aus einem Entwurf zum Journalplan*

Title supplied

25. In spring 1799, having moved from Frankfurt to Homburg in September 1798, Hölderlin conceived the plan for a 'poetic monthly', to be called *Iduna*. This text is probably the conclusion of the journal plan that Hölderlin promised to the publisher, Steinkopf, in his letter of 18 June 1799 (Letter 69). The opening words of the draft recur in this letter, where it is the poem that is to 'receive its due as a product of nature' in the essays Hölderlin envisages for the journal.

The Standpoint from which we should consider Antiquity/*Der Gesichtspunct aus dem wir das Altertum anzusehen haben*

26. The essay-fragment was likely written in June/July 1799, probably after 3 July. On the subject, compare Hölderlin's poem, 'An die Jungen Dichter'/'To the Young Poets' (*Selected Poems*, pp. 14/15); also his letters to Schiller of 20 June 1797 (Letter 46) and to his brother of 4 June 1799 (Letter 67). The central arguments are later developed in Letter 106 (to Böhlendorff, 4 December 1801).

The abbreviation in the opening sentence ('etc.') as well as the five interpolations here printed as footnotes indicate that the text is a draft which Hölderlin planned to expand at a later date.

27. 'Positive' here, as in Hegel, means nominal and fixed, as opposed to 'natural'.

28. The text breaks off here.

Note on Homer/*Bemerkung über Homer*

Title supplied

29. This note and the next two essays are probably linked to Hölderlin's plan to write a series of letters on Homer. The project is discussed in Letter 71 (to Neuffer, 3 July 1799) and is mentioned by Susette Gontard in her letter of 18 August 1799.

30. The text breaks off here.

'I am pleased . . .'/'*Mich freut es . . .*' and 'But most of all I love . . .'/'*Am meisten aber lieb' ich . . .*' (On Achilles)

Beissner: On Achilles (Über Achill)
Sattler: Brieffragmente über den Karakter Achills/Fragments of Letters on the Character of Achilles

31. These fragments are probably linked to the plan to write a series of letters on Homer detailed in the note to the 'Note on Homer'. They occur among the papers written for *Empedocles* and appear to have been written before the drama. Hölderlin announced an essay on the character of Achilles in Letter 66 (to Neuffer, 4 June 1799).

32. Homer, *Iliad*, Book 1.352.

33. *enfant gâté*: (French) spoilt child.

A Word on the *Iliad*/*Ein Wort über die* Iliade

34. This draft may be linked to the plan to write a series of letters on Homer detailed in the note to the 'Note on Homer'. Hölderlin announced an essay on the *Iliad* in Letter 66. The draft anticipates the ground covered in the next essay.

35. The manuscript breaks off here.

On the Different Modes of Poetic Composition/*Über die verschiedenen Arten, zu dichten*

36. This is a more developed version of the ideas contained in the previous essay, 'A Word on the *Iliad*'. The manuscript includes a translation of lines from Pindar, *Olympians*, 1. Beissner believes that this indicates Hölderlin's plan to connect the three character types linked to the 'tones' in this essay to the elements of water, fire and aether which are treated in Pindar's ode.

37. Hölderlin here refers to the doctrine of Thales echoed in Pindar, *Olympians*, 1.

38. The essay as we have it is written on two double sheets. The gap here was probably caused by the loss of a third sheet. The ending is also missing.

39. Homer, *Iliad*, Book 9.485–98, excerpt translated by Richard Lattimore (Chicago and London, 1951), p. 211. Hölderlin used the translation into German hexameters by the poet and scholar Johann Heinrich Voss (1793), to which he appended the following footnote: 'I hardly need to tell anyone that this is Voss's translation, and to those who do not know it yet, I confess that to my regret I only recently grew better acquainted with it.'

40. Sattler and Groddeck print this note in the main text.

41. This episode also occurs in Homer, *Iliad*, Book 9.185–91.

The Ground of the *Empedocles*/*Der Grund zum* Empedokles

Title supplied
Opening words: 'The tragic ode . . .'/'Die tragische Ode . . .'
Schmidt: On the Tragic (Über das Tragische)

42. This essay was written in connection with Hölderlin's drama, the *Empedocles*. A first plan for this was written in 1797, the first draft in December 1798/January 1799, and the second in spring 1799. The 'Ground' was written in late 1799, Knaupp thinks in October 1799 at the earliest. There followed a plan for the third version, and the third version itself.

After a brief introduction, the essay begins with a discussion of tragedy as such, the 'General ground', and then moves on to treat *Empedocles*. Empedocles (*c.* 492–432 BC), one of the pre-Socratic philosophers, came from Acragas in Sicily. He probably belonged to the aristocracy and was involved in Sicilian politics. The best-known legend about him relates that he ended his life by leaping into the crater of Etna, leaving a sandal behind him. This moment was to form the conclusion of Hölderlin's play.

43. *nefas*: meaning 'sin', 'crime', 'monstrous deed', 'something contrary to divine law'; the word recurs in the 'Notes on the *Oedipus*'.

44. Due to manuscript loss there is a large gap here (perhaps of two folio sheets).

45. **Nature and art**: a central pairing in Hölderlin's thought. Compare the poem 'Natur und Kunst'/'Nature and Art' (*Selected Poems*, pp. 74/75).

46. **aorgic**: a word probably of Hölderlin's own devising, meaning 'natural', 'tied to the elements', 'shapeless', or, in his words a few lines on, 'the incomprehensible, the unfeelable, the unlimited'. He uses it in contradistinction to 'organic', that which has form. The pairing resembles Nietzsche's later opposition between the 'Dionysian' and the 'Apolline' in *The Birth of Tragedy* (1872); as there, neither term can exist without the other. The word recurs elsewhere, notably in the 'Notes on the *Antigone*'.

47. **dissolves**: compare the reflections in 'The declining fatherland . . .'.

48. **annuls itself**: the German verb is *sich aufheben*, a word Hegel famously uses with three senses in play, though the main sense is 'annul' or 'cancel out'. The other meanings are 'transcend' and 'preserve'.

'The declining fatherland . . .'/
'Das untergehende Vaterland . . .'

Beissner: The Process of Becoming in Passing Away (Das Werden im Vergehen)

49. This was written after the third draft of *Empedocles*, probably right at the end of 1799. The essay's thesis of a 'becoming' in 'passing away' develops an argument possibly prompted by Fichte in his *Wissenschaftslehre* (*Theory of Knowledge*, 1794–5). It also rehearses a principle of Empedocles' philosophy.

50. The omission marks are in the manuscript.

51. Horace, *Odes*, Book 3.29.29ff.

52. The manuscript breaks off with a comma. The following fragmentary sentences (after the space) are at the bottom of the last page of the manuscript.

'When the poet is once in command of the spirit . . .'/
'*Wenn der Dichter einmal des Geistes mächtig* . . .'

Beissner: On the Procedure of the Poetic Spirit (Über die Verfahrungs-
weise des poetischen Geistes)

53. The essay may have been started in Homburg in 1799. Groddeck
    and Sattler place it in the first half of 1800, probably towards
    the end of Hölderlin's residence at Homburg. It is clearly a draft,
    in the first instance presumably written for the poet's own use,
    but fairly complete in itself, and represents his most sustained
    essay on poetic theory, revolving around the doctrine of the
    alternation of tones. The language of the original strains German
    syntax almost to breaking-point in the writer's quest for intellec-
    tual accuracy.

    After an extended introduction, the third paragraph introduces
    the three 'tones', but without naming them: the naive (actions or
    views, realities), the heroic (strivings, ideas, thoughts or passions,
    necessities) and the idealic (fantasies, possibilities). The tones are
    only once named together here, in the fourth paragraph.

54. **common soul . . . peculiar to each**: compare the formulation in
    Letter 74 (to Schelling, July 1799): 'the soul within the organic
    structure, being common to all members and particular to each'.

55. **hyperbolic**: not in the common sense but in the sense, derived
    from the Greek etymology, of 'going beyond itself' (literally,
    'throwing over and above').

56. There is a gap in the text before 'character'.

57. **naive . . . heroic . . . idealic**: compare the reflections in 'On the
    Different Modes of Poetic Composition', 'The lyric, in appear-
    ance idealic poem . . .' and the 'Poetological Tables'.

58. **intellectual intuition**: see the notes to 'Being Judgement Possi-
    bility' and 'Fragment of Philosophical Letters'.

59. **positive**: on the meaning of this word, see note 27 on 'The
    Standpoint from which we should consider Antiquity'.

60. The unfinished paragraph, printed here by Beissner, is treated by
    Sattler and Knaupp as a first draft of the footnote.

61. **solitude**: i.e. the state of the spirit before it has followed the rule
    of 'going out of itself', putting itself into relation with another
    sphere.

62. **S**: with this initial letter the main part of the essay breaks off.

63. This section seems to be an attempt to answer the question posed
    at (b) above about the consequences for 'poetic representation'.

64. *modus exprimendi*: 'means of expression'.

'Feeling speaks in a poem . . .'/'*Die Empfindung spricht im Gedichte* . . .'

65. This fragment is written in the middle of the manuscript of 'The lyric, in appearance idealic poem . . .', but Groddeck and Sattler argue that it was written earlier, probably during the composition of 'When the poet is once in command of the spirit . . .'.

    The argument reveals Hölderlin's concern to connect his doctrine of poetic tones with psychological states.

66. **energetic**: a word Hölderlin sometimes uses as a synonym of 'heroic'.

67. **the Diotima song**: Hölderlin refers here to one of his own poems to Diotima (i.e. Susette Gontard). Which is unclear, but a possible candidate is the one beginning 'Komm und besänftige . . .'/'Bliss of the heavenly Muse . . .' (*Selected Poems*, pp. 2/3).

'The expression, the characteristic . . .'/'*Der Ausdruk, das karakteristische* . . .'

Beissner: On the Parts of the Poem (Über die Parthien des Gedichts)

68. This fragment is written at the end of the manuscript of 'The lyric, in appearance idealic poem . . .', but Groddeck and Sattler argue that it was written first, probably during the composition of 'When the poet is once in command of the spirit . . .'.

    The 'parts' that Hölderlin here considers may perhaps be understood as the triadic 'sections' of a poem composed in a sequence of triads.

69. The fragment breaks off here.

'The lyric, in appearance idealic poem . . .'/'*Das lyrische, dem Schein nach idealische Gedicht* . . .'

Beissner: 'On the Difference between Poetic Kinds' ('Über den Unterschied der Dichtarten')

70. Groddeck and Sattler argue that this essay was written in summer 1800 at the earliest. The text appears to be an almost complete draft which, like 'When the poet is once in command of the spirit . . .', was presumably written for the poet's own use. It is closely connected with Hölderlin's Poetological Tables. The gaps in the text are not due to manuscript loss but to Hölderlin's breaking off and beginning again.

71. **metaphor**: Hölderlin apparently echoes the ordinary Greek meaning of the word, 'transposition' or 'transport'.

72. **a Pindaric ode . . . for Diagoras the Fencer**: *Olympians*, 7.

73. **aorgic**: see note 46.

74. **μηνιν αειδε θεα**: (Greek) the opening words of the *Iliad* – 'Sing to the goddess the wrath [of Achilles]'.

75. **necessary arbitrariness of Zeus**: mythical designation for the fundamental necessity for division inhabiting the unity of being. Four paragraphs on, Zeus is called 'the highest divisible'.

76. This paragraph is treated by Groddeck and Sattler as a draft for a closing passage to the section on tragedy, like those closing the sections on lyric and epic, which also focus on the 'basic tone'. They do not include it in the main text, and neither does Knaupp. We insert it here, following Beissner.

77. The text breaks off here.

'Does the idealic catastrophe . . .'/'*Löst sich nicht die idealische Katastrophe . . .*'

Beissner: 'Alternation of Tones' ('Wechsel der Töne'), borrowing a phrase from 'Note on Homer'

78. On Hölderlin's tone-theory, see Introduction (pp. xxxviii–xlv). The provisional, experimental status of these drafts needs to be borne in mind. They and the 'Poetological Tables' below belong with the essay beginning 'The lyric, in appearance idealic poem . . .'. They probably date from 1800.

79. **catastrophe**: Hölderlin is using the word in the etymological and literal sense of a 'down-turn' or 'overturning'. He means the point at which the sequence of tones is inverted, represented by the dash in the seven-step sequence below.

80. The words in brackets are thus in the manuscript, possibly indicating cancellation and certainly uncertainty.

81. Here Hölderlin uses normal script for the 'basic tone' and underlining (and initial capitalization) for the 'artistic character'.

Poetological Tables/*Poetologische Tafeln*

Given title

Beissner: included with 'Does the idealic catastrophe . . .' as 'Alternation of Tones'

82. These tables, closely linked in the manuscripts with the previous draft, set out more fully and in an alternative scheme what was

adumbrated there. See Introduction, pp. xxxvi–xli. L., T. and N. stand for 'lyric', 'tragic' and 'naive' (= epic); h, i, and n for 'heroic', 'idealic' and 'naive'.

83. **Aj.**: for *Ajax*, Sophocles' tragedy. 'Ant.' below is for *Antigone*. 'Aj.' was originally a correction of 'Ant.', and 'Ant.' a correction of 'Aj.', again suggesting an uncertainty on Hölderlin's part as to how the theory of tones could be applied.

84. These three big tables can be read horizontally and vertically. They set out the sequence of the 'artistic character' in each genre, dealing with them in the same order as above, first lyric, then tragic, then epic.

85. These final, numbered tables seem to set out in different form the sequence of tones for tragedy, first in a four-tone variant, then in the full seven-tone pattern.

'The tragic poet . . .'/'*Der tragische Dichter . . .*'

Beissner: Mixture of Poetic Kinds (Mischung der Dichtarten)

86. Groddeck and Sattler date the text not earlier than mid-June 1800. Beissner regards this piece as the 'quintessence' of Hölderlin's poetics, albeit with the qualification that it is difficult to understand.

Review of Siegfried Schmid's Play *The Heroine/Rezension zu Siegfried Schmids Schauspiel* Die Heroine

Given title

87. Siegfried Schmid sent Hölderlin his play, *The Heroine, or Tender Sense and Heroic Strength*, in February 1801, and this review seems to have been written soon afterwards, at Schmid's request. It was never published, and survives in a copy in Sinclair's hand. It shows us Hölderlin tentatively assaying aspects of his poetics in a public mode. There are correspondences with Letter 71 (to Neuffer, 3 July 1799), which is mostly about tragedy. Here Hölderlin considers comedy.

88. **Terence**: Roman playwright, active in the 160s BC.

89. **wings of Mercury**: Mercury, messenger of the gods, wore winged sandals.

'The meaning of tragedies . . .'/'*Die Bedeutung der Tragödien . . .*'

90. This text was formerly dated to Hölderlin's Homburg period, but Groddeck and Sattler argue that it was probably written at the time of the Sophocles translations, among other things noting a linguistic parallel ('light of life') with Letter 110 (to Böhlendorff, November 1802). It may have something to do with the unwritten 'introduction' to Sophocles mentioned in the next note.

Hölderlin's reflection represents his most compressed and elliptical definition of 'the tragic', expressed in the form of an equation. It belongs to the foundational texts in the German tradition of the philosophy of tragedy.

Notes on the *Oedipus*/*Anmerkungen zum* Oedipus

91. These notes, together with those on the *Antigone*, were written to accompany Hölderlin's Sophocles translation, published in April 1804. Although the publisher's announcement refers to 'ten years'' work, it is probable that Hölderlin only began these versions after abandoning *Empedocles*, perhaps as early as 1800, but more probably in Bordeaux, in 1802. In Letter 112 to his publisher, Wilmans (8 December 1803), he apologizes for the delay in submitting the manuscript. He never wrote the introduction mentioned in this letter, and his notes remain Hölderlin's most substantial statements on Greek tragedy. A second, closely related theme here, also pursued in the celebrated letter to Böhlendorff of November 1802 (Letter 110), is that of the aesthetic relation between ancient Greek and modern European art.

The line numbers below refer to those in Hölderlin's translation (in the Stuttgart edition) and in the original Greek.

92. μηχανη: (Greek) 'machine', 'instrument', 'device', 'way', 'means', 'art', 'skill', 'art exercised in a craftsmanlike way'; John Lavery suggests 'poetry which has an effect on the world', had 'practical results'.

93. *moyen*: the French word for 'means', here used in the sense of 'means of representation'.

94. **transport**: the word recalls the ordinary meaning of the Greek word 'metaphor'; compare 'The lyric, in appearance idealic poem . . .'.

95. *nefas*: see note 43 on 'The Ground of the *Empodocles*'.

96. Hölderlin lines 95-7; Sophocles lines 96-8.

97. Hölderlin 98; Sophocles 99.
98. Hölderlin 101; Sophocles 102.
99. Hölderlin 102–3; Sophocles 103–4.
100. Hölderlin 228–300; Sophocles 224–6.
101. Hölderlin 240–45; Sophocles 236–40.
102. Hölderlin 247–8; Sophocles 242–3.
103. Hölderlin 455–60; Sophocles 449–54. At line 458, Hölderlin alters 'immigrant' into 'dwells', i.e. 'someone who changes house' to 'someone who shares a house'.
104. Hölderlin 463–6; Sophocles 457–60. At line 465, Hölderlin alters 'having the same wife with' (literally, 'joint sower with') his father to 'in one bed'.
105. Hölderlin 930–32; Sophocles 914–16.
106. Hölderlin 967–9; Sophocles 950–51.
107. Hölderlin 979–80; Sophocles 962–3.
108. Hölderlin 981–90; Sophocles 964–72. In the Greek, 'no longer valid' refers to the oracles. The ambiguity arises in German.
109. Hölderlin 1027–8; Sophocles 1008–9.
110. Hölderlin 1036–40; Sophocles 1017–21.
111. Hölderlin 1053–6; Sophocles 1034–7.
112. Hölderlin 1079–82; Sophocles 1060–63.
113. Hölderlin 1095–104; Sophocles 1076–85.
114. *Της ψυσεως . . . εννουν*: The source for this quotation is the *Suidas* (a Greek lexicon, also known as the *Suda*, composed in Byzantium *c.* AD 1000), under the entry for Aristotle: 'ότι Αριστοτέλης της φυσεως γραμματευς ην, τον καλαμον αποβρέχων εις νουν' ('He was nature's scribe, dipping his pen in sense'). Hölderlin changes 'εις νουν' to 'εννουν', giving: 'He was nature's scribe, dipping the pen of good will'. This is now understood to refer to tragedians in general and to Sophocles in particular.
115. Hölderlin 1105; Sophocles 1088.

Notes on the *Antigone/Anmerkungen zur* Antigone

116. See the headnote to 'Notes on the *Oedipus*' for details of dating and context. As earlier in 'The lyric, in appearance idealic poem . . .', Oedipus and Antigone stand for two contrasting types of the tragic hero/heroine.
117. Hölderlin 466–8; Sophocles 449–51. At line 450, Hölderlin inserts 'my' before 'Zeus'.
118. I here follow Beissner's interpretation (*SW*, v, 207). The phrase

could be read to mean 'the dullness of the time which is appropriate to tragedy'.

119. Hölderlin 541–2; Sophocles 520–21.

120. Hölderlin 773–4; Sophocles 743–4.

121. **Hesperian**: i.e. 'towards evening', hence 'western', 'European'.

122. Hölderlin 1106–7; Sophocles 1064–5. Literally, 'But know well, indeed, you will not achieve many more wheels of chariot driver sun.'

123. Hölderlin 852ff; Sophocles 823ff. Hölderlin translates the whole passage thus:

> I have heard, that like the desert has become
> She, full of life, the Phrygian,
> Drawn from Tantalus in the womb, on Sipylus peak;
> Scraggy has become, like someone wearing
> Ivy chains, crumpled up
> In the slow long rock; and evermore with her,
> As men say, there stays winter;
> And washes her neck when fall snow-bright
> Tears from the fringe of her eyes. Right like her
> A spirit puts me to bed.

This departs considerably from the original. Hölderlin interprets Antigone's fate in terms of the relation between 'art' (the 'organic') and 'nature' (the 'aorgic'), which he had previously explored in 'The Ground of the *Empedocles*'. Niobe is an image of one in whom the organic, in its extreme, took on the form of the aorgic: organized life assumes the character of the inorganic. This entails a manifestation of the divine.

124. **the aorgic**: see note 46 on 'The Ground of the *Empedocles*'.

125. Hölderlin 987–8; Sophocles 949–50. Literally, 'And of Zeus was treasuring seed sowed of the golden rain.'

126. **antitheos**: 'contrary to divine', but also 'godlike'.

127. **Ajax and Ulysses**: in Sophocles' *Ajax*.

128. **δυσμορον**: (Greek) 'unhappy', 'ill-fated'; Hölderlin seems to use the word in the sense of 'bad fate', 'misfortune'.

129. **προφανηθι θεος**: Hölderlin, line 1199; Sophocles, line 1149 – (Greek) 'appear, O God!'

On the Fable of the Ancients/*Von der Fabel der Alten*

130. With the word 'fable' Hölderlin is using an obsolete word for myth, as also in Letter 114 (to Seckendorf, 12 March 1804), where he seems to define it as 'the poetic view of history'. Although the title uses 'fable' in the singular, the following notes refer to it as a plural. The text is probably from 1804.

131. **spirits**: in his Sophocles translations Hölderlin uses the word 'spirits' (*Geister*) for the gods. 'Connection between humans and spirits' is thus a definition of fable or myth.

Pindar Fragments/Pindar-Fragmente

Sattler: *Nine Pindar Commentaries* (*Neun Pindar-Kommentare*)

132. The dating of this text has been subject to some debate, and ranges from 1800 to 1805. Beissner argues that on stylistic grounds it must have been written some time after Hölderlin's Pindar translations of 1800 and proposes 1803; Sattler places it later, in 1805. Possibly the *Fragments* are the 'something' Hölderlin mentions in Letter 115 (to Wilmans, 2 April 1804). There are clear likenesses of language and preoccupation to the Sophocles 'Notes', but also differences.

The work represents a new kind of literary text, which unites ancient fragments (pieces of Pindar handed down by other classical authors) and an elliptic modern commentary into a single, lyrical whole.

Hölderlin's sources are here listed by ode number for the finished poems, and for the fragments by reference to the editions of Stephanus (1560), which Hölderlin owned and used, and of Snell (1964), the standard modern edition of Pindar's fragments.

133. Stephanus, p. 356; Snell, No. 43.
134. Pindar, *Pythians*, 4.180–89.
135. Stephanus, p. 360; Snell, No. 205.
136. Stephanus, p. 360, Snell, No. 109.
137. Stephanus, p. 358; Snell, No. 140b.
138. Stephanus, p. 350; Snell, No. 169.
139. Stephanus, p. 350; Snell, No. 214.
140. Stephanus, p. 350; Snell, No. 213.
141. Stephanus, p. 374; Snell, No. 30.
142. Stephanus, p. 364; Snell, No. 166.

APPENDIX

The Oldest Programme for a System of German Idealism/ Das älteste Systemprogramm des deutschen Idealismus

1. This text is the second page of a manuscript (the first page of which is lost) written in Hegel's hand. It is widely thought that the argument was formulated by Schelling, whose idea of 'myth' appears here, and was decisively influenced by Hölderlin's idea of art and beauty, as developed at the end of his novel, *Hyperion*. On various grounds, Jamme and Schneider in their critical edition argue for a dating of 1797: see Christoph Jamme and Helmut Schneider, *Mythologie der Vernunft. Hegels 'ältestes System-programm des deutschen Idealismus' – Kritische Edition* (Frankfurt, 1984). Jochen Schmidt puts it earlier, somewhere between summer 1795 and spring 1796, *Werke und Briefe*, Insel Edition, 2 vols. (Frankfurt, 1969).

List of Hölderlin's Letters Included in this Edition

30. To Friedrich Schiller. Nürtingen, 4 September 1795
31. To Johann Gottfried Ebel. Nürtingen, 9 November 1795
32. To G. W. F. Hegel. Stuttgart, 25 November 1795
33. To Johann Gottfried Ebel. Nürtingen, 7 December 1795
34. To Friedrich Immanuel Niethammer. Frankfurt am Main, 24 February 1796
35. To Karl Gok. Frankfurt, 20 March 1796
36. To Karl Gok. Frankfurt, 2 June 1796
37. To Christian Ludwig Neuffer. Frankfurt, June/July 1796
38. To Friedrich Schiller. Kassel, 24 July 1796
39. To Karl Gok. Kassel, 6 August 1796
40. To Karl Gok. Frankfurt, 13 October 1796
41. To G. W. F. Hegel. Frankfurt, 24 October 1796
42. To G. W. F. Hegel. Frankfurt, 20 November 1796
43. To Friedrich Schiller. Frankfurt, 20 November 1796
44. To Johann Gottfried Ebel. Frankfurt, 10 January 1797
45. To Christian Ludwig Neuffer. Frankfurt, 16 February 1797
46. To Friedrich Schiller. Frankfurt, 20 June 1797
47. To Christian Ludwig Neuffer. Frankfurt, 10 July 1797
48. To Karl Gok. Frankfurt, August 1797
49. To Friedrich Schiller. Frankfurt, August 1797
50. To Karl Gok. Frankfurt, ~ 20 September 1797
51. To Karl Gok. Frankfurt, 2 November 1797
52. To Karl Gok. Frankfurt, 12 February, posted 14 March 1798
53. To Friedrich Schiller. Frankfurt, 30 June 1798
54. To Heinrike Breunlin. Frankfurt, 4 July 1798
55. To Karl Gok. Frankfurt, 4 July 1798
56. To Christian Ludwig Neuffer. Frankfurt, August 1798
57. To Johanna Christiana Gok. Homburg, 10 October 1798
58. To Christian Ludwig Neuffer. Homburg, 12 November 1798
59. To Karl Gok. Rastatt, 28 November 1798
60. To Johanna Christiana Gok. Homburg, 11 December 1798
61. To Isaak von Sinclair. Homburg, 24 December 1798
62. To Karl Gok. Homburg, New Year's Eve 1798/1 January 1799
63. To Johanna Christiana Gok. Homburg, January 1799
64. To Johanna Christiana Gok. Homburg, early March 1799
65. To Susette Gontard. Homburg, Spring 1799
66. To Christian Ludwig Neuffer. Homburg, 4 June 1799
67. To Karl Gok. Homburg, 4 June 1799
68. To Johanna Christiana Gok. Homburg, 18 June 1799
69. To Johann Friedrich Steinkopf. Homburg, 18 June 1799
70. To Susette Gontard. Homburg, ~ June 1799

List of Correspondents: Biographical Notes

(Those whose surviving letters from Hölderlin have been translated complete are asterisked. Letter numbers are given in brackets at the end of each entry.)

*Böhlendorff, Casimir Ulrich (1775–1825), born in Kurland (Latvia), studied law at Jena from 1794 where he joined a revolutionary group and probably first met Hölderlin and Sinclair. In Switzerland he witnessed the French establish the Helvetic Republic in 1798 and wrote an account of it: *History of the Helvetic Revolution* (1802). He also published two plays. Returned to Kurland a disappointed man and took his own life. (106, 110)

Breunlin, Heinrike see Hölderlin, (Maria Eleonora) Heinrike.

Ebel, Johann Gottfried (1764–1830), doctor, naturalist and writer. Hölderlin met him in Heidelberg in 1795 on his way back home from Jena, and not long afterwards Ebel found him his second post as private tutor in Frankfurt. A good friend of the Gontard family, he was drawn to revolutionary Paris in 1796 and despite being disappointed by what he saw there stayed until 1802 when he attended to Susette Gontard on her death-bed. He wrote several successful books on Switzerland (where he lived permanently from 1810) which had some influence on Hölderlin. (29, 31, 33, 44, 81)

*Emerich, Friedrich Joseph (1773–1802), a lawyer in Wetzlar and supporter of the French Revolution. When the French took Wetzlar in 1796 he joined their army and then worked in the administration of Mainz. Hölderlin probably met him in summer 1799, and helped him publish some of his poems. In 1801 he resigned from his position in Mainz and wrote out of disappointment at the discrepancy between the revolutionary ideals and the political reality a number of articles highly critical of the French, which resulted in his being dispatched over the Rhine. Not long afterwards he died in Würzburg. (84)

*Goethe, Johann Wolfgang (1749–1832), the dominant German literary figure of his time in all genres, became known throughout Europe for his *Sufferings of Young Werther* (1774). Hölderlin met him in 1794 in Schiller's house in Jena and he came up in his correspondence with Schiller in summer 1797. He was a minister at the Weimar court and director of the theatre there. After a final meeting with Hölderlin in August 1797 in Frankfurt, Goethe described him to Schiller as 'rather weighed down and ailing, but genuinely endearing and with a modest, even anxious candour' (letter to Schiller, 23 August 1797). He regarded him as in Schiller's debt and advised him to write 'small poems'. (75?)

Gok, Johanna Christiana (1748–1828), Hölderlin's mother. Her first husband, Hölderlin's father, died in 1772, and her second, wine-merchant and mayor of Nürtingen, in 1779. Her father was a parish priest, her mother lived with her during most of Hölderlin's childhood and beyond. (1, 5, 6, 12, 13, 21, 22, 57, 60, 63, 64, 66, 73, 80, 83, 85, 86, 94, 97, 104, 107, 108, 109, 116–120)

Gok, Karl Christoph Friedrich (1776–1849), Hölderlin's half-brother. Unlike Hölderlin, his mother did not allow him to study, which is reflected in the often pedagogical tone of Hölderlin's letters to him. He became a successful civil servant. (11, 15, 18, 25, 35, 36, 39, 40, 48, 50, 51, 52, 55, 59, 62, 67, 93, 94, 101, 104, 105)

*Gontard, Susette (1769–1802), the mother of Hölderlin's charge in Frankfurt; she and Hölderlin fell in love soon after he arrived in 1796. She married her husband, Jakob Gontard (whose motto was 'Les affaires avant tout', literally, 'Business before all'), in 1786. Her grace and beauty struck others beside Hölderlin, who in his poetry addressed her as Diotima. She died of German measles caught from her children. (65, 70, 78, 79)

*Gonzenbach, Anton von (1748–1819), a magistrate and Hölderlin's employer in Hauptwil. His wealth came from the linen trade. Hölderlin's duties were to teach his two youngest children, Barbara Julia and Augusta Dorothea. (95)

*Hegel, Georg Wilhelm Friedrich (1770–1831), the philosopher, born the same year as Hölderlin and at the Stift with him 1788–93. The other main period of exchange was 1797 and 1798 when they were tutors in Frankfurt together. Some letters to him written from Jena have not survived, but their real influence on each other occurred in conversation. Together with Schelling, they invented German idealism. Hegel addressed his only poem, 'Eleusis', to Hölderlin in 1796. (17, 24, 32, 41, 42)

Hölderlin, (Maria Eleonora) Heinrike (1772–1850), Hölderlin's sister; he called her Rike. Married Christian Matthäus Theodor Breunlin in 1792 and lived in Blaubeuren, returning with her two children to live with her mother in Nürtingen after his death in 1800. (4, 8, 9, 54, 76, 87, 88, 89, 90, 92, 94, 96, 98, 104)

*Landauer, Christian (1769–1845), known to Hölderlin via Neuffer, became a good friend during trips to Frankfurt where his work as a draper often brought him. A democrat, he was convivial and fond of music, which made the months Hölderlin spent in his house in Stuttgart in the second half of 1800 one of the calmest and most productive periods of his life. Hölderlin addresses him in several poems. (99, 100)

*Mehmel, Gottlieb Ernst August (1761–1840), professor of philosophy at Erlangen and, together with Johann Georg Meusel, editor of the *Erlanger Literatur-Zeitung*. (91)

Nast, Immanuel Gottlieb (1769–1829), a clerk in Leonberg, west of Stuttgart, when Hölderlin knew him. Though he was gifted, his parents' circumstances did not allow him to study. He was Hölderlin's closest friend and main correspondent until the move to Tübingen in 1788 when their friendship petered out, but long after, in August 1828, he visited Hölderlin in the so-called tower. (2)

Neuffer, Christian Ludwig (1769–1839), at the Stift 1786–91, where with Hölderlin and Rudolf Magenau he formed a poets' club. He then took the normal route and became a priest in various parishes. His mother was Greek. He wrote conventional poems and translated Virgil's *Aeneid*. The friendship faded around 1800, but he is perhaps Hölderlin's most important correspondent. (3, 7, 10, 16, 19, 20, 23, 26, 27, 37, 45, 47, 56, 58, 66, 71, 82)

Niethammer, Friedrich Immanuel (1766–1848), coincided briefly with Hölderlin in the Stift and went on to study in Jena, where in 1793 he became professor of philosophy. In 1795 he founded the *Philosophische Journal*, from 1797 co-edited with Fichte. He was well known for his open house – in a diary entry of summer 1795 he records that Hölderlin, Fichte and Novalis met together there and spoke 'of religion and of revelation'. (34, 103)

*Schelling, Friedrich Wilhelm Joseph (1775–1854), the philosopher, knew Hölderlin in Nürtingen and came to the Stift in 1790. He was so precocious that the gap of five years between him and Hölderlin (and Hegel) was not apparent. He met Hölderlin for important talks in 1795 and 1796, and was visited by him in 1803 when he seems to have offered to approach the theatre in Weimar about his translations of Sophocles. (74)

*Schiller, Friedrich (1759–1805), the dramatist, poet, philosopher,

revered by Hölderlin from boyhood and like him a Swabian.
Hölderlin met him in 1793 and got his first job as a private tutor in
Waltershausen through him. In Jena Schiller took him under his
wing, publishing poems and an early fragment of *Hyperion* in his
journals – *Die Neue Thalia*, *Die Horen*, *Musen-Almanach* – and
finding him a publisher for the complete *Hyperion*. But Hölderlin
found his presence too much to bear and seems to have left Jena in
part to escape it. (14, 28, 30, 38, 43, 46, 49, 53, 72, 77, 102)

*Seckendorf, Leo von (1775–1809), studied law in Tübingen where
he met Hölderlin in 1792, then in Jena where he was among the
radical political groupings and knew Sinclair. Became a diplomat in
Württemberg and like Hölderlin was involved in Sinclair's trial for
high treason in 1805. He wrote, and published several of Hölderlin's
major poems in his *Musenalmanach* in 1807 and 1808. Died fighting
for the Austrians. (114)

*Sinclair, Isaak von (1775–1815), acquainted with Hölderlin in
Tübingen, they became close friends in Jena and lived together. He
was sent down from Jena in October 1795 for political activity, and
maintained links with revolutionary groups even after entering into
the service of the Landgrave of Hesse-Homburg. This eventually led
to his being accused of high treason in 1805, at which point several
letters to him from Hölderlin got lost. His hope was to establish the
ideals of revolutionary France in Germany. Twice he provided vital
support for Hölderlin in Homburg: 1798–1800 after the split with
the Gontard household, and 1804–6 when at his own expense he
arranged him a sinecure as a librarian at the court. He also wrote;
he took part in the wars of liberation against Napoleon in 1814.
The poem 'Der Rhein'/'The Rhine' is dedicated to him. (61)

Steinkopf, Johann Friedrich (1771–1852), a minor publisher with
whom Hölderlin proposed to edit his journal *Iduna*, which failed
due to lack of support from well-known writers. Steinkopf published
Neuffer's two poetic 'albums' (anthologies of new verse), and
carried on publishing books of mostly local interest, as well as
keeping a bookshop, until 1840. Schiller, advising Hölderlin not to
go ahead with the journal in August 1799, refers to Steinkopf as an
'insignificant beginner of a publisher'. (69)

*Wilmans, Friedrich (1764–1830), publisher of Hölderlin's Sophocles
translations and of the 'Night Poems'. He published many of the
German Romantics besides, as well as the maverick novelist Jean
Paul. (111, 112, 113, 115)

Index

PENGUIN CLASSICS

WAR AND PEACE
LEO TOLSTOY

'Yes! It's all vanity, it's all an illusion, everything except that infinite sky'

At a glittering society party in St Petersburg in 1805, conversations are dominated by the prospect of war. Terror swiftly engulfs the country as Napoleon's army marches on Russia, and the lives of three young people are changed forever. The stories of quixotic Pierre, cynical Andrey and impetuous Natasha interweave with a huge cast, from aristocrats and peasants, to soldiers and Napoleon himself. In *War and Peace* (1863–9), Tolstoy entwines grand themes – conflict and love, birth and death, free will and fate – with unforgettable scenes of nineteenth-century Russia, to create a magnificent epic of human life in all its imperfection and grandeur.

Anthony Briggs's superb translation combines stirring, accessible prose with fidelity to Tolstoy's original, while Orlando Figes's afterword discusses the novel's vast scope and depiction of Russian identity. This edition also includes appendices, notes, a list of prominent characters and maps.

'A book that you don't just read, you live' Simon Schama

'A masterpiece … This new translation is excellent' Antony Beevor

Translated with an introduction and notes by Anthony Briggs
With an afterword by Orlando Figes

PENGUIN CLASSICS

THE BEAST WITHIN
EMILE ZOLA

'He was driven by a single overriding need; he must appease the beast that raged within him'

Roubaud is consumed by a jealous rage when he discovers a sordid secret about his lovely young wife's past. The only way he can rest is by forcing her to help him murder the man involved, but there is a witness – Jacques Lantier, a fellow railway employee. Jacques, meanwhile, must contend with his own terrible impulses, for every time he sees a woman he feels an overwhelming desire to kill. In the company of Roubaud's wife, Séverine, he finds peace briefly, yet his feelings for her soon bring disastrous consequences. The seventeenth novel in the Rougon-Macquart cycle, *The Beast Within* (1890) is one of Zola's most dark and violent works – a tense thriller of political corruption and a graphic exploration of the criminal mind.

Roger Whitehouse's vivid translation is accompanied by an introduction discussing Zola's depiction of the railways, politics and the legal system and the influence of the studies of criminology and the Jack the Ripper murders on his novel. This edition also includes a chronology, suggestions for further reading and notes.

Translated with an introduction and notes by Roger Whitehouse

PENGUIN CLASSICS

THE EUROPEANS
HENRY JAMES

'They are sober; they are even severe ... But we shall cheer them up'

Eugenia, an American expatriate brought up in Europe, arrives in rural New England with her charming brother Felix, hoping to find a wealthy second husband after the collapse of her marriage to a German prince. Their exotic, sophisticated airs cause quite a stir with their affluent, God-fearing American cousins, the Wentworths – and provoke the disapproval of their father, suspicious of foreign influences. To Gertrude Wentworth, struggling against her sombre puritan upbringing, the arrival of the handsome Felix is especially enchanting. One of Henry James's most optimistic novels, *The Europeans* is a subtle and gently ironic examination of manners and morals, deftly portraying the impact of experience upon innocence.

Part of a series of new Penguin Classics editions of Henry James's works, this edition contains a chronology, further reading, notes and an introduction by Andrew Taylor exploring the novel's shifting patterns of opposites and James's portrayal of personal and national identity.

'This small book, written so early in James's career, is a masterpiece of major quality' F. R. Leavis

Edited with an introduction and notes by Andrew Taylor
Series editor Philip Horne

PENGUIN CLASSICS

THE MASTER AND MARGARITA
MIKHAIL BULGAKOV

'Magnificent ... a gloriously ironic gothic masterpiece ... had me rapt with bliss'
Patrick McGrath, *Guardian*

One spring afternoon the Devil, trailing fire and chaos in his wake, weaves
himself out of the shadows and into Moscow in Bulgakov's fantastical, funny and
frightening satire of Soviet life. Brimming with magic and incident, it is full of
imaginary, historical, terrifying and wonderful characters, from witches, poets and
Biblical tyrants to the beautiful, courageous Margarita, who will do anything to
save the imprisoned writer she loves.

Written in secret during the darkest days of Stalin's reign, when *The Master and
Margarita* was finally published it became an overnight literary phenomenon,
signalling artistic freedom for Russians everywhere.

A DEAD MAN'S MEMOIR
MIKHAIL BULGAKOV

'I confess quite frankly that what I produced was some kind of gibberish'

Sergei Maksudov has failed as a novelist and made a farce of a suicide attempt,
but only after a surprise break as a playwright on the Moscow stage does his
turmoil truly begin. Thrown uncomprehending into theatre life, he soon sees his
beloved play dragged into chaos by inflated egos, jealous critics, literary double-
dealers, communist censors and insanely bad acting. Full of affectionately drawn
characters, *A Dead Man's Memoir* is a brilliant, absurdist tale of the exhilaration
and black desperation wrought on one man by his turbulent love affair with
the theatre. Based on his own experiences at the famous Moscow Art Theatre
of the 1920s and 30s, it reaches its comic height in a merciless lampooning of
Stanislavsky's fashionable stage techniques.

PENGUIN CLASSICS

THE SHOOTING PARTY
ANTON CHEKHOV

'Why did I marry him? Where were my eyes? Where were my brains?'

The Shooting Party, Chekhov's only full-length novel, centres on Olga, the pretty young daughter of a drunken forester on a country estate, and her fateful relationships with the men in her life. Adored by Urbenin, the estate manager, whom she marries to escape the poverty of her home, she is also desired by the dissolute Count Karneyev and by Zinovyev, a magistrate, who knows the secret misery of her marriage. And when an attempt is made on Olga's life in the woods, it seems impossible to discover the perpetrator in an impenetrable web of deceit, lust, loathing and double-dealing. One of Chekhov's earliest experiments in fiction, *The Shooting Party* combines the classic elements of a gripping mystery with a story of corruption, concealed love and fatal jealousy.

Ronald Wilks's new translation of this work is the first in thirty years. It brilliantly captures the immediacy of the dialogue that Chekhov was later to develop into his great dramas. This edition also includes suggestions for further reading and explanatory notes.

Translated and edited by Ronald Wilks

PENGUIN CLASSICS

CHEKHOV: A LIFE IN LETTERS
ANTON CHEKHOV

'Medicine is my lawful wedded wife, and literature my mistress. When I've had enough of one, I can go and spend the night with the other'

From his teenage years in provincial Russia to his premature death in 1904, Anton Chekhov wrote thousands of letters to a wide range of correspondents. This fascinating new selection tells Chekhov's story as a man and a writer through affectionate bulletins to his family, insightful discussions of literature with publishers and theatre directors, and tender love letters to his actress wife. Vividly evoking landscapes, people and his daily life, the letters offer revealing glimpses into Chekhov's preoccupations – the onset of tuberculosis, his dual careers as doctor and writer, and his ambivalence about his growing reputation as Russia's foremost playwright and author. This volume takes us inside the mind of one of the world's great writers, and the character that emerges from these pages is resilient, generous, charming and life enhancing.

This is the first uncensored edition of the letters in any language, including previously unpublished material from the Russian archives, and the translation conveys the humour and warmth of Chekhov's prose.

Translated by Rosamund Bartlett and Anthony Phillips

With an introduction and notes by Rosamund Bartlett

PENGUIN CLASSICS

CONFESSIONS OF AN ENGLISH OPIUM EATER
THOMAS DE QUINCEY

'Thou hast the keys of Paradise, oh just, subtle, and mighty opium!'

Confessions is a remarkable account of the pleasures and pains of worshipping at the 'Church of Opium'. Thomas De Quincey consumed large daily quantities of laudanum (at the time a legal painkiller), and this autobiography of addiction hauntingly describes his surreal visions and hallucinatory nocturnal wanderings though London, along with the nightmares, despair and paranoia to which he became prey. The result is a work in which the effects of drugs and the nature of dreams, memory and imagination are seamlessly interwoven. *Confessions* forged a link between artistic self-expression and addiction, paving the way for later generations of literary drug-users from Baudelaire to Burroughs, and anticipating psychoanalysis with its insights into the subconscious.

This edition is based on the original serial version of 1821, and reproduces the two 'sequels', 'Suspiria De Profundis' (1845) and 'The English Mail-Coach' (1849). It also includes a critical introduction discussing the romantic figure of the addict and the tradition of confessional literature, and an appendix on opium in the nineteenth century.

Edited with an introduction by Barry Milligan

PENGUIN CLASSICS

THE LIFE OF SAMUEL JOHNSON
JAMES BOSWELL

'Johnson, to be sure, has a roughness in his manner, but no man alive has a more tender heart'

In Boswell's *Life of Samuel Johnson*, one of the towering figures of English literature is revealed with unparalleled immediacy and originality. While Johnson's *Dictionary* remains a monument of scholarship, and his essays and criticism command continuing respect, we owe our knowledge of the man himself to this biography. Through a series of wonderfully detailed anecdotes, Johnson emerges as a sociable figure with a huge appetite for life, crossing swords with other great eighteenth-century luminaries, from Garrick and Goldsmith to Burney and Burke – even his long-suffering friend and disciple James Boswell. Yet Johnson had a vulnerable, even tragic, side and anxieties and obsessions haunted his private hours. Boswell's sensitivity and insight into every facet of his subject's character ultimately make this biography as moving as it is entertaining.

Based on the 1799 edition, Christopher Hibbert's abridgement preserves the integrity of the original, while his fascinating introduction sets Boswell's view of Samuel Johnson against that of others of the time.

Edited and abridged with an introduction and notes by Christopher Hibbert

PENGUIN CLASSICS

REFLECTIONS ON THE REVOLUTION IN FRANCE
EDMUND BURKE

'To make a revolution is to subvert the ancient state of our country;
and no common reasons are called for to justify so violent a proceeding'

Burke's seminal work was written during the early months of the French
Revolution, and it predicted with uncanny accuracy many of its worst excesses,
including the Reign of Terror. A scathing attack on the revolution's attitudes to
existing institutions, property and religion, it makes a cogent case for upholding
inherited rights and established customs, argues for piecemeal reform rather than
revolutionary change – and deplores the influence Burke feared the revolution
might have in Britain. *Reflections on the Revolution in France* is now widely
regarded as a classic statement of conservative political thought, and is one of the
eighteenth century's great works of political rhetoric.

Conor Cruise O'Brien's introduction examines the contemporary political situation
in England and Ireland and its influence on Burke's point of view. He highlights
Burke's brilliant grasp of social and political forces and discusses why the book
has remained so significant for over two centuries.

Edited with an introduction by Conor Cruise O'Brien

PENGUIN CLASSICS

A HERO OF OUR TIME
MIKHAIL LERMONTOV

'I'm still in love with her … I'd give my life for her. But she bores me'

Proud, wilful and intensely charismatic, Pechorin is bored by the stifling world that envelops him. With a predatory energy for any activity that will relieve his ennui, he embarks on a series of adventures – encountering smugglers, brigands, soldiers, lovers and rivals – and leaves a trail of broken hearts behind him. With its cynical, immoral hero, Lermontov's novel outraged many critics when it was published in 1840. Yet it was also a literary landmark: an acutely observed psychological novel, narrated from a number of different perspectives, through which the true and complex nature of Pechorin slowly emerges.

Paul Foote's fine translation is accompanied by an introduction discussing the figure of Pechorin within the literary tradition of 'superfluous men' and the novel's influence on Tolstoy, Dostoyevsky and Chekhov. The edition also includes a chronology, explanatory notes and a historical note on the Caucasus.

'Vigorous and audacious … it retains its power as a psychological study'
Julian Barnes

Translated with an introduction by Paul Foote

THE STORY OF PENGUIN CLASSICS

Before 1946 ... 'Classics' are mainly the domain of academics and students; readable editions for everyone else are almost unheard of. This all changes when a little-known classicist, E. V. Rieu, presents Penguin founder Allen Lane with the translation of Homer's *Odyssey* that he has been working on in his spare time.

1946 Penguin Classics debuts with *The Odyssey*, which promptly sells three million copies. Suddenly, classics are no longer for the privileged few.

1950s Rieu, now series editor, turns to professional writers for the best modern, readable translations, including Dorothy L. Sayers's *Inferno* and Robert Graves's unexpurgated *Twelve Caesars*.

1960s The Classics are given the distinctive black covers that have remained a constant throughout the life of the series. Rieu retires in 1964, hailing the Penguin Classics list as 'the greatest educative force of the twentieth century.'

1970s A new generation of translators swells the Penguin Classics ranks, introducing readers of English to classics of world literature from more than twenty languages. The list grows to encompass more history, philosophy, science, religion and politics.

1980s The Penguin American Library launches with titles such as *Uncle Tom's Cabin*, and joins forces with Penguin Classics to provide the most comprehensive library of world literature available from any paperback publisher.

1990s The launch of Penguin Audiobooks brings the classics to a listening audience for the first time, and in 1999 the worldwide launch of the Penguin Classics website extends their reach to the global online community.

The 21st Century Penguin Classics are completely redesigned for the first time in nearly twenty years. This world-famous series now consists of more than 1300 titles, making the widest range of the best books ever written available to millions – and constantly redefining what makes a 'classic'.

The Odyssey continues ...

The best books ever written

PENGUIN 🐧 CLASSICS

SINCE 1946

Find out more at www.penguinclassics.com